Globalisation and SMEs in East Asia

STUDIES OF SMALL AND MEDIUM SIZED ENTERPRISES IN EAST ASIA SERIES

Series Editors: Charles Harvie and Boon-Chye Lee, *University of Wollongong, Australia*

This series incorporates both theoretical and empirical studies of various aspects of small and medium sized enterprises in East Asia, focusing on a number of key issues, problems and their survival in the wake of the regional financial and economic crisis. It examines the contribution of SMEs to national economies and how best to sustain their growth and performance. Selected geographic regions and/or industrial sectors are studied in greater depth for additional insight.

These enterprises are distinct in many ways from SMEs in other parts of the world. The studies will therefore contribute to an improved understanding of the roles played by East Asian SMEs in their domestic economies as well as within one of the most dynamic and rapidly developing regions of the global economy.

Titles in the series are:

1. Globalisation and SMEs in East Asia
   edited by Charles Harvie and Boon-Chye Lee

2. The Role of SMEs in National Economies in East Asia
   edited by Charles Harvie and Boon-Chye Lee

3. Sustaining Growth and Performance in East Asia
   The Role of Small and Medium Sized Enterprises
   edited by Charles Harvie and Boon-Chye Lee

4. Small and Medium Sized Enterprises in East Asia
   Sectoral and Regional Dimensions
   edited by Charles Harvie and Boon-Chye Lee

Globalisation and SMEs in East Asia

Edited by

Charles Harvie and Boon-Chye Lee

University of Wollongong, Australia

STUDIES OF SMALL AND MEDIUM SIZED ENTERPRISES IN EAST ASIA

Edward Elgar

Cheltenham, UK • Northampton, MA, USA

Published by
Edward Elgar Publishing Limited
Glensanda House
Montpellier Parade
Cheltenham
Glos GL50 1UA
UK

Edward Elgar Publishing, Inc.
136 West Street
Suite 202
Northampton
Massachusetts 01060
USA

A catalogue record for this book
is available from the British Library

Library of Congress Cataloguing in Publication Data

Globalisation and SMEs in East Asia / edited by Charles Harvie and Boon-Chye
Lee.
  p. cm. — (Studies of small and medium size entrprises in East Asia ; v. 1)
 Papers presented at an international conference, organized by the International
Business Research Institute of the University of Wollongong, Australia, held in
Wollongong on June 16-17, 2000.
 Includes bibliographical references and index.
 1. Small business—East Asia—Congresses. 2. Globalization—Economic
aspects—East Asia—Congresses. 3. Financial crises—East Asia—Congresses. 4.
Small business—East Asia—Finance—Congresses. I. Harvie, Charles, 1954- II.
Lee, Boon-Chye. III. Series.

HD2346.E18 G57 2002   2002018881
338.6'42'095—dc21

ISBN 1 84064 323 4

Printed and bound in Great Britain by MPG Books Ltd, Bodmin, Cornwall

To Sonya
(Charles Harvie)

To my mother and to the memory of my father
(Boon-Chye Lee)

Other books published by Charles Harvie

Contemporary Developments and Issues in China's Economic Transition (editor)
Causes and Impact of the Asian Financial Crisis (editor with Tran Van Hoa)
Vietnam's Reforms and Economic Growth (co-author with Tran Van Hoa)

Other books published by Boon-Chye Lee

The Economics of International Debt Renegotiation: The Role of Bargaining and Information

Contents

List of Tables

ix

List of Figures

Notes on Contributors

Gurmeet S. Bhabra is a Lecturer in the Department of Finance and Quantitative Analysis at the University of Otago, New Zealand, where he teaches applied investments and advanced corporate finance. He has also taught at the University of Pittsburgh and the Australian National University (executive education). He holds a PhD in finance from the Katz Graduate School of Business, University of Pittsburgh. His primary research interest is empirical corporate finance.

Hock-Beng Cheah is a Senior Lecturer at the School of Economics and Management, University College, University of New South Wales, Australia, where he teaches undergraduate and postgraduate courses. In the field of economics, his research interests are focused on entrepreneurship and economic development in the Asia–Pacific region. In the management field, his teaching and research interests include human resource management and organisational development. He was previously a Visiting Research Fellow at the Snider Entrepreneurial Centre, Wharton School, University of Pennsylvania, where he examined the 'Schumpeterian' and 'Austrian' conceptions of entrepreneurship, and proposed a new perspective of the entrepreneurial process. Since then he has explored more extensively the ramifications of this perspective of entrepreneurship for organisations, management and economic development.

Christopher Conca is an Assistant Professor of Information Systems at Appalachian State University. He received his PhD in information systems management from the University of South Florida in 1998. Dr Conca has worked in information systems in both the public and private sectors. His research interests include IS development, IS pedagogy, judgement and decision making, cognitive psychology, and general psychological issues relating to information system users. Dr Conca joined the faculty of ASU in 1996.

Leo Paul Dana was formerly Deputy Director of the International Business MBA Program at Singapore's Nanyang Business School. He has also served on the faculties of McGill University and INSEAD. He holds BA and MBA degrees from McGill University, and a PhD. from the Ecole des Hautes Etudes Commerciales. His area of expertise is in Emerging Markets. He is the author of 12 books, including *Entrepreneurship in Pacific Asia: Past, Present and Future* (World Scientific 1999), and *Economies of the Eastern Mediterranean Region: Economic Miracles in the*

Making (World Scientific, 2000), 90 journal articles, and nearly 100 case studies. He serves as Senior Advisor to the World Association for Small and Medium Enterprises, and as an editorial board member of several journals. Currently, Dr Dana is teaching at the University of Canterbury in New Zealand.

Hamid Etemad is Associate Professor of Marketing and International Business at the Faculty of Management, McGill University, Canada. A graduate of the University of California in Berkeley, he holds an MEng, an MSc, an MBA and a PhD. His research interests are in exporting, marketing, economic development, industrial strategy, globalisation and technology. Formerly Associate Dean and Director of the McGill MBA Program, he has also served as President of the Administrative Sciences Association of Canada.

Liz Fulop is Professor and Head of the School of Marketing and Management, Griffith University, Australia. Professor Fulop graduated with a PhD from the University of New South Wales. Her research interests are in business networks, R&D collaboration, regional development, SMEs, management and organisational issues. She has published on business networks, regional development organisations and policy, management learning, R&D collaboration between industry, research bodies and universities as well as across a range of management areas. She is the co-author of the first Australian management text to be adapted for publication in Europe. Professor Fulop has an involvement with an SME-based family business in the manufacturing sector. In addition she has been a consultant to a range of Australian government agencies.

Charles Harvie is an Associate Professor in the Department of Economics at the University of Wollongong, Australia. He is currently Deputy Director of his faculty's International Business Research Institute and Director of the Centre for SME Research and Development based at the University of Wollongong. He obtained his PhD in economics from the University of Warwick in 1986. He has taught in the UK, Australia, Thailand, Singapore and Vietnam in the areas of macroeconomics, international economics, monetary economics and transition economics. More recently his recent research interests have focused upon the Asian financial crisis, China's economic reforms, and the significance of innovation for SME export performance. Dr Harvie has published his research results in the form of numerous journal articles, books and book chapters.

David Ip is an Associate Professor in the Department of Anthropology, Sociology and Archaeology at the University of Queensland, and the Director of the Master's program in Social Planning and Development. He was born in Hong Kong and educated there as well as in the United States and Canada. He holds a PhD in sociology from the University of British Columbia, Canada. His main research interests lie in the study of Chinese immigrant entrepreneurs in Australia and he has published widely in this area. He is co-author (with Ikuo Kawakami, Karel Duivenvoorden and Lee Chang Tye) of *Images of Multicultural Australia* (Sydney: Multicultural Centre, The University of Sydney, 1994). He is also actively involved in consultancy work for the Australian international development assistance bureau, AusAid, and other international development organisations. Together with Constance Lever-Tracy and Noel Tracy, he is co-author *Diaspora Chinese and the Chinese Economy: An Emerging Synergy* (Houndmills, UK: Macmillan, and New York: St Martins, 1996).

Boon-Chye Lee is a Senior Lecturer in the Department of Economics at the University of Wollongong, Australia, where he also coordinates the International Economics and Business Integration program of the International Business Research Institute. He is a graduate of the Australian Graduate School of Management, University of New South Wales. His doctoral thesis, 'The Economics of International Debt Renegotiation', was subsequently published by Westview Press (1993). His more recent research interests have focused on SMEs, electronic money, and trust in Internet commerce. His research has been published in international journals including the *Asia–Pacific Journal of Management, Journal of International Financial Markets, Institutions and Money, Applied Economics Letters,* and *Netnomics,* and as book chapters.

Constance Lever-Tracy is a Senior Lecturer in the Department of Sociology and in the School of Political and International Studies, Flinders University of South Australia, Adelaide. She holds a PhD from Flinders University. She teaches and supervises student dissertations in the University's Masters program in International Relations, in Hong Kong and China. She was educated at the London School of Economics, University College London and Flinders University. She has a long-standing interest in international migration and in globalisation on which she has published widely, and is co-author (with Michael Quinlan) of *A Divided Working Class? Ethnic Segmentation and Industrial Conflict in Australia* (London and New York: Routledge and Kegan Paul, 1988).

John G. Powell is a Senior Lecturer in the Department of Finance and Quantitative Analysis at the University of Otago. He received his PhD in economics from the University of Toronto. He teaches finance at the University of Otago, New Zealand and has also taught at the Australian National University (as a visitor) and the University of New South Wales. He has published in the areas of financial economic theory, international finance, derivative securities, investments and economic psychology.

David Richards is currently Professor of International Business and Cross-Cultural Management in the Sunderland Business School, University of Sunderland, UK. He arrived in Sunderland in February 1998 from Darwin, Australia, where he was Associate Professor in International Management in the Graduate School of Business at Northern Territory University (NTU). Until 1986 he worked in higher education in the UK and, prior to going to NTU in 1990, was Head of Business and Management at the Brunei Institute of Technology, in Brunei, Southeast Asia. From October 1995 until June 1996 he was a Visiting Professor at the National Economics University in Hanoi, Vietnam, working on the MBA Project at the Centre for Management Learning. His research and teaching interests centre on international management, culture and organisational behaviour, with a special interest in cross-cultural and expatriate management and management learning. These interests currently focus on cross-cultural effectiveness, especially among expatriate managers, and on the means by which it may be learned and enhanced. He has published two books and a number of articles in refereed journals.

Donald G. Ross is an Associate Professor of Finance and Coordinator of the Financial Services Research Group at the University of Western Sydney, Blacktown campus, Sydney, Australia. He has written extensively on trade-related finance issues in relation to exporting SMEs.

Henry Sandee is a Senior Research Fellow at the Department of Development Economics at the Vrije Universiteit, Amsterdam. He received his PhD from the same university with a thesis on innovation adoption by small enterprises in Indonesia. In the 1984–86 period he worked at the University of Swaziland and from 1986–92 at Satya Wacana Christian University in Salatiga, Indonesia. Since 1993 he has been attached to the Vrije Universiteit involved in research and small enterprise development projects in Indonesia, Vietnam, the Philippines and Sri Lanka. He is presently involved in the design of business development services programs for clustered small enterprise in Indonesia.

Jing Shi is a Lecturer in the Department of Commerce at the Australian National University. His research interest falls in the area of initial public offerings, market efficiency and derivatives.

Kenneth Trimmer is an Assistant Professor of Computer Information Systems in the College of Business at Idaho State University. His educational background includes a BSc in business administration with a major in accounting from Bucknell University, an MBA from Western Carolina University, and an MAc from Washington State University. He completed his PhD at the University of South Florida in management information systems. He has extensive experience in accounting systems and productivity software with small- to medium-size businesses, having been a consulting manager for McGladrey & Pullen, as well as a proprietor of his own small business consulting practice. His current research interests involve conflict development in cross-functional information systems development teams, and critical success factors in the implementation of integrated business systems in SMEs.

Tim Turpin is a Professor and Director of the International Business Research Institute and the Centre for Research Policy at the University of Wollongong, Australia. He holds a PhD in sociology from La Trobe University, Australia. He has worked in government, private sector and university environments. He has researched and published widely on issues concerning research policy, cultural adaptation and the dissemination of knowledge. Over the past eight years he has carried out a range of research and consulting projects in China concerning the role of the state in developing regional innovation systems. Professor Turpin also teaches graduate programs on international relations, cross-cultural management and organisational behaviour.

Peter van Diermen is a Lecturer in the Department of Geography at the Australian National University, Canberra. He holds a PhD from the ANU. His research interests are in the areas of economic and industrial geography, small-scale business and employment in Asia, development and urbanisation in Southeast Asia, and sustainable livelihood in Indonesia. He is currently researching on the ecological footprints of Asian cities, Jakarta's urban environment, and informal employment in Indonesia. His teaching areas include sustainable development in the Third World, developmental issues in the Third World, and economic development in Southeast Asia.

Craig Van Slyke is an Assistant Professor of Management Information Systems at the University of Central Florida, USA, where he teaches courses in database and electronic commerce. He holds a PhD in information systems from the University of South Florida. Dr Van Slyke also spent ten years in the information technology industry in a number of capacities. His current research interests focus on issues related to the adoption of electronic commerce. Dr Van Slyke has published his research in a number of journals including *Communications of the ACM*, *Information Resource Management Journal*, *Annals of Cases on Information Technology Applications*, *Industrial Management and Data Systems*, and *Office Systems Research Journal*. He is also the co-author (with F. Belanger) of the forthcoming book, *Introduction to Electronic Business Technologies* (New York: Wiley).

Henry Wan, Jr is a Professor in the Department of Economics at Cornell University, USA, and a correspondence researcher at the Economics Institute, Academia Sinica, Nankang, Taiwan. He was a Goh Keng Swee Professor at the National University of Singapore, a visiting professor at Fudan University, Shanghai, the National Taiwan University, Taipei, Taiwan, and Boston University. He was also the President of the Chinese Economists' Association in North America. His research interests are in growth theory, international economics, East Asian studies and dynamic games.

Richard W. Wright is the E. Claiborne Robins Distinguished University Chair at the University of Richmond, USA. He served formerly as Director of International Management Studies at McGill University, as well as being a frequent visiting professor/scholar at other leading management schools around the world. Dr Wright holds a BA degree from Dartmouth College; an MBA degree from the Amos Tuck School of Business Administration; and a DBA in international management from Indiana University. He worked in the US diplomatic service and in private business before entering academia. Dr Wright is the author of ten books and research monographs in the field of international business, as well as numerous articles in leading scholarly journals. His most recent book, *International Entrepreneurship: Globalization of Emerging Businesses* (Greenwich, CO: JAI Press, 1999), explores the impact of globalisation on small businesses and entrepreneurial enterprises.

Tian Ze studied chemistry and worked in the industry in China prior to completing his Masters degree in business in finance at the University of Otago in Dunedin, New Zealand. He is currently working in the finance industry in China.

Acknowledgements

This book is a collection of invited papers by renowned international scholars of small and medium sized enterprises (SMEs). Its focus is upon identifying, and analysing, the resilience and coping strategies adopted by the East Asian SME sector in the aftermath of the 1997–98 financial and economic crisis. A number of dimensions are given emphasis, including: availability and access to finance; the role and significance of networking and franchising in the conduct of business; coping strategies for small business in the wake of the financial and economic downturn; issues and constraints facing the SME sector both before and after the crisis; the contribution of culture to business acumen and entrepreneurialism; technology transfer processes and the utilisation and application of information technology by SMEs; trends in regional SME labour markets; the impact on SMEs from electronic commerce; and the evaluation of foreign direct investment in the presence of political risk. Most of the chapters in this volume were initially presented, before final draft stage, at an international conference on SMEs in a Global Economy, organised by the International Business Research Institute of the University of Wollongong, Australia, held in Wollongong on 16–17 June 2000.

We would like to extend our appreciation and gratitude first and foremost to the contributors to the book, without whose dedicated, timely and scholarly contributions this volume would not have been possible. We are also grateful to numerous colleagues who commented on earlier drafts of each chapter. In particular, we wish to thank Gary Gregory, Matt Ngui, Constance Lever-Tracy and Tim Turpin. We are indebted to Catriona Sparks for her skilful formatting of the final drafts of each chapter, and to Robert Hood, Nadyne Smith and Priscilla Kendall for excellent administrative and typing assistance provided in getting the individual chapters to camera-ready stage.

We also wish to express our thanks to the International Business Research Institute, Faculty of Commerce, University of Wollongong, the University of Wollongong itself, and AusAid, for financial assistance provided during the completion of this project.

At Edward Elgar Publishing, we wish to thank Edward Elgar himself for his encouragement of, and support for, this book initiative from a very early stage, which provided the necessary impetus for its completion. In addition, we would like to thank Francine O'Sullivan for her patience and highly professional assistance.

Last, but not least, we would like to thank our respective families for their support and patience during the period of this project.

Charles Harvie and Boon-Chye Lee
Wollongong
June 2001

1 The Study of Small and Medium Sized Enterprises in East Asia

Charles Harvie and Boon-Chye Lee

1.1   INTRODUCTION AND OVERVIEW

The term 'East Asia' can be said to be a terminological convenience referring to a geographically proximate group of countries on the western rim of the Pacific stretching from Japan, Korea and China in the north to Australia and New Zealand in the south. Apart from superficial cultural similarities, particularly in the north, the heterogeneity of the region's economies, systems of government and economic organisation is perhaps the outstanding feature that strikes any observer of the political economy of East Asia. The economies of the region have followed very different developmental paths. The region encompasses developed economies (Japan, Australia, New Zealand), several newly industrialised economies that have in the last decade and a half or so joined the ranks of the developed nations (Korea, Singapore, Hong Kong and Taiwan), newly industrialising economies (Malaysia, Thailand, Indonesia) and a number of less-developed ones (including China and the Philippines). The peoples are culturally, religiously and ethnically diverse, with vastly differing levels of income, and are ruled by governments ranging from authoritarian regimes to democratically elected ones. Any attempt to study East Asia must therefore begin with a recognition of its diversity.

Such an economically heterogeneous environment provides rich material for the study of aspects of small and medium sized enterprises (SMEs) under different conditions. There are two ways in which such a study can be attempted. The first, the approach taken in this book, is to organise the study of SMEs according to common themes or topics; this allows the study of issues relevant to SMEs irrespective of where they are located. The second is to look at SMEs within the context of their particular economies and to focus on issues pertinent to them within their own environment; this is the approach taken in a companion volume, *Globalisation and SMEs in East Asia* (Harvie and Lee 2002).

The economic significance of SMEs has not been appreciated until comparatively recently. This is reflected in the relative neglect of issues relating to SMEs by policymakers and academics alike prior to the 1980s. That neglect is beginning to be rectified both at the national level and in international forums. Indicative of this is the gradual upgrading of interest in SMEs within the Asia–Pacific Economic Cooperation (APEC) forum. The APEC Committee of Trade and Investment was set up in 1993, and part of its brief included 'SME development'. In 1995, the SME Working Group was established as an *ad hoc* policy level group with an original two-year mandate that was subsequently extended twice. In 2000, the policy group was upgraded to the SME Working Group and granted permanent status (APEC 2001). These developments are in line with those in the European Union, and more generally in the Organisation for Economic Cooperation and Development (OECD). A key factor explaining these developments, which received a boost during the Asian economic crisis in 1997–98 that forms the backdrop to much of the analysis in this volume, is the increasing concern in recent years about countries' growth performances and high levels of structural unemployment, and the realisation of the significant role of SMEs in their economies. APEC figures indicate that they typically comprise more than 90 per cent of all business enterprises in a country and employ more than half of the workforce. These figures, however, mask the differences that exist between different countries. For example, SMEs in New Zealand and Singapore employ just over half of the workforce in those countries, but around three-quarters of the workforce in Japan and Taiwan, and around 90 per cent in Indonesia and Brunei (APEC 1998).

The diversity of the economies of East Asia means that they complement each other in many ways. For example, firms in one country have set up production facilities in other, lower-wage, countries. As economies and the enterprises in them progress up the development ladder and wage costs increase, they become less competitive and are forced to upgrade to remain competitive, abandoning the industries they previously occupied to other enterprises in countries similarly moving up behind them.

A good example of this is the Taiwanese personal computer (PC) industry, the hallmark of that country's reinvention of itself from a producer of low-quality manufactures to one capable of high-tech electronics. In two decades, through a concentration on high productivity, low costs and high quality, the Taiwanese PC industry built the country into the third largest producer of computer hardware in the world by 1999, contributing significantly to the country's remarkable growth. At the same time, as costs have increased, Taiwanese SMEs in the PC industry, in line with SMEs in other industries, have relocated production facilities to Mainland China, transferring technical know-how in the process. In 2000, China's production of computer hardware overtook that of Taiwan for the first time, with a production value of US$25.5 billion compared to Taiwan's US$23 billion (Goh 2001). It is noteworthy that around US$18 billion of Chinese production was attributable to Taiwanese firms based in the mainland. In order to stay competitive, Taiwanese firms are being forced to upgrade and seek ways of moving up the value chain. This upgrading is part of a broader trend of countries moving up the economic ladder that is evident elsewhere in the region and indeed around the world.

The example of the Chinese and Taiwanese computer industries also reflects a development of profound significance for the countries of the region: the rapid strides made by Chinese industry and enterprises in the last decade or so. Across a range of industries, Chinese enterprises have developed a level of expertise and competitiveness that is having a marked impact on the region. The country, with its seemingly inexhaustible pool of cheap but eminently educable labour, is posing a massive challenge to its neighbours. As Ohmae (2001) notes:

> Chinese companies ... are developing innovative, low-cost export businesses in apparel, vitamin supplements, food, watches, consumer electronics and appliances, plywood, footwear, and precision electronic and mechanical components. In the Pearl and Yangtse River deltas, there are more than 50 000 electronic component suppliers sophisticated enough to deliver their wares 'just in time' to the local Japanese and Taiwanese manufacturers ... In short, China is rapidly supplanting industries that took other Asian countries 15 years or more to build.

Held back by internal upheavals, wars and political turmoil for much of the last century, China appears to be finally 'finding its feet'. In the last decade the country has grown at an average annual rate of more than 10 per cent. It was relatively unscathed during the Asian crisis, and indeed proved a stabilising force by its refusal to devalue its currency against the US dollar. The rising economic prominence of China poses both problems and opportunities for its neighbours, whose enterprises will have to consider not just how they are to adapt for survival but also how they can best avail themselves of the opportunities offered by the fastest-growing consumer market in the world. How well the SMEs cope with the challenge posed by China will determine in large part the destinies of their economies.

1.2   A FRAMEWORK FOR UNDERSTANDING SMES

Figure 1.1 presents a broad conceptual framework that describes the operations of a typical SME or firm, and that serves to put the chapters in this volume in some perspective. The firm can be envisaged as a collection of different inputs (consistent with Coase 1937) which represent the resources the firm is able to marshal for the purpose of pursuing its goals. The inputs include finance, various technologies (including information technology: IT), human resources, general knowledge and experience, and entrepreneurial skills. However, like all economic agents, the firm is subject to resource constraints. The ways in which the firm seeks to maximise its use of the resources available to it and to overcome its resource constraints – for example,

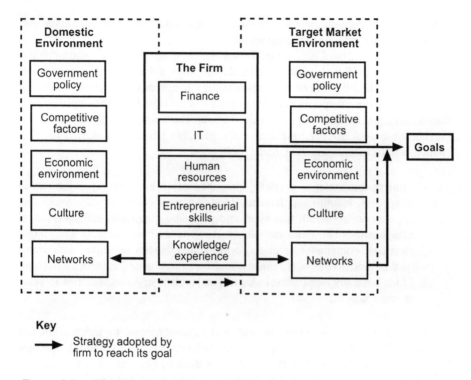

Key

→ Strategy adopted by
firm to reach its goal

Figure 1.1   The Firm in Its Economic Environment

by the use of business and social networks – is of particular interest.

The firm operates within its own domestic environment. This is shown in the diagram by the fact that it is partly in the Domestic Environment box. However, as a business it may also be targeting export markets, in which case it would also operate beyond its domestic borders. Therefore it would also be partly located in the Target Market box, and the performance of the firm is affected by conditions (for example, government regulations, the state of the market, competitive factors, infrastructure, the tax regime) in both the Domestic Market and the Target Market. Figure 1.1 illustrates the case where the firm has links with both domestic and international networks to facilitate its business activities and goals.

The 1994 APEC survey of SMEs revealed, among other things, that the key problems facing SMEs, in particular those interested or involved in exporting, include lack of access to the key resource inputs of finance and human resources in the form of skilled personnel, as well as problems of access to markets, because of lack of information and international protectionism (APEC 1994). The chapters in this volume address various aspects of these important issues. In addition, a number of other interesting issues are examined, including the impact of the Asian crisis on SMEs in the region, the contributions of SMEs to entrepreneurial activity and innovation, and the roles of different kinds of networks in different cultures.

1.3   STRUCTURE OF THE BOOK

Charles Harvie investigates the background to the 1997 Asian crisis, its impact on SMEs in the region and the role they play in economic recovery. Among other things, he finds that SMEs in general were more adversely affected than large enterprises, and that part of the reason was that they had less capacity for diversification of their product lines. Because of their strategic importance not just in providing employment opportunities and in curbing the monopoly power of the large enterprises but also in providing greater flexibility to the structure of the economy and in promoting regional trade and investment, governments have employed a range of measures to advance the development of SMEs in the aftermath of the Asian crisis.

Henry Wan Jr also emphasises the importance of industrial policy. He maintains that economies can reduce their vulnerability to financial crisis by strengthening their SMEs. Wan argues, with regard to the question of the contribution of SMEs to economic development, that not all SMEs are equal, and that those in manufacturing are more relevant (through opportunities for technology acquisition) than those in 'subsistence' industries. Government policy, which can determine the whole structure of industrial organisation, should therefore be addressed primarily to the former.

Henry Sandee, in referring to Anderson's (1982) proposed framework of the three phases of development of micro enterprises and SMEs in a country over time, distinguishes between these two classes of enterprise and provides a useful way of looking at them. The particular phase that a country's enterprises are at is a factor in how important SMEs are in the economy. Sandee refers, for example, to an observation by Hal Hill that the potential of SMEs for growth during the third phase, when large-scale firms become the growth engine of the manufacturing sector, depends on the policy stance adopted and whether opportunities for SMEs to complement large enterprises are encouraged. He then discusses the recent experiences of micro enterprises and of SMEs in Southeast Asia, which are broadly in line with trends elsewhere in the world. The speed with which many SMEs adapted to the crisis situation by concentrating on the production of basic goods is an example of their reputed flexibility in times of change and crisis. However, Sandee suggests that technical and financial support provided to those micro enterprises and SMEs that managed to obtain such support has not contributed to their growth. This is somewhat at odds with the current received wisdom and points to an issue that may merit further investigation.

On the important issue of access to finance, two different aspects are dealt with in separate chapters, one by Donald G. Ross and the other by Gurmeet S. Bhabra, John G. Powell, Jing Shi and Tian Ze. Ross examines the impact of the Asian crisis on the availability of trade finance for SMEs that were engaged in international trade. In the face of the withdrawal of financing from commercial sources at the height of the crisis, it was left to the export credit agencies and official aid financing, both bilateral and multilateral, to the region, in particular to Indonesia, Thailand and Korea, to prevent a complete drying up of financing to the region. SMEs were particularly hard hit and the lack of information which would have allowed creditworthy SMEs to be distinguished from those fatally impacted by the crisis meant that the former were tainted with the same brush as the latter. In many cases SMEs were forced to fall back on traditional family sources of financing and on countertrade initiatives.

Bhabra, Powell, Shi and Ze examine a different aspect of financing: specifically, they look at initial public offerings (IPOs) as a potential source of funding for SMEs in China and in Australia. They find that, in contrast to the Australian IPO market which is generally favourably disposed towards SMEs – indeed, SMEs play a major role in that market in Australia – Chinese companies have great difficulty obtaining not just IPO financing but financing generally, although this situation appears to be gradually changing in China. The importance of having regulatory structures and rules that support the IPO market (and, by extension, the financial markets generally) is highlighted in their analysis.

A different perspective is taken by Boon-Chye Lee and John G. Powell. They look at the issue of foreign direct investments by SMEs in the presence of political risk. Thus they adopt the perspective of potential investors and focus on the factors that are relevant in helping them arrive at a decision to invest or not. Noting that SME direct investments in a foreign country are subject to risks resulting from political acts, they present a simple model which allows such investments to be evaluated. Among other things, the model yields the intuitive result that foreign direct investments will have a lower value when the level of political risk which could have an adverse effect on investment projects is high.

The three chapters that follow turn to aspects of technology. One of the key factors behind the remarkable growth in productivity in the US in the latter half of the last decade is believed to be the increased use of information technology. While the debate on the significance and role of technology is still ongoing, recent studies such as Stiroh (2001) report that the productivity gains are related to the use of IT, and that the most IT-intensive industries experienced significantly larger productivity gains than other industries. The underlying assumption of the three chapters is that greater use of technology will help SMEs increase their productivity and innovativeness. Tim Turpin's chapter examines the impact of the Asian crisis on technology diffusion within clusters of firms in Indonesia. He finds that the crisis had a particularly severe impact on small Indonesian firms, but that it affected medium and large firms somewhat less severely. On the other hand, he finds that small firms contributed to recovery at a faster rate than medium and large firms, and suggests that this could be because a greater proportion of knowledge-intensive firms have survived the crisis than less knowledge-intensive ones. At the same time, there appears to be a move among small enterprises towards lower-value-added and less-knowledge-intensive industries. SMEs are also less connected to industry clusters than before. These trends do not augur well for diffusion of technology or for innovation, and Turpin suggests that policy reforms may be necessary to restore the links between large firms and SMEs in innovation clusters. The generalisability of his observations to other technologically dependent economies in the region will obviously depend on the degree to which their situations are similar to the Indonesian one.

Craig Van Slyke, Christopher Conca and Kenneth Trimmer discuss issues related to the requirements for the successful introduction of information technology into SMEs, including the reasons SMEs adopt technology and the ways in which technology diffusion can occur, and aspects of innovation. They examine the factors that can impede the use of IT by SMEs. The most significant of these are the lack of awareness or knowledge about IT and poor access to IT expertise; another important factor is the state of the national telecommunications infrastructure. Strategies for overcoming these barriers are then discussed.

Boon-Chye Lee's chapter, which is focused on SMEs and electronic commerce, looks at factors in the external environment that SMEs operate within, and how conducive those factors are to the uptake and implementation of electronic commerce strategies and technology by SMEs. Van Slyke et al. noted that external initiatives which encourage and support the use of IT can play an important role in influencing the key factors that impede its use by SMEs. Similarly, the importance of the role that government can play in providing an external environment conducive to e-commerce activities is highlighted. Aspects of this environment include: a reliable and efficient telecommunications infrastructure; a legal regime that recognises and supports contracts formed using e-commerce technologies, delineation of contractual rights and obligations between the parties to a transaction and of national jurisdictions in cross-border transactions; a technically literate workforce capable of performing the jobs required; an educated population that is able to use the technology and flexible enough to be willing to adapt to new ways of transacting goods and services. E-commerce offers the promise of greater productivity and competitiveness and SMEs are well placed to take advantage of its benefits, particularly in achieving scale economies not otherwise available to them.

Peter van Diermen notes that the contribution of SMEs to employment in East Asia outstrips their contribution to output. His chapter examines the impact of the financial crisis on the labour markets in South Korea, Indonesia, Malaysia, the Philippines and Thailand. A number of trends are identified. These include a downward shift in the size of businesses and a move towards casual employment, an increasing participation by females in the labour force as women take on a variety of work to supplement the household income, and the reduced mobility of labour across national boundaries as a governmental response to the problem of national unemployment.

Hock-Beng Cheah's chapter on entrepreneurship turns our attention to what is perhaps the key input associated with small businesses. He distinguishes between forms of entrepreneurship involving radical innovations and those involving relatively minor, incremental, and evolutionary adaptations to existing practices – what he terms 'creative entrepreneurship' and 'adaptive entrepreneurship', respectively. He uses the concept of adaptive entrepreneurship to illuminate and inform some of the sources of the SMEs' flexibility, drawing on examples in Hong Kong, China and elsewhere in Asia.

The chapter that follows, by Constance Lever-Tracy and David Ip, concentrates explicitly on Chinese small businesses in Taiwan, Hong Kong and Australia and their experiences during the Asian crisis. Based on interviews with 25 businesses, the study focuses on the survival strategies of these firms. From these interviews, a number of themes emerge. The first is the important role of networks in oiling the wheels of commerce. A distinction is drawn by a number of the interviewees between connections (*quanxi*), which are more 'instrumental and ... require deliberate cultivation' and networks (*renmo*), which are 'more organic, like your friends and neighbours'. The latter, which also include extended family, kinship and clan ties, are regarded as more reliable in times of travail. Another kind of network is the trust-based one that is built up over time between businesses and their customers. The second theme is the extreme financial conservatism of many of the businesses, which appear to shun debt. While this may be a condition forced upon them, banks being notoriously wary of lending to smaller businesses, it also appears to reflect something akin to being a business value. This value preserved many businesses from being overly exposed when the crisis struck and helped them weather the crisis.

Liz Fulop and David Richards draw a similar, though not identical, distinction between what they term 'contrived' networks, which are organised by third parties such as industry bodies or official authorities, and 'organic' networks which are formed without third-party intervention. The latter tend to crop up in high-context cultures, including China, Korea, Japan and Vietnam, where the external environment surrounding relationships is very significant in conveying nuances of meaning. By contrast, low-context cultures include the Anglo countries, Scandinavia and Germany, which are characterised by explicit communication codes, relatively impersonal authority and written rather than spoken contracts, among other things. Fulop and Richards investigate in some depth two of the more dominant network forms in the Asia–Pacific region, Chinese family business networks as an example of a high-context culture network, and Australian business networks as an example of contrived networking. They then draw some implications of the contrast between the two for network development for SMEs in the region generally.

Leo Paul Dana, Hamid Etemad and Richard W. Wright round off the volume with their discussion of franchises. This business form offers what they call an interdependent alternative to independent SMEs, noting that a franchise comprises a network of small firms distributing a proven product or service on behalf of a larger enterprise. Franchises can thus allow small enterprises to tap into economies of scale that are not possible without their franchisers. At the same time, large companies can achieve greater efficiency by incorporating smaller franchisees into their networks. An important advantage of franchises is that they present a lower risk profile than a typical independent SME and thus may be a more suitable form of business arrangement for the more risk averse or for those who are not innovators.

REFERENCES

APEC (1994), 'The APEC Survey on Small and Medium Enterprises', available at <www.actetsme.org>.

APEC (1998), 'Profile of SMEs in APEC Economies', available at <www.actetsme.org.sg>.

APEC (2001), 'Small and Medium Enterprises Working Group', at <www.apecsec.org.sg>.

Coase, R.H. (1937), 'The Nature of the Firm', reprinted in R.H. Coase (1990), *The Firm, the Market, and the Law*, Chicago: University of Chicago Press.

Goh, Sui Noi (2001), 'Taiwan PC Firms Feel Heat From China', *The Straits Times Interactive*, 2 August.

Harvie, C. and B.C. Lee (2002), *The Role of SMEs in National Economies*, Cheltenham, UK and Northampton, MA, USA: Edward Elgar.

Ohmae, Kenichi (2001), 'Asia's Next Crisis: Made in China', *The Straits Times Interactive*, 2 August.

Stiroh, Kevin (2001), 'Information Technology and the US Productivity Revival: What Do the Industry Data Say?', Staff Report No. 115, Federal Reserve Bank of New York, January, available at <www.newyorkfed.org/rmaghome/economist/stiroh/ks_itrev.pdf>.

2 The Asian Financial and Economic Crisis and Its Impact on Regional SMEs

Charles Harvie

2.1 INTRODUCTION

The economic performance of the East Asian economies[1] over a period of some forty years, was once described by the World Bank[2] as an economic miracle. A number of factors were advanced to explain the rapid and sustained rates of economic growth achieved by this group of economies. Foremost among these were good policy choices. This included the attainment of strong economic fundamentals: a stable macro economy, emphasising prudent monetary, fiscal and exchange rate policies, low interest rates, low inflation and a stable exchange rate; an emphasis on the accumulation of human capital; an effective and secure financial system; limiting price distortions; openness to foreign trade and investment; and implementing agricultural development policies. The attainment of strong economic fundamentals was supported by good policy choices in the area of selective interventions to support industrialisation and development: emphasis on export promotion; maintaining a low cost of borrowing; directed credit to priority sectors; and the selective promotion of key sectors or industries in the economy. This was also supported by strong institutions such as a high-quality civil service and other monitoring agencies. These strong policies and economic fundamentals were supported by market- or contest-based competition. In combination they supported the growth functions of accumulation (human capital, savings and investment), allocation (effective use of human capital in the labour market and high returns on investment) and productivity change (productivity-based catching-up and rapid technological change). The outcome from all of these was a win–win situation of rapid and sustained growth (rapid growth of exports, rapid demographic transition, rapid agricultural transformation and rapid industrialisation) with equity (equitable distribution of income, reduced poverty and improved social indicators).

Despite this glowing review from the World Bank, and the suggestion that the

East Asian economies should be seen as role models for other developing economies,[3] there were doubters. One of the most influential contributions in this regard was that of Krugman (1994), who argued that the economic growth attained by the East Asian economies could not be described as a miracle. In doing so he distinguished between intensive and extensive growth. The latter arises from increasing factor inputs to produce more output, while the former refers to expanding output with the same factor input. Extensive growth is not sustainable since ultimately returns to the variable factors must decline and hence also the growth of output. Only in the case of intensive growth, that is, gains in total factor productivity, is high growth sustainable. Krugman argued, based on his interpretation of available data, that the evidence suggested that East Asia's growth was predicated primarily on the basis of extensive growth, with little apparent evidence of significant gains in total factor productivity.[4] Consequently, Krugman argued, East Asian growth must inevitably decline.

By mid-1997 the East Asian miracle began to unravel, and Krugman's proposition appeared to be vindicated. However, this occurred not as a consequence of a slowing of economic growth[5] but rather as a consequence of a currency and financial crisis, which rapidly spread to become an economic crisis and, for some of the most severely afflicted economies, a severe social crisis. The floating of the Thai baht in July 1997 triggered a rapid currency devaluation and contagion that spread to other currencies across the region. The region was soon engulfed in a full-scale banking and financial crisis, and by 1998 an economic and social crisis of considerable magnitude. The effects of which are still ongoing.

The crisis has had a profound impact upon the corporate and financial sectors of the afflicted economies, particularly those of Indonesia, Thailand, Malaysia, the Philippines and Korea. It became recognised that the way in which business was conducted, the monitoring of the financial sector, the relationship between business and government, the need to place more emphasis on the development of the SME sector, and the conduct of macroeconomic policy would require radical restructuring and greater accountability and transparency in these countries. It is particularly in regard to the first of these that this chapter is focused. Restructuring of the corporate sector and enhanced corporate governance are essential for regional recovery. SMEs can make a major contribution to this recovery in terms of increased output, exports and employment, as well as enhancing the flexibility of these economies.

The remainder of this chapter proceeds as follows. Section 2.2 conducts an overview of economic developments in the region before and after the onset of the financial and economic crisis. Section 2.3 identifies alternative explanations for the crisis and isolates the key factors contributing to it, as well as identifying the policy responses adopted. Section 2.4 outlines the economic environment within which regional SMEs are operating in the wake of the crisis. Section 2.5 focuses upon the role of SMEs in the development process and the crucial role that they can play in the region in bringing about the necessary restructuring of economies, establishing globally competitive industries, expanding exports, generating employment and reducing regional income inequalities. Finally, Section 2.6 presents a summary of the major conclusions.

2.2   OVERVIEW OF THE ECONOMIC IMPACT OF THE CRISIS

Despite the previously impressive rates of economic growth and development attained by the East Asian economies, this did not prevent a financial, economic and social crisis of significant proportions occurring from mid-1997. Before discussing some of the key factors contributing to the crisis, it is important to identify the pre-crisis environment faced by the business community and the environment faced in the aftermath of the crisis. Tables 2.1a–2.1i summarise developments in some of the key macroeconomic indicators in the period before and after the crisis.

Impressive growth rates were achieved in the first half of the 1990s by this group of economies, ranging from an average 3.3 per cent over the 1990–95 period for the Philippines up to 10.6 per cent for China. The years 1996 and 1997 also registered an impressive regional growth performance, although this began to deteriorate in the second half of 1997. The year 1998 registered a major decline in regional GDP growth rates, with six of the economies registering a negative growth rate ranging from –0.5 per cent in the Philippines to –13.2 per cent in Indonesia. Even those economies

Table 2.1a
Macroeconomic Indicators, GDP Growth Rate,
Selected Asian Economies, 1990–99

	GDP growth rate				
Economy	1990–95	1996	1997	1998	1999
China	10.6	9.6	8.8	7.8	7.1
Hong Kong	5.0	4.5	5.0	–5.1	2.9
Indonesia	8.0	8.0	4.5	–13.2	0.2
Korea	7.8	6.8	5.0	–6.7	10.7
Malaysia	9.3	10.0	7.5	–7.5	5.4
Philippines	3.3	5.8	5.2	–0.5	3.2
Singapore	9.2	7.5	8.4	0.4	5.4
Taiwan	6.4	5.7	6.8	4.7	5.5
Thailand	9.2	5.9	–1.8	–10.4	4.2

Sources: IMF, 'International Financial Statistics', *Yearbook 1999*; IMF, *World Economic Outlook*, October, 2000.

Table 2.1b
Macroeconomic Indicators, Inflation Rate,
Selected Asian Economies, 1990–99

Economy	Inflation rate				
	1990–95	1996	1997	1998	1999
China	11.5	8.3	2.8	−0.8	−1.4
Hong Kong	9.3	6.0	5.7	2.8	−4.0
Indonesia	8.7	7.9	6.6	58.4	20.5
Korea	6.6	4.9	4.4	7.5	0.8
Malaysia	3.5	3.5	2.7	5.3	2.7
Philippines	10.9	8.4	5.0	9.7	6.7
Singapore	2.7	1.4	2.0	−0.3	0.1
Taiwan	3.8	3.1	2.0	1.7	0.2
Thailand	5.0	5.9	5.6	8.1	0.3

Sources: IMF, 'International Financial Statistics', *Yearbook 1999*; IMF, *World Economic Outlook*, October, 2000.

Table 2.1c
Macroeconomic Indicators, Unemployment Rate,
Selected Asian Economies, 1990–99

Economy	Unemployment rate				
	1990–95	1996	1997	1998	1999
China[a]	2.6	3.0	3.1	3.1	–
Hong Kong	2.0	2.8	2.2	4.7	6.2
Indonesia	3.7	4.9	4.7	5.5	6.4
Korea	2.4	2.0	2.6	6.8	6.3
Malaysia	3.7	2.5	2.4	3.2	3.4
Philippines	8.6	7.4	7.9	9.6	9.4
Singapore[b]	2.4	3.0	2.5	3.2	4.6
Taiwan	1.6	2.6	2.7	2.7	2.9
Thailand	1.7	1.1	0.9	3.4	3.0

Notes:
a   Urban areas only.
b   Ratio of unemployed to total labour force.

Sources: Asian Development Bank, *Key Indicators of Developing Asian and Pacific Countries*, 2000, Volume XXXI.

Table 2.1d
Macroeconomic Indicators, Saving/GDP,
Selected Asian Economies, 1990–99

Economy	Saving/GDP				
	1990–95	1996	1997	1998	1999
China	40.8	41.1	41.5	40.8	39.0
Hong Kong	35.7	32.3	33.4	32.3	–
Indonesia	32.7	30.1	31.5	28.4	19.5
Korea	36.3	34.0	33.7	34.2	34.2
Malaysia	37.3	42.9	43.8	48.5	47.0
Philippines	15.6	14.6	14.2	12.8	14.9
Singapore	45.9	49.5	50.4	50.6	49.9
Taiwan	27.5	26.6	26.4	26.0	26.1
Thailand	36.1	35.8	34.9	35.1	32.8

Source: Asian Development Bank, *Key Indicators of Developing Asian and Pacific Countries*, 2000, Volume XXXI.

Table 2.1e
Macroeconomic Indicators, Investment/GDP,
Selected Asian Economies, 1990–99

Economy	Investment/GDP				
	1990–95	1996	1997	1998	1999
China	38.5	39.6	38.2	38.8	38.3
Hong Kong	31.4	33.8	37.1	31.8	–
Indonesia	31.3	30.7	31.8	19.1	11.6
Korea	37.4	37.9	34.2	21.2	26.8
Malaysia	38.3	41.5	42.9	26.7	22.3
Philippines	22.7	24.0	24.8	20.2	18.6
Singapore	35.2	36.8	39.3	32.8	32.8
Taiwan	24.8	23.2	24.2	24.9	24.3
Thailand	41.0	41.7	32.9	20.3	20.7

Source: Asian Development Bank, *Key Indicators of Developing Asian and Pacific Countries*, 2000, Volume XXXI.

Table 2.1f
Macroeconomic Indicators, Interest Rate,
Selected Asian Economies, 1990–99

Economy	Interest rate				
	1990–95	1996	1997	1998	1999
China	10.11	10.08	8.64	6.39	5.85
Hong Kong	8.13	8.50	9.50	9.00	8.50
Indonesia	21.27	19.22	21.82	32.15	27.66
Korea	9.35	8.80	11.90	15.20	9.40
Malaysia	8.15	8.89	9.53	10.61	7.29
Philippines	18.52	14.84	16.28	16.78	11.78
Singapore	6.42	6.26	6.32	7.44	5.80
Taiwan	7.35[a]	5.80[a]	5.80[a]	5.30[a]	4.70[a]
Thailand	12.89	13.40	13.65	14.42	8.98

Note:
a   6-month time deposit rate.

Sources: IMF, *International Financial Statistics*, Various; Asian Development Bank, *Key Indicators of Developing Asian and Pacific Countries*, 2000, Volume XXXI.

Table 2.1g
Macroeconomic Indicators, Fiscal Balance/GDP,
Selected Asian Economies, 1990–99

Economy	Fiscal balance/GDP				
	1990–95	1996	1997	1998	1999
China	−0.9	−0.8	−1.8	−3.1	−3.5
Hong Kong	4.1	2.3	7.0	−2.0	−0.1
Indonesia	0.1	1.4	−0.7	−2.2	−2.2
Korea	−0.2	0.3	−1.5	−4.2	−5.1
Malaysia	−0.4	0.7	2.4	−1.8	−3.2
Philippines	−1.3	0.3	0.0	−1.9	−3.7
Singapore	13.1	10.6	11.8	3.4	2.5
Taiwan	−2.1	−1.3	−1.6	0.2	−1.3
Thailand	3.2	0.9	−0.3	−2.8	−3.3

Source: Asian Development Bank, *Key Indicators of Developing Asian and Pacific Countries*, 2000, Volume XXXI.

Table 2.1h
Macroeconomic Indicators, Current Account/GDP,
Selected Asian Economies, 1990–99

Economy	Current account/GDP				
	1990–95	1996	1997	1998	1999
China	1.4	0.9	3.2	3.0	1.5
Hong Kong	–	–	–	–	–
Indonesia	–2.3	–3.4	–2.3	4.4	3.8
Korea	–1.3	–4.7	–1.8	12.6	6.0
Malaysia	–5.8	–4.6	–4.9	13.7	16.9
Philippines	–3.9	–4.8	–5.3	2.0	9.2
Singapore	12.0	15.6	15.8	25.4	25.3
Taiwan	4.1	5.2	2.4	1.3	2.0
Thailand	–6.8	–7.9	–2.0	12.5	8.9

Sources: IMF, International Financial Statistics, *Yearbook*, 1999; Bank for International Settlements, 2000; IP Morgan; Asian Development Bank, *Key Indicators of Developing Asian and Pacific Countries*, 2000, Volume XXXI.

Table 2.1i
Macroeconomic Indicators, Export Growth Rate,
Selected Asian Economies, 1990–99

Economy	Export growth rate				
	1990–95	1996	1997	1998	1999
China	19.1	1.2	21.0	0.4	36.3
Hong Kong	15.6	4.0	4.1	–7.6	–2.5
Indonesia	12.8	10.9	7.0	1.1	3.7
Korea	13.2	4.1	4.2	–2.7	0.1
Malaysia	19.8	6.1	0.9	–6.8	14.7
Philippines	14.6	17.8	22.9	17.1	10.8
Singapore	17.8	5.8	0.2	–12.3	4.4
Taiwan	9.3	3.8	5.3	–9.4	9.9
Thailand	19.1	–2.6	3.4	–5.4	5.9

Sources: Asian Development Bank, *Key Indicators of Developing Asian and Pacific Countries*, 2000, Volume XXXI; IMF, International Financial Statistics, *Yearbook*, 1999 and Various; IMF, *World Economic Outlook*, October, 2000; Bank for International Settlements; JP Morgan; World Bank, *World Development Report 1999–2000*, Table 1, pp. 230–31.

maintaining a positive growth rate saw this decline noticeably. There was a clear recession in full swing across the economies of East Asia in 1998. In 1999, however, there was a dramatic turnaround, with all economies registering positive growth. The most impressive recovery being that of Korea, with a growth rate of 10.7 per cent. While there were clear signs of a recovery in 1999, the growth rates for most economies were considerably below that recorded prior to the crisis. A question mark also remained over the sustainability of the recovery.

The inflationary environment within which the business community had been operating, generally improved during the period of the 1990s. There were exceptions to this, particularly those countries most adversely affected by the crisis, in 1998, but by 1999, with the exception of Indonesia, inflation had been reduced to its lowest rate for the regional economies. Indeed in two economies, China and Hong Kong, the depth of the recession afflicting them was such that they experienced disinflation.

The unemployment rate remained relatively low throughout the 1990s for all of the East Asian economies, with the exception of the Philippines. The onset of the economic crisis in 1998 saw a noticeable increase in unemployment, with the exception of China and Taiwan. However, the official unemployment figures for China need to be treated with some caution, as they only refer to urban unemployed. Of all the economies in East Asia the performance of Taiwan has been the most impressive. Its unemployment rate barely changed over the 1996–98 period, although this rate was noticeably higher than that achieved in the first half of the 1990s.

The performance of the East Asian economies has been most notable in terms of their saving and investment rates, which are among the highest in the world. Their saving rate[6] was 30 per cent plus during the first half of the 1990s with the exception of the Philippines, which traditionally has had a much lower rate than that for the rest of the region. At the peak of the economic crisis the saving rate experienced a volatile performance across the region. Some countries saw the rate increase while others experienced a decline. The saving rate deteriorated most noticeably in Indonesia, and particularly in 1999.

On the other hand the investment rate,[7] not surprisingly, has been extremely volatile across the region, and was particularly adversely affected in the most financially and economically stricken economies. From being 30 per cent plus in the first half of the 1990s, again with the exception of the Philippines, the investment rate noticeably deteriorated in the crisis-afflicted economies – Indonesia, Korea, Malaysia, the Philippines and Thailand during 1998. Some of these experienced a slight improvement during 1999. The most noticeably affected economy was that of Indonesia, which experienced a decline in its investment rate from around 31–32 per cent up until 1997 to only 11.6 per cent by 1999 – a catastrophic reversal, from which it will be difficult to recover and to achieve previously impressive rates of economic growth. While the investment rate was relatively high during most of the 1990s, the quality of this investment and its productivity has been increasingly questioned. Much of this investment, as it turned out, was in unproductive assets, real estate and property, or simply added to excess capacity in a number of industrial sectors such as automobiles, steel, and semi-conductors. When the property market collapsed the return on this investment was very adversely affected.

The region is renowned for its prudent fiscal policy, and this is very apparent from Tables 2.1a–2.1i. During the first half of the 1990s these economies generally operated with a fiscal surplus (Hong Kong, Indonesia, Singapore and Thailand) or a small fiscal deficit (China, Korea, Malaysia and the Philippines). The exception is Taiwan, which operated with an average annual fiscal deficit equivalent to 2.1 per cent of GDP. Through 1996 and 1997 the fiscal position remained strong with either fiscal surpluses or small deficits. The onset of the economic crisis in 1998 resulted in a noticeable deterioration in the fiscal stance across all of the countries with the exception of Taiwan, which recorded a small fiscal surplus. Singapore also recorded a surplus but this was noticeably less than that recorded in 1997. By 1999, however, with the cost of financial and corporate sector restructuring mounting, in conjunction with declining taxation revenue, all of the East Asian economies, with the exception of Singapore, recorded fiscal deficits. Only in the case of Hong Kong did the size of the deficit decline as a percentage of GDP.

In terms of monetary and credit conditions, Tables 2.1a–2.1i identify developments in the nominal interest rates recorded across the region. Interest rates increased noticeably in the crisis-afflicted economies in both 1997 and 1998, easing again noticeably in 1999. A similar pattern can also be observed for Singapore. In Hong Kong, the interest rate increased in 1997 and declined in 1998 and 1999. In China and Taiwan a pattern of declining interest rates is apparent throughout the 1990s. However, it is important to compare and contrast developments in the real interest rate (the nominal rate deflated by the rate of inflation). In this regard it can be observed from Tables 2.1a–2.1i that in comparison to the first half of the 1990s, real interest rates, and hence the real interest burden of credit, increased noticeably during the period of the financial and economic crisis. The crisis-afflicted economies all experienced a noticeable increase in real interest rates in 1997, particularly in the cases of Indonesia, Korea and the Philippines, but thereafter there is a divergence in performance. Indonesia experienced a rapid reversal in the real interest rate, with this becoming negative in 1998, due to the rapid increase in inflation, but rising sharply again in 1999. A similar pattern is apparent for Thailand, although the volatility of these developments is considerably less than for the case of Indonesia. Korea experienced a continual increase in the real interest rate throughout the financial and economic crisis. Malaysia and the Philippines, on the other hand, have experienced a continual fall in the real interest rate since 1997. For China and Hong Kong the real interest rate has been increasing continually throughout the period of the 1990s. Singapore experienced an initial decline, rise and then decline over the 1997–99 period. Taiwan's real interest rate, on the other hand, initially increased, then decreased before increasing again.

While the aforementioned developments give a good indication as to the deteriorating domestic economic and business environment, external developments are key to explaining the extent of the rapidly deteriorating overall environment within the region. Tables 2.1h–2.1i, therefore, also provide information on external developments, focusing upon developments in the current account and export growth for the regional economies. Export growth slowed noticeably in 1996 for all of the economies with the exception of the Philippines.[8] A number of factors contributed to this slowdown: weakening global demand; a loss of competitiveness due to rising production costs and, most importantly, from a strengthening of exchange rates due to the relative strength of the US dollar,[9] particularly against the Japanese yen; the ongoing weakness of demand in the Japanese economy; the rise of China as a major competitor in export markets; and a decline in global prices for semiconductors, the production of which took place in a number of the regional economies.

Much of the growth of the East Asian economies in earlier periods was attributable to the growth of their exports. A decline in export earnings was of particular concern to these economies, given their increasing dependence on short-term capital flows, increasingly in the form of debt, to finance growing current account deficits. The economies most afflicted by the crisis were those experiencing relatively large current account deficits and a rising ratio of short-term external debt to foreign exchange reserves (Table 2.2). A slowdown in export earnings therefore led to increased difficulties in repaying short-term debt and in servicing the overall external debt, and reduced confidence by foreign investors in these countries.

Export growth remained relatively weak in 1997, with the exception of China and the Philippines, and certainly in comparison to its growth in the first half of the 1990s. In 1998 export growth collapsed with the spread of the financial and, more importantly, economic crisis in the region. Given the severe economic downturn across the region

Table 2.2
Short-term Debt/Foreign Exchange Reserves (%), 1990–98

	At end of period			
	1990–95	1996	1997	1998
China	44.2	24.2	22.5	19.2
Hong Kong	19.0	22.3	11.1	11.6
Indonesia	167.9	180.9	204.3	89.7
Korea	94.1	200.6	273.1	54.0
Malaysia	24.2	42.4	74.5	35.2
Philippines	176.4	80.8	166.2	79.1
Singapore	2.2	2.6	3.9	3.6
Taiwan	21.5	21.4	26.6	21.5
Thailand	100.6	101.1	135.4	82.7

Source: Calculated from Asian Development Bank, *Key Indicators Countries*, 2000, Volume XXXI.

Globalisation and SMEs in East Asia

at this time, and the fact that about 50 per cent of the East Asian economies' exports are to other East Asian economies, this inevitably contributed to a significant downturn in export growth. The crisis contributed to a collapse in regional domestic demand and reduced imports. Despite the collapsing regional currencies and improved international competitiveness, this was more than offset by collapsing market demand. While export growth for most countries declined, the decline in their imports was even more severe, resulting in a noticeable turnaround in the current account performance. As indicated in Table 2.1h, all of the East Asian economies experienced significant current account surpluses in 1998.

By 1999 a recovery of export and GDP growth across the region was under way. Export growth, with the exception of Hong Kong, became positive again, with the recovery of regional economic growth and current account surplus balances were maintained. Some of the export growth was quite spectacular, including that of China, Malaysia, Taiwan and Thailand in particular. A key issue relates to the ability of these countries to sustain this recovery, let alone their ability to return to growth rates experienced in the early 1990s. Growth of exports will remain crucial for the sustained recovery of the region. Strong growth in the US economy and the European Union (EU) will be crucial in this regard. The Japanese economy remains very weak, and cannot be relied upon as a market to assist in export growth expansion for the rest of East Asia.

The extent of the impact of the financial and economic crisis can also be seen from Table 2.3. Total GNP for each of the countries declined in 1998 relative to that achieved in 1997, and in some cases precipitously. In the worst case, that of Indonesia, total GNP declined from US$221 billion in 1997 to only US$130.6 billion in 1998. The country's GNP per capita declined from US$1100 in 1996 and 1997 to only US$640 in 1998. Declines in GNP per capita were also recorded in the other East Asian economies. Hence the impact of the financial and economic crisis has been considerable, requiring many years of recovery before pre-crisis levels of economic growth and GNP per capita can be re-established.

In sum, the financial and economic crisis has had a severe impact upon the region, resulting in declining domestic and regional demand, rising unemployment, falling investment, declining export growth, and an even more substantial decline in import growth, in general higher nominal and real interest rates, restricted access to credit, weakening fiscal balances, and improved current account and, by 1999, external debt positions. In the following section the main arguments advanced to explain the causes of the crisis, alternative viewpoints on policies required for recovery, and the contribution of the International Monetary Fund are discussed.

Table 2.3
Total GNP and GNP per capita, 1996–98

	Total GNP (US$ billion)				Per capita GNP (US$)			
	1996	1997	1998	1998[a]	1996	1997	1998	1998[b]
China	906.1	10 554.0	923.6	3 983.6	750	860	3 220	750
Hong Kong	152.5	163.8	158.2	147.1	24 160	25 200	22 000	23 660
Indonesia	217.3	221.5	130.6	568.9	1 100	1 110	2 790	640
Korea	482.5	485.2	398.8	569.3	10 590	10 550	12 270	8 600
Malaysia	91.5	98.2	81.3	155.1	4 330	4 530	6 990	3 670
Philippines	83.1	88.4	78.9	265.6	1 160	1 200	3 540	1 050
Singapore	93.1	101.8	95.5	90.5	30 590	32 810	28 620	30 170
Taiwan	282.9	292.6	268.6	–	13 230	13 560	–	12 330
Thailand	175.9	165.8	131.9	357.1	2 930	2 740	5 840	2 160

Notes:
a   Purchasing power parity (PPP), US$ billion.
b   Purchasing power parity (PPP), US$.

Sources: Asian Development Bank, *Key Indicators of Developing Asian and Pacific Countries*, Table 11, P. 17, 2000, Volume XXXI; World Bank, *World Development Report 1999–2000*, Table 1, pp. 230–31.

2.3   FACTORS BEHIND THE CRISIS

2.3.1   Panic Versus Fundamentals

What were the causes of the Asian currency, financial, and economic crises of 1997–98? Two main hypotheses and interpretations have emerged in the aftermath of the crisis. Each of these, of course, has important implications for the formulation of an appropriate policy response. According to one view, sudden shifts in market expectations and confidence were the key sources of the initial financial turmoil, its propagation over time and regional contagion. While the macroeconomic performance of some countries had worsened in the mid-1990s, as alluded to in the previous section, the extent and depth of the 1997–98 crisis could not be satisfactorily attributed to a deterioration in fundamentals, but rather to panic on the part of domestic and international investors somewhat reinforced by the faulty policy response of the International Monetary Fund (IMF) and the international financial community. Radelet and Sachs (1998 and 1999) present the most comprehensive exposition of this viewpoint. This view would advocate the provision of short-term financing[10] to increase the availability of liquidity in the form of useable foreign exchange reserves, to alleviate investor concerns and panic over the payment of interest on, as well as the retirement of, external short-term debt in particular.[11]

An alternative viewpoint suggests that the crisis reflected structural and policy distortions in the countries of the region. Fundamental imbalances triggered the currency and financial crisis in 1997, even if, once the crisis started, market overreaction and herding caused the plunge of exchange rates, asset prices and economic activity to be more severe than warranted by the initial weak economic conditions. In South Korea, Indonesia, Malaysia, the Philippines, Thailand, Singapore, Hong Kong, China and Taiwan, macroeconomic imbalances in these countries could be assessed within a broad overview of structural factors: current account deficits and foreign indebtedness, growth and inflation rates, savings and investment ratios, budget deficits, real exchange rates, foreign exchange reserves, corporate sector investment, measures of debt and profitability, indexes of excessive bank lending, indicators of credit growth and financial fragility, monetary stances, debt service ratios, dynamics and composition of capital inflows and outflows, and political instability. This position was at the heart of the IMF response to the crisis and is most comprehensively expounded by Corsetti et al. (1998). This viewpoint would emphasise the need to implement policies aimed at improving economic fundamentals.

2.3.2   Causes of the Asian Crisis – Background[12]

Central to an understanding of the roots of the Asian crisis is the multifaceted evidence on the structure of incentives under which the corporate and financial sectors operated in the region, in the context of regulatory inadequacies and close links between public and private institutions. The moral hazard problem in Asia magnified the financial vulnerability of the region during the process of financial market liberalisation in the 1990s, exposing its fragility *vis-à-vis* the macroeconomic and financial shocks that occurred in the 1995–97 period. The problem exhibited three different, yet strictly interrelated, dimensions at the corporate, financial and international levels.[13]

At the corporate level, political pressures to maintain high rates of economic growth led to a long tradition of public guarantees to private projects, some of which were effectively undertaken under government control, directly subsidised, or supported by policies of directed credit to favoured firms and/or industries.[14] Even in the absence of explicit promises of 'bail out', the production plans and strategies of the corporate sector largely overlooked cost and riskiness of the underlying investment projects.[15] With financial and investment policy enmeshed within a widespread business network of personal and political favouritism, and with governments that appeared willing to intervene in favour of troubled firms, markets operated under the impression that the return on investment was somewhat 'insured' against adverse shocks (Corsetti et al. 1998).

This provided the underpinnings of a sustained process of capital accumulation resulting in persistent and sizeable current account deficits. While borrowing from abroad to finance domestic investment should not raise concerns about external solvency, in fact it could actually be the optimal course of action for undercapitalised economies with good investment opportunities, the evidence for the Asian countries in the mid-1990s highlighted that the profitability of new investment projects was low. Investment rates and capital inflows in Asia remained high even after the negative signals sent by the indicators of profitability. In part, this occurred because the interest rate fall in industrial countries, especially in Japan, lowered the cost of capital for firms and motivated large financial inflows into the Asian countries up until 1997 (see Table 2.4). However, the crucial factor underlying the sustained investment rates was the financial side of the moral hazard problem in Asia, leading national banks to borrow excessively from abroad and lend excessively at home. Financial intermediation played a key role in channelling funds towards projects that were marginal if not outright unprofitable from a social point of view (Corsetti et al. 1998).

Considerable literature has been focused on a long list of structural distortions in the pre-crisis Asian financial and banking sectors: lax supervision and weak regulation; low capital adequacy ratios; lack of deposit insurance schemes; insufficient expertise in the regulatory institutions; distorted incentives for project selection and monitoring; outright corrupt lending practices; non-market criteria of credit allocation. All these factors contributed to the build-up of severe weaknesses in the undercapitalised financial system, where the most visible manifestation was a growing share of non-performing loans.

The adverse consequences of these distortions were crucially magnified by the rapid process of capital account liberalisation and financial market deregulation in the region during the 1990s, which increased the supply elasticity of funds from abroad.[16] The extensive liberalisation of capital markets was consistent with the policy goal of providing a large supply of low-cost funds to national financial institutions and the domestic corporate sector. The same goal motivated exchange rate policies aimed at reducing the volatility of the domestic currency in terms of the US dollar, thus lowering the risk premium on dollar-denominated debt (Corsetti et al. 1998).

The international dimension of the moral hazard problem hinged upon the behaviour of international banks, which over the period leading to the crisis had lent large amounts of funds to the region's domestic intermediaries with apparent neglect of the standards for sound risk assessment.[17] Table 2.4 clearly demonstrates the increasing significance of international bank, and other, sources of loans in Asia as a whole and particularly for the five crisis-affected Asian economies.[18] Underlying such an overlending syndrome may have been the presumption that short-term inter-bank cross-border liabilities would be effectively guaranteed by either a direct government intervention in favour of the financial debtors, or by an indirect bailout through IMF-supported programs. A very large fraction of foreign debt accumulation was in the form of bank-related short-term, unhedged, foreign currency-denominated liabilities. By the end of 1996, a share of short-term liabilities in total liabilities above 50 per cent was the norm in the region. Moreover, the ratio of short-term debt to foreign reserves, a widely used indicator of financial fragility, was above 100 per cent in Korea, Indonesia and Thailand in 1996 and 1997, and particularly so for Korea in

Table 2.4
Net Private Capital Flows to Emerging Markets, 1993–99 (US$ billion)

	1993	1994	1995	1996	1997	1998	1999
Emerging markets							
Total net private capital inflows	172.1	136.3	226.9	215.9	147.6	75.1	80.5
Net foreign direct investment	59.4	84.0	92.6	113.2	138.6	143.3	149.8
Net portfolio investment	84.4	109.6	36.9	77.8	52.9	8.5	23.3
Bank loans and other	28.3	−57.3	97.4	24.9	−44.0	−76.7	−92.5
Asia							
Total net private capital inflows	57.4	63.6	104.9	104.1	−1.4	−42.6	−27.0
Net foreign direct investment	33.9	47.1	46.6	53.1	55.5	58.3	49.9
Net portfolio investment	21.8	11.8	14.2	12.9	3.5	−17.9	−5.6
Bank loans and other	1.70	4.7	44.1	38.1	−60.4	−82.9	−71.3
Five crisis-affected Asian countries*							
Total net private capital inflows	31.8	36.1	74.2	65.8	−20.4	−25.6	−24.6
Net foreign direct investment	7.6	8.8	7.5	8.4	10.3	8.6	10.2
Net portfolio investment	17.2	9.9	17.4	20.3	12.9	−6.0	6.3
Bank loans and other	7.0	17.4	49.2	37.1	−43.6	−28.2	−41.1
Total net private capital inflows to the rest of the emerging markets							
Africa	−1.8	2.9	10.9	7.5	16.7	11.5	14.8
Europe	27.4	1.8	48.8	26.7	32.2	16.3	18.0
Russia	5.9	0.6	16.4	−0.1	1.4	−13.4	−16.2
Middle East	22.3	18.6	9.1	5.6	14.6	19.9	20.6
Western hemisphere	66.8	49.4	53.1	72.1	85.5	70.0	54.1
Brazil	12.0	6.7	32.5	34.3	23.3	13.8	13.3

Note: *   Indonesia, Korea, Malaysia, the Philippines and Thailand.

Source: IMF, World Economic and Financial Surveys, *International Capital Markets: Developments, Prospects, and Key Policy Issues*, September 2000.

1997 and then Indonesia in 1998 (see Table 2.2). The core implication of moral hazard is that an adverse shock to profitability does not induce financial intermediaries to be more cautious in lending, and to follow financial strategies reducing the overall riskiness of their portfolios. Quite the opposite, in the face of negative circumstances the anticipation of a future bailout provides a strong incentive to take on even more risk.

A number of country specific and global shocks contributed to the severe deterioration in the overall economic outlook in the Asian region, exacerbating the distortions already in place.[19]

The countries of Southeast Asia were also characterised on the eve of the crisis, as discussed in Section 2.2, as having weak macroeconomic fundamentals, including the following: sizeable and growing current account imbalances; high investment rates but declining efficiency and profitability; loss of international competitiveness arising from a stable currency *vis-à-vis* the US dollar, and rising domestic inflation; poor macroeconomic policy, focusing upon a fixed exchange rate in conjunction with capital account liberalisation; weak financial systems and institutional deficiencies; sizeable accumulation of foreign debt, characterised as being unhedged and short term.

As a result of the cumulative effects of financial and real imbalances, by 1997, the Asian countries appeared quite vulnerable to financial crises, either related to sudden switches in market confidence and sentiment or driven by deteriorating expectations about the poor state of fundamentals. In 1997 the drop of the real estate and stock markets, where sustained speculative trends were in part fuelled by foreign capital inflows, led to the emergence of wide losses and outright defaults in the corporate and financial sectors. Policy uncertainty stemming from the lack of commitment to structural reforms by the domestic authorities worsened the overall climate. From the summer of 1997 onward, rapid reversals of financial capital inflows led to the collapse of regional currencies amid domestic and international investor panic (see Table 2.5). Such a reversal was particularly prevalent for the five crisis-affected economies.

Table 2.4 summarises net capital inflows to emerging markets over the 1993–99 period. Asia as a whole received a significant proportion of this. The five crisis-afflicted economies were major recipients of private capital inflows, and this increasingly took the form of commercial bank and other loans. The rapid reversal of such capital flows in 1997 was mainly in the form of withdrawal of capital by international commercial banks.[20] Such a rapid reversal of capital provides the basis for the panic explanation for the crisis, which went well beyond that justifiable on the basis of economic fundamentals. Net outflows continued into 1998 and 1999. Net portfolio investment flows remained positive in 1997, becoming negative in 1998 and positive again in 1999.

It is worth noting from Table 2.4 that long-term net capital flows, in the form of foreign direct investment (FDI), remained positive in 1997 for the crisis-afflicted economies, and in fact increased in this year. Indeed, in 1998 and 1999, net FDI

Table 2.5
Exchange Rates, 1990–99 (per US$)*
1990–95 = 100

	1990–95	1996	1997	1998	1999
China	100	130.1	129.7	129.5	129.5
Hong Kong	100	99.8	99.9	99.6	100.1
Indonesia	100	114.1	141.7	487.7	382.6
Korea	100	104.9	124.1	182.8	155.1
Malaysia	100	96.1	107.5	149.9	145.2
Philippines	100	100.5	113.0	156.7	149.8
Singapore	100	87.0	91.6	103.2	104.5
Taiwan	100	104.1	108.9	126.9	122.4
Thailand	100	100.1	123.9	163.4	149.4

Note: *   A rise in the index number represents a depreciation of the local currency against the US$.

Sources: Calculated from IMF, *International Financial Statistics* (Various), and Asian Development Bank, *Key Indicators of Developing Asian and Pacific Countries*, 2000, Volume XXXI.

inflows remained strong for these countries. Table 2.6 confirms this by showing gross FDI inflows for the East Asian economies. These remained strong for all of the economies with the exception of the most adversely affected economy, that of Indonesia. Hence, in general, it can be said that long-term capital flows to the region

Table 2.6
Foreign Direct Investment, 1990–98
(US$ billion)

	1990–95	1996	1997	1998
China	19.4	40.2	44.2	45.6
Hong Kong	–	–	–	–
Indonesia	2.1	6.2	4.7	–0.4
Korea	1.0	2.3	2.8	5.1
Malaysia	4.2	5.1	5.1	5.0
Philippines	0.9	1.5	1.2	1.7
Singapore	5.5	7.9	9.7	7.2
Taiwan	–1.7	–2.0	–3.0	–3.6
Thailand	2.0	2.3	3.7	6.8

Source: Asian Development Bank, *Key Indicators of Developing Asian and Pacific Countries*, 2000, Volume XXXI.

remained strong throughout the crisis, boding well for the long-term growth and recovery of these economies. Clearly the problem lay with short-term capital flows, and suggested the need to focus attention upon restoring investor confidence as quickly as possible. However, the initial response was dominated by policy measures advocated by the IMF, as the crisis-afflicted economies turned to it for a financial rescue package.

2.3.3   IMF Policy Response

As a recipe for its loans the initial IMF response hinged substantially upon two key postulates: the need to reform the economies, with particular emphasis on fiscal discipline and banking sector restructuring; and the requirement to maintain high interest rates to avoid capital outflows and currency attacks. The targets and tactics of the IMF, however, did change over time as the situation in Asia progressively deteriorated, with requests from the IMF becoming less and less restrictive over time.

The IMF policies found many critics, and not just in East Asia (Radelet and Sachs 1998 and 1999). Several analysts argued that the high interest rates prescribed by the IMF to limit currency depreciation had severe repercussions on the economies of the Asian countries. Critics argued that interest rate hikes were not effective in slowing down currency depreciation, but rather worsened the extent of the crisis by leading to widespread banking and corporate bankruptcies. The effects of these policies have been described in terms of a vicious circle: the credit crunch imparted severe financial losses to otherwise solvent companies; the widespread fall in profitability translated into higher levels of non-performing loans and credit risk, exacerbating the crisis-induced recessions and, in turn, causing a further contraction in the supply of credit.

This view, however, was challenged on a key issue. Loose monetary policies in the early stages of a currency crisis contribute to exacerbating the extent of the depreciation, increasing the burden of foreign currency-denominated liabilities issued by banks and firms. In the presence of large external net liabilities a monetary expansion could actually produce financial distress and bankruptcies, setting in motion the same vicious cycle described above. Consistent with this argument is the view that the severity of the Asian crisis could in part be attributed to the unwillingness of the governments to undertake the appropriate restrictive measures at the right time.

While the appropriate interest rate policy was subject to widespread debate, it is agreed that high interest rates maintained beyond an 'emergency scenario' can have destabilising consequences. However, the crisis-afflicted countries exhibited a credit crunch which did not appear to be related to the level of interest rates, rather it had more to do with the inability of financially distressed banks to lend to a corporate sector labouring under the weight of severe debt overhang. Also the IMF's insistence on the closure of insolvent banks contributed to runs on financially healthy banks, as pointed out by Jeffrey Sachs.

Several commentators also argued that the fiscal policy requirements included in the IMF plans were unnecessarily, and harmfully, strict. At the onset of the crisis the Asian countries under attack were running low budget deficits or fiscal surpluses, as shown in Section 2.2, and were characterised by relatively low ratios of public debt to GDP, unlike the typical recipients of IMF funding assistance. Excessively tight fiscal policy, it is argued, made the crisis-induced recession worse. However, in support of the 'discipline view', it has been contended that loose fiscal policies at the onset of the crisis would have raised doubts about the policy makers' commitment to reduce the outstanding current account imbalances, jeopardising the credibility of their plans. Also, while fiscal deficits and debt were typically low before the crisis, in several Asian countries the projected fiscal costs of post-crisis financial bailouts were estimated to be in the range of 20 to 30 per cent of GDP. As these extra public liabilities translate into a permanent increase in the interest bill paid by Asian governments of 2–4 per cent of GDP per year, fiscal balances needed to be appropriately adjusted. It was only when the recessions rapidly materialised in the course of 1998 that the IMF progressively loosened its fiscal conditions to allow for cyclically adjusted fiscal deficits.

The breadth of the restructuring efforts required by the IMF raised concern that it had been playing an excessively intrusive role in domestic affairs. The criticism was that, by including in the programs a number of structural elements, the IMF was moving beyond its traditional macro-adjustment-related areas of competence (monetary and fiscal tasks) (see Feldstein 1998). The main counter-arguments were spelled out by Stanley Fischer in his reply to Feldstein (Fischer 1998c). To the extent that the Asian meltdown was attributable to structural problems rather than the traditional macroeconomic imbalances, an effective rescue strategy was bound to address the issues at the very core of the crisis. IMF lending to the Asian region would serve no purpose if the weaknesses of the financial sector, ranging from poor bank supervision and regulation to murky relations among governments, banks and corporations, were not removed by the appropriate structural reforms.

Concern was also expressed with the possibility that the IMF-led rescue packages contributed to moral hazard. Expectations of a bailout could lead investors and creditors to refrain from effectively monitoring their investment and lending strategies. Also, officials in debtor countries may pursue excessively risky courses of action, leaving a country more vulnerable to sudden shocks in fundamentals and shifts in market sentiment. While the residents of the country hit by a crisis suffer because of the crisis-induced recession, to the extent that the creditors are bailed out they do not bear a fair share of the burden of the crisis.

A number of objections were voiced against a simplistic reading of the problem. First, there is no direct evidence that the surge in capital flows to Asia after 1995 were related to expectations of international bailouts in the aftermath of the Mexican rescue package of 1994–95. The second objection regards the issue of who bears the costs of the crisis. The IMF repeatedly pointed out that a majority of private creditors, especially bond holders and equity investors, took a huge hit during the crisis. By the end of 1997, foreign equity investors had lost nearly three-quarters of their equity holdings in some Asian markets. None the less, commercial banks were to some extent spared. For instance, foreign banks operating in Korea demanded public guarantees on bank loans as a precondition for rolling over the existing loans, without forgiving any amounts due. The third objection goes against the argument that countries which rely on international support when things go out of control will follow unsound policies. Attaching conditions to assistance gives policy makers incentives to do the right thing. A fourth, and more substantial point, is that moral hazard may be the lesser evil, as the alternative response to a crisis, to leave countries and creditors to sort out their debts, may have much more dramatic and distortionary consequences. The lessons from the inter-war period and the 1980s point out that such a strategy requires complex negotiations over a long period of time, during which access to international markets is curtailed and long-term growth drastically lowered. A delay in taming a local crisis through the appropriate program of international assistance, and the failure to restore market confidence promptly, would greatly increase the chances of a systemic chain reaction across countries (Corsetti et al. 1998).

2.3.4   Capital Controls, Access to Capital and Debt Restructuring

Given the persistent and pervasive nature of the Asian crisis, the debate has encompassed such items as the reform of multilateral institutions, the future of economic and financial cooperation and, most importantly, the desirability of deregulation and liberalisation of international capital markets. The crucial question in the debate was whether exchange controls and limited capital mobility should become elements of an overall strategy of international crisis management and global restructuring. Here a distinction can be drawn between three related issues: (a) the case for controls on short-term capital inflows; (b) the case for controls on capital outflows in the event of a crisis; and (c) the optimal speed and sequencing of capital account liberalisation. Given the significance of the rapid withdrawal of short-term capital from the region in the second half of 1997, considerable interest has been focused upon the desirability and means for controlling such potentially destructive capital flows.

Many corporations have little access to working capital and are burdened by a massive stock of liabilities. Corporate debt to equity ratios that were already high before the crisis have grown even higher. Banks are under extreme stress. Partly as the result of high interest rates, which increase the rate of non-performing loans, and partly due to the attempt to recapitalise financial intermediaries at a rapid pace, the net worth of the banking system of the crisis-afflicted economies has drastically deteriorated. In such a context of financial distress and debt overhang, banks have been severely cutting credit to firms. In some cases this has been a decisive factor in inducing bankruptcy of corporations that in all likelihood would have been solvent in normal times. Contractions in trade credit are particularly painful, as such cuts undermine the firms' ability to import intermediate inputs and to produce and export domestic goods. An important indicator supporting this statement is the fact that, in spite of massive real depreciations, the exports from the crisis countries have not significantly increased in terms of volume.

Despite a decline in interest rates the credit crunch has still been severe in most countries. While the price of credit has been falling, banks that are effectively bankrupt or experience financial distress are unwilling to lend to corporate firms suffering from debt overhang so that loans are still drastically rationed. Perhaps a more effective way to assist the recovery of the Asian economies is to assist the recovery of production and exporting again, to be achieved through an accelerated debt-restructuring process that will recapitalise the banks, reduce corporate debt overhang, and provide firms with debt moratoria and new priority financing of working capital and trade. A comprehensive approach to bank and corporate restructuring is a key ingredient for the sustained recovery of the region.

2.4   IMPACT OF THE CRISIS ON, AND RESPONSE BY, REGIONAL SMES

2.4.1   Impact of the Crisis on SMEs

Section 2.2 identified the extent of the unfriendly domestic and external environment facing regional enterprises. SMEs have to operate within the macroeconomic environment of international and domestic markets, and as such are affected by changes in this environment. The major impact effects upon enterprises, including SMEs, arising from the crisis include: the price and volume of purchasing and sales both domestically and internationally; squeezed profit margins on existing products; reduced overall profitability arising from higher costs of inputs from higher domestic inflation and higher costs of imported inputs due to the collapse of the domestic currency, in conjunction with a decline in sales revenue; liquidity and cash-flow difficulties arising from customer bankruptcies and bad debts, difficulties in getting paid from similarly cash-constrained customers, and suppliers wishing to be paid as quickly as possible; a rising interest burden on outstanding loans; difficulties in gaining access to, and the cost of, temporary or longer-term finance from financial institutions; the need to strengthen efforts in regard to marketing; investment, particularly in research and development (R&D), is likely to be severely curtailed; and downsizing and potential loss of key personnel in an attempt to reduce costs.

Declining profits are likely to have had the broadest impact on SMEs, arising from changes in sales and purchasing. Weak exports and domestic demand resulted in falling orders and reduced prices, and a reduction in overall sales revenue. While the volume of raw material inputs required would also correspondingly fall, the cost of these, particularly if they were imported and denominated in US dollars, would increase in domestic currency terms with weakened domestic exchange rates. Thus SMEs experienced a reduction in post-tax profit because of a fall in sales volume and a reduction of profit margins on existing orders. As a result of the overall falling off in profits, some enterprises found themselves in severe operational and financial difficulties. Many SMEs were affected by the recovery of accounts receivable from other financially constrained enterprises and customers, and consequently the percentage of their customer bad debts increased.

Based on available data from Taiwan, by comparison with large enterprises the percentage of SMEs that found themselves affected by a fall in post-tax net profits, a reduction in the volume of orders and reduced raw material purchasing was significantly higher, demonstrating that the effects of the financial crisis on SMEs were far broader in scope than that experienced by large enterprises (Ministry of Economic Affairs 1999). In addition, the fall in the percentage of total operating revenue accounted for by exports was higher among SMEs than large enterprises. This indicates that SMEs were feeling the effects of the crisis in a wider range of product items or regions, or that, because of their small scale of operations, SMEs were unable to diversify their product lines so that when market demand fell the percentage of companies affected was that much higher (Ministry of Economic Affairs 1999).

Changes in the domestic financial environment, in particular, is liable to have had an impact upon SMEs in terms of access to financing, the interest rate burden, liquidity and other yardsticks of financial soundness. When a financial squeeze occurs it causes financial institutions to become more conservative in their lending to business enterprises, as a result of which SMEs have often not been able to secure the funding they needed, even on a short-term basis, creating cash-flow problems. As far as changes in interest rates are concerned, SMEs are traditionally viewed by financial institutions as having a relatively unsound financial structure. Thus, when the basic loan rate is raised, the increase in the interest rate charged to SMEs is often higher than the increase in the basic loan rate. Besides financial crises, Central Bank monetary policy, fluctuations in the foreign exchange market and the overall state of the economy can all lead to changes in interest rates, foreign exchange rates and the availability of financing, which in turn can affect an enterprise's operational and financial status.

During the financial crisis banks in afflicted economies were generally unwilling to make loans, although many large enterprises were still able to expand their loans. For SMEs, on the other hand, either because of the conservatism of the enterprise owners or because banks are generally less willing to make loans to them, the percentage of SMEs which increased their loans was far lower than that for large enterprises. Private loans, from family, friends and other network sources, remained an important potential source of support, even on a short-term basis, for SMEs during a financial crisis. Before the crisis, SMEs had considerably smaller dependence on bank loans in comparison to large enterprises. After the crisis, many regional governments, recognising the significance of SMEs in the recovery process, have attempted to expand access to finance for this key sector.

For many years SMEs have been playing an increasingly important role in exporting and investing overseas. Under these circumstances the occurrence of international financial crises is likely to have affected SME competitiveness in terms of foreign trade and also as regards the success of overseas investment projects, the import cost of raw materials, and other external factors. With the falling off in exports the percentage of operating revenue accounted for by this source will decline, putting more pressure on the need to generate sales from the domestic market instead. However, it is more difficult for companies to change their reliance on imported raw materials. Even those SMEs oriented solely towards domestic demand are still likely to be affected by developments in international markets, particularly those reliant on imported raw materials. In addition, international financial crises can also be expected to affect domestic financial markets, thereby having an impact upon SMEs' financing and domestic investment activities.

2.4.2   Strategies Used by SMEs in Response to the Financial Crisis

Both past and recent experience of the aftermath of economic crises demonstrate that interest rates and exchange rates can have a major impact on SME production, sales, cash flow and profits. The question of how to conduct risk avoidance operations in the midst of a financial crisis is thus an important issue. Under current economic and financial circumstances in Asia a key issue is how corporate governance of SMEs can be maintained, or enhanced, to a point where risk can be controlled, and where the relationship between cost and profit is stable and predictable. This can prevent excessive fluctuations from affecting the long-term development of SMEs. If SMEs are able to make effective use of risk avoidance strategies, tools and methods, they should be able to keep the impact of financial crises down to a minimum. In the following, emphasis is placed upon risk avoidance, risk management, market diversification, and other options as a means of keeping the impact of financial crises at a minimum.

Risk avoidance
SMEs in East Asia found themselves facing significant market, interest rate and exchange rate fluctuations during the period of the crisis. From the point of view of a business enterprise having to deal with major fluctuations in the state of the market, interest rates and exchange rates, the use of financial derivatives constitutes the most economical and fastest response strategy. Recent evidence from Taiwan (Ministry of Economic Affairs 1999) suggests that generally speaking, prior to the Asian financial crisis, the majority of SMEs considered credit risk (that is, the risk of their customers dishonouring their debts) to be the biggest risk they faced; this was true for almost every category of enterprise. However, after the Asian crisis, exchange rate risk was considered to be the greatest risk. Hence, there will be increasing interest for SMEs in exchange rate-related derivatives (such as advance sale or purchase of foreign currency, currency swaps and foreign currency options). For a relatively open economy with a high level of dependence on foreign trade, such as that of many of the East Asian economies, this means that the threat posed by exchange risk is a serious one, which obliges companies to make extensive use of derivatives to reduce their exposure

to risk. The other major forms of risk are credit risk and liquidity risk (risk related to market liquidity and cash flow).

Risk management

The basic strategies employed in risk management can be divided into five categories. These include strategies relating to production, sales, products and R&D, investment and organisation, and personnel. In the area of production strategies, many SMEs have already begun to increase their level of outsourcing so as to reduce the burden of production facilities. The use of outsourcing for production can reduce the amount that needs to be spent on fixed costs, thereby reducing the company's leverage, which in turn reduces the effect of fluctuations in operating revenue and net operating profit. SMEs making use of outsourcing as a method of risk management tend to be higher than that for large enterprises, and outsourcing has become an important characteristic of the production strategy of many SMEs.

As far as sales strategy is concerned, SMEs' most commonly used method of risk avoidance in this area is market diversification, followed by negotiation with customers to share exchange rate risk. Some SMEs are willing to sacrifice profits to maintain their market while a similar proportion adopt the opposite strategy, viewing market preservation as less important than profits. SMEs seem to emphasise market diversification more than large enterprises do.

In regard to product and R&D strategy, the main risk management methods employed by SMEs are product diversification and raising the level of product technology. The development of new products with high value added is another important product strategy. Mass market products are subject to a high level of competition and also tend to be particularly badly affected by the vagaries of the global economy.

In terms of their investment strategy many SMEs temporarily halted investment plans as a response to risk, while many chose strategic alliances to improve their position in terms of production or sales and to reduce the risk of overextending themselves. For many SMEs overseas investment, particularly with the severity of the crisis, played a relatively minor part in their overall investment strategy.

SMEs suffer from considerable restrictions in terms of both capital and personnel. This puts them at a disadvantage when it comes to R&D and marketing. In the context of a crisis SMEs need to retain their flexibility in terms of employment, but this should be done without losing key personnel, in key areas, essential for the long-term growth of the enterprise.

Market diversification

As a consequence of the financial crisis, evidence from Taiwan (see Ministry of Economic Affairs 1999) suggests that many SMEs changed the regions to which they exported. This was a reflection of the change in exchange rates and economic growth in different regions. Because of the worsening creditworthiness in some countries, particularly in some of the Southeast Asian nations, many SMEs in Taiwan changed the method of payment which they requested from their customers. While the changes in SME exports were fairly noticeable, the percentage of companies which made changes in purchasing and import quotations was lower. There were relatively few companies that made changes to their choice of production location or to their main products.

Export prices for SMEs in Taiwan changed by more than that for large enterprises, while those changing their import quotation was less. This situation reflects the fact that when it comes to negotiation over sales and purchasing prices, SMEs are in a weaker position than large enterprises. Being in a weaker position for price negotiation was also one of the reasons why SMEs' profits fell more than those for large enterprises.

Others

SME skill and information deficiencies suggest the need for government agencies to provide advice on financial planning. In addition, in the future, SMEs will need to secure more support from banks and actively communicate with them. They also need to be more active in the management of their own cash flow. SMEs also need to develop a more thorough understanding of the benefits offered by the different types of financial products available from banks; and they must also try to establish themselves as the indispensable suppliers of larger companies, so as to be able to secure their support.

2.5   IMPORTANCE OF THE SME SECTOR FOR RESTRUCTURING AND SUSTAINING ECONOMIC RECOVERY

The development of SMEs is largely recognised as being of primary importance for the generation of economic growth, export growth, the alleviation of poverty, the promotion of more pluralist societies, employment growth, and the generation of competition in domestic and international markets (World Bank). In market economies SMEs are the engine of economic development. Due to their private ownership, entrepreneurial spirit, their flexibility and adaptability as well as their potential to react to challenges and changing environments, SMEs can contribute to sustainable growth and employment generation in a significant manner. In Asia, with the liberalisation of economies, the restructuring of industries and, in some economies, the process of change of ownership, have resulted in governments facing difficulties due to the growing number of unemployed. Many of the crisis-afflicted countries in Asia are recognising that SME development will be a crucial factor in the process of industrial restructuring, employment growth, export growth, and providing the basis for a sustained recovery of regional economies. Parallel with ownership reform and privatisation, the number of SMEs is increasing.

SMEs are recognised as occupying an important and strategic place in APEC. They contribute significantly to the region's wealth and employment, as intermediate and final producers as well as consumers of goods and services. They are the primary vehicles by which new entrepreneurs provide the economy with a continuous supply of ideas, skills and innovation. Strong SME sectors attract and enable foreign investors to establish and expand domestic linkages. SMEs are also the source of future successful large enterprises. SMEs thus play a critical role in creating opportunities that make the attainment of equitable and sustainable growth possible.

The strategic importance of SMEs is recognised for a number of reasons, including the following:

- SMEs are contributing to employment growth at a higher rate than larger firms. The private sector, and in particular SMEs, form the backbone of a market economy, and in the long term are likely to provide most of the employment. SMEs tend to be concentrated in relatively labour-intensive activities, consequently playing an important role in employing the growing labour force in developing countries and alleviating the severe unemployment that threatens the survival of the poor. Labour intensity can be between 4–10 times higher for small enterprises.

- Support for SMEs will help the restructuring of large enterprises by streamlining manufacturing complexes, as units with no direct relation to the primary activity are sold off separately. Through this process the efficiency of the remaining enterprise might be increased as well.

- SMEs curb the monopoly power of large enterprises, offer them complementary services, and absorb the fluctuations associated with a modern economy.

- Through inter-enterprise cooperation, they raise the level of skills with their flexible and innovative nature. Thus SMEs can generate important benefits in terms of creating a skilled industrial base and industries and developing a well-prepared service sector capable of contributing to GDP through higher value added.

- A characteristic of small industrial enterprises is that they produce predominantly for the domestic market, drawing in general upon national resources and use and develop predominantly domestic technologies and skills.

- A structural shift from large enterprises, privately and state owned, to smaller privately owned SMEs will increase the number of owners, a group that represents responsibility and commitment to meeting changing market demands.

- An increased number of SMEs will bring more flexibility to society and the economy and might facilitate technological innovation, as well as provide significant opportunities for the development of new ideas and skills.

- New business development is a key factor for the success of regional development, particularly given the need to restructure and reconstruct many existing businesses and industries in the crisis-afflicted economies.

- SMEs not only play a key role in the economic development of individual economies, but, according to APEC, are also instrumental in promoting trade and investment activities among different economies. They are therefore instrumental in promoting the facilitation of a more open investment environment in the APEC region.

Because of this strategic importance a number of measures have been used to promote the development of SMEs in both developing and developed economies. These include:

- improvement of management training for SME managers. There is a general recognition that SME managers, especially in small firms in the start-up phase, have to carry an enormous burden, as they have to perform various functions simultaneously;

- reduction of administrative burdens for SMEs. Such firms have special difficulties in complying with too many regulations and procedures, especially in the start-up phase. SME managers have little time for this, and cannot afford consultants and lawyers to help them with advice and administrative requirements. There is a need for one-stop shopping;

- facilitate financing for SMEs. This is an important and sensitive issue, as many SMEs have continuous cash-flow problems, even without a financial and economic crisis. As practice shows, large banks are much more ready to give loans to larger enterprises than to small enterprises. Often SMEs have to pay a higher interest rate of between 2 and 6 per cent for bank credits in comparison to that of larger firms;

- stimulate industrial research and development activities in SMEs. Many SMEs perform little or no R&D, partly because they have no tradition of it and partly because they cannot afford it. Measures to increase industrial R&D in SMEs have to be created, especially if the SME is a supplier to a larger firm.

The Ottawa meeting of APEC, concerned with SMEs and their development, in September 1997, focused upon five key areas of importance to SMEs. These are access to: markets; technology; human resources; financing; and information.

- *Access to markets.* SMEs are recognised as facing special problems relating to their size and that, in the context of rapid trade liberalisation, they need to develop capacities to take advantage of opportunities arising from a more open regional trading system. The Internet is regarded as being of particular importance, as is the need to identify appropriate partners for joint ventures, to harmonise standards and professional qualifications, including investment laws and taxation procedures, and the protection of intellectual property rights.

- *Access to technology.* In a knowledge-based economy, applications of information and communications technology can be a great leveller for SMEs. However, when SMEs have limited access or understanding of these technologies, their prospects of acquiring and utilising these for their benefit is reduced.

- *Access to human resources.* Human resource development for SMEs requires a comprehensive approach, including: social structures and systems such as broad educational reforms; encouragement of entrepreneurship, business skills acquisition and innovation in society; mechanisms for self learning and ongoing training and enhancement of human resources; and appropriate governmental support programs.

- *Access to financing.* Many SMEs lack awareness of financing resources and programs available from commercial banks and other private sector and government sources, and they have difficulty defining and articulating their financing needs. Financial institutions need to be responsive to their needs and for continuing simplification of trade documentation.

- *Access to information.* Accurate and timely information is crucial for SMEs to compete and grow in a global market environment

An emerging consensus appears to have emerged relating to new approaches needed to improve the effectiveness of government strategies and programs supporting SMEs. In the field of micro finance, new approaches have emerged with the need to establish good practices for SME financing and for the provision of non-financial services to SMEs.

While government strategies to assist SMEs vary, depending upon the country's stage of development, there are some basic principles of successful SME development strategies. First, the creation of a level playing field. The fundamental key to a successful SME development strategy is the establishment of a business environment that helps SMEs compete on a more equal basis. To establish a level playing field, governments need to re-evaluate the costs and benefits of regulations that place a disproportionate burden on SMEs, implement regulations with the flexibility needed by SMEs, and place greater emphasis on competition and procurement policies to open SME access to markets. Second, to carefully target public expenditure to use scarce public resources effectively. Governments need to design a clear, coordinated strategy for SME development that carefully separates equity and efficiency objectives. Public expenditure should be confined to those services and target groups that are underserved by the market and for which there is a clear justification based on public goods or equity considerations. Using the methodology of micro finance, good practice in the delivery of services to SMEs can be judged according to the performance criteria of coverage, cost effectiveness, financial sustainability and impact. Finally, encourage the private provision of a wide array of financial and non-financial services. In most developing countries, SMEs do not have access to institutions and instruments appropriate to their needs. To ensure SME access to a diverse range of financial and non-financial services, governments should strive to develop private markets for services suitable for SMEs, stimulating market development on both the demand and supply sides.

2.6   SUMMARY AND CONCLUSIONS

This chapter has reviewed the economic and business impact of the Asian crisis, and reviewed the alternative interpretations of its key causal factors. The crisis has clearly had a significant impact upon regional growth, unemployment, inflation, investment, interest rates, exchange rates, export growth, and fiscal and current account balances. Of the two competing explanations for the crisis, this author comes down more on the side of the panic explanation. Two reasons are advanced for this. First, the extent of the adjustment of financial variables such as the exchange rate and interest rate went well beyond that justifiable purely on the basis of economic fundamentals. Second, these fundamentals were, in many ways, not considerably worse, and in some cases were actually better, than that experienced in the first half of the 1990s when no financial crisis occurred.

Rapid financial liberalisation, and the maintenance of relatively fixed exchange rates,[21] in conjunction with weak regulation and supervision of the financial sector, precipitated large inflows of private, and largely unhedged, capital inflows and the accumulation of external liabilities. The Asian economies became increasingly dependent on such inflows as current account deficits increased. These capital inflows became increasingly short term in nature during the 1990s, and in the form of debt owed to international commercial banks. It was the rapid withdrawal of funds by these international banks, mainly Japanese, in the second half of 1997 that brought about the banking and corporate sector crisis across the region culminating in the severe economic crisis during 1998. Initially, the IMF-funded rescue packages for the crisis-afflicted economies exacerbated the financial and economic crisis, most notably for Indonesia, although the harshness of the fiscal policy stance, in particular, was later reversed as the severity of the crisis intensified.

Regional SMEs could not avoid being adversely affected by the deterioration in the domestic and regional macroeconomic environment. Sales volume declined, product prices weakened in the face of intensified competition for business and weakened demand, and production and purchasing were consequently affected. Profit margins and overall profitability were squeezed. Liquidity and cash-flow difficulties followed as did bad debt and outstanding interest burdens. SMEs needed to put in place, either through their own initiatives and/or with the assistance of government, measures that would minimise risk arising from the impact of market, interest and exchange rate volatility, so as to ensure their long-run development. This requires improved corporate governance in the areas of risk avoidance, risk management strategies, market diversification, and improved access to information and finance.

The importance of SMEs for the recovery and sustained economic growth, development, and restructuring of the crisis-afflicted economies in East Asia, is widely accepted (World Bank, APEC and so on). SMEs are acknowledged to be strategically important: for industry restructuring; for employment growth; as a source of competition for large enterprises; for improving skills, flexibility and innovation; and for their potential to contribute to the promotion of regional trade and investment. Problems remain, however, in terms of access to markets, technology, human resources, financing and information. However, with improved and more effective government strategies and programs supporting SMEs, there is reason to believe that these can be overcome.

NOTES

1   These include Japan, the four tiger economies of Hong Kong, South Korea, Singapore and Taiwan, and the three newly industrialising economies of South-east Asia, Indonesia, Malaysia and Thailand.
2   World Bank (1993).
3   Japan, Hong Kong, Korea, Singapore and Taiwan had all effectively attained the status of developed economies by the 1990s.
4   Krugman's interpretation of the data has been questioned, see, for example, *The Economist* (1997), UBS (1996) and Sarel (1996).
5   Although this was inevitably affected by the resulting crisis.
6   Gross domestic saving as a proportion of GDP.
7   Gross domestic capital formation as a proportion of GDP.
8   Exports from the Philippines remained strong because of its greater reliance, in comparison to the other countries, upon exports to the US market in particular. The US economy remained very buoyant during this period.
9   Most of the economies focused upon effectively tied their currencies to the US dollar or a basket of currencies in which the weight of the US dollar was substantial.
10   Equivalent to the IMF acting as a lender of last resort.
11   Much of this debt was denominated in foreign currency, and therefore interest on it as well as its retirement had to be made in foreign currency.
12   Recent studies providing empirical evidence on the Asian crisis include Alba et al. (1998), Corsetti et al. (1998), Dornbusch (1998), Feldstein (1998), Goldstein (1998), IMF (1998), Radelet and Sachs (1998), and World Bank (1998). A large number of contributions on the crisis can also be found on Nouriel Roubini's Asian Crisis Homepage at <www.stern.nyu.edu/globalmacro/>.

13   The role of moral hazard in the onset of the Asian crisis has been stressed by a number of authors. See, for example, Fischer (1998b), Greenspan (1998) and Krugman (1998).

14   See IMF (1997).

15   See Pomerleano (1998) for an assessment of the corporate roots of the financial crisis in Asia.

16   See, for example, McKinnon and Pill (1996).

17   See, for example, Stiglitz (1998).

18   The major sources of these bank loans were Japanese and EU banks. US banks had considerably less exposure in East Asia. See, for example, Bank for International Settlements.

19   Whether cost competitiveness deteriorated in the rest of the region after the 50 per cent devaluation of the Chinese currency in 1994 is still a matter of debate. The thesis that a large part of China's recent export success reflects the devaluation that occurred in January 1994 and that this was one of the factors provoking the crisis in Southeast Asia has been espoused. However, recent studies – IMF (1997), Liu et al. (1998) and Fernald et al. (1998) – dismiss the thesis on the basis of several factors, most notably the fact that by 1993 about 80 per cent of Chinese transactions were already settled at the swap market rate, not the official rate, so that the official exchange rate devaluation influenced only about 20 per cent of the foreign exchange transactions.

20   In fact, mainly Japanese commercial banks.

21   Relative to the US dollar in particular.

REFERENCES

Alba, P., A. Battacharya, S. Claessens, S. Ghosh and L. Hernandez (1998), 'Volatility and Contagion in a Financially Integrated World: Lessons from East Asia's Recent Experience', paper presented at the PAFTAD 24 Conference, Asia–Pacific Financial Liberalisation and Reform, Chiang mai, Thailand, 20–22 May.

Corsetti, G., P. Pesenti and N. Roubini (1998), 'What Caused the Asian Currency and Financial Crisis?', mimeo, New York University. Also available at <www.stern.nyu.edu/globalmacro/>.

Dornbusch, R. (1998), 'Asian Crisis Themes', mimeo, Massachusetts Institute of Technology, February.

Economist, The (1997), 'The Asian Miracle: Is it over?', March, pp. 23–5.

Feldstein, M. (1998), 'Refocusing the IMF', *Foreign Affairs*, **77** (2), March–April, pp. 20–33.

Fernald, J., H. Edison and P. Loungani (1998), 'Was China the First Domino? Assessing Links between China and the Rest of Emerging Asia', Federal Reserve Board, International Finance Discussion Paper, No. 604, March.

Fischer, S. (1998a), 'The Asia Crisis: a View from the IMF', address at the Midwinter Conference of the Bankers' Association for Foreign Trade, Washington, DC, 22 January.

Fischer, S. (1998b), 'The IMF and the Asian Crisis', Forum Funds Lecture at UCLA, Los Angeles, 20 March.

Fischer, S. (1998c), 'In Defence of the IMF: Specialised Tools for a Specialised Task', *Foreign Affairs*, **77** (4), July–August.

Goldstein, M. (1998), 'The Asian Financial Crisis: Causes, Cures, and Systemic Implications, Policy Analyses in International Economics', No. 55, Washington, DC: Institute for International Economics.

Greenspan, A. (1998), Remarks before the 34th Annual Conference on Bank Structure and Competition, Federal Reserve Bank of Chicago, 7 May.

IMF (1997), *World Economic Outlook. Interim Assessment*, Washington, DC: International Monetary Fund, December.

IMF (1998), *World Economic Outlook*, Washington, DC: International Monetary Fund, May.

Krugman, P. (1994), 'The Myth of Asia's Miracle', *Foreign Affairs*, November/December, pp. 62–78.

Krugman, P. (1998), 'What Happened to Asia?', mimeo, Massachusetts Institute of Technology. Also available at <web.mit.edu/people/krugman/index/html>.

Liu, L., M. Noland, S. Robinson and Z. Wang (1998), 'Asian Competitive Devaluations', Working Paper 98-2, Washington, DC: Institute for International Economics.

McKinnon, R., and H. Pill (1996), 'Credible Liberalisation and International Capital Flows: The "Overborrowing Syndrome"', in T. Iti and A.O. Krueger (eds), *Financial Deregulation and Integration in East Asia*, Chicago: University of Chicago Press.

Ministry of Economic Affairs (1999), *White Paper on Small and Medium Enterprises in Taiwan, Small and Medium Enterprises Administration*, Taiwan, September.

Pomerleano, M. (1998), 'The East Asia Crisis and Corporate Finances: the Untold Micro Story', mimeo.

Radelet, S. and J. Sachs (1998), 'The Onset of the East Asian Financial Crisis', mimeo, Harvard Institute for International Development, Cambridge, MA, USA, March.

Radelet, S. and J. Sachs (1999), 'What Have We Learned, So Far, from the Asian Financial Crisis', mimeo, Harvard Institute for International Development, Cambridge, MA, USA, January.

Sarel, M. (1996), 'Growth and Productivity in ASEAN Economies', paper presented at an IMF conference, Jakarta, November.

Stiglitz, J. (1998), 'The Role of International Financial Institutions in the Current Global Economy', address at the Chicago Council on Foreign Relations, Chicago, 27 February.

Tran, V.H., and C. Harvie (eds) (2000), *The Causes and Impact of the Asian Financial Crisis*, Basingstoke, UK: Macmillan.

Union Bank of Switzerland (UBS) (1996), 'The Asian Economic Miracle', *International Finance*, **29**, Autumn.

World Bank (1993), *The East Asian Miracle: Economic Growth and Public Policy*, Washington, DC: World Bank, Oxford University Press.

World Bank (1998), *East Asia: The Road to Recovery*, Washington, DC: World Bank.

3 SMEs in the Globalised Developing Economies: Some Asia–Pacific Examples

Henry Wan, Jr

3.1 INTRODUCTION

During the financial crisis of 1997, the severity of its impact varied markedly within East Asia. Differences in industrial structure have often been held as a key factor. Today, four questions ought to be asked when we study SMEs in a developing economy:

1. How do these SMEs relate to its envisaged trajectory for development?

2. Whether and how SMEs improve the resilience of an economy in financial crises?

3. Are all types of SMEs equally relevant for the policy choice?

4. What is the impact of the development policy on those SMEs?

Different policies may lead to different outcomes. Choices enhancing the average rate of growth may increase its variance, making an economy vulnerable to financial crisis. For such issues, a comparative study is the proper approach. Research on SMEs is popular today because it is believed that the state of that sector matters, especially in avoiding financial crisis. Now there are SMEs and SMEs. How they contribute to an economy suggests which SMEs deserve more attention: is there room for improvement and do they provide much linkage in terms of serving as a channel for acquiring technology? Gas stations and barber shops the world over are alike. Handicrafts may be collectors' items. A machine shop is a handmaiden for

Thanks for the comments of Simone Clemhout, who first interested me in the topic of SMEs. I also appreciate the effort of an anonymous referee in my revision. All residual imperfections remain my responsibility.

development. It helps researchers on SMEs to clarify such issues beforehand, considering the nature of the subject and the state of the literature.

SMEs are heterogeneous, ranging from start-up firms in the Silicon Valley of the United States to the local traders in the South Pacific Islands. It has been suggested on various occasions that SMEs are responsible for the rapid American innovations in high tech, the high quality of Japanese products, the effective technology acquisition in Taiwan, the agile response to changing fashions in Hong Kong, the attraction of multinational investors to Singapore and poverty abatement in Bangladesh. Like plankton in ecology, SMEs have six properties: (a) minute in individual size, (b) transient in the average life cycle, (c) widespread in presence, (d) diverse in nature, (e) important both in their own right, and to the ambient system, and (f) close linkage to larger entities, either by metamorphosis, or through direct and indirect interactions.

Take the electronics industry, for example. SMEs affect various policy objectives in many economies. Thus, high-tech start-ups play a significant role in the New Economy of the United States, while large firms like Toshiba and Hitachi remain the pillars of strength for Japan but are closely assisted by SMEs in subordinate roles. The nature of SMEs also varies, not only from economy to economy but also from time to time. Once, the typical Taiwanese electronics firm was a small subcontractor assembling consumer electronics like radios and digital watches. The industry is now full of design houses for application-specific integrated circuits (ASICs). The state of SMEs is sensitive to industrial policy. Korean policy loans have favoured the large business groups versus the SMEs. Finally, the evolution and performance of SMEs are subject to economic laws, like the Law of Arrow (1962) on product innovation. All these facts are frequently stated in the literature. Thus, in accordance to well-known principles, the evolving SME sector forms an important channel for industrial policy, leading from industry structure to industry performance. In the 'globalised value chain', SMEs play a significant part under the framework of Porter (1990). This perspective should be kept in mind in the study of SMEs.

As a subject SMEs have already figured in the descriptions of Lancashire and Sheffield by Marshall (1919), and formed the focus of the pioneering work of Piore and Sabel (1984). In different economies they are studied for various reasons, from employment creation, the enhancement of income, the empowerment of the disadvantaged, to the acquisition or development of technology and the improvement of productivity. Now, SMEs in some sectors, say fast-food suppliers, are important for some policy objective, such as job creation, but hardly relevant for others, such as the development of technology. Since the focus of this chapter is on the growth of a developing economy, attention will be paid only to those related SMEs. Admittedly, such firms may in fact form only a minority of all the SMEs in certain economies.

Thus, by logic, our emphasis should be placed less on those traditional firms, or those which operate for subsistence rather than for profit, but more towards those in the globalised networks which might introduce technology by their direct or indirect interactions with the advanced economies. Yet, in the literature on SMEs, all firms of equal size are often treated alike in reporting the size distribution of firms. Little information is known about their likely contribution to growth potential. Hopefully, in future statistics compilation and sample surveys such concerns may be addressed.

Unless we wait until more data is generated under erroneous development policies, the alternative is to rely on the 'historical narratives' of individual firms and individual economies. Since one cannot afford to collect as many narratives as possible, we select nine types of economies in Section 3.2 cross-classified by the level of technology and the mode of operation of their SMEs, and attach one archetypal economy to each of these nine together with a brief 'stylised description'. From these, we next distil four working hypotheses on the evolution of the SME sector.

The Korean–Taiwanese comparison under the impact of the financial crisis of 1997 forms the heart of this chapter. SMEs play different roles in their alternative development trajectories. Japan is the template for the Korean policy in its heavy-chemical industry drive, and Taiwan has many firms that are clones of their Silicon Valley counterparts. That is why studies involving the future prospects of Korea and Taiwan must encompass Japan and the US of the present. Our ultimate motivation is not just about these economies, but to search for applicable implications. Hence, some other, certainly not all, nearby economies must be selectively considered.

According to this agenda, in Section 3.3, we infer from four hypotheses which SMEs utilise technology acquisition most effectively to aid development, and which firms are less effective in this area. Results are presented in Figure 3.1. These hypotheses also show how we can cross-classify the economy types and study their evolution, as done in Table 3.1. The Korea–Taiwan comparison is conducted in Section 3.4. Section 3.5 comments on the role of the government, using Japan, Korea and Taiwan as examples. Finally, Section 3.6 concludes by reviewing some of the important points from this chapter.

3.2 HIGHLIGHTS OF SMES IN SELECTED CIRCA-PACIFIC ECONOMIES

3.2.1 Nine Archetypal Economies

We consider three groups of economies. The first group includes Korea and Taiwan. We survey only some highlights of these two here, with a detailed comparison coming later. Next are Japan and the United States, which interact intensively with Korea and Taiwan. Japanese and American firms also serve as benchmarks for Korean and Taiwanese firms. The third group includes Colombia, the Fiji Islands, Malaysia, Hong Kong and Singapore. Each is useful in some unique way to compare with Korea and Taiwan, both to verify the 'consistency with reality' of our four hypotheses, and to provide a reference point for examining the impact of the financial crisis of 1997. These nine form a network of landmarks on the paths of development.

Korea
Even after its industrialisation under President Park, industries in Korea have adopted the Japanese 'closed system'[1] as their template for inter-firm linkage (see, for example, Kim and Nugent 1994). At one time, Japanese general trading corporations would intermediate for both Korean and Taiwanese SMEs, and earn huge profits from the operation. For example, Mitsubishi replaced its supply base at Kobe with Korean and Taiwanese subcontractors, as explained in Levy (1990). The Korean government then stepped in. Using large volume as a criterion, government banks selected 'general trading companies' (GTCs) to grant 'policy loans' at concession interest rates which were lower than the rate of inflation. The business groups then organised GTCs to both supplant the Japanese trading companies, but also exclude the SMEs from direct exports (see Fields 1995). They bankrupted some SMEs, bought out others, and reduced still others to the status of subcontractors, which even had to pay financial kickbacks to get orders (see Amsden 1989; also Kim 1997). Korean economists, like Kim (1997), often attribute the lower quality of Korean products – relative to Japanese products – to the weaker position of the Korean SMEs as compared to their Japanese counterparts. Supposedly, business groups are reluctant to see technically strong SMEs becoming independent.

Taiwan
Taiwanese SMEs are notable to international observers because they operate in an 'open system' and trade directly on the world market, often as subcontractors. Japanese general trading corporations have also played an important intermediation role. For example, Mitsubishi introduced the plastic shoe industry to Taiwan, and also financed skilled workers to set up their own shops in competition with their former employers (see Levy 1990). Unlike the situation in Korea, the government's attempt to promote large trading companies (LTCs) has been ineffective (see Fields 1995). Yet as the SMEs became better informed, better qualified and better trusted, they exported directly to the world market, sometimes with the help of the procurement agents of American retailers. For the bicycle industry, see the description of Crown and Coleman (1996). Thus in Taiwan, the process of the *elimination of the (Japanese) middlemen* – partial and incomplete as it is – came about by the market force of learning by doing, and not by a government initiative.

By directly interacting with buyers from advanced economies, the Taiwanese SMEs benefit from such contacts in the areas of technology and information. For example, we can quote Anthony Lo, President of Giant Manufacturing Co. on its former client, the Schwinn Bicycles Company, in 1992: 'Without Schwinn, we would never have grown to where we are today. We learned many basic things from them: quality, value, service' (see Tanzer 1992). Specific advice from their clients covered equipment selection, plant layout, and product design as documented in Crown and Coleman (1996). Eventually, that company grew into a world-class player on its own. The cluster of SMEs in satellite industries have made Taiwan highly competitive in several manufacturing industries, from machinery to electronics (see Hobday 1995). Even when rising wages made the textile industry less competitive, entrepreneurs could still profit from their human capital by relocating their factories to Mainland China.

The development of Taiwanese SMEs is closely related to international subcontracting. Both its micro structure and its operating principles are described in extensive detail in Shieh (1992). A case study there illustrates how a buyer of pyjamas from Sausalito, California placed an order, with attached design, through a trading company in Taipei. The order was then handled by a firm, 'industrial company', which made samples, monitored quality and recruited both workshops and individual home workers either directly, or through 'subcontractor heads'. None of the Taiwanese outfits had more than 10 members. From such field-work it is clear how those twin competitive advantages of Taiwan – low production cost and high flexibility – are related to the clustered SMEs in the subcontracting network. Low cost is the result of the competition among rival subcontracting chains as well as the high degree of utilisation of both the means of production and the labour force, including the use of stay-at-home workers, aborigines and a work-day as long as workers wish. High flexibility is the result of the breaking down of subcontracted jobs into their basic production operations, such as cutting, sewing, ironing, packing and so on, the training of each worker to do a number of basic operations, and the transfer of orders and tasks among different factories and workshops.

Still another type of SME arises around engineers and scientists who have studied and worked in advanced economies, in particular, the United States. These experienced persons are attracted home to start their own firms by the availability of low-cost foreign workers (from Thailand, for example), the local technicians from the existing electronics industries (such as radio and television assembly), and various suppliers of parts and components. Such high-tech SMEs combine technical effectiveness with market acumen and become a strength to the Taiwanese economy.

United States
Closely related to the operations of the Taiwanese SMEs, are their counterparts in the United States: not only as trading partners and sources of technology, but also as a template in several aspects.

The role of a trading partner. The last quarter of a century has witnessed the profound transformation of the American economic landscape. The rising standard of living brought with it higher labour costs and a tightening of safety and environmental standards in manufacturing. Thus, the operation of the product cycle resulted in the demise of many SMEs in various American labour-intensive industries, like footwear, and the erosion of other sectors such as traditional machine tools. Retailers of such products often searched for new sources of supply in developing economies such as in Taiwan. Since in other sectors, like various service industries such as e-commerce, new SMEs have stepped into the breach, the general picture of American employment has in no way deteriorated.

The role of the template. American SMEs demonstrate their function in at least four ways.

1. Their 'life trajectory'. What drove the recent American economic boom – the longest in history – owed much to an environment favourable to such high-tech SMEs as those in informatics and biotechnology. Some of these firms have grown into giants like Microsoft and Apple Computer. Others have been bought out after the successful introduction of their first fruits. Still others remain small over their entire life cycle, making contributions to technology, providing their employees with experience, and trading with or competing against larger firms. High-tech SMEs in Taiwan operate in a similar manner, though usually at a lower technological level.

2. Their specialised expertise. In economic terms many new firms are monopolistically competitive firms, each with some distinction. They are quite different from those SMEs in the industries phased out in America, like shoe-making, where SMEs produce *more of the same.* Thus in America itself, just as in some developing economies such as Taiwan though at a later stage, it is the intensified *division of labour* that transforms the SMEs from *perfect competition* to *monopolistic competition.* The emergence of expertise is clearly a sign of progress brought on by the globalisation of production. Just as classical economists have predicted: *the division of labour is decided by the size of the market.*

3. The inter-firm linkage. The special attribute of this American environment is 'the open system', in contrast to that which prevails across the Pacific in Northeast Asia. American SMEs are never tied down to specific large firms, and employees can also quit and join different businesses, or start up businesses on their own, without suffering much of a penalty. This also happens in Taiwan.

4. The disintegration and virtual integration in the high-tech sector. The computer industry was at one time highly vertically integrated with IBM as the archetype firm, with many smaller ones competing against it. Right now, Microsoft, Intel and Compaq as well as Dell are major players at the disintegrated level. The *barrier to entry* is clearly lowered for a disintegrated system, encouraging SMEs to join the market. At the same time close coordination remains possible, so that the industry achieves a virtual integration. The inter-firm relationship of an open system is fluid. Microsoft and Intel, former suppliers of IBM, may later serve Dell to rival IBM. In Taiwan, much smaller firms operate likewise at a specialised level, such as TSMC in pure chip foundry, Asutek in mother board and VIA in chipset making. Collectively, the cluster of close-by firms forms an *industrial district*, which was first studied by Alfred Marshall. In that sense, Silicon Valley is the direct descendant of Manchester and Sheffield. The principle of *external economy of scale* is alive and well.

From economic analysis the advantage of this environment is a higher pace of *product innovation* due to Arrow's Law, which predicts that an entrenched firm, with its established products, is likely to be slow to introduce new goods lest that action make current products technologically obsolescent. Vibrant SMEs are thus essential to technological dynamism.

Japan

Japanese industry derives its strength also from its large number of highly efficient SMEs, which operate in a *closed system*. Following traditions dating back to the Tokugawa period, each subcontractor is supposed to work primarily for a single client called the *primary parent*. Located in geographically concentrated fashion, and clustered in pyramid-style hierarchy, layers and layers of subcontractors serve the central assembly firm at the apex of the network. A third of the subcontractors may have an 80 per cent sales dependence on one single client. Work may be done for three or four other clients to even out the sales fluctuations and thus reduce unit costs (see Itoh and Urata 1994). The SMEs develop their own expertise and introduce various innovations, all aimed at reducing the cost and raising the quality for the glory of a brand name of the *primary parent*. Given sufficient time such synchronised efforts would yield so many incremental improvements to outcompete their American or European rivals, in products with a certain basic design.

From the economic point of view the *closed system* in Japan employs an *incomplete contract*, and encourages the SMEs and their chief client to invest in 'relationship-specific human capital' so that they can coordinate well. The large firms prefer to subcontract certain work outside to SMEs, rather than to carry out all operations inside their own firms, where their employees enjoy more extensive contractual rights (like job security in the system of 'lifetime tenure').

The strength of this system is that, supported by their central assembly firms in technology and information, the Japanese SMEs become very innovative, in spite of their small size. Occasionally, such small firms may grow large and become independent on the world market, like Shimano the producer of derailleurs for bicycles (see Crown and Coleman 1996). It remains true that on average most of such Japanese innovations are of the 'improvement engineering' type.

Japan is relevant to Korea in that Korean industrial policy consciously takes Japan as its template. It is also relevant for Taiwan in two ways, not only as a trading partner that supplies many key components but also as the cause of Taiwan's special advantage. The rapid response of the Taiwanese SMEs has made them valuable partners for American electronics firms in their revival against their Japanese competitors (see Borrus 1997).

Hong Kong

Ever after the Korean War when an embargo against China had temporarily eliminated entrepôt trade, local SMEs were solely responsible for reinventing Hong Kong as a vibrant, export-oriented, manufacturing economy. Based upon low labour cost, textiles, plastic products, toys and consumer electronics were all thriving industries. Two remarkable aspects of the economy are agile adaptation and continued progress. An illustration of the former is found in the quick adaptation of its entrepreneurs and the entire Hong Kong economy to the amazingly rapid rise and fall of the wig industry. The evidence of the latter is seen in the garment sector, where, as time goes on, the improvement in quality and reputation was such as to allow Hong Kong to graduate from a supplier of simple cotton textiles to the contract producer of top brand European design clothing. It has been suggested that these SMEs operate in the same manner as their Taiwanese counterparts, as discussed previously (see Findlay and Wellisz 1993).

However, with the worsening of its crowded conditions, Hong Kong reduced the flow of immigrant labour and shifted its economic base towards financial services. Since Hong Kong paid insufficient attention to technological education, after the Chinese economic reforms in late 1978 the exodus of industry began with the objective of escaping the high wage and high rents at home until little manufacturing remained. In a bitter-sweet finale many former Hong Kong SMEs have grown large, with their manufacturing base relocated in Guangdong Province, China, next door (see Sung 1997).

Singapore

Unlike Hong Kong, Singapore made a point of operating training programs for technical manpower according to the particular needs of multinational firms. Various favourable terms have been extended to investors producing goods with a high value-added margin. Perhaps because of these it has maintained its hold on its industrial sector, even though in the face of rising wages labour-intensive factories have migrated to Malaysia. SMEs became important for the government in the aftermath of the 1985 recession. Concerned that in future crises multinational firms may leave, the government further transferred technology to local SMEs. However, the emphasis is still for SMEs to serve the needs of multinational firms, rather than to directly export their products (see Chee 1992). Unlike Taiwan, export operation remains predominantly in the hands of multinational firms, and not local SMEs. The reason is still an issue of debate. According to Low and Lee (1990), Singaporeans are ready to go into business, but not in the manufacturing sector. One hypothesis is their 'crowding out' by the network of government-linked corporations (GLCs). Another reason may be the lack of scientists and engineers educated abroad.

Malaysia

Malaysia's exports have a high manufacturing content, but involve relatively low skill and are low value added. Presently, multinational corporations are quite important, with local SMEs, by and large, remaining peripheral. This pattern resembles Singapore more than Hong Kong in the past, or Taiwan in the present. What prevails in Malaysia is highly interesting, since the circumstances there resemble Singapore but without the presence of such specific institutions as the GLCs.

The Fiji Islands

Largely managed by South Asian immigrant entrepreneurs, SMEs in the Fiji Islands conduct manufacturing activities in an economy which is not yet extensively touched by the globalisation of production (see Fairbairn 1989). Textiles may be an exception. So far as SMEs are concerned, what prevails in the Fiji Islands today probably resembles Malaysia during the 1950s and 1960s and Taiwan in the late 1940s.

Colombia

SMEs in the garment sector do export their products but mostly to the Andean Group, where there is little pressure to be punctual in delivery, meticulous in quality control, or sensitive to customers' needs. Their entry to American and other high-income economies is largely unsuccessful, according to the study of Morawetz (1981).

The above descriptions are prepared to study SMEs operating under the product cycle, and not to review SMEs in the circa-Pacific economies proportional to their relative importance. As expected, some readers may interpret differently some details by various writers that have been reported here. For example, the appraisal of the SMEs of the Fiji Islands by Fairbairn (1989), the characterisation of Lall (1996) of the deindustrialisation of Hong Kong as disturbing, and the assessment of the influence of Japan's example on Korean policy by Kim (1997).

3.2.2 Four Hypotheses on the Types of SMEs

Based upon various 'historical narratives' in the above description of the nine archetypal economies, four tentative hypotheses are proposed.

The nature of output

First, it is our working hypothesis that in developing economies neither the traditional subsistence SMEs, nor those suppliers of differentiated final goods – no matter how refined – can make major contributions to the development process by themselves. Therefore, if development and growth form the objective of the study, what one must consider is not the number or relative share of all SMEs in an economy but rather those in the modern manufacturing sector.

The type of market

Second, it matters whether the SMEs are in an economy catering to developing economies or developed economies. When exporting to the latter market, discipline enforces requirements on tight specifications, punctual delivery and competitive pricing. To pass such a hurdle the labour force in a firm, and the firms in a supply network, must acquire certain technical capability, behavioural discipline and experience in organised effort. Such minimum requirements call for a once-and-for-all transformation for industrialisation. As a corollary, a customs union among the developing economies provides little help. One achieves at most the market size of a China or an India, but Chinese and Indian firms do not enjoy all that much advantage out of their sheer market size. This is why in history, sustained rapid growth is enjoyed only by those developing economies which participate in the worldwide product cycle. They gain information, technology and experience when they export manufactures to the developed lands.

Inter-firm linkages

Third, the nature of the supply network also makes a difference: is it an *open system* where a supplier can freely associate, or is it a *closed system* where each supplier is closely bound to one principal client, such that any outside work is done only on the latter's sufferance? Since technology is transferred by contact, and contact is broader in an open system, then openness must benefit economies in the developing phase.

Human capital

Finally, the skill requirement of production technology is crucial. In skill acquisition on-the-job experience matters, but there are limits. It is practically impossible to assign a worker with no formal education to a task requiring computer-aided design (CAD). Thus, to nurture high-tech start-ups a favourable general environment to SMEs is necessary, but insufficient. Even in an economy with thriving SMEs that produce garments, there would be no PC industry in its future if it is not ready to train technicians and engineers. One cannot replicate the development of Singapore or Taiwan if one is not ready to duplicate their program of human capital accumulation.

3.3   A TYPOLOGY AND SOME TENTATIVE INFERENCES

Gathering information from the above discussion we can first classify all SMEs in terms of their role, if any, in information and technology acquisition, as in Figure 3.1.

Next, the same information may be used to suggest how different types of economies interact with one another, and, at the same time, identify how, over time, the same economy may graduate from one economy type into another in the process of economic development. For this purpose we proceed to cross-classify the nine archetypal economies by two criteria, namely the stage of technology and the channels for output distribution as in Table 3.1.

The classification is far from exact, yet it can serve the purpose of studying the effect of SMEs on development and growth. What is relevant is their production technology, their modes of marketing, and the institutions developed under government policy. The nine economies are selected to highlight the diverse environment SMEs operate under. No two selected economies share the same environment.

3.3.1   Interactions Among the Various Economies

A few highlights can be outlined about the dynamics of the product cycle and how economies perform in the catching-up process. For reasons of history, America has

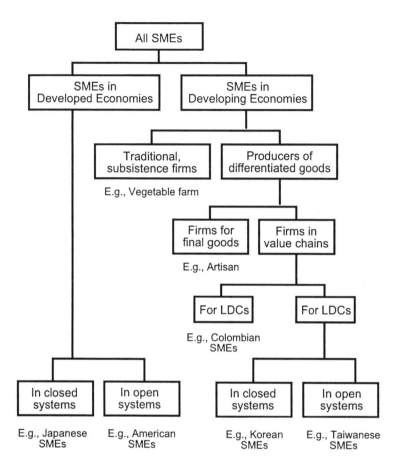

Figure 3.1   SME Classification

been the undisputed technological leader since the Second World War. Its vibrant high-tech start-up firms are apparently integral to the continued vigour of American technical leadership. Closely following is Japan, which challenges America with a cohesive, national agenda. The main focus has been *improvement engineering*, with SMEs assisting large firms in a 'closed system' of subcontractors to develop brand-name products with superior quality. Japan has enjoyed success up to the late 1980s, but its pace of progress has been somewhat blunted subsequently probably because of its industrial structure.

In both America and Japan, success led to rising wages and made cost cutting essential in competition. This encourages the outsourcing of certain operations abroad and bringing less developed countries (LDCs) into the system of globalised production.

Table 3.1
A Typology of the Archetypal Economies

	Sales by SMEs				
	Local		Global		
	At home	Nearby	Indirect		Direct
Economies			'Closed'	'Open'	
Advanced industrial			Japan		*US*
Medium industrial			Korea	*Hong Kong* Singapore	Taiwan
Early industrial		Colombia		Malaysia	
Pre-industrial	*Fiji Islands*				

Note: *Italics* means the industrial structure conforms to market forces.

Firms in both economies have saved the strategic part of the 'value chain' – R&D and over-all planning – at home. Under an 'open system', American firms outsource more operations than Japan. Economies like Colombia have not been very successful in catching up as yet. Next to Japan the newly industrialised economies (NIEs) of Korea, Taiwan, Hong Kong and Singapore have gone farther than others in catching up, each adopting a different policy but with SMEs playing a major part.

Korean policy makers regard Japan as the template, developing its own national agenda and 'closed system' even more strenuously than Japan. Taiwan and Singapore realise that because their economies are much smaller than Japan and Korea they must integrate their economies closely with the global system, and let their SMEs interact closely with foreign businesses. Taiwanese SMEs interact more directly with clients around the world, but Singaporean SMEs are focused on multinational firms already invested there. Each has made efforts to upgrade local technical manpower which provides the backbone of the local economy, working either with the multinational firms already there or through the SMEs. In comparison, Hong Kong has not paid that much attention to upgrading technical capability. Before the mid-1960s, because of its lack of bureaucratic regulations, the initial industrialisation of Hong Kong was very rapid and successful, relative to Korea and Taiwan. The production of their SMEs may be export oriented but firms are less forward looking. This led to de-industrialisation after the implementation of China's economic reforms.

Malaysia has pursued an economic policy dictated by its multi-racial society. Initially the SMEs were locally oriented, and mostly controlled by the minority

Chinese. They are similar to the SMEs in the Fiji Islands, or Singapore, before the arrival of multinational firms. The Islamic Malay majority are mostly rural, less educated and less cosmopolitan. For equity, and to avoid racial strife, massive efforts have been made to promote their interest in education, in employment, as well as in industry. The progress of such affirmative action programs is still slow. A faster pace is believed to be too disruptive and it might discourage badly needed foreign investment and lead to an economic downturn like that in the mid-1980s.

3.3.2   The Nine Economies and the Four Hypotheses on SMEs

We shall now draw implications from our hypotheses through comparisons among the nine diverse economies. They appear to be reasonably consistent with reality.

1. By the hypothesis on the nature of output, the economic development of the Fiji Islands is not likely to benefit from the SMEs related to tourism and handicraft. Textile exports by SMEs may yield more benefit.

2. By the hypothesis on the type of market, Malaysia is better positioned than Colombia to gain technology from the SME sector for development.

3. Among the four NIEs, the hypothesis on human capital is important. De-industrialisation occurred only in Hong Kong but not elsewhere, due to inadequate human capital formation. Broadly speaking, this may also explain the paucity of indigenous entrepreneurship in the Singaporean high-tech sector. Relative to both Korea and Taiwan, Singapore does not have a pool of scientists / engineers with practical experience abroad to draw upon. Malaysia shares the same weakness.

4. The principal difference between Korea, as well as Japan, and Taiwan, as well as America, concerns our hypothesis on inter-firm linkage, namely whether SMEs operate on the principle of a 'closed' or 'open' system. The former has the advantage of focused effort in improving product quality; the latter has its strength both in the acquisition of technology and the supply of innovative products. Like the Japanese, Koreans have worked strenuously for decades to nurture national industrial champions. Taiwan has developed more along American lines, with SMEs competing among each other at their own pace. The fact that American industries have not, overall, been overtaken by the Japanese also gives some explanation as to why over many decades the average growth of Taiwan has kept pace with that of Korea, even when the Korean government has adopted a more pro-growth stance. One reason may be that the 'open system' has considerable merit.

Additional points may be made regarding the 'open system'. Japan and Korea followed the Schumpeterian view: R&D must be undertaken in large firms. In comparison to Japan, the American anti-trust tradition favours SMEs, which serve as better launching pads of innovation by Arrow's Law. The American system delegates more design tasks than the Japanese to the adaptable SMEs in 'the China Circle' (Taiwan, Hong Kong, Singapore, South China). By the 1990s the coalition turned the table against Japan's slower large firms (see Borrus 1997). Free to take foreign orders under the open system, Taiwanese SMEs have acquired technology faster than their Korean counterparts. Their stronger technology makes the final product more competitive.[2]

Following the example of Japan, the Korean closed system has not provided that much of an advantage for its large firms in the world market. Yet it has weakened Korean SMEs, so that the long-term growth of Korea has not exceeded that of Taiwan. This prepares the ground for the next section.

3.4   SMES AND THE FINANCIAL CRISIS: THE KOREA–TAIWAN COMPARISON

In 1997 Korea sustained a serious debt crisis, but Taiwan was left largely unscathed. Since SMEs are prominent in Taiwan but weak in Korea, they are perceived as a protection against financial crisis. The truth is more complex. In 1997 active SMEs offered no protection to the economy of Hong Kong, which suffered then from a real estate bubble and not from external debt. Still, in the Korea–Taiwan comparison, Korean industrial policy invited trouble and resulted in a weakening of the SME sector.

In 1997 Korea was caught with: (a) the burden of private external short-term debt with short maturity, (b) low foreign exchange reserves and (c) trade and current account deficits. The dilemma was, without devaluation, the continued trade deficit would exhaust the reserves, yet with devaluation the foreign debt – denominated in foreign currency – would balloon beyond many firms' ability to pay at maturity. Both the heavy external debt and the low foreign exchange reserves were caused by heavy private investment, which even exceeded the extraordinarily high Korean savings, resulting in the need to utilise foreign savings in the form of debt. The trade deficit occurred because the Korean export mix was capital intensive with a low supply elasticity and a downwardly inflexible wage structure, thus making it particularly vulnerable to the volatile terms of trade. In a nutshell, foreign saving was borrowed for domestic investment to produce outputs with highly unstable prices.

Superficially, Korean industrial policy resembled that of Japan. Yet with a higher initial human capital, Japan could export the products of its heavy industries on the basis of their quality and reputation rather than low price. There was no need to run a trade deficit or raise foreign debt. Nor are Japanese large firms reluctant to allow SMEs to improve their technology. Large firms and heavy industry are not by themselves the trouble. The question is, how have firms become large?

This kind of massive investment was made in Korea only because of the presence of 'moral hazard'. As investors the business groups gambled for private gain, but at 'socialised risks'. They had become 'too big to fail', and could present the state with a *fait accompli*, counting upon the government banks for financial succour. The volatility of the export price and the concentration of the output mix became a concern for the state, and not for the investor.

Taiwan and Korea are similar in situation, but different in industrial structure. Both are poor in resources. Neither enjoys cutting-edge technology. To survive and thrive they must export manufactures. What they export reflects how they produce and who makes the investment decisions. Korea specialises in goods produced with internal economies of scale: oil tankers, cars, steel and memory chips. Heavy fixed equipment in capital-intensive industries are naturally controlled by large firms. To cross-subsidise such projects across industry lines, it is natural that business groups would arise to even out the funding requirement at different phases of the investment projects. Such industries often have militant unions and hence downwardly inflexible wages. Large fixed costs also imply inelastic supplies.

Taiwan opted for an alternative choice, with many SMEs seeking niche products in the world market. The staple products include bicycles, machine tools, computer peripherals and application-specific integrated circuits. SMEs often have a more flexible wage structure, and highly elastic supply schedules. Business groups also form over time, but often as suppliers of domestic needs rather than export staples. Adaptability in a changing market becomes Taiwan's means for survival. For what they produce, for example, bicycles, firms such as Giant Manufacturing may also become the largest producer in the world. Even so each is likely to be relatively small in the whole economy, with little chance of getting special state support because of its sheer size. In terms of high foreign exchange reserves, no foreign debt, and frequent trade surpluses, it is Taiwan rather than Korea that resembles Japan.

3.5 THE ROLE OF THE GOVERNMENT

In Table 3.1, there are two parallel lines of evolution: Korea–Japan, under the closed system, and Taiwan–US, under the open system. Both Korea and Taiwan have not only maintained their industries, which Hong Kong has had difficulty in doing, but have also witnessed the flowering of indigenous entrepreneurship, active on the world market (which is still largely absent in Singapore). This degree of success may be attributed to a sufficient supply of 'public goods', including law and order, utilities and infrastructure, a stable macro economic environment, and last – but not the least – an adequate pace of human capital formation. Yet, as the last section indicates, there are major distinctions between the development policies of these two economies. This was made clear during the crisis of 1997.

In open systems the networks of different economies penetrate mutually. So far, firms like Vitelic and VIA have moved back and forth between the United States and Taiwan. In upgrading the economy further, Taiwan faces no more challenging barriers than those facing Finland or Switzerland. In closed systems, the question, 'is Korea going to be the second Japan?' is harder to answer, in view of the differences in the macro economic performances of these two economies.

Although Korea is twice as populous as Taiwan, it is not the size but the policy choice which made the two economies develop along such different paths. After all, beyond tariff protection, neither America nor Canada – both followers of Britain in industrialisation – had ever adopted any industrial policy similar to those of Korea or Japan. Neither America nor Canada could be said to be 'too small' for that type of policy.

Actually, between Taiwan and Korea, differences in policy emerged, but not because Taiwan adopted any special measures which promoted its SMEs as a class. Nor have high-tech SMEs been favoured over high-tech large firms. It was in Korea that a conscious choice was made to create large firms and large business groups quickly, soon after President Park seized power in a coup. To legitimise his military rule, Park personally took on the task of supervising Korean growth. He arranged for government banks to grant selected business groups short-term loans at negative real interest rates. Over those few that grew rapidly, he imposed personal control. In principle the state could bankrupt any firm any time by calling in the loans, and President Chun did cause the Kukje Group to fail (see Fields 1995). But in the end, under President Kim Young Sam, the state could bankrupt no business group that was 'too big to fail', without triggering a crisis.

In contrast to Taiwan it is quite clear that the Korean policy weakened SMEs and prevented them from becoming adaptable exporters, because of the degree and manner in which business groups were promoted. Financed by the state, the business groups set up general trading corporations to exclude the Korean SMEs from foreign markets. In contrast to Japan, the Korean policy did not cause large firms to nurture SMEs as innovative subcontractors, but rather to exploit them for immediate gain. Unable to build up brand loyalty for their products the Korean large firms had to search for comparative advantage in industries with high capital intensity and significant internal returns to scale, such as shipbuilding and dynamic random access microchips (DRAMs). This made the Korean economy constantly short of investment funds and the Korean trade balance highly susceptible to fluctuations in the terms of trade.

We should not get the impression that the best government policy is always a passive policy. Market failure often develops in a market economy, and the government should act to ameliorate such shortcomings. For example, clustered SMEs provide external economies to one another. Such a development can be assisted by the government through well-designed industrial parks and government-sponsored research facilities. This is what Taiwan has done in the electronics industry. In a sector with a rapid turnover of firms, what is important is that the SME sector generally is in good health and not that every individual SME must continue to thrive for ever. That is an antidote against moral hazard.

3.6 CONCLUSION

SMEs are not a panacea against financial crisis, yet an economy may become vulnerable to crisis because the SME sector is weak. Although not all SMEs are suitable for development a healthy SME sector is helpful in its various roles, including as an incubator for efficient large firms. SMEs can thrive without active government assistance, however the state can play a useful role against market failure. Overall, human capital formation is perhaps the most important factor in the long run.

NOTES

1   To be explained below.
2   See Chu and Li (1996) on Taiwan's bicycles.

REFERENCES

Amsden, A.H. (1989), *Asia's Next Giant: South Korea and Late Industrialisation*, Oxford: Oxford University Press.

Arrow, K.J. (1962), 'Economic Welfare and the Allocation of Resources for Invention', in National Bureau of Economic Research, *The Rate and Direction of Inventive Activity*, Princeton, NJ: Princeton University Press, pp. 609–25.

Borrus, M. (1997), 'Left for Dead: Asian Production Networks and the Revival of the US Electronics', in Barry Naughton (ed.), *The China Circle: Economics and Electronics in China, Taiwan and Hong Kong*, Washington, DC: Brookings Institution Press, pp. 139–63.

Chee, P.L. (1992), 'Potentials and Problems of SMI', in Kim Seung Jin and Suh Jan-Won (eds.), *Co-operation in Small and Medium-scale Industries in ASEAN*, Kuala Lumpur: Asian and Pacific Development Centre, pp. 75–114.

Chu, W.W. and J.J. Li (1996), 'Growth and Industrial Organisation: A Comparative Study of the Bicycle Industry in Taiwan and South Korea', *Journal of Industrial Studies*, **3** (1), 35–52.

Crown, J. and G. Coleman (1996), *No Hands: The Rise and Fall of The Schwinn Bicycle Company, An American Institution*, New York, NY: Henry Holt.

Fairbairn, T. (ed.) (1989), *Island Entrepreneurs: Problem and Performances in the Pacific*, Honolulu, HI: East-West Center, Pacific Islands Program.

Fields, K. (1995), *Enterprise and the State in Korea and Taiwan*, Ithaca, NY: Cornell University Press.

Findlay, R.E. and S. Wellisz (eds) (1993), *Five Small Open Economies*, New York: Oxford University Press.

Hobday, M. (1995), *Innovation in East Asia: The Challenge to Japan*, Aldershot: Edward Elgar.

Itoh, M. and S. Urata (1994), 'Small and Medium-size Enterprise Support Policies in Japan', Policy Research Working Paper 1403, Washington, DC: World Bank.

Kim, L. (1997), *Imitation to Innovation: The Dynamics of Korea's Technological Learning*, Boston, MA: Harvard Business School Press.

Kim, L. and J.B. Nugent (1994), 'The Republic of Korea's Small and Medium-Size Enterprises and Their Suport Systems', Policy Research Working Paper 1404, Washington, DC: World Bank.

Lall, S. (1996), *Learning from the Asian Tigers: Studies in Technology and Industrial Policy*, New York, NY: St Martin's Press.

Levy, B. (1990), 'Transactions Costs, the Size of Firms and Industrial Policy: Lessons from a Comparative Case Study of the Footwear Industry in Korea and Taiwan', *Journal of Development Economics*, **34** (1–2), 151–78.

Low, L. and T.Y. Lee (1990), *Local Entrepreneurship in Singapore, Private and State*, Singapore: Times Academic Press.

Marshall, A. (1919), *Industry and Trade: A Study of Industrial Technique and Business Organization; and of their Influences on the Conditions of Various Classes and Nations*, 2nd edition, London: MacMillan and Co. Ltd.

Morawetz, D. (1981), *Why the Emperor's New Clothes are not Made in Colombia: A Case Study in Latin American and East Asian Manufactured Exports*, Oxford: Oxford University Press.

Piore, M.J. and C.F. Sabel (1984), *The Second Industrial Divide: Possibilities for Prosperity*, New York: Basic Books.

Porter, M.E. (1990), *The Competitive Advantage of Nations*, New York: Free Press.

Shieh, G.S. (1992), *'Boss' Island: The Subcontracting Network and Micro-entrepreneurship in Taiwan's Development*, New York: P. Lang.

Sung, Y.W. (1997), 'Hong Kong and the Economic Integration of the China Circle', in Barry Naughton (ed.), *The China Circle: Economics and Electronics in China, Taiwan and Hong Kong*, Washington, DC: Brookings Institutions Press, pp. 41–80.

Tanzer, A. (1992), 'Bury thy Teacher', *Forbes*, **21** (December), 1221.

4   SMEs in Southeast Asia: Issues and Constraints in the Pre- and Post-crisis Environments

Henry Sandee

4.1   INTRODUCTION

This chapter discusses evidence on the impact of the financial and economic crisis on SMEs in the manufacturing sector in Southeast Asia. We rely mostly on case studies because of the lack of aggregate and/or sectoral overviews. Many case studies suggest that SMEs have been weathering the crisis better than large firms (Cameron 1999; Hill 1999; and Rasiah 1999). In this chapter we look at possible explanations.

It is relevant to make a distinction between micro enterprises and SMEs. We shall discuss both in this chapter. Micro enterprises are a key asset in poverty alleviation strategies as they offer easily accessible jobs to households to make ends meet. Such enterprises are particularly important during periods of economic distress. In Southeast Asia there is evidence of recent growth of micro enterprises due to the loss of better-paid jobs in other sectors of the economy. SMEs play a different role in economic development. The benchmark for support to SMEs should be their contribution to productive employment generation. There is evidence to suggest that SMEs do well during periods of economic growth when small-scale entrepreneurs are able to profit from new market opportunities (Hill 1995). This chapter argues that we cannot understand the recent performance of SMEs without taking into consideration the dynamics of SMEs during the years of rapid economic development as well. We concentrate the analysis on the country that we know best: Indonesia.

An earlier draft of the chapter was presented at an ADB-OECD workshop on SME financing in Asia, 3–4 July 2000, Asian Development Bank, Manila.

This chapter is structured as follows: Section 4.2 presents a framework on micro enterprise and SME dynamics with special reference to the manufacturing sector. In particular, it looks at the changing size structure of employment during the process of industrialisation. Section 4.3 discusses trends in micro enterprise and SME development in Southeast Asia prior to the crisis. Section 4.4 presents evidence on the impact of the crisis on SMEs in the region. We argue that the tendency of SMEs to cluster may partly explain their relatively good performance in recent years. Section 4.5 looks at the experiences with direct technical and financial support to SMEs before and since the crisis. We pay attention also to changes in the policy environment since the crisis. Section 4.6 summarises the major findings from this chapter.

4.2   MICRO ENTERPRISES, SMES AND ECONOMIC DEVELOPMENT

4.2.1   Trends in the Development of the Manufacturing Sector

Anderson (1982) published a frequently quoted article on the role of small enterprises in economic development.[1] He distinguishes three distinct phases regarding the relative importance of micro enterprises and SMEs through time. Phase one refers to the early stage of industrial development during which cottage and household industries (CHIs), mainly micro enterprises, are predominant in terms of both employment generation and number of production units. Large factories in this phase are mainly foreign or state owned and they have few linkages with the domestic economy. The second phase is characterised by increased urbanisation and expanding cash markets that give rise to a shift from traditional household activities to growing specialisation of the entrepreneurs in small-scale production with more use of hired labour and apprentices in addition to family workers. CHIs are displaced increasingly by SMEs in a growing number of manufacturing subsectors. Countries like Cambodia, Laos, and possibly Vietnam appear to be in this phase. Large firms become more important too while there is evidence of their increased integration in the domestic economy through subcontracting and other types of business linkages. In phase three, large-scale firms become the engine of growth of the manufacturing sector. Scale economies become prominent with respect to plant, management, marketing and distribution in countries like Thailand, Malaysia, the Philippines and Indonesia. CHIs decline further in importance while SMEs *may* remain, playing a vital role in the development of the manufacturing sector through growing involvement in subcontracting. Hill (1995) adds that the SME growth potential in a country during this phase depends very much on the policy environment: does it offer opportunities for SMEs to develop alongside large firms through manufacturing complementary outputs or concentrating on niche markets? The extent of concessionary finance, investment incentives, tariff structures, government subsidies and so on determines the importance that big firms attach to subcontracting and the opportunities for small firms to find viable market opportunities.

4.2.2   Micro- and Small-firm Dynamics: New Evidence

Liedholm and Mead (1999) have recently published a very important book based on extensive fieldwork concerning small enterprises and economic development in selected developing countries (mainly in Africa). It advances the discussion in at least two ways. First, recent evidence suggests that in many developing countries micro enterprises do *not* decline in absolute importance when the aggregate economy develops. Field evidence shows that many new micro enterprises are started each year although many others also cease operation. However, there is a *net* stream of micro businesses in most developing countries. Micro enterprises have remained more important than expected some 20 years ago because other sectors of the economy do not generate sufficient jobs. Second, Liedholm and Mead (1999) show that only a few per cent of micro enterprises graduate to become small firms with ten or more workers. The great majority of micro enterprises are non-growing enterprises that remain fully reliant on (unpaid) family labour. Nevertheless, graduates are of importance since they generate a considerable number of jobs.

Micro enterprises and SMEs face different constraints. There are clear drops in the importance of marketing and capital as main constraints when firms grow, suggesting that SMEs are participating in more dynamic factor and product markets compared with micro enterprises. SME activities are generally more attuned to market opportunities compared with micro enterprises.

Importantly, Liedholm and Mead found that most SMEs are *not* micro-enterprise graduates but firms that started with both family workers *and* paid labourers right from the start. This is very relevant for policy makers as it suggests that the micro-enterprise sector may often not be the seedbed for the emergence of small-scale entrepreneurs.

Liedholm and Mead's field evidence is also relevant to understand recent developments in Southeast Asia. Their findings suggest that when the economy as a whole is growing, small enterprises add to their workforce. At the same time many micro enterprises close down while also there is less pressure to start new micro businesses. During good times, SMEs are able to profit from new market opportunities that arise. By contrast, the opposite forces are at work during an economic downturn. Under such circumstances, many SMEs remain stable in terms of employment or perhaps shed some workers, while a shortage of employment opportunities in the overall economy increases the pressures on people to start their own new business even though these may generate only very low incomes.

4.2.3   Small-enterprise Clusters

In recent years, there is more optimism concerning the growth and export prospects of small manufacturers in developing countries (Schmitz and Nadvi 1999). There is evidence that the SME sector *can* be resilient and dynamic during both economic good *and* bad times, and this is attributed partly to the importance of clustering of small manufacturing enterprises. Clusters can be simply defined as sectoral *and* spatial concentrations of firms. For example, we do not find one or two tailors in a certain village, but tens or hundreds of them working side by side. Clustering offers opportunities to work together (joint action) and generate external economies. Consequently, growth constraints faced by individual small-scale manufacturers are less severe in clusters. In clusters, small-scale entrepreneurs may benefit from external economies that arise through collective purchase of inputs and/or collective marketing efforts. Clusters offer opportunities for joint action by small-scale entrepreneurs: together they may mobilise financial and human resources. This facilitates technological upgrading and penetration of dynamic market segments as it brings down transaction costs. 'In summary, the argument is that ... [clustering] breaks down the investment into riskable steps, that the enterprise of one creates a foothold for the other, that ladders are constructed which enable small enterprise to climb and grow' (Schmitz and Nadvi 1999, p. 1506).[2] Evidence from Southeast Asia suggests that a substantial part of SME exports originate from clusters of small enterprises. Clustering facilitates penetration in distant markets because of the cost advantages in production and marketing.

4.3   TRENDS IN SME DEVELOPMENT IN SOUTHEAST ASIA (BEFORE THE CRISIS)

4.3.1   Changes in the Size Structure

Hill (1995) provides an overview of SMEs in the region during the period of rapid industrialisation and economic growth since the mid-1980s. Hill notes that micro enterprises and SMEs typically employ 30–60 per cent of the manufacturing workforce in the region. There is a shift towards larger industrial units over time in the region. This is to be expected as periods of economic growth offer new opportunities to SMEs while many micro enterprises close down.

There are data problems when we want to assess the changing role of SMEs during the process of economic development in Southeast Asia. Hill (1995) notes that the best data set is available for Singapore, which shows that the biggest shakeout has occurred in the initial stages of the export-industrialisation growth process. During the later stages SMEs may regain their role in the industrialisation process when these enterprises develop their technological capabilities and are able to function as reliable counterparts in subcontracting relationships. However, Hill notes that this will happen only when the government policy stance stimulates SMEs to play their potential role.

Hill (1995, pp. 13–14) discusses the SME shares in distinct subsectors of the manufacturing sector in Indonesia, Malaysia and the Philippines. Table 4.1 summarises his findings for selected subsectors. For the purpose of comparison, SMEs have been defined as firms with a workforce of up to 200 workers. The table shows that SMEs are significant 'in labour intensive industries, where an ability to adapt to customer-oriented requirements is an advantage, and in which scale economies and brand names are not generally significant' (Hill 1995, p. 13). Examples include leather products, footwear, furniture, structural clay products, and metal products.

We are able to present a more recent overview of trends for Indonesia only. The Economic Census results of 1986 and 1996 allow us to study changes in the composition of the Indonesian manufacturing sector over a period of 10 years. Table 4.2 shows that micro and small firms continue as the locus of most employment in Indonesia's manufacturing sector. As of 1996 nearly half of all workers were found in units of five workers and two-thirds in ones of under 20. About a quarter are found in establishments of 100 or more workers and probably close to a fifth in those of over 500 workers (Berry et al. 1999).[3]

Timmer (1999, p. 85) notes that labour productivity rose dramatically in the 1986–96 period for medium and large-scale manufacturing enterprises. Rice and Abdullah (2000) confirm this. The fact that the employment size structure did not change significantly in the 1986–96 period suggests that productivity improvements have occurred over most of the size structure. This would imply that micro enterprises and SMEs have been dynamic, too, with rapidly increasing levels of productivity that allows them to remain competitive *vis-à-vis* large firms.

Table 4.1
SME Shares in Selected Industries
(% share of SMEs in industry value added)

ISIC	Industry	Indonesia	Malaysia	Philippines
311	Food products	69.5	53.1	19
313	Beverages	26.6	9.9	7
322	Garments	57.3	24.5	12
331	Wood products	23.6	69.2	25
332	Furniture	94.7	na	35
364	Bricks, tiles	93.7	na	na
381	Metal products	38.7	63.3	46
383	Electric equipment	18.2	20.5	12
Total		20.5	38.7	21

Source: Adapted from Hill (1995, p. 14).

Table 4.2

Size Composition of Indonesian Manufacturing Establishments, 1986 and 1996

Year	Size of establishment (number of workers)	Number of establishments	Employment (thousands of workers)	Per cent of Employment	Labour Product- ivity
1986					
	< 5	1 422 593	2 700.1	50.8	
	5–19	98 129	787.7	14.8	2366
	20–99	12 902	493.2	9.3	12 627
	100 and up	2 894	1 328.4	25.1	na
	Total	1 536 518	5 309.4	100.0	
1996					
	< 5	2 415 285	4 830.5	44.6	na
	5–19	242 067	1 873.2	17.1	2 985
	20–99	16 317	623.8	5.7	9 913
	100 and up	6 680	3 591.1	33.0	24 268
	Total	2 703 346	10 918.6	100.0	

Sources: Sensus Ekonomi1 1986 and Rice and Abdullah (2000), who draw also on unprocessed data from Badan Pusat Statistik for small enterprises in 1996 (from the 1996 Economic Census).

There is evidence that similar productivity growth has taken place among SMEs in other countries in the region. Rasiah reports productivity increases for Malaysia for small firms participating in subcontracting networks in the electronics industry. Berry and Rodriguez (1999) note that SMEs in the Philippines appear to have recovered from a long period of decline. Between 1967 and 1988, the employment share of establishments with more than 100 workers grew from 22 per cent to over 28 per cent. At the same time the employment share of SMEs (10–99 workers), though it did rise, remained small compared to other countries of the region, at just less than 10 per cent in 1988. Taking the whole period from 1975 to 1994 there was a tendency for labour productivity gaps of the larger establishments *vis-à-vis* the 10–40 worker category to rise and also the smallest enterprises gained on this group. Nevertheless, the SME sector recorded productivity growth albeit slowly (Berry and Rodriguez 1999). Rodriguez and Tecson (1998) present recent evidence that suggests that changes in trade policy have had an important effect on the industrial sector in the Philippines. Recent liberalisation created an environment that favoured dynamic SME development through lowering barriers to imports of intermediate and capital goods. However,

Rodriguez and Tecson (1998) argue that the recent dynamics of SMEs in the Philippines still appears weak compared to neighbouring countries because a number of other policies (labour, tax, and credit regulations) are still biased towards bigger establishments.

4.3.2 The Importance of Clustering, Business Linkages and Technological Upgrading for SME Development

Liberalisation policies in many countries of the region have enabled export-oriented industrialisation and have offered new domestic and export market opportunities to SMEs. These new opportunities emerged through increases in both intermediate and final demand. Clustering and, to a lesser extent, subcontracting have been important mechanisms through which both micro enterprises and SMEs have participated in economic development. It is often overlooked that a substantial part of SME exports from the region originate from clustered micro and small enterprises involved in subcontracting relationships or other forms of vertical business linkages.

Data on clusters, though, remain scarce so far. Table 4.3 shows the importance of clusters for the province of Central Java in Indonesia, which is the heartland of micro- and small-enterprise employment in the country. In Indonesia the Ministry of Industry and Trade provides a listing of so-called *sentra industri* or clusters. *Sentra industri* are defined as geographical groupings of at least 20 similar enterprises. Exceptions, however, are made for groupings of small enterprises that export (part of) their products. In such cases, smaller groupings are also registered as clusters. The *sentra industri* data suggest that there are only limited differences in average firm size in clusters between the main industrial subsectors, such as food processing, textiles, wood products and structural clay products. Firms in clusters are very small and they employ on average 2–3 workers only. Sandee et al. (1994) and Klapwijk (1997) estimated the importance of clusters in the province of Central Java:

1. There were some 4200 *sentra industri* in Central Java in 1989. Together these clusters employed some 50 per cent of all manufacturing workers.

2. Since the majority of clusters in Central Java are groupings of small-scale and cottage enterprises, we have also estimated the share of clusters in employment generated by all such enterprises. We found that clusters provided some 63 per cent of all employment in cottage and small-scale manufacturing.

Table 4.3 summarises the main characteristics of *rural* industry clusters in Central Java. It ranks clusters according to the value of investments in equipment, which is an indication of the different barriers to entry (Weijland 1999). The table shows that clusters are diverse. Bamboo weaving, ceramics, palm sugar and so on are marginal activities that are carried out by rural households in the absence of more rewarding income-generating employment. In such clusters the advantages of clustering are confined to lower transaction costs in input collection and marketing output. In contrast,

Table 4.3
Rural Clusters by Subsector in Central Java: Weight, Cluster Size
and Investment, and Yearly Gross Output, 1989

Product	Percentage of cluster total	Enterprises per cluster	Investments per enterprise (Rp. 1 000)	Gross output per enterprise (Rp. 1 000)
Bamboo weaving	21.5	69.4	11.8	751
Ceramics	1.4	64.8	17.1	680
Palm sugar	17.8	120.0	27.6	599
Tempe	10.7	28.0	38.6	4 854
Textiles weaving	0.8	45.2	51.9	4 404
Krupuk	5.6	59.1	76.8	4 340
Bricks	6.2	41.5	87.1	3 147
Tailoring	3.0	18.3	97.5	1 977
Furniture	4.5	38.9	112.7	5 187
Batik	3.3	96.7	117.8	1 536
Roof tiles	4.7	65.0	148.7	1 814
Farm tools	1.2	33.4	154.3	3 273
Leather	0.4	35.4	241.7	9 761
Tahu	2.4	33.6	299.5	11 853
Embroidery	0.8	86.3	385.7	46 482
Garments	0.8	47.1	731.6	13 143
Other	14.9	44.0	177.2	5 474
Total	100.0	63.9	85.6	3 446

Sources: Klapwijk (1997, p. 76) and Weijland (1999, p. 1522).

embroidery and garments appear more dynamic and these activities require substantial investments and output. Products of the latter clusters are marketed over much wider areas than the marginal clusters.

Technological upgrading appears to have been a major source of SME dynamics. There is evidence that innovation adoption is widespread among SMEs in the region and that it has resulted in productivity growth. Clustering and business linkages are important arrangements for 'delivery' of technological change. Both lower the barriers to innovation adoption by offering small firms opportunities to share the costs with others (either other producers or traders) (Rasiah 1999; Tran Van Hoa 1999; Sandee et al. 2000; Tambunan 2000).

Various authors have noted the unfavourable biases in government policy for SME development, and it is widely acknowledged that the performance might even improve in the absence of such biases. Rice (2000, p. 11) argues for Indonesia that 'even though small manufacturing enterprises did not appear to grow quite as rapidly as medium–large ones during this period, they performed very well. They should be able to perform even better in the future with more supportive economic policies, including little or no bias against them, unlike in the past'.

Finally, the relatively good performance of SMEs during the years of rapid growth seems not to be explained by effective promotion policies through provision of technical and/or financial assistance. Evidence from the region suggests that technical assistance has not been very useful to promote SME growth. In general, small producers rate financial assistance higher than technical assistance. The main point however is that, irrespective of the effectiveness of assistance, the percentage of small enterprises that have received some kind of support is so low that it cannot be considered as an important engine of SME growth (Pernia and Pernia 1986; Sandee et al. 1994).

4.3.3   A Case Study: Changes in Roof-tile Production in Indonesia

A case study on the Indonesian tile industry may be useful to illustrate the changes in the size structure of the manufacturing sector during a period of rapid growth. The roof-tile sector is characterised by the coexistence of distinct types of firms and production technologies ranging from cottage industries with traditional hand-driven equipment to medium-sized firms with power-driven presses and mixers. Small firms use clay as the main input while larger firms rely on cement. In the 1986–93 period we studied selected tile clusters each representing a specific type of firm and technology. Primarily the hierarchy imposed by the structure of demand explains the coexistence of different types of firms and technologies. Different technologies generate different types of output, with different prices, for different groups of rural and urban consumers. Economic development in Indonesia during the period of study resulted in higher per capita incomes which made it possible for households to spend more money on building or upgrading of dwellings. This resulted in a shift of demand towards more expensive tiles. Some tile clusters were able to adjust to these shifts in demand by upgrading technology and in the production of higher quality (and more expensive) tiles while other clusters closed down. The transformation in the tile industry had a positive impact on employment with small firms employing an increasing number of paid workers. However, many women, who were previously highly active in cottage enterprises, lost their access to the industry. Technical and/or financial support by government agencies or non-governmental organisations (NGOs) has played no role in the changes in the tile industry. The lowering of subsidies on cement, which is the main input for large-scale tile manufacturers, has been an important boost for small-scale manufacturing of tiles as it has raised the prices of cement tiles (Wahjana 1994; Sandee 1995).

4.4   THE IMPACT OF THE CRISIS

4.4.1   Introduction

There is a widespread impression that smaller enterprises have been weathering the crisis better than larger companies because they are less reliant on formal and import markets, and, presently, on very costly borrowed funds. Furthermore, these enterprises tend to produce 'necessities' rather than 'luxuries', for which demand is unlikely to stagnate much, even during a crisis. Likewise it is argued that the crisis has led to more liberal policies to counter foreign capital withdrawal from the region. The depreciation of currencies in many countries has been favourable for smaller enterprises that are generally less dependent on imports compared with their larger counterparts. Below, we make a distinction between evidence on micro enterprises versus SMEs. Furthermore, we shall pay specific attention to SME developments in Indonesia.

4.4.2   Micro-enterprise Development

There is evidence of the growing importance of micro enterprises for employment generation in various countries in the region. Webster (1999) notes this for Vietnam. Foreign investment has dropped to a small fraction of levels seen a few years ago. The number of private companies, mainly SMEs, grew very rapidly following liberalisation and rapid economic growth. However, in recent years of economic adversity, the growth rate has slowed down importantly. Consequently, the micro-enterprise sector remains the main provider of jobs and incomes for the majority of the Vietnamese population, and its role is expanding in recent years. White (1999) mentions for Thailand that the share of self-employment has risen from 53.8 to 54.4 per cent in the 1997–98 period while it had constantly been decreasing prior to the crisis. White adds that the immediate impact of the crisis affecting several countries in the region has been greatest in the urban areas. In such areas, the most substantial increase has been in badly paid self-employment. In urban concentrations such as Jakarta, Bangkok and Manila the laying off of workers in large-scale enterprises has not resulted in massive return migration to the rural areas. Many laid-off workers have remained in the cities and found relief in the informal sector.

The ILO (2000) notes for Cambodia that the majority of the population is active in micro enterprises and retailing with textile manufacture, weaving apparel, wood and wood products, grain milling and sugar processing being the main industrial activities. Micro enterprises are very important in both rural and urban areas in Cambodia and their role is increasing over the years. The crisis has contributed to further growth of the micro enterprise sector.

Most general statistical evidence on trends in the labour market comes from the large annual Susenas survey (carried out during the month of January, in the middle of the rainy season when agricultural activity is likely to be most prominent).

Comparison of the figures for 1995, 1997 and 1998 shows that those with their own business but no workers moved up some 4 per cent while those with temporary or unpaid workers dropped the same amount (Berry et al. 1999). This shift was apparent in both urban and rural areas, and has characterised the economy as a whole, not just manufacturing. Since a substantial part of self-employment trade and service activities have a 'last resort' character it is likely that the adjustment process has involved a shift to such marginal activities. In Indonesia the social safety-net programs and the expansion of micro credit schemes have contributed also to the expansion of micro enterprises. The programs and schemes have improved access of urban and rural households to grants and subsidised loans which have been used to start up micro business ventures especially in activities with low entry barriers.

We may conclude that, as expected, the micro enterprise sector has expanded in most countries of the region. It is a distress strategy for those that have lost their access to better-paid jobs elsewhere in the economy. There are signs of involutionary growth with more enterprises serving the same clients. Trends in this sector in Southeast Asia are in accordance with Liedholm and Mead's evidence on expansion of the micro-enterprise sector during economic downturns.

4.4.3   The Crisis and SMEs: Indonesian Experiences

SMEs with a high input content have suffered from substantial increases in prices; which sometimes went up more than 400 per cent in Indonesia in a period of a few months only. SMEs that concentrate on the domestic market are confronted with sluggish demand on domestic markets from both intermediary and final consumers. By contrast, SMEs that aim at export markets are in a very favourable position to penetrate new markets because of the steep decline of the value of many currencies in the region. Evidence so far indeed shows the diversity in impact on SMEs and their adjustment strategies to the changes in the economic environment since the outbreak of the crisis.

The Akatiga Foundation (1999) in Bandung has carried out a survey on the impacts of the crisis on SMEs in various provinces in Indonesia. The Foundation is involved in monitoring the performance of 800 SMEs. It reports that during 1997–98 some 28 per cent of the producers showed improved performance, while the remainder lost or saw no significant change. Export-oriented firms did better than their domestic counterparts. The study also showed that SMEs in Java suffered more than those on other islands of the archipelago, and those in urban areas more than their rural counterparts. The Akatiga survey identified various coping strategies by small-scale entrepreneurs to deal with economic adversity, including working at lower profit margins and lowering labour costs.

Musa and Priatna's (1998) survey on access to credit for small and medium enterprises during the crisis, based on a sample of some 300 firms in eight provinces and various sectors, reports that self-finance has remained the main source of funds for investment and working capital. More than 75 per cent of small firms were fully reliant on own funds to finance business activities and less than 13 per cent had access to formal finance, with the number declining slightly since the outbreak of the crisis. The limited exposure of small-scale business activities to borrowed funds from the formal sector is presumably one of the factors explaining the resilience of these activities during the current period of economic distress. The main coping mechanisms of the sampled firms include the use of cheaper inputs to replace expensive (imported) materials and the downsizing of the labour force. Of respondents, 80 per cent have seen their business shrink (though only 21 per cent report laying off workers); in 12 per cent of cases it stayed constant and 8 per cent have achieved an increase, the latter occurring mainly in those activities which export and have limited need for imported materials.

Scattered evidence from surveys undertaken by the Ministry of Co-operatives and Small and Medium Enterprise Development taken together with the cited Susenas data and with basic economic logic, leave little doubt that the SME sector has on balance felt some negative impact from the crisis. The crisis creates pressure for firms to adopt adjustment strategies to cut costs and to redirect output to new market opportunities whenever possible. The Susenas evidence to the effect that there have been no major changes in the structure of manufacturing employment suggests only modest job loss in small-scale firms. Either most firms have been able to cope without major reductions in their workforce, or the creation of new firms has offset such reductions. Of course the picture may become different if economic recovery does not come soon, and more drastic adjustment strategies may be needed.

A look at specific industries helps to identify the range of effects from the crisis. There is evidence of rapid growth and employment generation in the small-scale furniture industry, especially in Jepara but also in North Sulawesi (Akatiga Foundation 1999; Jellinek and Rustanto 1999; and Sandee et al. 2000). This industry exemplifies an economic activity that uses domestic inputs and has plenty of export potential. Large and small firms in the furniture industry are developing long-term linkages to overcome the present insecure environment. Foreign actors play an important role as intermediary between domestic production networks and international buyers, and also contribute to easing the credit constraint due to the collapse of the Indonesian banking system. Policy has contributed positively to the transition through the development of the provincial harbour to accommodate container transport, the simplified procedures for foreign investors, and the improved facilities for clearing exports. As for the impact of the recent events on the smaller enterprises, some of those already engaged in exporting (usually indirectly) are being pressured by contractors and large firms to sign long-term contracts; some may become disguised wage labour. The fast growth has produced greater standardisation and a stricter division of labour and tasks among firms. Prior to the crisis the small firms had access to various trade networks. Sandee (1998) wonders whether these changes will diminish the overall flexibility of the industry and have a negative effect on regular quality upgrading, which has been the norm in the past and will remain much needed in the future.

The experience in the construction materials sector contrasts considerably with that of furniture, as befits its non-tradable character. Wiradi (1998) reports that brick making in certain villages in West Java has collapsed as a consequence of the substantial decline in urban building activities. Sandee (1998), however, found that tile and brick makers in specific villages of Central Java maintained pre-crisis production levels, through a gradual replacement of urban markets by rural ones. The relatively good condition of farmers in the area and the channelling of funds from the social safety-net programs into rural building activities fuelled this replacement.

4.4.4   Impact of the Crisis on SMEs in Other Countries in the Region

Berry and Rodriguez (1999) discuss the impact on the SMEs in the electronics and car parts industries in the Philippines. SMEs dominate the assembly industry in electronics while large firms dominate the production of parts; by contrast, in the automotive industry the production of parts is dominated by SMEs while larger firms concentrate on the assembly of parts. Both industries were aiming primarily at export markets prior to the crisis and these markets have remained buoyant. There is also some evidence that the domestic markets for car parts has been quite resilient because the crisis has led to a postponing of purchases of new cars and increased the demand for replacement parts.

Rasiah (1999) shows for Malaysia that the successful participation of SMEs in the export trade does not always come about spontaneously through communication and collaboration among SMEs and big domestic firms and multinationals. Rasiah argues that government trade and industrial policy has hampered the development of subcontracting linkages. There are, however, certain regional governments (at the state level) that have been able to foster commercial and sustainable linkages between big firms and SMEs. These regional governments were able to enhance effective coordination between markets, institutions and firms that has been beneficial to subcontractors. Their proactive support to local SMEs has bridged the gaps between these firms and the larger enterprises and multinationals.

Webster (1999) found for Vietnam that many SMEs are now facing tough times, and they are very vulnerable. 'Most are producing low-entry barrier, low margin products within export industries that are among the most "rootless" in the world, e.g., garments and footwear. Firms that are selling these products through trading agents are mostly selling Vietnamese labour, which is currently better value than that of competing countries even though its productivity is generally quite low' (Webster 1999, p. 8). Vietnamese SMEs are under pressure as the depreciation of many currencies in the region forces them to accept even lower returns to stay in the market. Consequently, SMEs are lacking resources to expand their business. In the mid–1990s foreign buyers were still highly interested and, with the dong exchange rate more competitive, they were 'knocking at the doors' of many private SMEs. Since the crisis this is no longer the case, and small-scale entrepreneurs are faced with the demands of operating in a much more competitive marketplace. Vietnamese SMEs that aim at the domestic market are facing problems too as the downturn of the Vietnamese economy has negatively influenced their business opportunities.

For Cambodia, the ILO (2000) reports that economic liberalisation during the 1990s has permitted a strong revival of the private SME sector. Examples are given of the brick and tile, rice-milling and construction industries. In addition, the tourist industry offers major opportunities to SMEs. Also in this country, however, there is evidence of mounting problems for SMEs as a consequence of the economic crisis that has hit the region.

Régnier's (2000) study on SMEs in Thailand during the crisis evaluates the distress among SMEs during the crisis and the subsequent IMF-led structural adjustment policies. His study argues that a significant proportion of small entrepreneurs have revealed a capacity for resilience. Many small firms were able to adjust to the new economic situation. There are plenty of examples of SMEs that have gone bankrupt but the overall trend is adjustment. Régnier found that the crisis had a negative impact on collaboration among small firms, and individual entrepreneurs have 'turned to the core fundamentals of [their] own business and [have] tried to keep it standing through the storm' (Régnier 2000, p. 153).

4.5   PROMOTING MICRO ENTERPRISES AND SMES: BEFORE AND DURING THE CRISIS

4.5.1   Introduction

The previous section has shown the importance of the macro economy on the development of the smaller enterprises in the economy. Liberalisation, trade and industry policies have much influence on the prospects for both micro-enterprise and SME development. A depreciation of currencies and high interest rates are of significant influence, and have been beneficial for those enterprises that are not dependent on imported items and which do not rely on formal credit.

It is the case, without doubt, that ongoing macro policy adjustments remain of the highest importance to foster micro enterprises and SME development in the region. Strengthening the legal and regulatory framework is often mentioned as one of the key elements of small-enterprise development strategies. There is, for example, a great need to streamline the licences and permits that SMEs need to start, continue, or expand their businesses. In addition, the promotion of domestic and international competition by removal of entry barriers and tariff and non-tariff barriers will be beneficial to SME development especially for those in export trade. The creation of a more enabling environment for micro-enterprise and SME development is not only to be achieved through policy adjustments at the national level, but it requires also a proactive role by regional governments. Several international donors intend to concentrate on these policy issues in the foreseeable future. Likewise, there is evidence through the region that incentive systems, tax holidays and such measures are not accessible to all enterprises but only to firms that have reached a certain threshold in terms of fixed assets, turnover or employment. Consequently, they are favouring larger enterprises and SMEs are not facing a 'level playing field'.

4.5.2 Supporting the Development of Micro Enterprises and SMEs

In all countries of the region, governments have launched a range of technical and financial support programs to foster the development of small enterprises. Throughout the years these programs have frequently been improved with more attention being paid to sustainable support through private sector involvement that remains beneficial to target groups after withdrawal of public funding. In this section we shall review programs for technical and financial assistance in the region and assess whether, and eventually how, these programs have changed in the wake of the economic and financial crisis. This section is based mainly on Indonesian experiences.

Technical training programs in the region are frequently executed under the auspices of the Ministry of Industry through agencies for small enterprise development. Such agencies have networks of offices at the provincial and local level to execute the technical assistance programs. For example, specialised officers are concentrated at the provincial level and visit the districts in accordance with the execution of local programs, while general training and extension officers are posted directly at the local level. In Southeast Asia, there exists a range of credit programs for micro- and small-enterprise development. Some programs are aimed specifically at enterprises, while others have a broader scope and focus on all types of business plans that are submitted by rural and urban households. Prior to the crisis there was a trend towards the development of credit schemes on a non-subsidised basis to promote the execution of sustainable programs. Some schemes focus on credit to groups only, but most schemes have an individual approach. Increasingly, credit applications in the region need to be accompanied by business plans in order to decrease possible default. There are a limited number of examples of credit programs that are provided in conjunction with technical assistance. In such cases, financial assistance is frequently considered a follow-up to technical support.[4] We shall discuss the impact of various schemes below.

Small industry clusters are important for manufacturing employment generation in the region. Some countries in the region have specific programs for clustered small manufacturing enterprises. Examples are Thailand and Indonesia where a substantial part of total manufacturing employment is concentrated in rural industry clusters (Allal 1999; Sandee and Van Hulsen 2000). Cluster development features highly on the agenda of the Indonesian, and also Thai, government because it offers opportunities to offer support to a large number of small producers at relatively low costs. In addition, learning effects are likely to be high in clusters, and assistance may concentrate on selected producers who are highly motivated and who are expected to play a leading role in local change processes.

4.5.3   Support to Micro and Small Enterprises

There is limited evidence on the impact of technical and financial support to promote small-enterprise development (Pernia and Pernia 1986; Sandee et al. 1994; Sandee 1998; and Sandee and Van Hulsen 2000). Technical support is provided at low cost. In most cases government officers with low salaries are responsible for the provision of a range of support services. In general, support concentrates on supply-side measures, such as training and credit, because these are cheaper to provide than demand-side measures such as strengthening links between small and big firms and stimulating participation in exhibitions and trade fairs. The latter requires more substantial involvement of support agencies in terms of finance and manpower.

Review studies show low participation rates in technical and financial support programs. It was estimated that for the province of Central Java (Indonesia) fewer than 10 per cent of micro enterprises and SMEs had participated in technical and financial assistance programs during the 1970–92 period. The majority of micro and small enterprises have not received any assistance so far, and with existing budgets it will take many years before a majority of the target group will have participated in support programs.

Review studies also show that the impact of both technical and financial assistance to *micro-enterprise* development is *limited*. The majority of these enterprises can be labelled as dormant, in the sense that they produce basic products for poor consumers mainly in rural areas. Their output is of little interest to urban traders and they are highly dependent on the growth of incomes in their direct surroundings. Training and credit will not be sufficient to bring about change (innovation adoption) in enterprises that are firmly embedded in traditional rural trade patterns. For example, palm-sugar producers were taught to use new production methods, while there is general agreement in Indonesia that the market for processed palm sugar is saturated. Assistance is biased towards male producers, and women are significantly underrepresented among the beneficiaries although they dominate the micro-enterprise sector in most countries in the region. The effectiveness of assistance is further dampened by its non-recurring nature. In fact, it is unrealistic to expect that a two-day training session and financial assistance of some US$25 (very common features of support) will be the turning point for micro enterprises to make the switch to dynamic production and marketing channels.

Additionally, review studies find evidence in the region of a positive relationship between support and employment growth in many SMEs. Assistance can be highly relevant in the case of dynamic SMEs. Among such enterprises there is demand for technical and financial services to *accommodate* growth processes that have been put on track by producers and buyers. For example, SME producers of woven cloth in Java (Indonesia) are frequently requested by traders to manufacture new designs in accordance with rapid changes of preferences among consumers. Such sale prospects stimulate producers to participate in training courses and, in many cases, they are willing and able to pay for such services. In dynamic clusters there are frequently intensive inter-firm linkages, and patterns of collaboration facilitate the diffusion of technical and financial assistance among the producers in the cluster.

4.5.4   Support During the Crisis

There are two contrasting trends in the support to the small-enterprise sector since the outbreak of the crisis. First, there is a tendency to provide more subsidised support to *micro* enterprises given the key role that they play in poverty-alleviation strategies. Second, there is growing attention for sustainable business development services (BDS) and commercial credit for *small- and medium-scale* enterprises, with greater involvement of private sector managed delivery mechanisms. In this section we shall look briefly at recent experiences with financial and technical support in the region since the crisis.

Technical assistance for micro-enterprise development has become less important *vis-à-vis* financial assistance in response to the crisis. In many countries, development agencies were confronted with budget cuts. There are few examples of international donor agencies that have been willing to replenish technical support budgets. This does not come as a surprise as it is widely acknowledged that technical support to micro enterprises has not been very useful in stimulating change and creating new jobs. Moreover, review studies have revealed that technical support is not rated very highly. By contrast, both national governments and international donor agencies have given high priority to the provision of financial assistance with subsidised interest rates. The 'credit boom' has been an important factor explaining the expansion of the micro-enterprise sector. Improved access to (micro) credit has been important for many micro enterprises to counter the cost increases and sluggish demand during the crisis. There is awareness, however, that this is not a strategy for sustainable micro-enterprise development in the long run, but it plays, undeniably, a key role in poverty alleviation strategies and social safety-net programs.

Support to SMEs in the region has developed differently since the crisis. Access to credit has worsened as a consequence of the crisis, which has led to a credit crunch that appears to have been compensated only for micro enterprises through the creation of new subsidised credit facilities. This has been a constraint for SME development. We note that SMEs that participate in export networks have been less hit by the credit crunch because of financial support arrangements that are provided by buyers, traders and big (foreign) firms through subcontracting relationships. These alternative sources of credit have been crucial for successful expansion of SMEs in the export sector. By contrast, the crisis has stimulated attention for the creation of sustainable BDS schemes for SME development. Such schemes should be increasingly managed by the private sector, and there is growing attention for the involvement of the private sector in the provision of business services. Private provision of BDS is expected to be more effective *and* sustainable. It is also expected that private BDS will concentrate on dynamic small- and medium-scale entrepreneurs as these will be the mostly likely target group that need services to accommodate their business plans, *and* they are able to pay for such services.

We can be more specific for Indonesia. Current donor and government-sponsored discussions in Jakarta focus on the following issues. First, there is attention for the enhancement of a competitive business environment that will be more conducive for SME development. Implementation of anti-monopoly and bankruptcy laws is important to foster 'a level playing field' for big and small firms. Also, ensuring simple and clear regulations by local authorities brings down the transaction costs of setting up and expanding small businesses. Second, a streamlining of credit schemes is discussed with the aim of increasing financial support for sound investments. Using market-based rates for credit and improving the banks' ability to lend to SMEs are highlighted. Third, business development services are under review with the aim of improving the performance of government technical assistance programs. The establishment of trade fairs and information centres is under consideration as an effective means to transfer information and technology to small firms.

The Indonesian reality shows, however, that there is a gap between current discussions and the willingness of government agencies to actually make changes in existing technical and financial support schemes. Government-sponsored assistance to small enterprises in Indonesia is deeply embedded in the basic philosophy that it is an obligation of the government to guide and uplift the weaker groups in society that are working overwhelmingly in small businesses. *Pembinaan* (guidance) and *golongan ekonomi lemah* (weaker economic groups) are basic concepts in past, present and, mostly likely, future government approaches. The strong and long-term commitment of the Indonesian government to *pembinaan* deserves to be taken into account by both Indonesian and donor-driven initiatives to reform assistance programs for small-enterprise development. In other words, it will be hard to change past policy, and this is exacerbated by the fact that there is surprisingly little insight into the effectiveness of existing programs. The success and effectiveness of the assistance programs is typically measured by whether the annual outreach targets have been achieved. Government officials view the growth of the small-enterprise sector, and its resilience during the crisis, as an indicator that service provision is bearing fruit (Sandee 1995; Tambunan 2000).

Despite the discussions between donors and government agencies referred to above, the Indonesian government has proposed new initiatives for small-enterprise development which remain firmly embedded in its basic philosophy towards 'weaker groups' in society. The proposed schemes support a government-guided SME development program based on subsidised and guaranteed credit schemes, tax incentives, the selection of thrust sectors, licensing and new regulations. Credit guarantee schemes are to be developed according to Japanese experiences, and technical support centres are to be set up at the provincial level financed exclusively by soft loans from state banks. Furthermore, tax incentives will be introduced to small producers that want to upgrade their technology. There is clearly a gap between donor-driven initiatives and recent government proposals. A hard and careful look needs to be taken at both, and there is a need for empirical support for effective policies and programs based on both Indonesian and international practices. In the meantime it appears not very realistic to expect major shifts in policy support for SMEs, and donor agencies may want to take a cautious approach in the interim.

4.6 CONCLUSIONS

The development of the micro-enterprise and SME sector in Southeast Asia in the pre-crisis situation follows trends observed throughout the world. Micro enterprises become somewhat less important when economies grow rapidly, while SMEs have adjusted more favourably to the liberalisation policies and export-industrialisation strategies. SMEs have profited from increases in domestic and export demand. Their performance might even have been better in the case where the policy stance was less biased towards larger firms. Direct technical and financial support has contributed little to the overall performance of the SME sector in the region. Small-firm dynamics are explained chiefly by their ability to profit from emerging market opportunities albeit in the context of an unfavourable policy stance.

During the crisis micro enterprises have gained importance. This was to be expected given the important role that they play in poverty-alleviation strategies and providing 'last resort' employment. Their re-emergence appears to be a sign of poverty rather than a sign of progress. The SME sector was confronted with declining domestic demand and a credit crunch. However, their concentration on production of basic goods that are also demanded highly during economic adversities, and their limited dependence on formal finance, has enhanced their ability to react flexibly to the new economic situation. SMEs participating in export networks have benefited greatly from the crisis and ensuing depreciation of currencies.

Finally, technical and financial support has reached only a minority of micro and small-scale enterprises in the region. There is virtually no evidence that support has contributed to firm growth of those that did have access. Since the crisis there has been an expansion of financial support to the smallest enterprises. Presently, there are projects and programs under preparation that aim at greater involvement of the private sector in the provision of business development support and strengthening of financially sustainable schemes for small-firm development. At least some of the new initiatives deviate substantially from current practices, and it is expected that many new programs and projects will encounter resistance during their execution.

NOTES

1   See also Tambunan (2000) for a summary of patterns of change and development of SMEs in the process of economic development.

2   Schmitz and Nadvi (1999, p. 1506) mention that probably the best example of cluster development by riskable steps is the Taiwanese computer industry, which gave rise to global players but started as a cluster of small firms.
3   See Rice and Abdullah (2000) for a detailed and thorough comparison of the development of small and medium/large manufacturing enterprises from 1986 to 1996 by sector.
4   This section is based on Sandee et al. (1994).

REFERENCES

Akatiga Foundation (1999), 'Crisis Impact Monitoring Study on Small-scale Enterprises', Report to the Asia Foundation, Jakarta: Akatiga Foundation.
Allal, M. (1999), 'Business Development Services for Micro and Small enterprises in Thailand', Working Paper no. 1, Project ILO/UNDP THA/99/003, Bangkok: International Labour Organisation.
Anderson, D. (1982), 'Small Industry in Developing Countries: A Review of Issues', *World Development,* **10** (11), 913–48.
Berry, A. and D. Mazumdar (1991), 'Small-scale Industry in the Asia and Pacific Region', *Asian-Pacific Economic Literature,* **5** (2), 35–67.
Berry, A. and E. Rodriguez (1999), 'Dynamics of SMEs in a Slow-growth Economy: The Philippines in the 1990s', paper prepared for a World Bank conference on small and medium-scale enterprises, Chiang Mai, Thailand.
Berry, A., E. Rodriguez and H. Sandee (1999), 'Firm and Group Dynamics in the Role of SME Sector in Indonesia', paper prepared for World Bank conference on small and medium-scale enterprises, Chiang Mai, Thailand.
Cameron, L. (1999), 'Survey of Recent Developments', *Bulletin of Indonesian Economic Studies,* **35** (1), 3–40.
Gibson, A. (2000), 'The Development of Markets for Business Development Services: Where We Are and How To Go Further', paper presented at an International Conference on BDS in Vietnam, Hanoi.
Hakemulder, R. (1999), 'Promoting Local Economic Development in a War-affected Country. The ILO Experience in Cambodia', Geneva: Employment and Training Department, International Labour Organisation.
Hill, H. (1995), 'Small–medium Enterprise and Rapid Industrialisation: the ASEAN Experience', *Journal of Asian Business,* **11** (2), 1–31.
Hill, H. (1999), *The Indonesian Economy in Crisis: Causes, Consequences and Lessons,* Singapore: Institute of Southeast Asian Studies.
International Labour Organisation (1999), *Towards Full Employment: Prospects and Problems in the Asia and Pacific Region,* Geneva: ILO.
International Labour Organisation (2000), 'Report on Micro and Small Enterprise Development for Poverty Alleviation in Cambodia', Bangkok: ILO.

Jellinek, L. and B. Rustanto (1999), 'Survival Strategies of the Javanese during the Economic Crisis', Consultancy Report to the World Bank, Jakarta.

Klapwijk, M. (1997), *Rural Industry Clusters in Central Java, Indonesia*, Tinbergen Institute Research Series, No, 153, Vrije Universiteit, Amsterdam.

Knorringa, P. (forthcoming), 'Cluster Trajectories and the Likelihood of Endogenous Upgrading', The Hague: Institute of Social Studies.

Liedholm, C. and D.C. Mead (1999), *Small Enterprise and Economic Development. The Dynamics of Micro and Small Enterprises*, London and New York: Routledge.

Musa, A. and Priatna, P. (1998), 'The Policy Reform for Capital and the Impact on SMEs', Report to the Asia Foundation, Jakarta.

Pernia, E. and J. Pernia (1986), 'An Economic and Social Impact Analysis of Small Industry Promotion: A Philippine Experience', *World Development*, **14** (5), 637–51.

Rasiah, R. (1999), 'Small and Medium Machine Tool Firms and Subcontracting. Links with Microelectronics Multinationals in Malaysia', paper prepared for a World Bank conference on small and medium-scale enterprises, Chiang Mai, Thailand.

Régnier, P. (2000), *Small and Medium Enterprises in Distress. Thailand, the East Asia Crisis and Beyond*, Aldershot, UK: Ashgate.

Rice, R. (2000), 'Small Enterprises as an Essential Part of the Indonesian Development Strategy', Partnership for Economic Growth Project, Jakarta.

Rice, R. and I. Abdullah (2000), 'A Comparison of the Development of Small and Medium/Large Indonesian Manufacturing Enterprises from 1986 to 1996 by Sector', Partnership for Economic Growth Project, Jakarta.

Rodriguez, E. and G. Tecson (1998), 'Liberalisation and Small Industry – Have Manufacturing SMEs in the Philippines Benefited?', *Small Enterprise Development*, **9** (4), 14–22.

Sandee, H. (1995), *Innovation Adoption in Rural Industry. Technological Change in Roof Tile Clusters in Central Java, Indonesia*, Amsterdam: Free University.

Sandee, H. (1998), 'Promoting Small-scale and Cottage Industry Clusters in Indonesia', *Small Enterprise Development*, **9** (1), 52–6.

Sandee, H., R.K. Andadari and S. Sulandjari (2000), 'Small Firm Development During Good Times and Bad. The Jepara Furniture Industry', in C. Manning and P. van Diermen (eds), *Indonesia in Transition. Social Aspects of Reformasi and Crisis*, Indonesia assessment Series, Singapore: Institute of Southeast Asian Studies, pp. 184–98.

Sandee, H., P. Rietveld, H. Supratikno and P. Yuwono (1994), 'Promoting Small-scale and Cottage Industries in Indonesia: An Impact Analysis for Central Java', *Bulletin of Indonesian Economic Studies*, **30** (3), 115–42.

Sandee, H., and S. van Hulsen (2000), 'Business Development Services for Small and Cottage Industry Clusters in Indonesia: A Review of Case Studies from Central Java', paper presented at International Conference on Business Development Services in Vietnam, Hanoi.

Schmitz, H. and K. Nadvi (1999), 'Clusters and Industrialisation: An Introduction', *World Development*, **27** (9), 1503–14.

Tambunan, T. (2000), *Development of Small-scale Industries during the New Order Government in Indonesia*, Aldershot, UK: Ashgate.

Timmer. M.P. (1999), 'Indonesia's Ascent on the Technology Ladder: Capital Stock and Total Factor Productivity in Indonesian Manufacturing', *Bulletin of Indonesian Economic Studies*, **35** (1), 35–56.

Tran Van Hoa (1999), 'Micro and Small-scale Enterprises in Central Vietnam. An Empirical Study', Masters thesis, Nagoya University, Japan.

Van Diermen, P. (forthcoming), 'Small and Medium Enterprise Development in Indonesia', Workshop Proceedings, Asian Development Bank, Manila.

Wahjana, J. (1994), 'Women and Technological Change in Rural Industry: Tile Making in Java', *Economic and Political Weekly*, **29**, April 30, 19–33.

Webster, L. (1999), 'SMEs in Vietnam: On the Road to Prosperity', Private Sector Discussions No. 10, Mekong Project Development Facility, Hanoi.

Weijland, H. (1999), 'Micro Enterprise Clusters in Rural Indonesia: Industrial Seedbed and Policy Target', *World Development*, **27** (9), 1515–30.

White, S. (1999), 'Creating an Enabling Environment for Micro and Small Enterprise Development in Thailand', Working Paper No. 3, Project ILO/UNDP THA/99/003, Bangkok, International Labour Organisation.

Wiradi, G. (1998), 'Rural Java in a Time of Crisis: With Special Reference to Curug Village, Cirebon, West Java', paper for a workshop on The Economic Crisis and Social Security in Indonesia, Berg-en-Dal, The Netherlands.

5 Trade Finance for East Asian SMEs and the Asian Financial Crisis

Donald G. Ross

5.1 INTRODUCTION

The Asian financial crisis had dramatic impacts on most East Asian SMEs, including the loss of funding sources, higher interest rates and collapsing markets. There was also, however, a special class of difficulties for those East Asian SMEs trading internationally. These enterprises were buffeted by an extremely hostile trade finance environment while, at the same time, many lost their key trading support as their local commercial banks collapsed.

Just what were the trade finance issues affecting East Asian SMEs? In its most basic sense, trade finance is about getting paid for your exports and paying for your imports. This primary focus on payments is crucial as cash is the lifeblood of the enterprise. Receiving and making international payments sustains the operations of trading SMEs. However, additional dimensions of trade finance also need to be examined if we are to understand just how the Asian financial crisis impacted on East Asian SMEs. These dimensions include an examination of how SME trading ability was impacted by foreign exchange rate movements, export credit risk changes, diminishing capital goods and services financing, and disruptions to normal international cash management practices.

This chapter examines these multiple dimensions of trade finance for East Asian SMEs in the light of the Asian financial crisis. There are great differences among East Asian countries in terms of their social differences, their financial and trading infrastructure, how they were impacted by the crisis, and the approaches they took to manage it. Still, the contention that the Asian financial crisis was heavily related to a

The author would like to thank participants at the SMEs in a Global Economy conference, colleagues in the Financial Services Research Group of the University of Western Sydney, and an anonymous referee for helpful comments on earlier drafts of this chapter.

contagion effect directly related to a loss of confidence directs us to focus on the larger trade finance issues without delving into the specific hardships faced by individual trading SMEs. This focus on the common trade finance factors at play allows us to proffer common guidance on how to keep SMEs trading in such adverse conditions.

The chapter proceeds as follows. Section 5.2 focuses upon trading East Asian SMEs and the impact of the varying foreign exchange rate movements experienced in the region, their relative impact on importing and exporting activities, and available risk management practices. Section 5.3 looks at export credit risks for exporting SMEs in East Asia during the crisis, with particular emphasis on foreign buyer risks, country risks, and alternative export credit risk transference options. Section 5.4 looks at capital goods and services financing changes affecting East Asian SMEs in terms of project financing issues, export credit agency attitudes, and aid financing to the region. Section 5.5 looks at East Asian SMEs and their bank service provider relationships, how SMEs were affected by blocked cash and drying liquidity conditions, and the re-awakening of countertrade initiatives in the light of the crisis. Finally, Section 5.6 presents a summary of the major conclusions from this chapter.

5.2   FOREIGN EXCHANGE RATE MOVEMENTS

The substantial foreign exchange rate devaluations experienced by many East Asian currencies were among the most visible signs of the Asian financial crisis. This section looks at East Asian SME trading in terms of the varying foreign exchange rate movements experienced in the region, their relative impact on importing and exporting activities, and available risk management practices.

The East Asian currencies were mostly linked to the US dollar, either formally through a peg or informally through central bank operations that maintained a stable exchange rate against the dollar. Although the Asian financial crisis put downward pressure on all East Asian currencies, the degree of foreign exchange rate devaluation was extremely diverse. Some countries such as Korea, Thailand and Indonesia experienced strong devaluations, while other countries such as Singapore and Taiwan experienced more moderate devaluations, while still others, most notably Hong Kong and China, retained their original peg against the dollar.

From a trade finance perspective, the key question is how did these varying rates of devaluation affect the ability of East Asian SMEs to continually trade? The answer is even more variant than the currency movements. While home currency devaluations are generally considered 'good' for exporting activities and 'bad' for importing activities, there is much more to be considered. Two key dimensions of foreign exchange rate exposure are transactions exposure and economic exposure. These two foreign exchange rate exposures can also be considered in terms of exporting and importing activities.

In trade finance, transaction foreign exchange exposure deals with foreign exchange losses on transactions already entered into. This exposure can adversely affect firms both when exporting, when they lose from a drop in the home currency value of an export receivable denominated in a falling currency, and when importing, when they lose from the increase in the home currency value of an import payable denominated in a rising currency. Key risk factors that heavily impact on the amount of transaction-based, foreign exchange exposure include invoicing currency, the credit period offered, and the relative volatility of the target currency.

The reliance on US dollar invoicing for most of East Asia's SME exports resulted in substantial transaction gains for some exports and devastating losses for some imports. Especially hard hit would be those firms importing for their local markets on credit terms requiring the establishment of US dollar letters of credit with the order. As these credit terms could involve a transaction exposure period often in excess of 90 days, these importing firms may have been locked into a US dollar obligation costing two or three times as much as originally budgeted. Substantial transaction based, foreign exchange losses would also have been incurred by East Asian firms exporting within the region on buyer currency terms when the invoicing currency devalued against their own currency.

Economic exposure deals with losses in the value of the firm from adverse foreign exchange rate movements. Here the focus is on changes to the firm's competitive advantage and on maintaining markets. Firms engaged in exporting from countries that suffered substantial devaluations were generally winners.[1] In an attempt to capitalise on the increased price competitiveness of its exports, Indonesia embarked on a major export expansion program in an effort to rebuild its economy after the substantial devaluation of the rupiah (*Project Finance* 1997, p. 50). On the other hand, SMEs exporting from countries with moderate or low devaluations would have seen their competitiveness reduced *vis-à-vis* intra-regional suppliers with substantial home currency devaluations. For example, Hong Kong SMEs selling on hard currency terms would be much less price competitive than Korean SMEs when selling into the US market. The Hong Kong SMEs would also run the risk of market loss for their exports to those East Asian markets that had suffered substantial devaluations.

There are a number of risk management practices available to deal with the transaction- and economic exposure-based, foreign exchange risks faced by East Asian SMEs. Transaction based, foreign exchange rate risk can often be managed by shortening credit terms and shifting the invoicing currency. Other bank instrument methods used to hedge foreign exchange risks generally become too expensive, or are unavailable, in the extreme conditions that characterised the Asian financial crisis. Economic-based, foreign exchange rate risk is usually managed by production and marketing changes to either reduce the hard currency costs associated with the exported goods and services, or to reposition the exported goods and services so that they are marketed more on non-price factors. For trading SMEs positively affected by the foreign exchange rate changes, the large movements in their home currency or the relative improvements in their price competitiveness provided an opportunity for market building and increased profitability.

Of course, the intense atmosphere surrounding crises such as the Asian financial crisis rarely allow such risk management approaches to be undertaken in a calm and rational manner.[2] Malaysia's experience in the crisis at the time of introducing its currency controls is illustrative of the difficult medicine that must often be taken to restore confidence in the markets. As such, Rasool Khan, Managing Director of the Bank of Nova Scotia in Malaysia, noted in *Euromoney* (May 2000, p.104):

> [W]here you have a situation like we had in 1997, you cannot think of free trade, you have to think of stability first. The ringgit was hitting 4.20 to the dollar before the 3.80 peg was imposed. At that time, the general feeling was that the ringgit could go to 7.50. That was the mood, every Malay was talking about what it would do to their money. It was bad. Sentiment can drive things a long way.

In addition to restoring confidence and removing the need for foreign exchange rate hedging, Malaysia's US$3.80 peg also resulted in an undervalued ringgit that had a positive impact on Malaysian SME exporters. Of course, the flip side of an undervalued currency and currency controls is overvalued imports that are difficult to secure hard currency for. This situation could have hit SMEs importing into Malaysia hard, depending on their relative importing and exporting activities. Those firms which were able to restructure their import payment obligations, perhaps by arranging special trading accounts or using offshore affiliates, would have been relatively better able to secure the imported raw materials and components crucial for their domestic and re-export markets.

Finally, when considering the relative impact of large foreign exchange rate movements on importing and exporting activities as well as the general economic and political state of the country, it is worth noting that foreign exchange rate movements are often overdone in the market. This was certainly the case for those East Asian countries suffering foreign exchange rate devaluations caused by rumours and other baseless information circulating in the market. Government priorities under such circumstances should be geared towards calming the market through better information flows and smoothing macroeconomic policies.

5.3   EXPORT CREDIT RISK CHANGES

The Asian financial crisis and its resultant heavy mortality of larger commercial enterprises, banks and SMEs alike substantially elevated trade credit risks within the region for both East Asian firms and exporters into the region alike. The negative impact of these commercial collapses was further exacerbated by the lack of clear credit information on the relative health of the larger commercial enterprises, banks and SMEs involved. This is so as clear credit information, and its resultant confidence, would have allowed trading to continue on normal terms for enterprises that were still financially sound. This section looks at export credit risks for exporting SMEs in East Asia during the crisis, with particular note to foreign buyer risks, country risks and alternative export credit risk transference options.

Foreign buyer risks, namely, default on payment obligations, financial insolvency, refusal of goods and termination of contracts, increased dramatically within the region during the crisis. Many firms were made uncompetitive by the soaring costs of imported raw materials. Other firms were lost due to their inability to service their US dollar-denominated debt with substantially devaluated home currency cash flows, plunging real estate losses, and their own bad debt losses to customers unable to pay. In the light of such adverse trading conditions and the inability to clearly assess individual firm credit risk, exporters typically would substitute foreign commercial bank risk for foreign-buyer risk by insisting on bank letters of credit for payment. Unfortunately, many of the commercial banks relied upon by exporting SMEs in East Asia were themselves failing due to overexposure to real estate-related loans and other bad debts.

An interesting dimension of this overall decline in buyer and bank creditworthiness in the region, was the manner in which news of the declining creditworthiness was released and acted upon. While London-based trade financiers were still willing to accept Indonesian credits in December 1997, Singaporean-based credit insurers were reporting increased buyer defaults throughout the region, including Indonesia, at that time (*International Trade Finance* 1997b). Clearly, there was a local market advantage where regional traders were able to structure against the increasing risks before traders from outside of East Asia. At the same time, margins for all types of commercial and bank guaranteed credit were increasing throughout the region. In December 1997, Korean and Thai banks who would ordinarily be financed were no longer wanted in the secondary debt market, while Indonesian banks were financed only at much higher spreads (175 basis points vs 40 basis points) (*International Trade Finance* 1997b).

Country risks of losses from import and export restrictions, currency inconvertibility, and, in the case of Indonesia, war, revolution and insurrection risks, also deteriorated dramatically within the region. Scarce foreign exchange was, in some countries, allocated to more essential imports, or, depending on the degree of corruption, allocated to those able to persuade bank officials to make it available to them. This situation would have placed SMEs at a particular disadvantage *vis-à-vis* medium- and large-sized enterprises, given the relatively lesser influence of individual SMEs. War, revolution and insurrection risks took their toll by making it impossible to deliver contracted goods and services. In some cases, enterprises owned by certain ethic groups were targeted and burned to the ground.

Risk management of these heightened foreign buyer and country risks can be undertaken in a number of ways. These include avoiding the risk by insisting on secure credit terms, reducing the risk by reducing the shipment sizes or by shortening the exposure period, and transferring the risk to another party through export credit insurance or export receivable discounting. Insisting on secure credit terms, such as payment in advance or letters of credit confirmed by acceptable banks, in many cases was impossible as the weakened buyers were simply unable to fund purchases in advance, or establish the letters of credit required. Risk reduction by reducing shipment sizes to more acceptable exposure limits or by insisting on quicker repayment terms was probably used by many of the coping SME exporters in the region, as well as those exporting into the region from outside. However, such risk-reduction strategies carry their own cost in terms of reduced efficiency and lost sales opportunities. They also tend to be restricted to those SMEs with specialised products, or other forms of market power, able to force buyers to accept less-than-optimal credit and trading terms.

In many cases, export credit insurance, especially from official export credit agencies, provided essential risk management support. Often, officially supported,[3] export-credit insurance was the primary means of maintaining trading arrangements. The Export Finance and Insurance Corporation's (EFIC) *1998 Annual Report* (p. 13) highlighted this role, from the perspective of an insured Australian exporter:

> [Our] buyer in Indonesia is hurting at the moment. We've invested a lot of time and money into Indonesia and we will do everything we can to stay committed to our buyer. However, he has problems paying on time because of the current situation and we've worked actively with EFIC to minimise our losses.

This was especially so when commercial banks inside and outside the region curtailed their normal activities until they could better gauge the relative extent of the crisis and the strength of their banking counterparties. A clear preference for foreign banks with local branches was exhibited among banks and export credit agencies staying open in the region during the crisis (*International Trade Finance* 1997b). Unfortunately, trading SMEs in East Asia would have been systemically disadvantaged by such a preference as the large foreign banks would have been focusing their commercial attention and resources on the larger domestic and multinational companies.

Additional evidence suggesting that the SME sector was specifically disadvantaged in terms of trade finance is provided by the primary sector support programs put in place in many of the East Asian countries during the crisis. For instance, Bank Indonesia introduced a trade receivable discounting scheme that allowed selected, large Indonesian companies to borrow at SIBOR or SIBOR +1 per cent. This scheme was criticised by many on the basis that scarce trade finance 'was going to the companies that needed it least' and that it was actually inhibiting local banks from entering the international trade finance area (*Project Finance* 1997, p. 50).

5.4 CAPITAL GOODS AND SERVICES FINANCING

The Asian financial crisis brought about a profound change in how the rest of the world viewed the emerging economies of East Asia. Without hyperbole, infrastructure financing in East Asia went from being the world's hottest market to being in a deep freeze. This section looks at capital goods and services financing changes affecting East Asian SMEs in terms of project financing issues, export credit agency attitudes, and aid financing to the region.

The initial stages of the crisis brought about a collapse of project financing business in East Asia. This was due to new projects being shelved as project sponsors and foreign lenders began to 're-do the numbers' in the wake of the major regional devaluations to determine whether the projects retained the ability to service their US dollar debt packages. Blow-outs in the current account, the flight of capital from regional markets, and a collapse of local tax revenues also contributed to a number of high-profile project cancellations as regional governments sought to adjust to the new reality. Finally, many projects stalled when local cost financing dried up as the domestic banks were unable to continue supporting infrastructure projects given large losses on their domestic real estate loans.

Attitudes among project financiers varied substantially both within the banking community and over time. As noted above, many project financiers simply suspended their financing activities in the region until they had a better understanding of the situation. On the other hand, even in August 1997, Citibank was reputedly still bullish on the region as it reportedly 'discovered opportunity among the turmoil' as deposits poured into its Bangkok branch, as locals fled troubled Thai financial institutions (Philips 1997). Presently, there remains a 'wait and see' attitude among many project financiers to see which local banks will survive and stay involved. Many do not anticipate a strong resurgence in project financing in the region until 'the end of the restructuring phase, when banking systems in Japan, Indonesia, Thailand, and Korea have been recapitalised [and] when non-performing loans have been either written-off or hived into separate bad banks' (*Project Finance* 1998c, p. 30).[4]

Export credit agency attitudes were far more generous to East Asia generally, and East Asian enterprises particularly, than were the world's commercial banks. This more supportive behaviour was due to the role of export credit agencies in expanding their own nation's trade, as well as the use of export credit agencies as a vehicle by which certain countries channelled their assistance to East Asia during the crisis. New financing lines of credit were opened to keep up the flow of raw materials, and, as mentioned earlier, official export credit insurance was used to support established trading relationships. Even so, export credit agency opinions and support varied substantially over the course of the crisis as well as between the export credit agencies. For some export credit agencies, the resilience of their lending and insurance support to the region was bolstered by their 'national interest accounts'. These accounts allow export credit agencies to extend financing and credit insurance into riskier markets while being indemnified by their national governments.

Official aid financing by many of the world's leading economies to the region was also stepped up. Bilateral aid financing was generously offered, in particular, to assist Thailand, Korea and Indonesia cope with the crisis. Multilateral aid financing was also bolstered in the region by new lines of credit offered by the Asian Development Bank and the World Bank. The use of these aid packages served to prevent a complete drying up of infrastructure and trade financing.

The collapse of large infrastructure projects within the region had a substantial impact on SMEs. This is particularly so as many of the region's trading SMEs were involved in supplying goods and services to the many project sponsors. The sharp downturn in the construction industry, in particular, resulted in a substantial amount of excess capacity and business failure among the SME sector.

5.5   INTERNATIONAL CASH MANAGEMENT PRACTICES

Collapsing commercial banks, blocked cash receipts and payments, and drying liquidity within the national financial systems of East Asia brought many East Asian SMEs to their knees. New ways of coping with the collapse of the financial system were required, and some 'not-so-new' ways were reintroduced. This section looks at East Asian SMEs and their bank service provider relationships, how SMEs were affected by blocked cash and drying liquidity conditions, and the reawakening of countertrade initiatives in light of the crisis.

East Asian SMEs were especially hard hit by the collapse of the local commercial banks they relied upon for their trade finance banking. This was primarily due to the holistic banking relationships SMEs generally have with their banks, but was probably exacerbated by the greater reliance on personal relationships in business than is the case for Western SMEs. Building new relationships takes time, and it would be very difficult for SMEs to initiate and cement appropriate banking relationships under the very trying circumstances of the Asian financial crisis. Likewise, as noted earlier, East Asian SMEs were not able to access the regional branches of the large multinational banking groups who were able to maintain trade finance flows. This is so as the large, multinational banks would focus only upon the largest enterprises in the East Asian region.

Blocked cash and drying liquidity conditions in East Asia also would have been proportionally much harder on SMEs than on larger domestic enterprises. SMEs generally lack the political clout to receive prioritisation to scarce foreign exchange, or to the export credit support made available by other nations to maintain trade. In some cases, blocked cash was also due to formal currency controls that effectively frustrated SME payments abroad. Drying liquidity conditions also resulted in bank reticence to lend for extended periods, as many teetering local banks sought to maintain highly liquid assets in the light of their own problems. Finally, the tightening of bank credit would have affected the ability of exporting SMEs to even access local trade credit as raw material suppliers demanded immediate cash settlement in order to reduce their own credit exposure and liquidity needs.

Just how severely these blocked cash and drying liquidity conditions affected individual trading SMEs is a function of their alternative financing sources. Some SMEs were able to access more traditional, family network sources of financing. Others were able to rely on relatively more patient, established trading relationships with overseas affiliates or long-established suppliers and customers. Clearly, much of the damage caused to trading SMEs operating without these informal trade support mechanisms could have been avoided by the establishment of specialised trade finance entities backed by the individual East Asian countries. These entities, whether established independently or simply as departments separated from general commercial bank operations to carry out their trade support functions, could have continued to operate confidently to support trading SMEs with governmental guarantees of their intermediary functions.

Finally, countertrade initiatives were a natural response to the blocked cash conditions brought about by the Asian financial crisis. Indonesia signed a number of banking arrangements with other central banks in the region to cushion trade and investment within the region (*Project Finance* 1997, p. 50). Likewise, the Philippines and Malaysia signed a bilateral trade payments agreement to try to balance trade flows and reduce foreign exchange risk (*Trade Finance* 1998, p. 8). The Philippines also looked to countertrade to help make payment under state procurement contracts and to make foreign companies enter counterpurchase arrangements valued at up to 50 per cent of the state contract (*Trade Finance* 1998, p. 8). Unfortunately, these countertrade initiatives mostly serve larger commercial and state-owned enterprises without providing much direct benefit to trading SMEs. This is largely because of the heavy administrative costs involved in negotiating not just the export sale but also the related purchase. The extended periods between cash disbursement for production and delivery of the primary exported product and cash receipt from the related sale and collection of the linked purchase goods would also tend to stretch the cash conversion cycle beyond the self-financing capacities of most SMEs.

5.6   CONCLUSIONS

The impact of the Asian financial crisis on the trading ability of East Asian SMEs was widely variant both between the countries of the region, and between the trading SMEs within each country. Some SMEs were assisted by a collapsing local currency through a boost to relative and absolute competitiveness. Other SMEs were wiped out by an inability to pass on devaluation-induced price increases on imported goods and services. Generally, though, SMEs were victimised by spiralling bad debts largely outside their control, as well as by bank collapses that destroyed their ability to finance their international trade activities. Most enterprises felt the general pain inflicted on their national economies through the cancellation of large infrastructure projects and the collapse of domestic growth rates. Likewise, foreign exchange shortages and controls frustrated many SMEs in their efforts to continue trading.

A common factor in most of these adverse circumstances was the general collapse of the confidence required for continued trading. Looking back at the crisis, it is apparent that many trading SMEs have been able to reposition and move forward. The inability to distinguish between those trading SMEs that were fatally impacted by the crisis and those able to reposition and survive is largely due to the lack of quality and timely information. Having access to this information would have allowed parties dealing with East Asian SMEs to more quickly and confidently determine firm strength, and then renegotiate the terms under which trading activities could continue.

A similar conclusion can be drawn regarding the assessment and management of the country risks affecting East Asian trade. Countries such as Malaysia and Hong Kong, SAR, were able to reduce the amount of damage to their trading SMEs by re-instilling a sense of order and confidence to the marketplace. Noting the overwhelming importance of the banking sector to East Asian SME trading leads us to support government actions used to shore up the banking sector's trade support activities. A quicker and more aggressive separation of international trade facilitation services from general bank operations could have substantially reduced the amount of harm visited on trading SMEs by the collapse of their primary trading support.

Moving forward in East Asia requires a heightened appreciation for the role of trading SMEs in the region's economic development, and the consequential development of new infrastructure to better serve their trade finance needs. Among the many gifts of a healthy SME sector to a national economy is the great benefit of economic diversification when primary industries weaken. To truly enjoy this benefit, the SME sector needs to be prioritised when developing policies to reduce the damaging effects of systemic collapses such as the Asian financial crisis.

NOTES

1   If one does not consider the impact of the high domestic interest rates, business failure, and political instability that often accompany local currency devaluations. These factors can lead to reduced reliability of supply, ability to achieve delivery deadlines, quality of productand so on, which, although not traditionally considered as trade finance issues, can dramatically impact upon the ability of exporting firms to deliver as promised.

2   For those exporters and importers on the wrong side of the currency movements, there is little reason for 'calmly' watching their hard-earned business success being taken away. Sometimes, even the very best-managed businesses are wiped out by foreign exchange rate movements such as those experienced in the Asian financial crisis.

3   Officially supported, export credit insurance is backed by governmental, as opposed to private, export credit insurers. While the mode of delivery varies among countries from direct underwriting by state corporations to private insurers underwriting with a government guarantee, the effect of risk transference to the sponsoring government is the same. Many governments, such as Australia's, took on extra risk to sustain the flow of goods and services to the harder hit East Asian markets.

4   Quoting Angus Amour, Head of Structured Trade and Project Finance at EFIC.

REFERENCES

Abdullah, M.A. (2000), 'Globalised Economy and the Strategic Importance of SMEs in Malaysia's Industrial Structure', *Proceedings of the SMEs in a Global Economy Conference*, Wollongong, Australia, 16–17 June, Wollongong: IBRI, pp. 3–14.

Ahmad, Z.A. (2000), 'How the Malaysian Automotive SMEs Survived the Crisis', *Proceedings of the SMEs in a Global Economy Conference*, Wollongong, Australia, 16–17 June, Wollongong: IBRI, pp. 15–22.

Asiamoney (1997), 'The Horrible Truth of the Exchange Rates', London, September, pp. 33–5.

Cheah, H.B. (2000), 'Recovering from the Crisis: The Role of Entrepreneurship and SMEs in Asia,' *Proceedings of the SMEs in a Global Economy Conference*, Wollongong, Australia, 16–17 June, Wollongong: IBRI, pp. 85–101.

Chen, H.L., Chow, E.H. and Lim, I.F. (2000), 'Impacts of the Asian Financial Crisis on Taiwan's Small and Medium Enterprises', *Proceedings of the SMEs in a Global Economy Conference*, Wollongong, Australia, 16–17 June, Wollongong: IBRI, pp. 102–12.

Euromoney (2000), 'If Controls Go, Will Confidence Falter?', **373** (May), 100–109.

Export Finance and Insurance Corporation (1998), *1998 Annual Report*, Sydney, Australia.

Gregory, G. (2000), 'Globalisation of Small and Medium Enterprises (SMEs) in Korea: A Response to the Asian Financial Crisis', *Proceedings of the SMEs in a Global Economy Conference*, Wollongong, Australia, 16–17 June, Wollongong: IBRI, pp. 205–21.

Hayashi, M. (2000), 'Support Mechanisms for the Development of SMEs in Indonesia: the Case of Automotive and Motorcycle Parts Industry', *Proceedings of the SMEs in a Global Economy Conference*, Wollongong, Australia, 16–17 June, Wollongong: IBRI, pp. 271–92.

International Trade Finance (1997a), 'Asian Crisis: Tigers Feel the Pinch but Export Finance Remains Available', London, 12 September, pp. 1–2.

International Trade Finance (1997b), 'South-east Asian Debt Overhang Threatens Financing Flows; Cost of Credit Rises', London, 19 December, pp. 11–14.

Mansor, S.A., R. Mustafa and F. Soetrisno (2000), 'State Support for SMEs in Malaysia: Pre and During Economic Crisis', *Proceedings of the SMEs in a Global Economy Conference*, Wollongong, Australia, 16–17 June, Wollongong: IBRI, pp. 406–13.

Philips, M.M. (1997), 'Firms Play Cool in Southeast Asian Heat – Currency Crisis Fails to Deter Global Players with a Long View', *Wall Street Journal*, Eastern Edition, 11 August, p. 42.

Project Finance (1997a), 'BI Outlines Key Role for Countertrade Deal', December, p. 50.

Project Finance (1997b), 'Caterpillar Signs Indonesian Countertrade Deal', December, p. 50.

Project Finance (1998a), Boost for Thai Trade', April, p. 24.

Project Finance (1998b), 'Countertrade Initiatives Proliferate in Asia', April, p. 24.

Project Finance (1998c), 'EFIC Takes the Asian Pill', November, p. 30.

Project & Trade Finance (1997a), 'Vietnam Receives Downgrades', August, p. 18.

Project & Trade Finance (1997b), 'Thai Devaluation Sparks Project Rethink', August, p. 19.

Project & Trade Finance (1997c), 'Asia Embraces Countertrade', August, p. 19.

Project & Trade Finance (1997d), 'Thailand Sobers Before Sell-offs', October, pp. 23–4.

Ross, D.G. (1999), *Export Finance: A Guide for Australian Managers*, Sydney: Waratah Export Finance Services Pty Ltd.

Skotnicki, T. (2000), 'Asia Looms Even Larger', *Business Review Weekly*, 8 September, pp. 52–8.

Trade Finance (1998), 'Phillippines Moves on Trade Initiative', September, p. 8.

Victorio, A. (2000), 'The Aftermath of the Asian Financial Crisis: Some Evidence and Policy Recommendations', *Proceedings of the SMEs in a Global Economy Conference*, Wollongong, Australia, 16–17 June, Wollongong: IBRI, pp. 611–17.

White, C. (2000), 'Hanvit Bank Leading the Korean Comeback', *Euromoney*, **373** (May), p. 20.

6 Financing Issues: SME IPOs in China and Australia

Gurmeet S. Bhabra, John G. Powell, Jing Shi, and Tian Ze

6.1 INTRODUCTION

A major outcome of the Asian financial crisis has been a much more restrictive financing environment for companies throughout Asia, a trend that is perhaps inherently sensible given the excesses and waste that occurred prior to the crisis. The exit of 'hot money' from East Asia and the depletion of countries' financial resources during the crisis have limited the region's financing sources. The ability of SMEs to obtain domestic financing could therefore have an important influence on SMEs in East Asia. This chapter examines initial public offerings (IPOs) as a potential source of funding for SMEs in China and Australia.

The contrast between the ability of SMEs to obtain funding through IPOs in China and Australia is extreme. It is very difficult for SMEs in China to access funds through IPOs because of the listing requirements and quotas imposed by the Chinese government. Firms must have solid profit histories and must also obtain government approval to go public, a constraint that would appear to put this source of financing beyond the reach of most SMEs. This was especially so prior to 1996 when IPO quotas were very restrictive, and large state-owned enterprises (SOEs) used up the quotas when they were forced to convert to shareholding companies due to the unsustainable financial assistance which would otherwise have been required by unprofitable SOEs (Han 1997). The Chinese government's recent money shortages have had the surprising effect of easing the restrictions on firms going public because firms with growth opportunities requiring significant investments are now encouraged by the government to go public due to the government's inability to provide funding (Cao 1998). This easing still does not reverse an overall appearance of quite limited access of Chinese SMEs to the IPO market.

Australia is at the other extreme since numerous small resource companies and technology start-ups frequently access the IPO market to fund their expansion or to allow private investors to liquidate their holdings. The capital markets of Australia therefore share a feature of the United States market whereby small companies often have ample opportunity to go public.

The sharp contrast between the experience of SMEs' ability to access IPO funding in China and Australia raises the question of whether the apparent inability to finance SMEs through IPOs in China reflects the ability of small companies to find other, less costly sources of finance. Or does it instead reflect 'the inability of small companies to access public equity markets? And in the latter case, which are the main obstacles obstructing their access to the stock market?' (Pagano et al. 1998, p.62). Analysis of the size of companies initially going public in China and Australia also raises the question of whether small companies play an important role in the cyclical pattern referred to as hot and cold markets for IPOs. These important questions are examined by analysing the empirical relationship between IPOs of SMEs and larger companies in China and Australia. Institutional features of each country's IPO market would be expected to affect this relationship, so the first two sections of the chapter outline institutional details of the IPO markets in China and Australia that are pertinent to SMEs and also briefly mention alternative financing sources available to SMEs in these countries. The third and fourth sections examine data on the volume and underpricing of SME IPOs as well as larger company IPOs in China and Australia. The results indicate that SMEs play a dominant role in the Australian market and are sometimes an important part of the Chinese IPO market as well, thus indicating that prospects for SME financing through IPOs are favourable in Australia and have recently become more reasonable in China. There are still times when financing through IPOs is extremely difficult, however, so the conclusion looks at general implications of the chapter's results concerning trends in SME access to funding via IPOs and other financing alternatives.

6.2   SME FINANCING IN CHINA

SME activity is surprisingly vigorous in China, but much of the financing for SMEs has tended to be provided through informal channels because of problems with the Chinese banking system and the absence of venture capital funding (*The Economist* 2000). Formal equity financing through IPOs was not initially an option for SMEs because Chinese corporate shares were first issued on the Shanghai and Shenzhen stock exchanges so that the government could partially privatise state-owned enterprises as part of its economic liberalisation program. The Shenzhen Stock Exchange has since become known as a home for private company IPOs such as joint-venture companies, however, so SME financing through IPOs is now more of a possibility. The rest of this section outlines institutional features of the Chinese stock markets and the Chinese IPO process in order to outline why IPO financing of SMEs, while possible, is relatively difficult.

6.2.1 Chinese Stock Markets

The Shanghai Securities Exchange, China's first recognised stock exchange, officially opened during December 1990; a few months later, in April 1991, the Shenzhen Stock Exchange opened. By the end of 1991 there were 91 companies with locally designated A shares listed on either the Shanghai or the Shenzhen exchanges, and this number had increased to 765 by 15 August, 1997, with the Shanghai Securities Exchange having a slight majority of the total number of listings.

The stock markets in China operate using the latest computer technology. Most quoted companies now follow international accounting standards and hire respected accounting specialists to audit their books.[1] At the prevailing exchange rate of Yuan 8.3184/US$, the 1997 market capitalisation on the Shenzhen Securities Exchange was equal to US$93.8 billion, an amount which was less than the size of the Japanese or US markets but greater than the Australian market.

Chinese Share Categories

The process of privatising government-owned enterprises (GOEs) and start-up firms requires that they be established as shareholding companies. Shares in these firms are sold to public investors, employees, legal entities and state-owned enterprises. Most stock sales are partially sold to the public. Shares held by legal entities and the government usually represent more than 50 per cent of the total capitalisation.[2] This provides a mechanism for the government to retain control of the process of liberalising and privatising the financial ownership of industry.

Currently, there are four types of share ownership:

1. *Sponsor shares*, which are state-owned shares held by state institutions and government departments in order to retain control of companies. They are strictly non-tradable.

2. *Oriented Legal person shares*, which can only be owned by other state-owned enterprises. They cannot be listed on exchanges, other than a small number traded on the Security Trading and Automatic Quote System (STAQS) and National Electronic Trading System (NETS).[3]

3. *Staff shares*, which are held by employees of the company. They are non-tradable until firms permit their conversion to tradable shares.

4. *Public shares*, subcategorised as either 'A' shares designated for local investors or B, H, S or N shares designated for non-Chinese investors, with the latter having little immediate relevance for SMEs because only large companies can currently issue shares to foreign investors. 'A' shares trade only in the Chinese currency, renminbi or yuan, and trading is officially restricted to Chinese citizens. 'A' shares dominate the Chinese stock markets in terms of market capitalisation and level of activity.

6.2.2　Chinese IPO Issuing Features

The Shanghai and Shenzhen exchanges initially opened on an experimental basis, but the government soon established the China Securities Regulatory Commission (CSRC) in 1992 to regulate and supervise the exchanges. At that time a company with net assets over 150 million yuan and a three-year profit record could submit a listing application to the local government for approval. The local government recommended approved companies to the Securities Commission, which then recommended the companies to the CSRC for final approval. As a result a company seeking to list shares on one of the exchanges might need to wait some years,[4] especially since a quota on the total value of shares that could be listed every year has been decided upon by the central government based on economic development goals. The quota was then allocated to each local government in China. A tight quota of only 5 billion yuan in 1995 was doubled in 1996 and increased to 30 billion yuan the following year (Cao 1998), thus considerably relaxing but not eliminating this constraint on the ability of companies to obtain funds through an IPO. Regulations on the requirements for listing have also been relaxed recently; this important trend will be discussed further in the conclusion.

IPO issue prices in China are calculated using a company's earnings per share (EPS) times a price–earnings ratio (PE ratio). The PE ratio of an issuing company is normally fixed at a number between 15 and 17, so the only crucial part left in determining an IPO price is the calculation of EPS. Before 1997, there were six different methods for calculating EPS that an issuing company could choose. These methods were:

1. forecasted EPS at the end of the issuing year;

2. EPS at the end of the issuing year, as derived from accounting information for the current and past years;

3. (EPS of last year + forecasted EPS using method 1)/2;

4. (EPSs of the last two years + forecasted EPS using method 1)/3;

5. (EPSs of the last two years + derived EPS using method 2)/3; and

6. average EPS for the past three years.

The problem with the existence of six different EPS methods was that every issuing company could choose an EPS method to suit their specific requirements, so investors were often confused as to what the reported EPS of the issuing company actually represented. From 17 January 1997, the Chinese government regulated the calculation of EPS by choosing method 6 as the method for calculating the EPS of the issuing company. This method would tend to hurt SMEs that had existed for only a short time because costs associated with the start-up of the SME would initially decrease the EPS.

Chinese IPO Share Allocation Methods

The Chinese IPO market is still developing, but there are currently three IPO share allocation methods used. All methods involve a lottery process. The IPO price is pre-determined by the process described in the previous section, and investors bid for the quantity of shares they desire at this price. The first two share allocation methods require investors to deposit the full amount of bidding money into a prespecified bank at the time of application. The deposit depends upon the quantity of shares bid times the issuing price of the shares. This amount cannot be withdrawn until completion of the IPO.[5] It can be up to three months, under one variant of the deposit method, before deposited funds are returned if they are not needed for share purchases. Under the third IPO allocation method, investors can purchase a potentially unlimited number of deposit certificates over a specified time period.

The proportion of shares bid for that the investor successfully obtains under the first allocation method is equal to the ratio of the total shares available divided by the total shares bid for by all investors. New issues under this method are only available in the geographic region of the issuer. This feature causes a great deal of uncertainty concerning lottery odds and it also penalises investors from other regions. A high maximum quantity of the new issue that can be purchased by institutional and retail investors under this method also leads to excess bidding and speculation. In one variant of this method, the unused bidding money is not returned to the investors right away after the completion of the issuing process because it is deposited as a term deposit for three months. This method therefore has the highest bidding costs for investors. The major advantage of this method is that a proportion of the new issue is guaranteed to each bidder.

The second IPO allocation method, currently the most popular, does not guarantee that investors will get any IPO shares since winning bids are drawn in a lottery. Major advantages of this method are its coverage (the new issue is available to any investor in the country) and its simplicity relative to the other allocation methods. Another important advantage is that the maximum quantity an investor can bid for is 0.1 per cent of the total available shares; this partially eases the problem of speculation resulting from excess bidding by wealthier investors and institutions. The opportunity to win is still generally low for retail investors, however, due to small investors' limited availability of funds (Zhu 1997). Limited funds and lottery odds that are often very low create a disincentive for retail investors to bid, especially since there is no guarantee that bidders will receive any of the new issue.

Under the third IPO allocation method, a claiming number is assigned to each deposit certificate and a lottery process determines the winning numbers. Each winning deposit certificate is entitled to the purchase of a prespecified quantity of new shares, with non-winning deposit certificates being refunded.

All of these methods require the costly deposit of funds and involve considerable risk that shares bid for will not be obtained. This tends to restrict the field of major players in the Chinese primary market to institutional investors and a relatively small number of rich individuals, because a large investment is required at the time of bidding if investors are to receive a sizeable investment (Zhu 1997). Dai (1997) argues that institutional investors' control of the primary market is the major cause of speculative behaviour in the secondary market.

The high costs of bidding, combined with other features of the IPO process such as the conservative procedure for determining the issue price, ensure that there is hardly any risk that investors will not make a profit if they obtain an allocation of an IPO; the first day's trading price is almost always a (low digit) multiple of the issue price (Zhu 1997). High initial IPO returns (underpricing of IPOs) also tend to be accentuated by huge demand for new equity relative to the limited supply in the primary market (Dai 1997). The extreme level of underpricing of Chinese IPOs represents a considerable cost to SMEs that are financed by IPOs because it means that the original owners are, in effect, giving away most of the value of the SME to the IPO investors for free. The extent to which the drawbacks of, and restrictions on, IPO financing of SMEs in China limit IPOs of SMEs is ascertained in the fourth section of the chapter.

6.3   THE AUSTRALIAN IPO MARKET

Features of the Australian IPO market are generally fairly consistent with procedures used throughout most of the world, so only a brief outline of the institutional details of the Australian IPO market is required. The outline serves to emphasise the contrast between the ease with which SMEs can access financing in Australia versus China.

6.3.1   Institutional Features of the Australian IPO Market

The process of raising equity capital in Australia is regulated by the Corporation Law as well as by the Listing Rules of the Australian Stock Exchange. The Corporation Law was enforced in January 1991. It prohibits the offer for subscription or issue of an invitation to subscribe for securities unless a prospectus has been lodged with the Australian Securities and Investment Commission (ASIC). The Corporation Law requires all the statements included in a prospectus to be true and to not be misleading. The current financial position of the company is presented in the prospectus, with disclosure of details of assets, liabilities, profits and losses being specifically required. It is interesting to note, however, that there is no explicit requirement that profit forecasts are to be contained in the prospectus, whereas a profit forecast in the prospectus is a compulsory requirement for Chinese companies.

The size of IPOs in Australia ranges from about AU\$2 million to AU\$2 billion, with many small IPOs involving companies in mineral exploration (Bruce et al. 1997). Australia is recognised as a major source of natural resources and the stock exchange traditionally has contained a relatively large proportion of resource sector stocks compared to other exchanges. Resource sector listings averaged 31 per cent as a proportion of listed stocks over the 1974–93 period, peaking at 41 per cent in 1991 (Brailsford and Shi 2000). Mineral exploration is considered to be a very high-risk activity, so enterprises engaged solely in this kind of business activity are almost always totally equity funded (Bruce et al. 1997).

An IPO is initiated in Australia once the board of directors of a company has approved the IPO. After the IPO is initiated, a prospectus outlining the offering terms has to be lodged with and registered by ASIC. Investors are then invited to apply for shares by completing an application, usually attached to the prospectus, and sending the required application money to the company's share registrar or to the underwriter of the issue. Larger offerings tend to have more than one underwriter, and the lead underwriter apportions some of its risk to sub-underwriters before or during the offering period. The sub-underwriting positions tend to be taken by institutional investors, although broking firms, merchant banks and individuals also sometimes perform this function (Bruce et al. 1997).

There are two important features of the Australian IPO market. First, the prospectus details the number of shares to be issued and an issue price (or an issue price range), neither of which can be changed during the course of the issue. This differs from many other national markets where the issuing company distributes a draft prospectus to the market and institutional investors respond by indicating the quantity of shares they are prepared to buy at different possible issuing prices, with the offering price and institutional allocations being determined immediately prior to the listing date. Ritter (1987) argues that this feature of the US IPO market reduces the uncertainty associated with each issue, thus implying that Australian IPOs would be associated with higher uncertainty.

A second important feature of the Australian IPO market is the requirement that all shares on offer must be sold or taken up prior to the commencement of trading of the shares on the Australian Stock Exchange. When there are unsold shares at the closing date of an offer, the underwriter is obligated to purchase the remaining shares from the issuing company.

6.3.2 Underwriting Agreements in Australia

There are two common types of underwriting agreements in Australia. In the traditional approach, known as a 'stand-by' agreement, investors apply for shares by sending an application form along with the necessary application money to the company's share registrar or the underwriter. The underwriter fulfils a dual role of marketing the offering, taking up shortfalls between issued minus subscribed shares, and allocating shares among bids if the offer is oversubscribed. Underwriting of IPOs therefore takes the form of a 'stand-by' agreement.[6] To reduce the risk faced by the underwriter, a portion of the risk is normally laid off with a sub-underwriter prior to or during the offer period.

A new technique called 'book-building' has been introduced in recent years, especially for larger offerings that have arisen from the privatisation process for government-owned enterprises. It is an open price technique. Its features include the ability to publicise the offering prior to registration, settlement of the offer price after presentations to investors, and the ability to register interest prior to official registration by retail investors. This has led to greater flexibility and efficiency. Book-building allows supply and demand to be matched more closely because pricing can be adjusted as investor demand is canvassed, and it minimises the time between pricing of a new issue and the IPO date. Retail applications must normally be lodged prior to the closing of the book-build process, however, so the price initially paid by applicants is decided upon using three alternative approaches. The first approach is called 'constrained open pricing' and it sets a maximum price for such applications. Any difference between this maximum price and the book-build price for successful applications, plus the remaining application monies lodged for unsuccessful applications, is refunded. The second approach allocates shares at the book-build price up to a maximum number set by the applicant's application money. The third approach offers the shares on a partly paid basis, with the initial instalment set at a fixed amount per share which is payable on application. The difference between the book-build price and the initial instalment has to be paid as the final instalment after the book-build process.

The ability to tailor the IPO price towards investor demand favours the financing of SMEs through IPOs in a number of ways. The IPO share issue price can usually be adjusted as investor demand is ascertained so that the SME is sold to the public at a price that is relatively close to its fair market value. This ensures that the original SME owners are giving away less of the value of the firm to new investors in an IPO. The adjustment of the IPO issue price towards fair value also prevents excessive bidding involving the costly deposit of funds, and also reduces, but does not eliminate, the risk associated with bidding for an IPO, thus reassuring most investors that the IPO process is fair and reasonable. This, in turn, would widen the base of potential IPO investors, something of especial importance for SMEs since a lack of information regarding SMEs, relative to other companies, already tends to limit the potential pool of investors SMEs could attract to an IPO.

6.3.3   IPOs of SMEs in Australia

Institutional features of the Australian IPO market, as well as the overall Australian financial system, have been, and continue to be, relatively favourable for financing SMEs. A decline in the number of SME IPOs following the 1987 stock market crash and the 1990 recession prompted the government to attempt to improve opportunities for SMEs, however, via a Pooled Development Fund (PDF) program in 1992. The program's objective was to encourage the provision of equity capital to Australian SMEs, with a key attraction being tax exemptions on dividends and capital gains on companies with less than AU$30 million in total assets (Hall 1995).

The Bendigo Stock Exchange has recently offered to become a stock exchange that caters exclusively to Australian SMEs (Switzer 1999). All three levels of government have backed the proposal, and it is hoped that exchange-imposed regulation of SMEs would make institutions feel more comfortable about extending equity and debt financing to SMEs.

6.4 THE EMPIRICAL RELATIONSHIP BETWEEN SME IPOS AND TOTAL CHINESE IPOS

This section empirically examines SME IPOs in order to determine whether SMEs make up a large and significant component of the total number of IPOs in China. This helps to determine whether Chinese SMEs have had access to financing via the IPO market. The analysis also indicates current trends in SME financing via IPOs as well as whether SMEs play an important role in the cyclical behaviour of Chinese IPOs.

6.4.1 Data

The data set is obtained from Shenzhen Security Information Limited and has been collected by hand. The data set consists of 735 firm-commitment domestic A-share IPOs between December 1990 and April 1998, 360 of which were listed on the Shenzhen Stock Exchange (SZSE) and 375 on the Shanghai Securities Exchange (SHSE). Foreign-designated B, H and N share offerings are not included in the data set because most of these shares are offered as secondary offerings after a firm has already listed in the local markets, and also because only large companies tend to be allowed to issue foreign shares (Cao 1997).

Chinese IPO firms are divided into three groups: those with 1995 total asset values less than US$30 million, between 30 million and 100 million, and larger than 100 million. The exchange rate used in this study to convert yuan amounts to US dollars is 8.5. The 1995 value of total assets of a firm is used as a proxy for the total asset value of the firm when it went public. For those firms going public before (after) 1995 the total asset value would generally be lower (higher) than the 1995 value, thus introducing a small potential bias into the analysis. It can be noted that the Chinese accounting system differed significantly from international accounting standards (IAS). This was especially true before 1993, but the introduction of the Accounting Standards for Business Enterprise on 1 July 1993 brought Chinese accounting practices closer to international standards (see also Winkle et al. 1994; and Davidson et al. 1996). Mills and Cao (1996, p. 28) state that 'the impact of IAS adjustments on the profit and loss accounts and the net asset value of most Chinese companies is quite substantial, with a discrepancy of more than 20 per cent between IAS and the Chinese accounting system being quite common'.

Correlations among the monthly number of IPOs and average initial returns (IPO underpricing) are reported in Figure 6.1. The IPO initial return, IPO underpricing, is defined as $IR = (P_1 - P_0) / P_0$, where P_0 is the initial offering price and P_1 is the closing price on the first day of stock market trading.

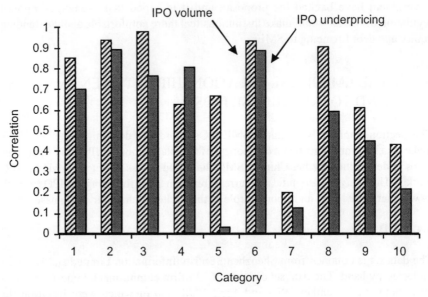

Figure 6.1   Chinese IPO Volume and Underpricing Correlations

Categories:
1 = All IPOs vs IPOs with total assets less than US$30 million;
2 = All IPOs vs IPOs with total assets between US$30 million and US$100 million;
3 = All IPOs vs IPOs with total assets less than US$100 million;
4 = All IPOs vs IPOs with total assets greater than US$30 million;
5 = IPOs with total assets less than US$30 million vs IPOs with total assets between US$30 million and US$100 million;
6 = IPOs with total assets less than US$30 million vs IPOs with total assets less than US$100 million;
7 = IPOs with total assets less than US$30 million vs IPOs with total assets greater than US$100 million;
8 = IPOs with total assets between US$30 million and US$100 million vs IPOs with total assets less than US$100 million;
9 = IPOs with total assets between US$30 million and US$100 million vs IPOs with total assets greater than US$100 million;
10 = IPOs with total assets less than US$100 million vs IPOs with total assets greater than US$100 million.

6.4.2   Chinese A Share IPOs of SMEs and other Companies

The total number of IPOs in China follows a cyclical pattern that appears to be even stronger than the hot and cold IPO markets documented in the United States. The maximum number of IPOs in a year was 207 in 1997, which was slightly higher than the number in 1996. The minimum number of IPOs was 5 in 1990 when the Shanghai Securities Exchange was officially set up. Another extreme IPO low occurred in 1995 following a peak period in 1993 and 1994. IPOs on each exchange (Shenzhen and Shanghai) follow patterns similar to the overall pattern for the total number of IPOs in China.

The monthly number of IPOs follows an extremely cyclical pattern, as indicated by the graph of monthly IPOs presented in Figure 6.2. Figure 6.2 presents the number of IPOs per month of all companies as well as companies with total assets (TA) less than US$30 million as well as less than US$100 million. Table 6.1 provides additional detail on the number and percentage of IPOs by SMEs in particular time periods.

Figure 6.2 reveals that there were three sharp peaks of total IPOs in 1994, 1996 and 1997, but only two peaks in 1996 and 1997 for IPOs for companies with total assets less than US$30 million. It can be noted that there were periods when few SMEs accessed financing via IPOs; indeed, there are periods when virtually no IPOs of any type occur.

During the six years prior to 1996, less than 10 per cent of all IPOs were for companies with total assets less than US$30 million. There was a ten-fold increase in this number to over 200 in the three years from 1996 to 1998 – this is all the more significant because numbers for 1998 are incomplete. The overall trends therefore present a very encouraging picture for SME financing in China. Relaxation of IPO regulations and quotas has created more opportunities for SMEs recently. Further relaxation of governmental constraints should create additional opportunities in the future, especially since the development of the Chinese stock market and the volume of Chinese IPOs have been determined by government policies rather than by market fundamentals.

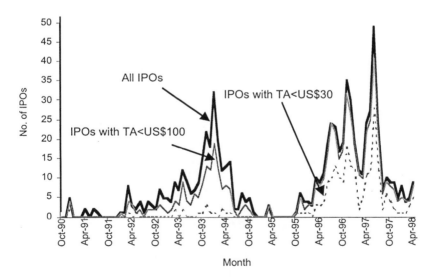

Figure 6.2   Number of IPOs on the SHSE and the SZSE, by Month

Table 6.1
Percentage of Companies with Total Assets (TAs) Less than US$30 Million and US$100 Million

	Total assets <US$30m	Total number	%	Total assets < US$100m	Total number	%
1990–95						
Shenzhen	7	126	5.56	66	126	52.38
Shanghai	16	173	9.25	103	173	59.53
All	23	299	7.69	169	299	56.52
1996–98						
Shenzhen	109	234	46.58	206	234	88.03
Shanghai	91	202	45.05	183	202	90.59
All	200	436	45.87	389	436	89.22
1990–98						
Shenzhen	116	360	32.22	272	360	75.56
Shanghai	107	375	28.53	286	375	76.27
All	223	735	30.34	558	735	75.92

6.4.3   Underpricing of Chinese A-share IPOs

A number of studies have already documented the extreme level of underpricing of Chinese IPOs. This study has IPO underpricing data for the Shenzhen market only. Maximum underpricing of an IPO in the data set is an amazing 4 800 per cent! Figure 6.3 illustrates average monthly underpricing of Shenzhen IPOs in order to demonstrate that underpricing in China is also extremely cyclical, with much higher peaks of underpricing than in most other countries of the world.

Table 6.2 indicates how underpricing differs between the IPOs of SMEs and other sized companies. SME underpricing was actually lower at first, but more recently it has significantly exceeded the overall level of IPO underpricing. The difference in the level of SME underpricing in the early period was insignificant, presumably because of high volatility and the fact that only 4 of the 70 IPOs were for firms with assets less than US$30 million. Table 6.2 also indicates that original SME owners receive less than a quarter of the value of each share they issue to the public (assuming that the first day closing price represents fair value). This extreme level of underpricing certainly reduces the appeal of using IPOs to finance SMEs in China.

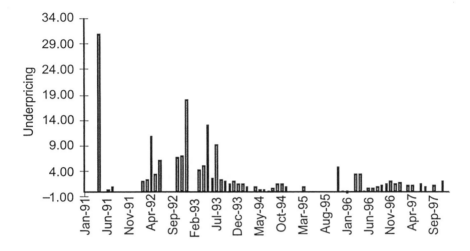

Figure 6.3   Underpricing of IPOs on the SZSE, by Month, 1991–97

Table 6.2
Underpricing of IPOs of Different Sizes on the Shenzhen Stock Exchange

	1991–93	1994–97	1991–97	p-value of t-test (1991–93 vs 1994–97)
Total assets <US$30m	1.71	3.25	3.20	
US$30m<Total assets<US$100m	4.81	2.87	3.31	0.0988
Total assets<US$100m	4.46	3.04	3.25	0.1573
Total assets>US$100m	4.88	1.34	2.85	0.0196
All	4.67	2.72	3.15	0.0322
p-value of t-test (Total assets <US$100m vs Total assets >US$100m)	0.8044	0.0029	0.5943	

6.4.4   Volume of SME IPOs in Relation to Overall IPO Activity in China

Evidence concerning the monthly level and average underpricing of SMEs initially going public in China raises the question of whether small companies play an important role in the cyclical pattern referred to as hot and cold markets for IPOs. Figure 6.4 overlays the stock market index level with total IPO volume and SME IPO volume to explore these inter-relationships. Hot and active IPO periods generally correspond to stock market upturns. A 'hot' IPO period occurred when Chinese stock exchanges were first being established, possibly due to initial investor overenthusiasm for a new investment opportunity. An active IPO period also corresponded to the 1997 Chinese stock market boom. IPOs of SMEs are highly correlated with overall IPO and stock market cycles in the post-1995 time period only. It will be left to future research to explore whether these inter-relationships are causal or coincidental.

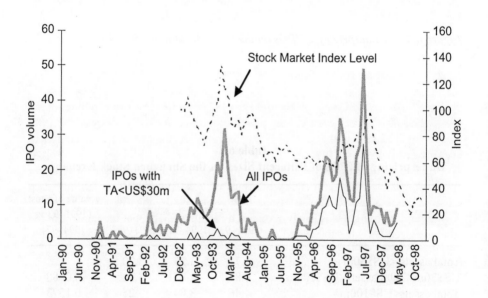

Figure 6.4   Chinese IPO Volume and Stock Market Index Level

6.5 THE EMPIRICAL RELATIONSHIP BETWEEN SME IPOS AND TOTAL AUSTRALIAN IPOS

Australian IPO data can also be examined in order to provide an indication of whether SMEs in Australia have reasonable access to financing via the IPO market. A major difference between the Australian and Chinese IPO market that is noticed immediately is the less extreme level of underpricing in Australia, although Australian cycles in IPO activity and underpricing are still quite pronounced. The examination of Australian IPO volume and underpricing in the following subsection indicates whether SMEs play an important part in this cyclical behaviour.

6.5.1 Data

The Australian data is obtained from the Securities Data Corporation. Australian IPO firms are divided into three groups, one with total equity less than AU$10 million, a second group with total equity between 10 million and 30 million, and a final group with total equity larger than AU$30 million.

Correlation among different groups for the monthly number of IPOs and average initial returns are reported in Figure 6.5.

6.5.2 Australian IPO Volume

Peaks in Australian IPO volume occurred in 1987 when 170 firms went public, and in 1994 when 70 IPOs occurred. A long period of relative inactivity followed the 1987 stock market crash, and the level of IPO activity still had not recovered to anywhere near pre-crash levels by 1998.

Figure 6.6 and Table 6.3 outline monthly IPO volume in Australia for different sized companies. IPOs with equity offerings of less than AU$10 million made up most of the total number of offerings in the late 1980s, thus indicating that the Australian IPO market was easily accessed by smaller SMEs, but the number of the smallest-sized IPOs has decreased significantly in the 1990s. SMEs with net equity less than AU$30 million have played a dominant role in the IPO market throughout the whole period. It is still worth noting, however, that there were times during the early 1990s when no SME IPOs occurred.

6.5.3 Australian IPO Underpricing

Australian IPO underpricing is extremely volatile, but it is hard to classify it into traditional 'hot' and 'cold' periods other than an obvious 'hot' period leading up to the 1987 stock market crash. Australian IPO underpricing instead seems to display a high but fairly constant overall level of underpricing, interspersed with intermittent sharp underpricing spikes as well as months when returns are actually negative.

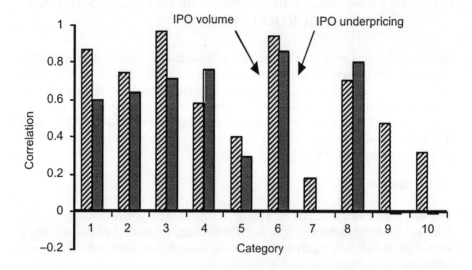

Categories:
1 = All IPOs vs. IPOs with total equity less than AU$10 million;
2 = All IPOs vs. IPOs with total equity between AU$10 million and AU$30 million;
3 = All IPOs vs. IPOs with total equity less than AU$30 million;
4 = All IPOs vs. IPOs with total equity greater than AU$30 million;
5 = IPOs with total equity less than AU$10 million vs. IPOs with total equity between AU$10 million and AU$30 million;
6 = IPOs with total equity less than AU$10 million vs. IPOs with total equity less than AU$30 million;
7 = IPOs with total equity less than AU$10 million vs. IPOs with total equity greater than AU$30 million;
8 = IPOs with total equity between AU$10 million and AU$30 million vs. IPOs with total equity less than AU$30 million;
9 = IPOs with total equity between AU$10 million and AU$30 million vs. IPOs with total equity greater than AU$30 million;
10 = IPOs with total equity less than AU$10 million vs. IPOs with total equity greater than AU$30 million.

Figure 6.5   Australian IPO Volume and Underpricing Correlations

Monthly averages of IPO initial returns in Australia are shown in Figure 6.7. The average monthly initial return on the first day of stock exchange listing for the whole period is 23 per cent.

Table 6.4 indicates whether initial returns for SMEs and larger companies are different. SMEs actually have lower initial returns, although the difference is not significant. The results indicate that original owners of SMEs in Australia are able to sell their shares at a price fairly close to the initial trading value of the shares.

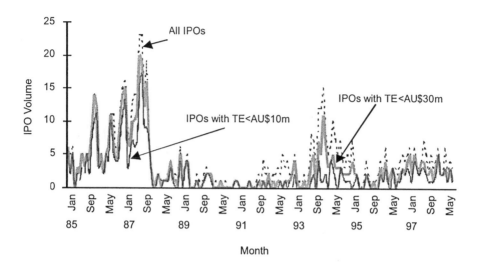

Figure 6.6   Number of Australian IPOs, 1985–98

Table 6.3
Percentage of Companies Going Public with Total Equity Less than
AU$10 Million and AU$30 Million

	Total Equity <AU$10m	Total number	%	Total Equity <AU$30m	Total number	% ,
1985–89	242	356	68	310	356	87
1990–98	107	314	34	184	314	59
1985–98	349	670	52	494	670	74

6.5.4   Volume of SME IPOs in Relation to Overall IPO Activity

Figure 6.8 overlays the stock market index level with total IPO volume and SME IPO volume. It demonstrates that SME IPO volume in Australia was highly correlated with overall activity as well as the level of the stock market prior to the 1987 stock market crash, and all three series have retained a correlation. IPO underpricing is

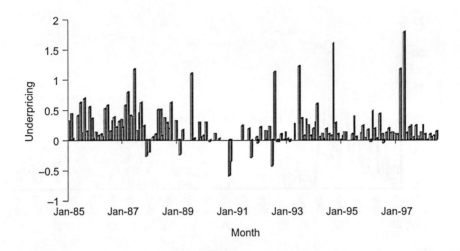

Figure 6.7   Underpricing of Australian IPOs, by Month

Table 6.4
Average Initial Returns for Different Groups during Different Periods

	1985–89	1990–99	1985–98	*p*-value of t-test (1985–89 vs 1990–98)
Total equity <AU$10m	0.24	0.16	0.22	0.1493
AU$10m<Total equity<AU$30m	0.59	0.22	0.39	0.0478
Total equity <AU$30m	0.32	0.18	0.27	0.0177
Total equity >AU$30m	0.39	0.28	0.31	0.2856
All 0.33	0.22	0.28	0.0492	
p-value of t-test (Total equity <AU$30m vs Total equity > AU$30m)	0.4543	0.2233	0.4451	

fairly idiosyncratic, however, but there is a high overall correlation among the underpricing series, especially in the earliest time period (see Figure 6.5). Once again, it is left to future research to explore whether these relationships are causal or coincidental.

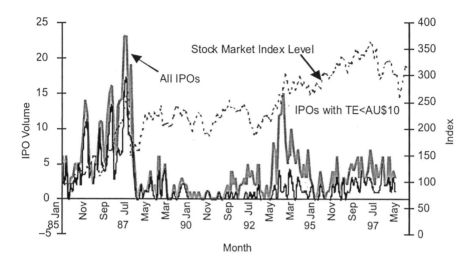

Figure 6.8   *Australian IPO Volume and Stock Market Index Level*

6.6   CONCLUSION

A comparison of the Chinese and Australian experiences of SMEs tends to indicate that Australian equity markets have been very favourably disposed towards financing of SMEs. Up until the 1990s it could be argued that the Australian IPO market was actually a market for SMEs. SMEs still play a dominant role in the Australian IPO market; indeed, recent high-profile multi-million dollar high-technology floats have featured companies that, up until the IPO, would fit the definition of an SME. IPO financing is one element only of the financing opportunities available to SMEs in Australia, with traditional bank financing being the most important source of funds (APEC 1994), and a limited supply of venture capital fund financing also being available, thus creating a relatively favourable environment for financing SMEs.

By contrast, obtaining finance in China is very difficult for all companies, with informal funding being the dominant source of financing for SMEs. This chapter's findings tend to indicate that a lack of access to IPO funding for Chinese SMEs is symptomatic of general financing difficulties in China rather than being an indication of the efficiency of alternative sources of funding for SMEs. SMEs are, nevertheless, starting to play a very important role in the increasingly active Chinese IPO market, with Shenzhen leading the way with foreign-affiliated joint-venture companies and Shanghai playing an equally important role for other Chinese SMEs. The experience of SMEs in other countries of East Asia with respect to financing are somewhere in between the extremes of China and Australia, but would tend towards the Chinese experience of government restrictions gradually being freed up with a resultant up-tick in SME IPO activity.

The recently announced Growth Enterprises Market in Hong Kong, a secondary-level listing venue for smaller companies, could greatly improve the SME financing situation in China, since many of the companies are expected to be Chinese based (WSJ.com 1999). A proposed merger between the Shanghai and Shenzhen exchanges could also help, since Shenzhen would then become a home for technology start-ups and other SMEs. Continued liberalisation of the Chinese economy and relaxation of constraints should be even more important for Chinese SMEs, however, since a high domestic level of savings could be funnelled towards smaller corporations more efficiently than presently occurs via informal domestic capital markets.

Empirical results suggest that there are still occasions when SMEs have very limited, or even non-existent, access to IPO financing, even though SMEs often have good access to the IPO market in Australia and the access of SMEs to the IPO market in China has improved markedly. SMEs also appear to play an important role in the overall cyclical pattern of IPOs.

NOTES

1   See the *Newsletter of the Chinese Finance Association*, **3** (39), 30 June 1997.
2   The size of government ownership ranges from approximately 0 per cent to 80 per cent.
3   Only publicly traded shares ('A' shares and 'B' shares) can be traded on the Shanghai and Shenzhen exchanges.
4   Note: Cross-listing on both stock markets is not allowed.
5   Each investor is only allowed to open one such account.
6   The underwriter has to buy any shares that are not fully subscribed at the issue price. The issuer receives the total funds raised, equal to the total number of shares issued times the offer price, minus an underwriting fee and flotation costs.

REFERENCES

APEC (1994), *APEC Survey on SMEs: Member Report of Australia*, Singapore: APEC Secretariat.
Brailsford, T. and J. Shi (2000), 'The Cyclical Behaviour of the IPO Market in Australia', Working Paper, Australian National University.
Bruce, R., B. McKern, I. Pollard and M. Skully (1997), *Handbook of Australian Corporate Finance*, 5th edition, Sydney, Australia: Butterworths.

Cao, H. (1997), 'The Effect of Returning of Hong Kong on the Structure of Chinese Security Market', *China Securities*, 3 March, p. 4.

Cao, F.J. (1998), *The Development, Regulation and Internationalism of Chinese Security Market*, Beijing: China Finance Publishing.

Chinese Finance Association (1997), *Newsletter*, **3** (39), 30 June.

Dai, H.L. (1997), 'Asymmetry in Issuing and Trading, and its Relation to Speculation', *China Securities*, 17 April, p. 4.

Davidson, R.A., A.M. Gelardi and F.Y. Li (1996), 'Analysis of the Conceptual Framework of China's New Accounting System', *Accounting Horizons*, **10**, 58–74.

Economist, The (2000), 'China Survey', April 8, pp. 14–21.

Hall, C. (1995), 'Economic Development and the SME Sector in Australia: Issues and Evidence', in E.U. Park (ed.), *Small and Medium-sized Enterprises and Economic Development*, Seoul: Korea Development Institute, pp. 13–49.

Han, Z.G. (1997), *Chinese Security Market is in a Great Changing Period*, Beijing: Economic and Science Publishing.

Henry, M.K. and Y.V. Hui (1998), 'Underpricing and Aftermarket Performance of IPOs in Shanghai, China', *Pacific-basin Finance Journal*, **6**, 453–74.

Loughran, T., J.R. Ritter and K. Rydqvist (1994), 'Initial Public Offerings: International Insights', *Pacific-basin Finance Journal*, **2**, 165–99.

Mills, R.W. and Y. Cao (1996), 'Accounting and Financial Reporting in China', *Management Accounting,* **74**, 26–8.

Pagano, M., F. Panetta and I. Zingales (1998), 'Why Do Companies Go Public? An Empirical Analysis', *Journal of Finance,* **53**, 27–64.

Ritter, J. (1987), 'The Costs of Going Public', *Journal of Financial Economics*, **19**, 269–81.

Su, D. and B.M. Fleisher (1999), 'An Empirical Investigation of Underpricing in Chinese IPOs', *Pacific-basin Finance Journal*, **7**, 173–202.

Switzer, P. (1999), 'Lifeline on the Way from Bendigo', *The Australian*, 31 May, p. 39.

Winkle, G.H., F. Huss and X.Z. Chen (1994), 'Accounting Standards in the People's Republic of China: Responding to Economic Reforms', *Accounting Horizons*, **8**, 48–57.

WSJ.com (1999), 'Asia Briefs', Dow Jones and Company, 20 July edition.

Zhu, W. (1997), 'An Analysis of Miracle in the New Issue', *China Securities*, 15 April, p. 3.

7 Small and Medium Enterprises: Evaluating Foreign Direct Investments in the Presence of Political Risk

Boon-Chye Lee and John G. Powell

7.1   INTRODUCTION

SMEs can be important catalysts for economic growth in developing countries, especially for economies where excessive or intrusive regulation limits the ability of larger private or public companies to operate in an efficient, dynamic manner. Financing of SMEs can be problematic in developing countries, however, if local savings are insufficient to finance countries' investment requirements or are being channelled, perhaps inappropriately, into larger projects or larger company investments. The Inter-American Development Bank (IADB) and, to a lesser extent, the European Bank for Reconstruction and Development, therefore, emphasise the important role that foreign direct investment (FDI) can play in the financing of SMEs, and both development banks discuss in detail their strenuous efforts aimed at enhancing this role. A similar emphasis is much less apparent at the Asian Development Bank (ADB), but it is still possible to detect that the ADB envisages an important role for FDI in Asian SMEs. The ADB explicitly recognises that investments in SMEs will not be forthcoming, however, if local capital markets are non-existent or dysfunctional, local property rights are inadequate, or local government regulations and policies hinder investors. ADB private-sector initiatives in the least-developed countries therefore often focus on financial sector infrastructure and policy initiatives to alleviate these types of potential political risk concerns for Asian SME investors.

While statistics on foreign direct investments in and/or by SMEs in East Asia are scanty at best, the phenomenon is by no means unimportant. Hall (2002) estimates that FDI by SMEs contributes around 50 per cent of all cases of FDI, and between 5 and 10 per cent by value. The analysis of foreign direct investment is therefore an important exercise, but one fraught with difficulty because political risks such as potential expropriation, restrictions on currency convertibility, or inadequate property right protections can create a wedge between the underlying returns to FDI and the level of FDI returns which can be repatriated. Recent events in the Asia–Pacific region, including insurrection in Fiji, civil unrest in Indonesia and Malaysia's attempts to restrict foreign investment repatriation, emphasise the importance of political risk concerns of foreign direct investors. The traditional approach used to evaluate FDI in the presence of potential political risk has relied upon *ad hoc* downward adjustments of cash-flow expectations or else upward adjustments of the discount rate used to estimate FDI present values. Both these approaches have been arbitrary and seem unsatisfactory and inconsistent with theory. The door has therefore been wide open for an approach that explicitly recognises that when foreign direct investors become involved in a country they issue the local government with an option to impose political risk losses on foreign investors. The losses may or may not be to the benefit of the local government but are always costly to foreign direct investors.

Mahajan (1990) recognised the option granted by foreign investors to FDI host governments by evaluating the ability of governments to expropriate FDI in a Black–Scholes option-pricing framework (Black and Scholes 1973). This chapter explores how the Mahajan (1990) model can be improved upon, and it also provides an alternative model for evaluating FDI in the presence of all types of political risk. The alternative approach draws upon the notion that FDI returns can be evaluated using a combination of investments that mimic the political risk and underlying profitability of an FDI project. This approach allows FDI projects to be valued in the presence of political risk because an investment combination with similar payoffs to the FDI project should have the same initial value. The analysis begins with the observation that investments in a particular country – including sovereign debt and FDI – fall within the jurisdiction of the same government, and therefore they are subject to risks stemming from the policies of the same government and political events in the same country. It is important to note that political risk affects different investments to varying degrees at different points in time, but the modelling approach only requires the intuitive assumption that *ex ante* perceptions of potential political risks be related, as will be discussed further when the model is presented. This means that it is possible to put together a combination of investments, including sovereign debt instruments, which mimics the repatriable income profile of a particular FDI project. The replicating investment combination is made up of assets with prices that are readily observable, so the valuation of the FDI project becomes relatively straightforward. This valuation approach provides a simple and intuitive indication of whether a particular FDI project will be value enhancing for offshore investors.

This chapter explores the connection between political risk and foreign direct investment in SMEs by providing a framework for evaluating FDI in the presence of political risk, thus allowing the importance of political risk for FDI in SMEs to be assessed. The chapter proceeds as follows. Section 7.2 looks at how political risk can affect foreign investments, including SME FDIs, and also examines the extent to which SME FDI in Asian developing countries is important as well as whether it is subject to political risk concerns. Section 7.3 introduces and examines the Mahajan (1990) approach for evaluating the expropriation risk of FDI. Sections 7.4 and 7.5 present a general model for evaluating FDI political risk and the solution of the model and its implications, respectively. Finally, Section 7.6 presents a summary of the substantive conclusions from this chapter.

7.2   FOREIGN INVESTMENTS AND POLITICAL RISK

Three main avenues of investment typically exist for foreign investors in a country: debt instruments issued by entities, including the host government, domiciled in the country; shares in listed companies located in the country,[1] and foreign direct investment (FDI). These investment avenues are all subject to varying degrees of risk, including political risk.

For the purposes of this chapter, we define political risk generally as arising from any politically motivated actions that have an impact on investment returns in a country. Political risk covers a wide range of possible actions, from acts of terrorism and kidnappings directed at the foreign personnel of companies to foreign exchange restrictions. Sovereign risk, which arises from the actions of the government, is part of political risk. We make no distinction between these risks in this chapter.

Of the three main investment avenues, sovereign debt and FDI are perhaps more subject to political risk factors because, unlike indirect equity investments, they are more difficult for investors to disengage themselves from quickly when the investment climate becomes unfavourable. In addition, investors tend to be more closely involved with the management of the investments, either directly, in the case of FDI, as equity partner–owner–managers of the investment or indirectly, in the case of debt, by way of a relationship with the government of the day. This closeness also makes it more difficult for them to withdraw from the investments. SMEs are usually more flexible to manage, are less visible, and involve smaller capital outlays for foreign investors, so on the one hand they should be less subject to political risk. Foreign investors might often find that SMEs are more difficult to sell, however, and owners will tend to be less sophisticated in dealing with international risks. The net result is that political risk appears to be an important problem of fairly equal magnitude for large and SME foreign direct investors alike (see, for example, APEC 1994).

For foreign investors, the absence of a legal or other mechanism which guarantees unhindered access to investment returns adds a 'country risk' element to their investments (Eaton and Gersovitz 1983). In the case of FDI, the severest form of political risk that investors are subject to is the threat of outright expropriation by the host government. Expropriation risk can be somewhat countered by the reverse threat of retaliatory economic sanctions, by the use of 'knowledge-based, firm-specific assets' that are more difficult to seize, and by employing smaller plants which utilise more labour-intensive technologies so that capital investment costs can be recouped more quickly (Eaton and Gersovitz 1983; Markusen 1991). Even if FDIs can often be afforded a degree of protection from outright expropriation, however, they are still vulnerable to more subtle or indirect forms of political risk. These include currency inconvertibility, war damage, civil strife damage, actions against company personnel (like kidnapping), and limits on remittances (repatriation risk). Similarly, foreign creditors are vulnerable to debt moratoria or outright repudiation although, as in the case of FDI, these risks are tempered by the availability of economic sanctions.

Although actual losses incurred by FDI and debt investments do not necessarily occur contemporaneously, during difficult economic circumstances these forms of investment are particularly vulnerable to the actions of national governments. Debt-service moratoria or restrictions on capital repatriation, for example, are commonly employed by countries in these situations in order to halt capital flight or further depletion of stocks of international reserves. This will tend to put downward pressure on prospective values of debt and FDI projects even during good times, thus implying that investors' prospective assessments of potential political risk losses for FDI and sovereign debt are correlated. This has led Bekaert (1995) to assert that a crude measure of all political risk is actually the secondary market price of sovereign debt, and he cites instances where foreign investor perceptions and sovereign debt prices moved sharply in tandem. Country risk ratings also tend to take into account sovereign debt and foreign investment political risk factors (Howell and Chaddick 1994). All of these considerations imply that sovereign debt and FDI values will tend to be correlated.[2]

The threat of political risk implies that an element of extra return is necessary before offshore investors find that FDI is value enhancing. Exactly how much extra return is required by foreign direct investors when it is possible that foreign governments will impose political risk losses on investors is determined in this chapter using a valuation approach which replicates FDI payoffs. It is possible, however, to empirically outline some very general profitability measures for different regions of the world. Africa appears to have had the highest average return on equity for FDI of around 25.5 per cent per annum in 1993 (United Nations 1995), possibly reflecting the extreme level of political risks sometimes encountered which discouraged foreign investors from pursuing all but the most profitable investment projects. This compares to an average return on equity of 16.6 per cent per annum in other developing regions of the world and an 8.6 per cent per annum average return on equity in the developed world for FDIs in 1993 (United Nations 1995).

While differences in the relative depth and sophistication of capital markets no doubt account for some of the observed regional disparities in rates of return, differences in political risk levels are also important. Political losses faced by foreign direct investors during the period from 1987 to 1992 have been estimated by Howell and Chaddick (1994). These range from a low of 0 (no recorded losses) in developing countries – Kenya, Malaysia and Nigeria to a high of 9 (out of a possible 10) in

Czechoslovakia as well as Yugoslavia, and a 7 for Vietnam and Saudi Arabia, where 10 represents maximum losses (see Table 7.1). These losses are due to factors such as corruption, payment delays, personnel restrictions, expropriation, and inconvertibility, all of which contribute directly to political risk losses incurred by foreign direct investors. Howell and Chaddick (1994) also examined variables used by political risk forecasting agencies which are highly correlated with political risk loss realisations. The most important of these variables appear to be exchange controls, international borrowing liability, payment delays, labour costs, equity restrictions, bad neighbours and authoritarianism. Countries with the worst 1986 scores for these variables included Sudan, Uganda, Iran, Ethiopia and Iraq.

Table 7.1
FDI Political Risk Losses, 1987–92
(proportion of total investment lost)

Latin America	Index	Sub-Saharan Africa	Index	Other	Index
Argentina	1	Ghana	2	Algeria	0
Brazil	2	Kenya	0	China	4
Chile	4	Nigeria	0	Czechoslovakia	9
Ecuador	2	South Africa	4	Egypt	3
El Salvador	3	Zaire	5	Greece	4
Guatemala	3	Zambia	4	Hong Kong	2
Mexico	3	Zimbabwe	3	Indonesia	3
Peru	4			Malaysia	0
Venezuela	4			Morocco	3
				Pakistan	1
				Philippines	2
				Poland	3
				Russia	2
				Saudi Arabia	7
				South Korea	2
				Taiwan	3
				Tunisia	1
				Turkey	2
				UAE	4
				Vietnam	7
				Yugoslavia	9

Note: 0 = no political risk losses, 10 = maximum political risk losses.

Source: Lee and Powell (1998), adapted from Howell and Chaddick (1994).

In order to distinguish between political risk losses facing foreign direct investors and foreign government debt investors, the Political Risk Services' forecasting variables (outlined in Howell and Chaddick 1994), which pertain to government debt investors, can be used. These include exchange controls, fiscal or monetary expansion, and international borrowing liability. Countries that score badly on these government finance variables but do relatively better on overall political risk, thus implying a low FDI risk to government debt risk ratio, include Venezuela and Indonesia. Mexico and Saudi Arabia were in the opposite situation of having a relatively high FDI risk to sovereign debt risk ratio.

FDI in SMEs in Asia is increasingly important, as indicated by Japanese and Korean efforts to attract foreign investors to invest in SMEs (japan.sme.com 2000; korea.sme.com 2000) as well as Asian Development Bank initiatives in most developing countries in Asia. Chinese joint-venture activity between domestic companies and foreign multinationals is often implemented via SMEs and is extremely important in the development of the Chinese economy (see Chapter 6 in this volume). Political risk is obviously a crucial concern for investors in China, and is important for foreign investors in many Asian developing countries. In fact, less-developed countries with the greatest tendencies towards political risk will often have a higher proportion of FDI in SMEs precisely because the economies are small and underdeveloped, thereby tending to preclude an extensive presence of large-scale foreign activity.

7.3   THE EXPROPRIATION OPTION

Mahajan (1990) recognised the option granted by foreign investors to FDI host governments by evaluating the ability of governments to expropriate FDI in a Black–Scholes option-pricing framework. The Mahajan (1990) model assumed that governments would seize foreign investments when it was in their economic interest to do so. The 'cost of exercise' is the compensation provided to foreign investors whose assets are seized plus the cost of sanctions imposed by the local government, and the expected value of these costs are assumed to be constant in the model. The benefit of exercise would be the value of the investments seized, so expropriation will occur when it is in the economic interest of the host government to do so, as defined by the cost of exercise being less than the value of what is seized.

The Mahajan model, while providing the important implication that expropriation can be an economic decision made by the host government according to its own economic interests, overlooks the equally important point that governments often impose or else 'create' political risk losses that appear to be in no counter-party's direct interests. It can also be observed that outright expropriation has become much less of an issue during the last couple of decades, but total political risk losses have remained extremely important.

On a more technical level, the Mahajan (1990) paper misses the important point that the cost of 'exercising' the host government's expropriation option is non-constant. The exercise cost will tend to be highly correlated with the value of what is being seized; compensation will necessarily be higher when the value of what is being seized is greater, and foreign retaliation will also be more intense when considerable value is being lost. The expropriation option should therefore be modelled as an exchange option, with the important implication being that the estimated value of the host government's option to expropriate will be considerably lower. The intuition for this result is the observation that the host government receives less when expropriating, because during the only times when it would want to expropriate the required cost of doing so is higher.

7.4   A GENERAL MODEL FOR EVALUATING FDI POLITICAL RISK

This section provides a more general evaluation of the effect of political risk on FDI. An event tree representation is used to depict political risk in stylised form, thus clarifying the possible outcomes facing FDI projects in the presence of political risk. FDI projects are then valued using a payoff replication approach. The valuation procedure relies upon the observation that political risks that affect FDI projects also tend to hurt sovereign debt investors, so a portfolio of foreign government debt as well as other investment holdings can be used to replicate FDI project payoffs.

In the stylised model there are two representative countries. The 'home' country (designated by a subscript h, when required) is a developed economy that is home to a firm considering FDI ('the firm'). The foreign country (designated with a subscript f, when necessary) provides FDI opportunities for the firm but is subject to political risk. The foreign country might also provide indirect equity investment opportunities.

The firm can invest at home in a project similar to the potential FDI activity, or it might have the opportunity to invest in the foreign country's indirect equity investment opportunity. Each dollar invested at home (or in a particular indirect equity investment opportunity in the foreign country) at time $t = 0$ provides potential time period $t = 1$ total returns equal to u dollars if returns are favourable or d dollars if the investments go badly. The probability of the home investment return (or the foreign indirect equity investment return) being favourable is p, as illustrated in Figure 7.1. It is assumed for simplicity that foreign indirect equity investments are not subject to political risk; this assumption could be relaxed at the cost of some complication.

In the stylised model it is assumed that FDI project profitability in the foreign country is proportionately related to the home investment returns (or the returns of a particular foreign indirect equity investment opportunity), with the proportionality factor being α. $\alpha > 1$ corresponds to the situation where FDI is more profitable than home investment (or indirect equity investment) due to the firm having a competitive

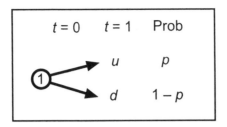

Figure 7.1   *Foreign Investment Equity Investment Returns*

advantage in the foreign country. Underlying FDI returns at time $t = 1$ to a dollar invested by the firm in FDI projects in the foreign country are a high return of αu with probability p or a low return of αd with probability $1 - p$ (see Figure 7.2).[3] The model ignores idiosyncratic risk of FDI projects that, in any event, can be diversified away by investors and so should not affect valuations.

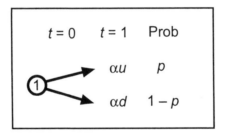

Figure 7.2   *Underlying Foreign Debt Investment Returns*

A drawback to FDI is the possibility that some of the FDI returns might not be available to the firm due to political risk losses. Political risk considerations include potential confiscation, repatriation restrictions, punitive taxation, foreign exchange controls, or other political interventions and misadventures. Losses due to political risks can occur when FDI returns are high as well as low. It is assumed in the stylised model that realised political risk losses at time $t = 1$ are R per dollar initially invested with probability q if FDI returns are favourable or L per dollar invested with probability m if returns are low (see Figure 7.3).

Socio-political considerations suggest that government actions giving rise to political risk losses are more likely when FDI returns are unfavourable. In this situation

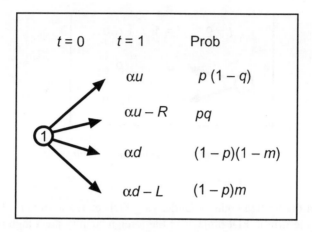

Figure 7.3   *Repatriable Foreign Direct Investment Returns*

some of the foreign country's industries would be generating lower profits and therefore lower government revenues, thus creating an incentive for the government to try to cover any revenue shortfalls by, for example, imposing additional taxes or restrictions on the repatriation of profits. Difficult economic times might also provide a trigger for civil unrest that could affect the profits of the companies concerned. The overall implication is that the probability and extent of political risk losses will generally be greater when FDI returns are low ($m > q$ and $L > R$).

Government actions that create political risk also tend to affect the foreign government's debt securities. Sovereign debt political risk losses incurred by foreign investors can include payment delays, foreign exchange convertibility restrictions, excessive withholding taxes, and partial or outright default. If political risk losses occur when FDI returns are high then they are expected to impose a loss of a proportion T of the face value of one period foreign government debt (D_f) whereas political risk losses anticipated in low FDI return situations imply losses of a proportion U of the debt face value (see Figure 7.4). It is further assumed that the expected level of sovereign debt political risk losses is proportionate to the expected level of FDI political risk losses, so

$$\frac{T}{R} = \frac{U}{L}.$$ (7.1)

This assumption makes the stylised model's solution simpler to obtain, and is consistent with the observation that, ahead of time, investors fear that political risk could affect sovereign debt as well as foreign direct investments, thus giving rise to the highly correlated valuation effects on each when perceived political risk levels

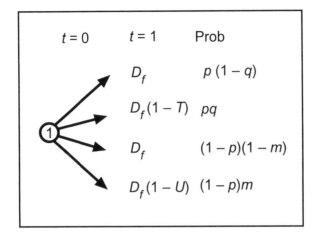

Figure 7.4   Repatriable Foreign Government Debt Returns

change (Bekaert 1995). The assumption does not rule out the important possibility that realised losses will be non-proportionate for sovereign debt and foreign equity, but instead deals solely with expectations.

The initial cost at time $t = 0$ of one period foreign government debt with face value D_f is $D_f/(1 + r_f)$, where r_f is the appropriate one-period foreign government debt interest rate.

Risk-free debt of the multinational's home country is guaranteed to provide total returns equal to the risk-free debt's face value D_h due to the assumed absence of political risk in the home country. The initial cost at time $t = 0$ of domestic risk-free government debt is $D_h/(1 + r_h)$. The local debt value is translated into the foreign country's currency via a forward exchange rate. Foreign exchange risk is abstracted from in the model because of the implied ability to hedge the risk in the model, thus allowing the analysis to concentrate on the effects of political risk in the model.

7.5   THE MODEL'S SOLUTION AND IMPLICATIONS

The approach used to solve the model relies upon the concept of replicating (mimicking) the firm's FDI returns by examining an investment portfolio which provides the same payoffs as the FDI project in each of the four alternative return scenarios at time $t = 1$. Figure 7.3 indicates that the alternative FDI payoffs at time $t = 1$ are αu (Scenario 1), $\alpha u - R$ (Scenario 2), αd (Scenario 3), or $\alpha d - L$ (Scenario 4). The cost of initially creating this replicating investment portfolio provides at time $t = 0$ indication of the value of the FDI project from the perspective of the firm considering the FDI project. The intuition for this result is that when two alternative investments (the replicating portfolio and the FDI project) have the same eventual payoffs then they should have the same initial values (see, for example, Dixit and Pyndick 1994).

An investment portfolio created at time $t = 0$ which will replicate FDI payoffs at time $t = 1$ consists of k dollars invested in the foreign indirect investment opportunity, D_h dollars of domestic risk-free debt maturing at time $t = 1$, and D_f dollars of foreign government debt maturing at time $t = 1$. This replicating portfolio has a payoff (see Figures 7.1 and 7.4) of $ku + D_h + D_f$ in Scenario 1, $ku + D_h + D_f(1 - T)$ in Scenario 2, $kd + D_h + D_f$ in Scenario 3, or $kd + D_h + D_f(1 - U)$ in Scenario 4. In order to mimic the time $t = 1$ payoffs to one dollar invested in the FDI project the investment and debt holding values k, D_h, and D_f must be adjusted so that the replicating portfolio payoffs are equated with the FDI project payoffs in every scenario. This requires:

$$ku + D_h + D_f = \alpha u \tag{7.2}$$

in Scenario 1, where the lefthand side of the equation is the return to the replicating portfolio in this scenario whereas the righthand side is the repatriable FDI payoff in the same scenario. Similarly, in Scenario 2:

$$ku + D_h + D_f(1-T) = \alpha u - R \tag{7.3}$$

is required,

$$kd + D_h + D_f = \alpha d \tag{7.4}$$

is required in Scenario 3, and in Scenario 4 the requirement is

$$kd + D_h + D_f(1-U) = \alpha d - L. \tag{7.5}$$

The solution of equations (7.2) through (7.5) implies

$$k = \alpha, \tag{7.6}$$

$$D_f = \frac{R}{T}, \tag{7.7}$$

and

$$D_h = -D_f. \tag{7.8}$$

The total cost of the replicating portfolio (equations (7.6) to (7.8)) at time $t = 0$ is

$$\alpha - \frac{R}{T}\left[\frac{1}{1+r_h} - \frac{1}{1+r_f}\right],$$

where r_f and r_h are the appropriate one-period interest rates on foreign government debt and domestic borrowings maturing in one time period. The cost of the replicating portfolio provides a time $t = 0$ valuation V_0 of a dollar invested by the firm in the FDI project since investments which have the same eventual payoffs should have the same initial values:

$$V_0 = \alpha - \frac{R}{T}\left[\frac{1}{1+r_h} - \frac{1}{1+r_f}\right]. \tag{7.9}$$

The first term of FDI valuation equation (7.9) adjusts the value of FDI according to its profitability, whereas the second term of the valuation equation takes account of the potential for FDI political risk losses. A firm's competitive advantage raises the value of a dollar of FDI by a factor α, as the first term of equation (7.9) indicates. The potential for political risk reduces the firm's valuation of FDI below the level α, however, as the second term of equation (7.9) reveals. A higher magnitude of potential FDI political risk losses (R) lowers the valuation of FDI from the firm's point of view, especially when political risk also increases the interest rate r_f which investors demand when investing in foreign government debt.[4] These last two considerations, taken together, imply that FDI has a lower value when the foreign country is perceived to have a lot of potential political risk that is likely to be harmful to FDI projects. In this situation an element of extra return is necessary to compensate FDI investors for the additional political risks they have to bear relative to indirect equity investors (Eaton and Gersovitz 1984). In extreme cases, excessive perceived FDI political risk losses lower the valuation of FDI in the country towards zero.

The FDI valuation equation (7.9) indicates that, from the parent firm's perspective, the value of FDI (V_0) exceeds its cost if

$$\alpha - 1 > \frac{R}{T}\left[\frac{1}{1+r_h} - \frac{1}{1+r_f}\right]. \tag{7.10}$$

This condition provides the intuitive result that increasing the multinational's FDI projects is only value enhancing if the additional profitability of the FDI project ($\alpha - 1$) exceeds a measure of the expected political risk losses of the project (the right-hand side of condition (7.10)).

Implementation of valuation equation (7.9) requires estimates of investment profitability, government debt interest rates, and potential political risk losses. FDI profitability is project specific and must therefore be estimated for each project, but the other input variables can be directly estimated. Estimates of the risk premium demanded by sovereign debt investors in the foreign country $(r_f - r_h)$ can be obtained from debt prices (see, for instance, the Monday edition of the *International Herald Tribune*). Political risk forecasts can also be used to infer an appropriate risk premium for foreign government debt. The potential for political risk losses facing foreign direct investors (R) and foreign debt market investors (T) can be estimated using past loss realisations as well as political risk forecasts (Howell and Chaddick 1994).

The valuation approach described in this chapter indicates that governmental negotiations with potential foreign direct investors could focus on potential FDI political risk losses (parameter R) and the FDI profitability level α. For example, in negotiating the initial FDI agreement with the government, the foreign firm should take care that the agreement is not too skewed in either party's favour (unlike some cases in the past where the government was disadvantaged relative to multinational foreign direct investors because of a lack of technical expertise and negotiating skills). Otherwise, this can be a source of resentment and increase the probability of political action in the future, and it can also increase the size of potential FDI political risk losses R. Conversely, the foreign host government would be ill-advised to press its advantage to the point where it will suffer in the long run by making FDI unattractive.

Our analysis of FDI political risk also suggests that foreign direct investors should discuss all of these considerations with the foreign government, thus helping foreign direct investors to be more accurate about their evaluation of potential returns under different scenarios. Governments might actually want to initiate this discussion if it reduces foreign direct investors' qualms about potential political risk losses.

7.6   CONCLUSION

This chapter has presented a simple model for valuing FDI from the point of view of foreign firms, including SMEs, facing potential political risks. The key assumption of the model is that political risk losses affect the government debt market as well as FDI, thus allowing repatriable FDI returns to be 'replicated' using foreign and local debt holdings as well as foreign indirect equity investments. Once this assumption is made and FDI payoffs are mimicked, a valuation of FDI projects follows directly since it can be observed that two investments that have the same payoffs in all situations should have the same initial value. The model's solution supports the intuition that FDI has a lower value when the foreign country is perceived to have a lot of potential political risk which is likely to be very harmful to FDI projects, so an increase in FDI is only value enhancing if the additional profitability of the FDI project exceeds a measure of the expected political risk losses of the project.

The valuation model is important for Asian developing countries subject to political risk where FDI will tend to be in SMEs, and will be especially applicable in China where even large multinational FDI has tended to be in the form of smaller joint ventures with local Chinese companies. The Asian Development Bank therefore makes political risk initiatives its primary private sector focus in the least-developed Asian countries.

NOTES

1   This form of investment is often referred to as indirect equity investment or portfolio investment.
2   This will be the case even if actual losses suffered by FDI and debt investors do not occur together.
3   The model implies that underlying FDI project returns and the returns to the foreign indirect equity investment opportunity being examined move up or down proportionately, as would happen if the firm's FDI project faces operational risk factors which are similar to the risk factors facing the indirect investment opportunity. The model can be altered or extended to relax this feature.
4   It would appear that the value of FDI is increasing in the potential political risk losses facing sovereign debt investors (T), but this interpretation is incorrect because higher potential sovereign debt losses lead to an increase in the foreign interest rate r_f demanded by sovereign debt investors.

REFERENCES

APEC (1994), *APEC Survey on SMEs: Member Report of Australia*, Singapore: APEC Secretariat.

Asian Development Bank (2000), *Country Reports*, Manila: Asian Development Bank.

Bekaert, G. (1995), 'Market Integration and Investment Barriers in Emerging Equity Markets', *The World Bank Economic Review,* **9**, 75–107.

Black, F. and M. Scholes (1973), 'The Pricing of Options and Corporate Liabilities', *Journal of Political Economy*, **81**, May-June, 637–59.

Dixit, A. and R. Pindyck (1994), *Investment Under Uncertainty*, Princeton, NJ: Princeton University Press.

Eaton, J. and M. Gersovitz (1983), 'Country Risk: Economic Aspects', in R.J. Herring (ed.), *Managing International Risk*, New York: Cambridge University Press, pp. 75–99.

Eaton, J. and M. Gersovitz (1984), 'A Theory of Expropriation and Deviations from Perfect Capital Mobility', *Economic Journal*, **94** (March), 16–40.

Hall, Chris (2002), 'Profile of SMEs and SME Issues in East Asia', in C. Harvie and
    B.C. Lee (eds), *The Role of SMEs in National Economies in East Asia*, Cheltenham,
    UK and Northampton, MA, USA: Edward Elgar.
Howell, L.D. and B. Chaddick (1994), 'Models of Political Risk for Foreign Investment
    and Trade: An Assessment of Three Approaches', *Columbia Journal of World
    Business*, Fall, pp. 70–91.
Lee, B.C. and J.G. Powell (1998), 'Globalised Investing and the Political Risk Aspects
    of International Sovereign Debt and Foreign Direct Investments', in A. Levy-
    Livermore (ed.), *Handbook of the Globalisation of the World Economy*,
    Cheltenham, UK and Northampton, MA, USA: Edward Elgar, pp. 100–22.
Mahajan, A. (1990), 'Pricing Expropriation Risk', *Financial Management*, **19** (4),
    77–86.
Markusen, J.R. (1991), 'The Theory of the Multinational Enterprise: A Common
    Analytical Framework', in E.D. Ramstetter (ed.), *Direct Foreign Investment in
    Asia's Developing Economies and Structural Change in the Asia–Pacific Region*,
    Boulder, CO: Westview Press.
United Nations (1995), *Foreign Direct Investment in Africa*, Washington, DC: United
    Nations Conference on Trade and Development in Geneva.

8 The Role of SMEs in the Diffusion of Technology among East Asian Economies

Tim Turpin

8.1 INTRODUCTION

During the past two decades there has been a significant rise in investment in research and development among the economies of the Asia–Pacific region. This trend has been consistent with increased national emphases on promoting knowledge-based economies. For almost all countries, gross expenditure on R&D (GERD) increased through the 1980s and into the 1990s. For South Korea, between 1981 and 1995, GERD (expressed as a percentage of GDP) increased from 0.6 to 2.4 per cent; for Japan during the same period it increased from 2.3 per cent to 3.0 per cent; for Singapore, from 0.3 per cent to 1.2 per cent; for Australia, from 1.0 per cent to 1.6 per cent; and for Chinese Taipei, from 0.9 per cent to 1.7 per cent. By the end of the 1980s, national investment in R&D in South Korea was nearly 16 times higher than it was during the late 1970s. In Taiwan, overall R&D investment grew by a factor of 12 during the 1980s (Turpin et al. 1998). The largest component of growth in these R&D investments came from the private sector.

The trend towards building knowledge-based economies has led to increased levels of innovation. This can be observed in indicators such as patent registrations. Between 1986 and 1996 Japanese patents registered in the US rose from 13 219 to 23 089, for South Korea they rose from 49 to 1 496 and for Singapore from 4 to 84 (Bourke and Butler 1995). For the region as a whole, however, development has remained uneven. Some economies stand out as major producers of technology; others remain

The author wishes to acknowledge the important contribution to this chapter made by Ms Eka Yosida, from the Research Office for International Collaboration, University of Wollongong, Australia, and Dr Widyantoko Sumarlin from BPP Teknologi Jakarta.

predominantly technology users. For the 'users' their technological capability depends very much on their capacity to remain strategically linked to international systems of innovation. Although the 'users' may be more dependent they can nevertheless derive technological benefit by being linked to such systems.

Similarly, while a small number of technologically powerful firms generally dominate patenting activity, and derive considerable benefit from doing so, many of the more dependent firms are able to derive some technological benefit by being linked to clusters of firms that comprise an innovative system. Thus, while the components that comprise innovation systems may be unequally linked, they collectively contribute to the diffusion of technology and knowledge.

Although an increasing number of SMEs are major contributors to technological change, the majority remain very much technologically dependent on large firms or on strategic alliances within clusters of firms. In the wake of the financial crisis this raises some important questions. To what extent has the crisis had an impact on these arrangements? Are SMEs any more or less able to gain access to new technologies or know-how? What are the consequences for the diffusion of technology? What does this mean for the more technologically dependent economies in the region? These are the key questions addressed in this chapter.

The chapter proceeds by initially discussing the general role of SMEs in the production and diffusion of technology. It is argued that while it is generally recognised that SMEs are performing an increasingly central role in national systems of innovation, the diversity of enterprises usually captured in national data sets provides little help in making other than superficial observations. In order to develop more analytical rigour, Hill (1998) has proposed a typology that focuses on (a) SMEs engaged in horizontal or vertical linkages with larger firms, or (b) those producing in specialised niches outside the commercial domain of larger enterprises (Hill 1998, pp. 27–71). While this is a useful way to develop new studies, existing data limit the extent to which such finer-grained analyses can be pursued.

The analysis in this chapter seeks to overcome some of the data limitations by drawing together three separate but complementary data sets. The first is a national collection that offers an overview of the impact of the financial crisis on Indonesian small, medium and large enterprises. Because Indonesia was one of the countries most severely affected by the crisis it offers a useful case for exploring its impact on the relationship between small, medium and large firms. The second set of data is drawn from a national survey of firms across different industry sectors concerning their business experiences through the same period. Finally, a regional case study is introduced to provide more detailed insight into the experiences of a sample of manufacturing firms.

On the basis of the three data sets, it is argued that the financial crisis has had a far more immediate impact on small enterprises in Indonesia than it has on medium or large firms. This is not altogether surprising, but the important point made here is that this could be undermining the innovation potential of clusters that incorporate small and large firms. This could be occurring not so much because the crisis has put businesses out of business, although it has certainly done that, but because it has weakened innovation links between small and large enterprises. Some alternative policy approaches may be required to enable small but innovative enterprises to contribute to, and benefit from, the diffusion of technological advance.

The chapter proceeds as follows. Section 8.2 focuses upon the role of SMEs in the production and diffusion of technology in the Asia–Pacific region. Section 8.3 focuses upon SMEs in the context of knowledge-based organisational alliances. Section 8.4 focuses upon the contribution of SMEs to technology diffusion in Indonesia. Section 8.5 discusses in some detail the impact of the financial crisis, between 1997 and 1999, on Indonesian SMEs, and attempts to identify whether the crisis has had an adverse impact on links for access to technology between SMEs and larger firms or technology enabling institutions. Section 8.6 draws upon a study of nearly 200 000 enterprises across 27 provinces in Indonesia to identify the impact of the crisis upon SMEs in the country. A case study of the experiences among manufacturing SMEs in Central Java is presented in Section 8.7. Section 8.8 provides conclusions, and implications for technology and innovation.

8.2   THE ROLE OF SMES IN THE PRODUCTION AND DIFFUSION OF TECHNOLOGY IN THE ASIA–PACIFIC REGION

SMEs comprise well over 90 per cent of all enterprises in the Asia–Pacific region. They provide employment for over half of the workforce and contribute somewhere around 50 per cent of the region's GDP (Hall 1995). The majority of SMEs, however, particularly in the less industrially developed countries, do not make intensive use of technology.

With increased growth across the economies of the region, and increased access to new technologies, a considerable proportion of SMEs have benefited from the 'entrepreneurial engine' of leading-edge industries (Hall 1995, V-b–10). Many of these firms have moved beyond their traditional commercial or production base as local 'suppliers' to become successful high-growth enterprises in national and regional economies (Liu 1995). In some countries, such as Singapore, industrial development has coincided with a move towards larger firms. In 1965, for example, 8.3 per cent of all establishments in Singapore employed more than 100 workers. By contrast, in 1992, the proportion had risen to 18 per cent (Hill 1998, p. 277). However, it is clear that even in industrially developed countries, SMEs remain a major force in economic production. Further, while it might be anticipated that the proportion of SMEs in an economy might be lower as per capita GDP increases, this does not follow for all ASEAN (Association of Southeast Asian Nations) countries (Hill 1998, p. 293). One possible explanation for this is that with increased industrialisation, the profile of SMEs changes. That is, as an economy becomes more technologically independent, a more technological SME emerges.

In Australia, a small player in the global economy, the leading edge of the national 'value-added' export drive is commanded by 700 SMEs (Australian Manufacturing Council 1993). The same trend can be observed in the United Kingdom, the US, many other European countries, and Japan (Sengenberger et al. 1990). In Taiwan, SME development has been explicitly supported by public R&D organisations for the purpose of 'spinning off' new small-firm industries while at the same time facilitating the transfer and assimilation of advanced technologies (Wade 1990). In countries such as Indonesia and China, in spite of the apparent dominance of large conglomerates or state-owned enterprises, there is evidence that much of the domestic manufacturing innovation is produced by small- and medium-sized firms (see Hill 1998).

However, while SMEs have performed an important role in economic development their contribution to national systems of innovation remains ambiguous. For example, SMEs are generally considered to be users of technology rather than producers (Bessant 1999). Exceptions, as Bessant points out, are in the knowledge-intensive fields. However, irrespective of whether they are technology producers or users, their role in the diffusion of technology is significant. Many SMEs are linked to large technology-intensive firms as suppliers or customers. In addition, many small firms are interlinked with networks or clusters that include substantial technological input from publicly funded research institutions (Bessant 1999, p. 602). A recognition of this 'diffusion' role has led to a greater emphasis on SMEs in national policies for technology development (Wong 1996). It remains to be seen how appropriate this emphasis is in the context of structural changes since the onset of the financial crisis.

8.3   SMES AND KNOWLEDGE-BASED ORGANISATIONAL ALLIANCES

Three factors stand out that suggest structural changes through the last few decades have placed SMEs in a more central role in the diffusion of technology than was previously the case. First, a growing number of studies have shown that SMEs are particularly important elements in fast-moving knowledge-intensive sectors such as IT and biotechnology. Their organisational flexibility has meant that they can become drivers, rather than simply users, in the development and uptake of new technologies in organisational networks and alliances or industry clusters. Second, the decline of the centralised laboratory has meant that SMEs, through networked R&D alliances, now perform a more significant role in national R&D efforts. This has placed a greater emphasis on clusters rather than individual firms as the organisational base for innovation. Third, government policies for technology and innovation have placed greater emphasis on developing innovation or knowledge systems rather than on developing 'single-tier' technology capability. This has placed a greater emphasis on the mechanisms for linking firms, sectors and institutions rather than on building capabilities for specific sectors.

8.3.1   SMEs and Knowledge-based Networks

In economies based on new and intensive technologies it is access to knowledge rather than the ownership of knowledge that counts. Networks or industry clusters provide a mechanism for SMEs to gain access to new knowledge and new technologies. It is *networks* not *entities* that matter (Marceau 2000).

Within innovation networks their smaller size has enabled SMEs to adapt quickly to new technological opportunities. SMEs in the Taiwan economy grew much faster during the 1970s, and after this period they were able to compete successfully with many of the larger firms (Schive 1995, p. 10). A recent study has shown that these smaller firms were able to advance during the 1970s because they were equipped with a more flexible set of technologies, and were more adaptive to the external environment than their larger counterparts (Schive 1995).

Similar observations can be made from Australian studies. An Australian innovation survey, for example, found that the larger the firm the more likely it was to engage in innovative activities, but the mode or nature of innovation differed according to size of firm (Australian Bureau of Statistics 1994). The survey findings showed that the pace of innovation among small firms was faster and involved smaller amounts of capital investment. For small firms (fewer than 20 employees) the median time to reach commercialisation was 6–12 months, whereas for firms with over 100 employees the median time was one to two years. Further, the median cost for small firms was lower, AU$10–50 thousand compared to over AU$100 000 per innovation activity for large firms. This finding was more pronounced for process innovation than product innovation.

A more recent study in Japan concluded that Japanese SMEs rely heavily on research alliances with enterprises from different industries and research institutes belonging to local governments. The study concluded by noting that SMEs played a crucial role in Japan in supporting a national innovation system, and were central to maintaining Japan's high innovative capacity (Sugasawa and Liyanage 1999).

In China, the rapid growth of township and village enterprises has been facilitated through complex networks of affiliations and alliances between scientists, engineers, academics and business entrepreneurs (Harvie and Turpin 1997). As Christerson and Lever-Tracy (1996) have noted, the impressive growth among these Chinese enterprises reflects a pattern of development in the industrial development of the 'third Italy'. In this context, they note the salience of horizontal alliances that include local governments as key ingredients in responding to fast-changing market niches.

8.3.2   Decline of the Centralised Laboratory

Another structural change affecting the role of SMEs in diffusing technology has been the decline of the centralised laboratory. A significant feature of the commercial and public sector research environment through the 1990s has been the shift away from the centralised laboratory towards smaller research units with flexible and adaptable research alliances. In the United States, for example, there has been a trend through the past decade towards the devolution of R&D strategic management to business divisions or units (Whittington 1991). Forecasts made in the United States through the 1990s suggested that approximately half of all major firms expected to increase their participation in alliances and joint ventures (Roberts 1995). In Australia, it is already apparent that almost half of industrial R&D investments are made in organisations external to the investing firm or agency. Similarly, in Japan a recent survey indicated that over 60 per cent of major firms expected to be 'highly dependent' on external technology sources (Roberts 1995).

Further impetus to the decline of the centralised laboratory has come from a recognition by governments that SMEs have been able to work more effectively with universities in exploiting technological breakthroughs, than have larger firms. The US government has consequently given preferences to small firms in legislation concerning technology licensing rights (Etzkowitz and Stevens 1995).

Since the 1980s China has embarked on a concerted program to link publicly funded research to the market demands of its rapidly expanding economy. Research institutes, universities and large state-owned enterprises in China have since become embedded in new and flexible alliances across a whole range of business enterprises (Turpin and Liu 2000). However, many of the most innovative R&D structures in China are emerging around complex networks of affiliations or alliances of scientists, engineers, academics and business entrepreneurs (Turpin et al. forthcoming). It thus appears that across the world and among different cultural and political systems, the idea of the centralised laboratory, driven by long-term corporate strategies, appears to be giving way to more collective approaches to R&D investment involving complex organisational arrangements. In this context SMEs have the potential to perform quite central, as well as peripheral, roles in the development and diffusion of technologies.

8.3.3   SMEs as Components of National and Regional Innovation Systems

Another structural change that has influenced the technological capacity of SMEs has been the way that governments have shifted their attention away from developing specific technologies, and more towards options for creating knowledge or innovation systems (Belloti and Tunalv 1999). Focusing on developing a knowledge *system* that emphasises the 'structured' arrangement of institutions, communities and organisations that intersect through the production, use and diffusion of knowledge.

In Indonesia, for example, the focus on developing strategic industries through the 1970s and 1980s has shifted toward investigations of ways to draw SMEs into industry clusters (Hill 1998). In the Republic of Korea the previous policy emphasis on large firms has more recently been identified as problematic for building a sustainable national innovation system (Kim 1997). In many countries SMEs have provided a target for policies that seek to transcend rural and urban modes of industrialisation, and the informal and formal sectors of production (Chamarik and

Goonatilake 1994). In this context, it is their capacity to interconnect with other components of systems as much as their inherent capacity to generate technology that is seen as important. As Holbrook has pointed out, the great fragility of many local systems of innovation, particularly those in developing countries, is a direct result of their being 'weakly institutionalised' (Holbrook et al. 1999). This is not simply a matter of size or age of the systems. Rather, it is a matter of the *systematic* nature and sustainability of interaction between the elements that make up the system.

Some countries developed policy initiatives specifically intended to link SMEs to science and technology (S&T) institutions. Taiwan, for example, responded to development challenges by establishing an Industrial Technology Research Institute to support the growth of small firms (see Mathews and Cho 2000). In Indonesia, through the 1980s, where small-scale industry had become a high priority for government, a number of technical service units (UPTs) were established to enhance technological capability among SMEs. While these developments reflected a recognition among policy makers of the need to promote innovation among SMEs, they also contributed to bringing SMEs into a more central role in innovation systems.

8.3.4   Implications for SMEs in Less Industrially Developed Economies

The above discussion suggests that the role of SMEs in the production and diffusion of technology has been undergoing some transformation. It was argued that three key factors have contributed to this: the emergence of knowledge-based organisational networks; the decline of centralised R&D laboratories; and an increased emphasis in government policies for promoting systems of innovation. While there are considerable differences in the status of technological capability among SMEs across economies in the region, these enterprises appear to be subject to these influences, in some way, in almost all countries.

Among the less industrially developing economies, technological capability often tends to be concentrated in foreign and joint-venture firms or within large but somewhat segmented state-owned enterprises. The task for government policy is not only to attract technology from foreign sources but also to confront the more difficult task of 'capturing' and diffusing such capabilities more generally throughout their economies. In other words, they face the task of attracting *and* embedding international technological capability in their own local innovation systems. SMEs can perform an important role in this process. However, one of the major difficulties for these countries is that their local systems are fragile and are weakly connected to national institutions and larger production enterprises. The recent financial crisis could be a factor further adding to this fragility. The following sections in this chapter explore the extent to which this has occurred among firms in Indonesia.

8.4   SMES AND TECHNOLOGY DIFFUSION IN INDONESIA

8.4.1   The Policy Context

During the mid-1990s numerous reports noted that the Indonesian economy was performing reasonably well, if not better than expected, in terms of moving its productive orientation towards high-growth industries (Ray 1999). Overall, the national workforce grew by nearly 22 per cent between 1987 and 1996, outstripping the rate of population growth at around 15 per cent. The size of the manufacturing workforce grew by 85 per cent during the same period to reach 10.8 million people. The workforce in large and medium enterprises (LMEs) expanded even more rapidly (by 134 per cent) to comprise 4.2 million employees in 1996. Manufacturing employed a rising proportion of the workforce, from around 8 per cent in the late 1980s to over 12 per cent in 1996. Total GDP doubled in real terms, the output from manufacturing grew at more than twice the rate for GDP and manufacturing output from LMEs grew, in real value, more than three-fold.

However, several weaknesses were beginning to emerge. Despite the growth of the non-oil sectors, several studies observed that only limited structural change in the economy had occurred. Moreover, it was noted that compared to other countries in the region there was little transformation occurring in key social institutions such as those associated with finance, governance, public policy and knowledge production. Other weaknesses attracting attention were the segmentation of the skilled workforce, the concentration of R&D among state-owned firms and research institutions (Mans 1996); and the spatial segmentation in the manufacturing sector (Hill 1998). Further, although the non-oil manufacturing sector had grown rapidly there remained a high level of dependency on low skill and natural resources. By the late 1990s low-technology extractive-based industries still accounted for over 60 per cent of the value of output. While some of the high- and medium-technology sectors had grown rapidly, this was from a low base. There was only limited evidence of development of local supplier industries to support export-oriented assembly. The rate at which product qualities and designs were being upgraded to achieve higher competitiveness also appeared limited.

Behind these industrial limitations was a weakly integrated science and technology system (Mans 1996). In short, it was becoming clear that a comparatively weak technological capability within Indonesian firms and institutions had been a major barrier towards improving export growth in knowledge-intensive, high-growth industries. Not surprisingly, therefore, the long-term development plans through the 1990s placed an unprecedented level of importance on science and technology. These efforts included new programs to build closer links between public and private sector enterprises and promote innovation through research institutes and UPTs. The latter were specifically targeted towards raising technological capability among SMEs, particularly in small-scale industrial estates.

8.4.2   The Onset of the Financial Crisis

The financial crisis served to exacerbate industrial weaknesses that were already emerging in the Indonesian economy. What started as a monetary problem, rapidly turned into a national crisis affecting almost every social and economic institution across the country. Firms that produced goods and services for the domestic market were hard hit by weakening exchange rates. They faced increasing costs for imported basic materials and weakening demand in domestic markets. As the political consequences of the crisis began to unfold many large enterprises and public institutions, built-up and maintained under the military dominance of the Suharto regime, began to unravel. At the same time the depth of the crisis undermined the capacity of smaller firms to upgrade their technological capability and respond to export opportunities provided by the devalued exchange rate. Instead, most were driven to further their technological dependence on foreign firms or state institutions.

One immediate impact of the crisis on the nation's S&T capability was a substantial reduction in public expenditure on R&D budgets. Already small in terms of proportion of GDP (0.2 per cent) and predominantly carried out in public institutions or large state enterprises (80 per cent), the national R&D budget served to undermine already limited R&D infrastructure. In addition, public technological capability provided through UPTs were also reduced. Technology-dependent firms, particularly SMEs, were likely to be particularly disadvantaged by these events (Hidayat et al. 1998). The reduction in public R&D infrastructure combined with reduced foreign technological investment and a reduced capacity among local firms to maintain a technological edge, carried the potential to introduce even more weaknesses to the country's technological capacity

The following sections investigate the impact of the financial crisis, between 1997 and 1999, on Indonesian SMEs. One of the major questions addressed is whether the crisis has had an adverse impact on links for access to technology between SMEs and larger firms or technology enabling institutions. If SMEs have come to occupy a more central role in innovation systems, and if they have been adversely affected by the recent crisis, then it is likely that there will be broader consequences for the diffusion of technology within the economy more generally.

8.5   A NATIONAL OVERVIEW OF THE IMPACT OF THE CRISIS ON SMES

National data on SMEs in Indonesia is limited and it is only recently that data have been collected systematically by enterprise size and industry sector. The Ministry of Cooperatives and SMEs began collecting data on small firms in 1992. In 1997 the collection became more detailed and allowed for comparisons between small, medium and large enterprises. Data are now collected on small, medium and large firms based on financial classifications of assets and turnover. Small enterprises are classified as those with assets of less than Rp. 200 million.[1] Medium and large enterprises are classified as those with assets in excess of this figure. In addition, enterprises with a turnover of less than Rp. 1 billion annually are classified as small; those with a turnover of between Rp. 1 and 50 billion are classified as medium; and those with over Rp. 50 billion are classified as large. While this definition is problematic for international comparisons it still serves to provide for an exploratory analysis of the relationship between large and small enterprises, so defined in Indonesia.

In Indonesia the largest proportions of small enterprises are concentrated in agriculture, forestry and fisheries; trade and restaurants; and manufacturing. The next largest concentration is in the service sector. Table 8.1 shows the sectoral distribution of small enterprises by sector for the years between 1991 and 1999. Data for 1994 and 1995 were not available. These data show that until 1997 there is evidence of a gradual trend away from enterprise concentration in agricultural production and towards greater concentration in the trade and service sectors. Manufacturing remained fairly consistent at around 7 per cent of all small enterprises. Between 1997 and 1998, however, there is a sharp reversal of this trend.

Comparative data for medium and large enterprises for the same time series is not available. However from 1997 comparative data were collected. Table 8.2 shows the comparative data for small, medium and large enterprises for the years 1997 and 1998, the most severe years of the crisis. Table 8.3 presents the same data as percentage change between the two years.

While the number of firms overall was reduced by over 7 per cent during the two-year period the most dramatic change was in the finance sector. For small firms the decline in total enterprises operating over the two-year period was even more dramatic. However, in all sectors except trade/restaurants SMEs experienced a greater decline in total numbers than medium or large enterprises, and reflect a stronger growth in agricultural production enterprises. Medium and large enterprises reflect similar patterns of change, but one that is quite different from the pattern reflected in the experiences of small enterprises. Figure 8.1 illustrates these different patterns.

8.5.1 Labour Absorption by Enterprise, Size and Sector

Data are also available on the numbers of people employed by size of enterprise and industry sector for 1997 to 1999. The data for 1997–98, presented in Figure 8.2, show a similar pattern to that illustrated in Figure 8.1 for the same year. Taken together, these data suggest that during the two-year period small enterprises experienced a decline in the manufacturing and service sectors but growth in the agricultural sector. The pattern is far less marked for medium and large enterprises.

The labour force absorption data for 1998–99 suggest a more stable situation, with only two sectors showing further contraction (Figure 8.3). For 1998–99 the data show a similar pattern for labour absorption, irrespective of enterprise size. The data for the three years combined, 1997–99, show the result of concentrated growth over

Table 8.1
Number of Small Enterprises by Broad Economic Sector, 1992–98

Sector	1992	%*	1993	%*	1996	%*	1997	%*	1998	%*
Agriculture, forestry and fisheries	21 298.6	63.7	21 761.8	64.3	22 533.9	57.9	22 511.6	56.7	23 097.9	62.8
Mining and quarrying	87.4	0.3	90.0	0.3	192.1	0.5	204.4	0.5	137.2	0.4
Manufacturing	2 484.9	7.4	2 581.0	7.6	2 748.5	7.1	2 817.4	7.1	2 104.9	5.7
Electricity, gas and water	16.8	0.1	20.7	0.1	13.2	0.0	13.4	0.0	7.3	0.0
Construction	863.7	2.6	866.2	2.6	203.1	0.5	199.2	0.5	122.9	0.3
Trade, hotel and restaurants	5 825.6	17.4	5 950.7	17.6	9 436.4	24.3	9 986.5	25.2	8 325.3	22.6
Transportation and communication	1 176.5	3.5	1 212.6	3.6	1 731.1	4.4	1 852.4	4.7	1 507.6	4.1
Finance	20.0	0.1	38.3	0.1	67.3	0.2	71.3	0.2	18.5	0.1
Services	1 669.1	5.0	1 346.0	4.0	1 976.8	5.1	2 048.3	5.2	1 439.9	3.9
All sectors	33 442.6	100.0	33 867.3	100.0	38 902.4	100.0	39 704.5	100.0	36 761.5	100.0

Note: * Total rounded to 100.
Source: Ministry of Cooperatives and SMEs, 'Statistics of Cooperatives and SMEs' (1999).

141

Table 8.2

Number of Small, Medium and Large Enterprises by Economic Sector, 1997 and 1998

Sector	1997			1998			All enterprises	
	Small	Medium	Large	Small	Medium	Large	1997	1998
Agriculture, forestry and fisheries	22 511 588	1 543	57	23 097 871	1 562	58	22 513 188	23 099 491
Mining and quarrying	204 413	504	51	137 284	555	56	204 968	137 895
Manufacturing	2 817 379	10 495	694	2 104 856	9 545	631	2 828 568	2 115 032
Electricity, gas and water	13 434	370	41	7 319	375	41	13 845	7 735
Construction	199 253	7 811	170	122 945	7 097	154	207 234	130 196
Trade, hotel and restaurant	9 986 510	26 944	513	8 325 351	22 081	421	10 013 967	8 347 853
Transportation and communication	1 852 401	2 432	117	1 507 629	2 064	99	1 854 950	1 509 792
Finance	71 334	6 023	294	18 519	4 419	216	77 651	23 154
Services	2 048 349	4 327	160	1 439 915	4 191	155	2 052 836	1 444 261
Total units	39 704 661	60 449	2 097	36 761 689	51 889	1 831	39 767 207	36 815 409

Source: Ministry of Cooperatives and SMEs, 'Statistics of Cooperatives and SMEs'(1999).

142

Table 8.3
Proportional Change in Numbers of Small, Medium and Large Enterprises,
by Industry Sector, 1997–98

Sector	Percentage change		1997–98	Overall change 1997–98
	Small enterprises	Medium enterprises	Large enterprises	All enterprises
Agriculture, forestry and fisheries	2.60	1.23	1.75	2.60
Mining and quarrying	−32.84	10.12	9.80	−32.72
Manufacturing	−25.29	−9.05	−9.08	−25.23
Electricity, gas and water	−45.52	1.35	0.00	−44.13
Construction	−38.30	−9.14	−9.41	−37.17
Trade, hotel and restaurant	−16.63	−18.05	−17.93	−16.64
Transport and communication	−18.61	−15.13	−15.38	−18.61
Finance	−74.04	−26.63	−26.53	−70.18
Services	−29.70	−3.14	−3.13	−29.65
Total	−7.41	−14.16	−12.68	−7.42

Source: Ministry of Cooperatives and SMEs, 'Statistics of Cooperatives and SMEs' (1999).

the two years in the agricultural sector, already the largest sector by far, and with minimal change in the trade, hotel and restaurant sector (Figure 8.4).

These data suggest that the economic crisis has had a disproportionate impact on SMEs. Further, they suggest a retreat among small enterprises away from manufacturing and service sectors and a return to agriculture. But, how has this general trend been experienced at the firm level? What might these changes mean for the capacity of small firms to upgrade or maintain their technological capability? What might this mean for small firms and their role in national innovation systems? While the data are suggestive, and a useful starting point for the present analysis, they do not allow for insights into these more specific questions. In order to extend this enquiry, the following section introduces additional data provided by the Department of Cooperatives.

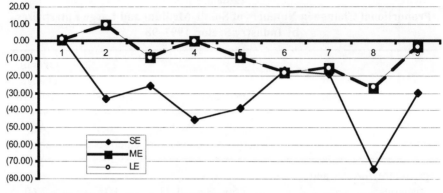

1=Agriculture, forestry, fisheries   4=Electricity, gas and water   7=Transport and communication
2=Mining and quarrying   5= Construction   8=Finance
3=Manufacturing   6=Trade, hotel, restaurants   9=Services

Source: Ministry of Cooperatives and SMEs, 'Statistics of Cooperatives and SMEs' (1999).

*Figure 8.1   Percentage Change in Number of Small, Medium and Large Enter-
               prises by Economic Sector, 1997–98*

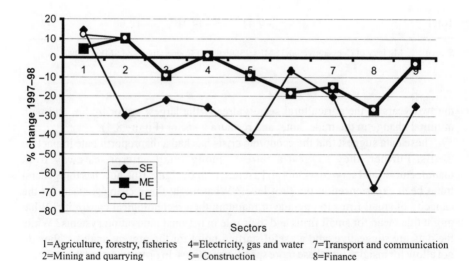

1=Agriculture, forestry, fisheries   4=Electricity, gas and water   7=Transport and communication
2=Mining and quarrying   5= Construction   8=Finance
3=Manufacturing   6=Trade, hotel, restaurants   9=Services

Source: Ministry of Cooperatives and SMEs, 'Statistics of Cooperatives and SMEs' (1999).

*Figure 8. 2   Percentage Change in Labour Absorption among Small, Medium
                and Large Enterprises by Economic Sector, 1997–98*

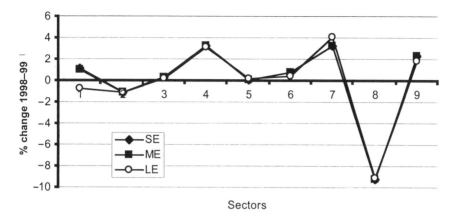

1=Agriculture, forestry, fisheries   4=Electricity, gas and water   7=Transport and communication
2=Mining and quarrying   5= Construction   8=Finance
3=Manufacturing   6=Trade, hotel, restaurants   9=Services

Source: Ministry of Cooperatives and SMEs, 'Statistics of Cooperatives and SMEs' (1999).

Figure 8.3   *Percentage Change in Number of Small, Medium and Large Enterprises by Economic Sector, 1998–99*

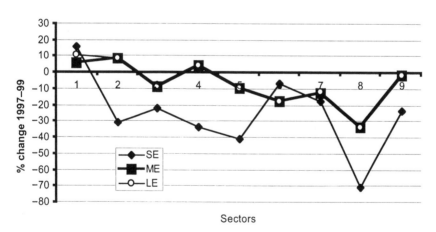

1=Agriculture, forestry, fisheries   4=Electricity, gas and water   7=Transport and communication
2=Mining and quarrying   5= Construction   8=Finance
3=Manufacturing   6=Trade, hotel, restaurants   9=Services

Source: Ministry of Cooperatives and SMEs, 'Statistics of Cooperatives and SMEs' (1999).

Figure 8.4   *Percentage Change in Labour Absorption among Small, Medium and Large Enterprises by Economic Sector, 1998–99*

8.6 A NATIONAL SURVEY OF SME EXPERIENCES THROUGH THE FINANCIAL CRISIS

In order to gain more insight into the impact of the financial crisis on small enterprises the Department of Cooperatives carried out a study of nearly 200,000 enterprises across 27 provinces. The study collected information from firms operating in selected sectors that would indicate the extent of: (a) decreased levels of business; and (b) cessation of a major business activity. Some results from this survey are shown in Table 8.4.

According to the survey, 18 per cent of all small firms ceased a major business activity and over 25 per cent experienced decreased business activity during 1998. Again these data reinforce the observation that the impact across sectors has been variable. The data show the impact to be most severe in the manufacturing and agriculture sectors. Explanations for this are complex and likely to involve many factors. For example, some sub-sectors were more adversely affected by the rising costs of raw materials than others. While some sectors derived short-term benefit from a reduced exchange rate there was also an immediate adverse impact from the reduced purchasing power of local users and consumers. Further, while there was

Table 8.4
Percentage of Small Enterprises that have Stopped and
Decreased Business, 1998

	Sector	Sample size (enterprises)	Decreased business (%)	Stopped business (%)
1	Agriculture, forest and fisheries	3 246	42.76	31.15
2	Mining and quarrying	2 515	50.42	22.74
3	Manufacturing	69 604	27.71	35.41
4	Electricity, gas and water	0	0.00	0.00
5	Construction	1 847	11.53	5.41
6	Trade, hotel and restaurants	84 752	19.73	4.89
7	Transport and communication	668	6.14	10.03
8	Finance	0	0.00	0.00
9	Services	13 271	40.58	4.42
	Total	175 903	25.19	17.70

Source: 'Analysis of Monetary Crisis Impact on Small Enterprises', Data and Information Centre, Department of Cooperatives, Indonesia, 1998.

potential for some firms to benefit from increased export orders the reduction in imports led to a shortage of containers for export shipping.

On the positive side, however, the data on labour absorption for 1998–99, suggest a realignment between small firms and their larger counterparts. This positive note is reinforced by further data from the Department of Cooperatives. These data show that SMEs were actually increasing their contribution to GDP from 1997–99 while the contribution from both medium and large firms contracted (see Table 8.5). This suggests that while a considerable number of small firms went out of business between 1997 and 1999, those that were doing well continued to do so. Perhaps the impact of the crisis has been most severe on those most technologically dependent.

Again, what might this mean for the role of SMEs in industry clusters and networks and what does it mean for the status of innovation and the diffusion of technology? A case-study approach allows for a more detailed investigation of this issue. Two regional case studies carried out in the immediate post-crisis period provide some insights into the technology status of SMEs in the manufacturing sector. These studies were carried out in order to assess whether the concept of an Industrial Service Centre (ISC) might be appropriate for providing technical services to clusters of SMEs rather than to single firms. The two case-study regions were Tegal in Central Java and the Sukambumi district of West Java. Only the Tegal case study is reported here, however, similar findings emerged from the Sukambumi study.[2]

Table 8.5
Contribution of small, medium and large enterprises to GDP: 1997–99

	Contribution to GDP		
Size of enterprise	1997	1998	1999
Small	37.96	40.89	41.89
Medium	19.84	17.28	17.47
Large	42.20	41.83	40.64

Source: Department of Cooperatives, Jakarta.

8.7   A CASE STUDY OF EXPERIENCES AMONG MANUFACTURING SMES IN CENTRAL JAVA

The district of Tegal lies within the jurisdiction of the provincial government of Central Java. It is located on the northern shore, bordering West Java. Although it contributes only 5 per cent of Central Java's total regional output it has maintained a consistently high growth rate (around 12 per cent between 1992 and 1997).

The local economy is dominated by the agriculture sector, but there has been a trend away from agriculture towards manufacturing. In 1992 manufacturing accounted for 16 per cent of the district's output. By 1997 the proportion had increased to just under 25 per cent (a proportion consistent with the national manufacturing output).

Local data collections allow manufacturing to be disaggregated into four product groups: agriculture, forestry and fisheries; chemical; multifarious; and metal, machinery and electronics.

In all four manufacturing groups, SMEs make major contributions to production. The most significant contribution has been in the metal, machinery and electronics group (see Table 8.6).

Each of the four product groups combine a number of major product categories. The product categories within each of the four product groups that comprise the manufacturing classification are shown in Table 8.7. This table provides a profile of the numbers of firms and their level of production in manufacturing in the district. These data show the product categories where SMEs are most predominant. For example, in the chemicals product group, acetylene gas and plastic bottles are dominated by two firms producing over 20 per cent of all chemicals. In contrast, 2 622 firms producing non-pressed bricks provide only 16 per cent of all production in the same group. Similarly, in the multifarious product group 35 firms engaged with weaving (0.3 per cent of all firms in the group) produced 18 per cent of the total product group output. However, 3 058 firms producing garments (27 per cent of all firms in the group) produced only 17 per cent of the total product group output.

Table 8.6
Manufacturing Production by Product Group and Size of Enterprise, Tegal District, 1995

Product group	Total enterprises	Total production (m. Rp)	Total number of large enterprises	Total production of large enterprises (m. Rp)	Total production of SMEs	% production of SMEs
Agriculture, forest, fisheries	8 872	65 020	6	11 122	53 898	82.9
Chemical	4 712	32 159	3	7 734	24 425	76.0
Multifarious metal, machinery	11 290	168 164	8	36 327	131 837	78.4
Electrical	2 958	38 999	2	1 089	37 910	97.2
All product groups	27 832	304 342	19	56 272	248 070	81.5

Source: Industry service of the District of Tegal (Dinas Perindustrian, Kabupaten Tegal).

The metal, machinery and electrical group has the highest proportion of SMEs (see Table 8.6). In this group a large number of smaller firms tend to dominate the production of small items such as nuts, bolts, washers and hinges. Kitchenware production, which includes items such as ovens and oven components, aluminium rice cookers, copper frying pans and teapots, also has a high concentration of small firms. Automotive vehicle components also comprise a large number of small firms. This primarily involves the production of fuel tanks, front mountings and similar components. There are few companies that make high precision items. Few firms are in the business of producing machinery. Of those that do it is mainly food-processing machines or machinery for producing roof tiles or ceramic products. In terms of the largest number of firms the largest cluster is concerned with producing agricultural tools (774 firms). In contrast, there is only one firm producing hydraulic presses. Experiences with the acquisition of technology at the firm level in the metals, machinery and electronics group provides the focus for more detailed study in the following section

8.7.1 Experiences of Manufacturing SMEs in the Metal Product Group in the Tegal Region

This section summarises the results of 12 in-depth interviews with directors of firms in the metalwork sector. In addition to the 12 case studies further data were collected from 20 firms through a postal survey. The main focus of the interviews and the survey was on documenting the source and type of technical assistance supporting production within the firm. In particular, information was sought on the capacity of existing technical service units to support the technological capability of SMEs in the immediate post-crisis period. Further, the interviews explored whether the concept of an 'Industrial Service Centre' directed specifically towards the provision of industrial training, product testing, upgrading of machinery and quality improvement might assist SMEs to upgrade their technological capability.

A major concentration of SME manufacturing in the Tegal district is in the *Lingkungan Industri Kecil* (LIK) – small-scale industrial estate. Since the 1980s technological development in the estate has been supported by a technical service unit (UPT) under the Department of Industry and Trade. Nine of the case-study firms were located within the LIK. However, the interviews and survey showed that even small firms beyond the industrial estate had relied at some stage on the UPT for technology development. While manufacturing output from the metals sector is predominantly produced by SMEs, the case-study interviews identified a high degree of technological dependency on the part of SMEs. In addition, the major incentive to innovate among SMEs stems from their links to large or foreign firms. In the absence of such links it appears that SMEs face both increased barriers *and* decreased incentives to innovate.

A major question for the issues raised in this chapter is: to what extent are cluster-

Table 8.7
Manufacturing Sector by Product Groupings, Enterprises and Production,
Tegal District, Central Java, 1995

Product group	Total enterprises	Total production (m. Rp)	Average production per firm (m. Rp)
Agric., Forest, Fisheries Group	**8 872**	**65 020**	**7.3**
Soybean and tempe	4 687	25 392	5.4
Tea processing	30	12 333	411.1
Chip and kerupuk	1 211	10 493	8.7
Fish drying & smoking	340	4 670	13.7
Mineral water	2	2 130	1 065.0
Sauces, shrimp paste, etc.	135	2 264	16.8
Cakes, pastry, etc.	1 257	1 587	1.3
Ice cube, etc.	194	1 524	7.9
Others	1 016	4 627	4.6
Chemical Group	**4 712**	**32 159**	**6.8**
Lime, plaster	220	7 600	34.5
Roof tile	1 306	5 606	4.3
Non-pressed brick	2 622	5 250	2.0
Plastic bottle	1	4442	4442.0
Acetylene gas	1	3 225	3 225.0
Structural cement products	88	3 029	34.4
Clay and houseware products	162	631	3.9
Car windshield	90	630	7.0
Paper, cardboard	2	600	300.0
Goods made from used tyres	194	435	2.2
Pesticides	1	301	301.0
Others	25	410	16.4

Product Group	Total Enterprises	Total production (mill. Rp)	Average production per firm (mill. Rp)
Multifarious Group	**11 290**	**168 164**	**14.9**
Wooden furniture & fixtures	1 941	48 253	24.9
Weaving	35	30 259	864.5
Garment	3 058	28 804	9.4
Saw mill products	502	21 771	43.4
Non-garment textiles	1 545	8 786	5.7
Footwear	154	8 625	56.0
Gold accessories	47	5 096	108.4
Shuttle cocks	213	4 463	21.0
Bamboo & coconut weaving	2 043	3 153	1.5
Leather products	150	2 174	14.5
Rattan craft products	2	1 689	844.5
Wood craft & carving	2	1 580	790.0
Kitchenware (wood, bamboo, rattan)	1 327	1 291	1.0
Leather processing	45	1 028	22.8
Others	226	1 192	5.3
Metal, Machinery & Electronics Group	**2 958**	**38 999**	**13.2**
Nails, bolts, screws, etc.	218	7 410	34.0
Kitchenware	347	3 952	11.4
Fabricated metal (building)	42	2 715	64.6
2- & 3-wheel vehicle components	577	2 081	3.6
Metal castings	14	1 278	91.3
4-wheel vehicle body rebuilding	2	1 132	566.0
Agricultural tools	774	1 008	1.3
Bicycle and becak accessories	515	1 000	1.9
Metal furniture	35	764	21.8
4-wheel vehicle components	22	505	23.0
Hydraulic press machines	1	470	470.0
Loud speaker components	1	227	227.0
Others	410	16 457	40.1

Source: Industry service of the District of Tegal (Dinas Perindustrian, Kabupaten Tegal).

based UPTs able to support technology development among SMEs in the post-crisis environment?

Links between sectors, customers and suppliers

In general there was evidence of only limited trading between the metalwork SMEs and other industry sectors in Tegal. The majority of products were traded with customers outside the region, mainly in Jakarta. Few firms had regular customers within Tegal. Most trading was based on direct subcontracting with assemblers while others were directed to wholesalers. However, subcontracting among local enterprises was common. There appear to be two reasons for this. First, because subcontracting serves the purpose of complementing existing production facilities among smaller firms, and second because most firms have limited production capability and are unable to cope with large orders when they become available. Many only entered the metalwork business after they obtained an order from a customer even though small in quantity. After finding an initial customer few firms attempted any promotion effort. Even after many years most customers continued to be those that made first contact. Nearly all firms interviewed planned their production on a job-order basis rather than orienting it to a general market. Most had regular monthly orders combined with *ad hoc* orders.

In summary most SMEs in the metals group were highly dependent on a very small number of customers, often only one. Links between customers and suppliers were predominantly with firms outside the local cluster. Links between firms in Tegal were largely horizontal links between similar firms, carrying out the same form of production utilising similar technologies and processes.

Access to technology

Practically all machinery and maintenance was sourced from outside the district. Among the surveyed firms almost all machinery was purchased secondhand. Only one firm used numerically controlled machine tools. Most production facilities were 'minimally maintained'. Exceptions were a small number of firms in receipt of foreign technical assistance. Most products did not require a high level of precision. Nor was there a strong demand for high production quality. Although technical capabilities were sufficient for current manufacturing purposes they did not allow for innovation beyond present capacities. A major factor inhibiting innovation appeared to be the lack of a demanding customer or market. Product testing was not required for most products and most products allowed for loose tolerance. This also applied to firms supplying auto parts. Dyes and fixtures were mostly produced in-house and this, coupled with a lack of demand for high quality, provided little incentive for innovation.

Access to technical skills

Few firms actively sought training to upgrade skills among their employees. Most relied on major customers for skills improvement. A major constraint often cited for upgrading firm skills was the high level of job mobility and the relatively large proportion of workers paid on a 'job-order basis'. In other words, without sustainable growth or continuity in manufacturing orders there was little chance of acquiring and retaining higher-skilled technical personnel.

Impact of the financial crisis on technological services

Through the early 1990s the government was becoming aware of the need to support technology upgrading among firms other than state strategic industries and state enterprises. Support for the development of industry clusters was seen as one potential mechanism for achieving this. The national government's decision to set up a series of technical service units as described earlier, was intended to drive innovative capabilities within the manufacturing sector. These were regarded as important for assisting firms to upgrade machinery, systems and skills and gain access to shared major infrastructure items. However, the onset of the financial crisis has apparently limited the capacity of the state to maintain these units. As a result, in the Tegal district, larger items such as rolling machines have now been relocated to a limited number of industrial zones.

Further, for many firms that have made technological progress, their capabilities are already beyond what the state can provide through the UPTs. These firms explained that while they initially relied on the UPT for technical support their internal technology capacity was now superior to the support available through the UPT. In other words, it appears that the technological capabilities of the service units have not been able to keep pace even with the limited capability of those outside the small-scale industrial estates. For those firms within the industrial estates, their reliance on UPTs and their level of technology remained unchanged. The financial crisis has further eroded the capacity of UPTs to appropriately service the technology needs of SMEs in this sector.

In summary, it appears that the SME metalwork firms in this district have a number of common characteristics. They are dependent on a small number of customers outside their immediate region, both for orders and for technological expertise. While the state has supported development opportunities for small firms in metals manufacturing through technical assistance units, such units appear to have outlived their usefulness. The financial crisis appears to have accelerated this process.

There appear to be horizontal links between small production firms but these contribute to similar modes of production with little scope for transferring upgraded skills or technologies. Firms surveyed in the industrial estate in Tegal have continued to be dependent on the limited and increasingly isolated technical capabilities of technical service units. Firms beyond the industrial estate cluster, while more independent, also appear to be more isolated from demands or capacity to innovate.

Finally, the crisis seems to have impinged on small manufacturing enterprises in this metals sector in three inter-related ways. First, there has been a reduction in market demands from customers to engage in innovation; secondly there has been a reduction in the supply of skills and increases in the cost of new components or machinery; and third, there has been reduced access to appropriate technical facilities or services.

8.8   CONCLUSIONS: IMPLICATIONS FOR TECHNOLOGY AND INNOVATION

The data presented at the beginning of this chapter suggest that the impact of the economic crisis on small Indonesian firms has been particularly severe. They suggest a sharp distinction between the impact on small firms and the impact on medium and large firms. Further, this distinction between small enterprises on the one hand and medium and large on the other, appears to be sustained across all major sectors. The distinction between the experiences of the two groups appears to be most extreme in the finance, construction, energy and mining sectors. Evidence emerging from the Department of Cooperatives' survey is showing that economic activity among small firms in the manufacturing and the service sectors has also been markedly affected.

However, additional data suggest that while this may be the case, SMEs are contributing to recovery at a faster rate than medium or large firms. An explanation for this could be that among those small firms that have survived, there is a greater proportion of knowledge-intensive firms. In other words, it could be that it is the knowledge-intensive firms that have been best placed to withstand the hard times – or even benefit from them. The evidence from many countries in the Asia–Pacific region is showing that the more dynamic and innovative SMEs have achieved that position by maximising their involvement in technology-based networks or alliances. Such networks typically involve suppliers, customers, scientific institutions and in some cases, government agencies. Of particular salience in most systems, or innovation clusters, is the dynamic interaction between small and large enterprises. The case study included in this chapter suggests that an emerging industry cluster in the metals manufacturing product group, while productive and technologically progressive through the period of rapid economic growth, has not been able to sustain growth or technological progress through the more difficult times.

Two factors appear to be converging here. First, there appears to be a retreat among small enterprises to low value-added or less knowledge-intensive industries. This is not surprising given that sustained capital investments are required to maintain a firm in technology-intensive activities. Second, it appears that SMEs are recovering but they are more isolated and less connected to the industry clusters that were emerging through the 1980s. SMEs in the metals manufacturing product group in Tegal, for example, appear to be more independent but less close-knit than they were before the crisis.

While these firms are surviving, such a trend does not appear conducive, in the longer term, to the diffusion of technology or to innovation. It is also counter to the changing role of SMEs in innovation systems discussed earlier in this chapter. Rather than a retreat among small enterprises towards more isolated modes of production, there is a need for increased interaction and alliances between the various parts of the innovation system. This includes technical alliances between small and large firms, between suppliers and customers, and between public and private sector enabling institutions. Thus, while small enterprises appear to be absorbing a considerable proportion of the unemployed population and contributing to increased GDP, they are playing less of a role in diffusing *beyond* industry-specific clusters.

The crisis seems to have emphasised a particular fragility among small enterprises in national innovation systems. The data presented here are only sketchy and there are many factors that might be contributing to the changing status of small, medium and large firms and their relationships to one another. Sketchy as the data may be, there is evidence that the financial crisis has left SMEs in Indonesia particularly vulnerable to dislocations in vertical or horizontal links to larger firms and technical support networks. This is likely to lead to their disconnection from national or transnational innovation systems. If this occurs their role in acquiring and diffusing technology in the national system is likely to be diminished.

There are policy implications. If critical pathways between large firms and SMEs in innovation clusters have been disturbed, then policy reforms for their reconstruction may be required. For example, a reconstruction of the technical services originally provided through the UPT model, but with a more appropriate and specific technical focus, might serve to coalesce and promote pockets of innovation. In any case, as attempts at reform progress, there will be an increasing need for industry-specific policy research to inform and assess their impact on technological capacity and innovation among SMEs.

NOTES

1   At the time of writing, July 2001, US$1 was equal to Rp 8 000.
2   The case-study interviews and survey were carried out by Dr Widyantoko Sumarlin from BPP Teknologi. The author is grateful for the material provided by Dr Sumarlin for inclusion in this chapter.

REFERENCES

Australian Bureau of Statistics (1994), *Innovation in Australian Manufacturing: 1994*, Catalogue No. 8116, Canberra: AGPS.

Australian Manufacturing Council (1993), *Emerging Exporters: Australia's High Value Added Manufacturing Exporters*, Melbourne: Australian Manufacturing Council.

Belotti, C. and C. Tunalv (1999), 'Acquisition of Technological Knowledge in Small and Medium-sized Manufacturing Companies in Sweden', *International Journal of Technology Management,* **18** (3/4), 353–71.

Bessant, J. (1999), 'The Rise and Fall of "Supernet": A Case Study of Technology Transfer Policy for Smaller Firms', *Research Policy,* **28**, 601–14.

Bourke, P. and L. Butler (1995), *International Links in Higher Education Research*, National Board of Employment, Education and Training, Commissioned Report No. 37, Canberra: AGPS, May.

Chamarik, S. and S. Goonatilake (1994), *Technological Independence: The Asian Experience*, Tokyo: United Nations University Press.

Christerson, B. and C. Lever-Tracy (1996), 'The Third China? China's Rural Enterprises as Dependent Subcontractors or as Dynamic Autonomous Firms?', paper presented to the Asia-Pacific Regional Conference of Sociology, Manila, 28–31 May.

Etzkowitz, H. and A.J. Stevens (1995), 'Inching Toward Industrial Policy: The University's Role in Government Initiatives to Assist Small, Innovative Companies in the US', *Science Studies*, **2**, 13–31.

Hall, C. (1995), 'Investing in Intangibles: Improving the Effectiveness of Government SME Advisory Services in the APEC Region', in *Report of APEC Symposium on HRD for SMEs*, Chinese Taipei: APEC, China Productivity Centre, pp. 2.1–2.36.

Harvie, C. and T. Turpin (1997), 'China's Market Reforms and Its New Forms of Scientific and Business Alliance', in Clement A. Tisdell and Joseph C.H. Chai (eds), *China's Economic Growth and Transition*, New York: Nova Science, pp. 257–91.

Hidayat, M., K. Ajidarmo, R. Priambudi and W. Sumarlin (1998), 'The Impact of the Economic Crisis and Its Policy Implications on Technology Development in Indonesia', paper presented to the Science and Technology Policy Asian Network Workshop, Science and Technology Policy for Asia–Pacific Economies in the 21st Century, Hanoi, June.

Hill, H. (1998), *Indonesia's Industrial Transformation*, Sydney: Allen & Unwin.

Holbrook, A., L. Hughes and J. Finch (1999), 'Characteristics of Innovation in a Non-metropolitan Area: The Okanagan Valley of British Columbia', Centre For Policy Research on Science and Technology, Report 9901, Simon Fraser University.

Kim, L. (1997), *Imitation to Innovation: The Dynamics of Korea's Technological Learning*, Boston, MA: Harvard Business School Press.

Liu, P. C. (1995), 'The Role of SMEs in Economic Development of Chinese Taipei', in *Report of APEC Symposium on HRD for SMEs*, Chinese Taipei: APEC, China Productivity Centre, pp. 6.1–6.37.

Mans, D. (1996), 'Focusing Indonesia's Technology Support Institutions on Effective Technology Diffusion', in *Indonesia – Industrial technology Development for a Competitive Edge,* Indonesian Discussion Paper Series, Washington: World Bank, pp. 33–47.

Marceau, J. (2000), 'Australian Universities: A Contestable Future', in *Why Universities Matter,* Sydney: Allen & Unwin, pp. 214–34.

Mathews, J.A. and D.S. Cho (2000), *Tiger Technology: The Creation of a Semiconductor Industry in East Asia,* Cambridge: Cambridge University Press.

Ray, D. (1999), 'How Competitive is Indonesia in the Emerging Global Knowledge Economy?', in *Proceedings of the AIBSEAR International Conference*, Academy for International Business South East Asia Region (AIBSEAR), July, pp. 286–98.

Roberts, E.B. (1995), 'Bench-marking the Strategic Management of Technology', *Research – Technology Management*, **38** (1).

Schive, C. (1995), 'Industrial Policies in a Maturing Taiwan Economy', *Journal of Industry Studies*, **2** (1).

Sengenberger, W., G. Loveman and M. Piore (1990), *The Re-emergence of Small Enterprises: Industrial Restructuring in Industrial Countries*, Geneva: International Institute of Labour Studies.

Sugasawa, Y. and S. Liyanage (1999), 'Technology and Business Opportunities for Small and Medium Enterprises in Japan: The Role of Research Networks', *International Journal of Technology Management*, **18** (3–4), 308–25.

Turpin, T., S. Garrett-Jones, P. Burns and X. Liu (forthcoming), *Innovation, Technology Policy and Regional Development: Evidence from China and Australia*, Cheltenham, UK: Edward Elgar.

Turpin, T. and X. Liu (2000), 'Balanced Development: The Challenge for Science, Technology and Innovation Policy', in Charles Harvie (ed.), *Contemporary Developments and Issues in China's Economic Transition*, Basingstoke, UK: Macmillan, pp. 191–211.

Turpin, T., H. Spence, S. Garrett-Jones and A. Marsh (1998), 'South-East Asia and the Pacific Rim', in H.J. Moore (ed.), *World Science Report*, Paris: UNESCO Publishing Elsevier, pp. 212–36.

Wade, R. (1990), *Governing the Market: Economic Theory and the Role of Government in East Asian Industrialisation*, Princeton, NJ: Princeton University Press.

Whittington, R. (1991), 'Changing Control Strategies in Industrial R&D', *R&D Management*, **21** (1), 43–53.

Wong, P.K. (1996), 'Developing Technology Managers in Singapore: Issues and Challenges', in Karen Minden and Wong Poh-Kam (eds), *Developing Technology Managers in the Pacific Rim: Comparative Strategies*, New York: East Gate Books, pp. 62–92.

9 Requirements for SME Information Technology

Craig Van Slyke, Christopher Conca and Kenneth Trimmer

9.1 INTRODUCTION

Small business development is a critical component to the growth of developing economies. According to the Asia–Pacific Economic Cooperation (APEC) forum, in member countries SMEs account for 95 per cent of all enterprises and employ over 80 per cent of the workforce. Further, SMEs account for between 30 and 60 per cent of GDP in member countries. In addition, the use of information technology is also increasing in East Asia. According to the World Information Technology and Services Alliance (WITSA), information and communication technology (ICT) spending is growing faster in the Asia–Pacific region (excluding Japan) than in any other area of the world. In fact, Vietnam boasts the world's fastest-growing ICT market with a 35 per cent compound annual growth rate. Recovering economies such as Indonesia, Thailand and Korea enjoy increasing ICT spending as their currencies become stronger (WITSA 2000). When one couples the importance of SMEs in East Asian economies with the trend towards increasing ICT use in the region, it becomes clear that understanding issues related to SMEs' use of information technology (IT) is important. The purpose of this chapter is to discuss a number of issues related to the requirements for successful introduction of IT into the small to medium sized enterprise.

Our discussion is organised as follows. In Section 9.2 we describe how SMEs utilise information technology, focusing on traditional usages as well as emerging applications and technologies. Section 9.3 identifies key factors that influence small business managers' decisions to adopt or reject IT-related innovations. Section 9.4 discusses how resource poverty, in various areas, can translate into barriers to the successful introduction of IT in SMEs. Section 9.5 discusses how barriers to IT use by SMEs arising from a lack of both slack financial and human resources, as well as a lack of knowledge among both employees and management, can be assisted by external sources including that of consultants, not-for-profit organisations, business partners and governmental entities. The section highlights four barriers and potential solutions based upon the external sources. Section 9.6 discusses a number of recommendations, broken down according to stakeholder, for facilitating SME IT use. Finally, Section 9.7 presents a summary of the major recommendations and conclusions from this chapter.

9.2   HOW SMES USE INFORMATION TECHNOLOGY

Small- to medium-sized businesses can utilise a wide-ranging set of computer applications within their organisations. However, as opposed to their larger counterparts, SMEs have a tendency to utilise packaged versus customised or hybrid systems, due primarily to their overall lack of resources. Because SMEs also have a tendency to employ generalists rather than specialists, the focus of the applications they employ initially address general productivity issues. Historically, SMEs have had a tendency to automate basic activities within the organisation such as word processing and accounting. These activities tend to be routine, are often mundane, and they are readily automated, particularly because they can be both recurring and relatively structured. Once employees in an organisation become familiarised with basic computerised applications, products that could be utilised for non-recurring and/or unstructured activities are more easily embraced by the SME. Such applications include spreadsheets, databases, industry-specific software, and computer aided design (CAD). The nature of these applications, generally shrink-wrapped software, allows the SME to focus on their business as opposed to information technology issues. The applications are commonly supported either through toll-free helplines, or through contracts with a local IT specialist. Therefore, the concept of outsourcing is inherent to SMEs, as they typically lack the slack resources necessary to engage the specialist on a full-time basis.

SMEs have also traditionally purchased turnkey systems. Such systems were often proprietary as well as industry specific. Early adoption of IT by SMEs was often accompanied by mid-sized systems such as the IBM System 34 and 36 or the DEC PDP series of hardware. These early systems often contained industry-specific business and accounting solutions. The advent of the microcomputer, and a plethora of productivity software and business solutions, enabled more SMEs to embrace IT, in addition to allowing early adopters options beyond their proprietary solutions. The remainder of this section presents further discussion of the types of applications utilised by SMEs, and the changing nature of the applications.

9.2.1   Traditional Uses of IT by SMEs

SMEs have historically utilised IT for productivity, data management and accounting/ financial applications. In addition, many SMEs have also embraced specialised applications, ranging from customised accounting and business solutions to CAD and materials requirements planning (MRP). In addition to providing tangible benefits to the organisation, the systems were often cost justified.

9.2.2   Office Productivity

Addressing office productivity was often a primary justification for the initial adoption of IT in the SME. Correspondence with outside organisations involved in the supply chain was greatly facilitated by the adoption of word processing software. Early word-processing software utilised a skill set present in the administrative portion of SMEs, typing. Although characteristics of word processors such as word wrapping were new to many, making the transition from the typewriter to the word processor, the basic concept underlying this software class was readily embraced by the SME. In addition to word-processing software, many SMEs also adopted electronic spreadsheets. Long employed in a manual environment by the SME for scheduling purposes, forecasting and subsidiary journals, electronic spreadsheets provided the organisation with enhanced productivity opportunities, and in many cases contributed to strategic advantages for the SME. As with word-processing software, the electronic spreadsheet enabled those in the SME to automate and extend mental models that existed within the framework of the organisation.

The management of data offered by IT, in the form of first flat-file database management products and then relational database management systems (DBMSs), provided SMEs with an opportunity to extend their operations and enable employees to extend their productivity beyond the framework that existed within the typical SME. Maintaining lists of customers, contacts, vendors and employees provided the SME with the opportunity to combine some of their word-processing functions with mail-merge technology, offering the SME a competitive advantage that previously had accrued to organisations with either large IT investments or large numbers of employees.

As the existence of DBMSs became wider spread and more 'user friendly', SMEs were able to utilise the DBMSs to develop lightweight end-user applications to help address their specific needs. These applications provided the SME with an opportunity to address needs specific to their markets and business rules.

Other specialised applications for SMEs, such as CAD and manufacturing control systems (MCSs), again provided the smaller organisation with capabilities previously available only to those organisations with larger IT budgets and staff. The advent of a number of CAD products for microcomputers and workstations provided the SME with the opportunity to develop sophisticated, flexible designs. MCSs allowed the smaller organisation the opportunity to increase the quality of their manufactured outputs, and to reduce their overall number of defects, again providing them with competitive advantages previously only available to larger organisations.

In addition to productivity enhanced by word processing, spreadsheets, DBMSs and more specialised applications such as CAD and MCSs, a wide range of accounting and business software was also available and often used by SMEs. The use of accounting-oriented applications provided the SME with a broad range of reporting and record-keeping abilities.

9.2.3   Shrink-wrapped versus Hybrid Business Software

The marketplace for business software and the SME began with the porting of robust applications from larger platforms to minicomputers, then microcomputers. In addition, the availability of UNIX and Xenix operating systems, and corresponding microcomputer hardware and software environments, allowed even the smallest of organisations to employ multiple-user business solutions. As local area networks became more robust and software publishers developed more comprehensive applications, the SME was able to obtain the business and financial reporting capabilities that were previously the domain of larger, well-funded organisations.

In 1990, over 200 integrated general-purpose business information systems were available for SMEs (Anonymous 1990). In addition, products for specialised industries such as construction, manufacturing (MRPs), legal, medical, point-of-sale, distribution, and a number of specialised or 'vertical' markets were available as shrink-wrapped software solutions. These products were often customisable, either internally through the specific software controls or with user-friendly structured query language-based report writers. In addition, some products readily provided external interfaces to allow customised applications to integrate with the shrink-wrapped software.

A set of proprietary products was also available to the SME. Such products were focused towards vertical markets, and often had been previously developed for a competitor. This set of products, with the assistance of the original developer, provided the SME with an opportunity to have a set of truly customised software applications. In addition, the advent of DBMSs also provided the SME with an opportunity to have a third party develop products that addressed the specific needs of their organisation, without the exorbitant development costs that can accrue to such projects in larger organisations. The existence of these accounting and business information systems helped set the stage for the emerging applications that are now critical for the success of the SME.

9.2.4   Emerging Applications

Many SMEs are subject to pressures due to their existence on a particular supply chain. SMEs that are primary suppliers to larger organisations, and those who are dependent upon large organisations for a significant proportion of their resale goods, have been subjected to electronic data interchange (EDI) and corresponding inter-organisational systems. For many SMEs, the decision to employ an EDI environment and an integrated system was an easy call – it was demanded by the larger organisation.

Many EDI systems are now moving to the World Wide Web (Web). Transactions on the Web, part of electronic commerce (e-commerce), can be from business–business

(B2B); business–consumer (B2C); or consumer–consumer (C2C). The SME should focus on the first two of these types. In addition, the Web also provides the SME, should their business plan call for it, the opportunity to extend their market far beyond their geographic domains. Such Web-based marketing provides an SME with essentially enhanced mail-order capabilities, enabling them to reach a wider marketplace than even partnerships with mega-corporations such as Wal-Mart. E-commerce has existed in the form of EDI for many years. Proprietary systems led to standards within the driving corporations or industry. These systems are now transforming into products with browser-based interfaces.

The ease of use and connectivity of the Web provides other advantages to the SME involved in a business partnership. Inter-organisational systems within these partnerships can provide a wide range of benefits. Access to supply chain partners' information systems allows better planning for the SME's production schedule. It also helps enable just-in-time (JIT) processes. In addition, should the larger trading partner provide expert systems or artificial intelligence products to its partners, the SME can derive additional competitive advantages from their association.

For the SME, security in their EDI system has not, previously, been a great issue. The majority of EDI environments passed through virtual private networks (VPNs), or other highly secure processing centres. However, due to the inherent open nature of the Internet, as SMEs move their EDI and other marketing strategies to the Web the reliability and security of their transactions may be compromised. This is less an issue with the B2B form of transaction, as trading partners on the supply chain will often have a privacy policy in place. The issue becomes more critical as the SME opens its market to the consumer and begins B2C transactions. For example, with Web-based marketing the SME can provide direct service to the potential customer, whether a business or an individual consumer. With direct services, the SME must perform a secure and private transaction with the consumer. Such B2C transactions open the SME to potential risks of firewall penetration and information assurance risks. When adopting a B2C transaction strategy, the SME must have a strategy to detect and prevent any intrusion. However, in the case of an SME that has an independent distribution network, Web-based marketing could drive the prospective purchaser to a 'local' retailer that stocks their products, thus benefiting the SMEs' supply chain partner. Consumers in this environment may be relying on a static set of Web pages, receiving responses only through electronic mail (e-mail) correspondence. This environment is less sensitive to security issues, particularly when housed on a server provided by a service provider.

The growth of the Web has also fostered a nearly ubiquitous electronic mail (e-mail) environment. An email address has become a requirement for the SME much as a fax number and telephone had become necessary previously. E-mail can act as a compliment to all other forms of Web-based commerce, or it can be the sole function performed through the Web. At a minimal level, organisations can take advantage of the asynchronous nature of e-mail. Sending an e-mail message with instructions and a printable order attached can facilitate the procurement phase of supply chain management. The asynchronous nature of e-mail communication can, by itself, provide the SME with a form of a virtual business environment.

It should be noted that little of this is new. The Internet, EDI and e-mail have existed for years. Another 'old' strategy is also beginning to re-emerge. As the use and acceptance of enterprise resource planning (ERP) systems becomes more widespread, ERP vendors must seek strategies to expand their market presence. A new business strategy, application service providers (ASPs), is emerging. Some ASPs provide access to database instances driven by robust ERPs, such as those offered by SAP. This service, much like Ross Perot's timesharing strategy for EDS, helps drive the cost of service down to levels more affordable for the SME. In addition, SME-focused ERP providers such as Great Plains provide Web-based B2C services that are integrated into their business information systems.

9.2.5   Summary

SMEs have traditionally used information technology to automate many of their repetitive processes. Many have evolved from automating somewhat simple tasks such as basic word processing, to operating full-scale marketing programs integrated with their entire business operations and financial information. The rapid expansion of the World Wide Web is creating an environment that SMEs should be ready to utilise. The ability of SMEs to adapt to the changing nature of technology and to utilise it to improve their overall supply chain environment may determine their longevity.

9.3   WHY SMES ADOPT INFORMATION TECHNOLOGY

In order to comprehend the requirements for IT use by SMEs, it is important to understand factors that are thought to influence small-business managers' decisions to adopt or reject IT-related innovations. Diffusion of innovation theory can help us gain this understanding. In this section, we provide an overview of the portion of diffusion theory related to adoption decisions. We begin with a brief overview of diffusion theory. Then, we discuss a number of factors that have been demonstrated to influence adoption. This is followed by a discussion of the influence of prior adoptions and communications networks on the adoption decision.

9.3.1   Diffusion of Innovation Theory

The term innovation refers to an idea, practice or object that is seen as being new by a potential adopter (Rogers 1995; Tornatzky and Fleischer 1990). There are two characteristics of an innovation that are important to consider. First, central to the concept of an innovation is that the innovation is new *to the adopter*, which means that although a technology may have been in existence for many years, if a potential adopter perceives the technology to be new, to that adopter the technology is an innovation. The Internet illustrates this point. Though the technology of the Internet has been in existence for several decades, to many potential adopters the Internet is new, and thus is an innovation. Similar arguments could be made for many information technologies, including personal computers, decision support systems and collaboration technologies. Although these information technologies have existed for many years, to a large number of small businesses, they are innovations. As a result, diffusion of innovation theory may prove useful in determining how to induce IT adoption in SMEs.

The process by which the use of an innovation spreads through a social system is known as diffusion (Mahajan and Peterson 1985). Diffusion of innovation is a widely studied research area and has been applied in literally thousands of studies involving hundreds of innovations (Rogers 1995). Information technology innovations have been widely studied using diffusion theory as a basis (Prescott and Conger 1995). Prescott and Conger (1995) provide a comprehensive model of the factors influencing diffusion, as shown in Figure 9.1. The components of the model are briefly discussed below as they apply to SME IT adoption.

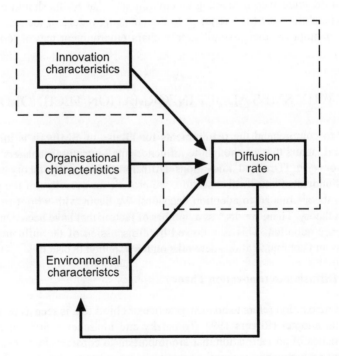

Figure 9.1   Prescott and Conger Information Technology Diffusion Model

An interesting question concerning SME adoption is that of the level of analysis. The factors related to adoption differ according to whether the adoption is at an individual or organisational level. For example, perceptions of the characteristics of an innovation have been demonstrated to influence individual adoption, while factors such as top management support and competitive pressures are related to organisational adoption. Normally, it is questionable to apply individual-level factors to organisational-level adoption decisions. However, many SMEs are so dominated by the enterprise's top manager (often the owner) that the level of the adoption decision becomes cloudy. Since, to our knowledge, there is no definitive evidence as to which set of factors best apply to SMEs, we include both individual and organisational level factors in our discussion. Others have included both in empirical studies (for example, Premkumar and Roberts 1999).

Organisation characteristics

A wide variety of organisational characteristics are thought to impact the adoption on new technologies. Kwon and Zmud (1987) include formalisation, the informal communications network, and the degree of specialisation and centralisation as factors which may impact IT implementation. Other organisational characteristics have been studied. These include organisation size (Fuller and Swanson 1992; Grover and Gosslar 1993; and Premkumar et al. 1997), degree of formalisation (Grover and Gosslar 1993), and management support (Hoffer and Alexander 1992; Grover 1993; Grover and Gosslar 1993; and Premkumar et al. 1997).

Organisational factors have been included in studies of SME information technology adoption. For example, top management support is related to the adoption of Internet-related technologies (Premkumar and Roberts 1999). The size of the SME is also thought to be related to IT adoption (Premkumar and Roberts 1999; and Thong and Yap 1995). Although size is related to SME adoption of IT, this may actually be reflective of the availability of slack resources, including financial and human resources. It is important to understand that a major barrier to the adoption of IT by small businesses is resource poverty. It makes sense that larger SMEs may have more resources to dedicate to IT projects. It is not surprising that organisational size not only impacts whether an SME uses IT, but can also influence the extent of IT adoption – the higher the level of IT expertise, the more extensive the IT utilisation.

The organisation's skill in the use of information technology is also an important factor influencing adoption decisions. Clearly, a lack of expertise in IT can hinder an SME's adoption of the technologies. However, equally important is the impact of IT expertise on the awareness of the capabilities of IT. Without knowledge of the capabilities of IT, SMEs are far less likely to recognise opportunities to apply IT to the organisation. Even when aware of the potential of IT application, SMEs with low IT expertise may feel that they are unlikely to be successful in applying the technologies. It is possible to obtain outside expertise – in fact many SMEs rely on IT vendors and consultants to supply the requisite knowledge. However, the financial resource poverty faced by many SMEs may preclude this approach. Interestingly, the

IT knowledge of the chief executive officer (CEO) may also have an impact on adoption decisions (Thong and Yap 1995) for many of the reasons just stated. In addition, the CEO's attitude towards IT may depend, in part, on his or her IT knowledge. The more positive the CEO's attitude, the more favourably he or she will view IT adoption (Thong and Yap 1995).

The CEO's attitude towards IT is doubly important because top management support is a critical factor in the success of IT projects (Igbaria et al. 1997). This is true of IT projects in small and large organisations. Regardless of the size of the organisation, or the nature of the project, the support of top management smoothes many project hurdles. Top management has the ability to marshal resources in order to help projects succeed. In smaller SMEs, the only top manager in the organisation may be the owner. Combining this reality with the importance of top management support to IT success makes clear how more IT-aware CEOs may be more likely to adopt and implement information technologies in their organisations.

The level of IT support and training may also impact the adoption and acceptance of IT by SMEs. Note that these factors refer to the level of support and training internal to the organisation, external support is discussed in a later section. The availability of internal IT support has a positive impact on the IT success. In addition, internal IT support impacts perceptions of the characteristics of IT. As discussed in a later section, these perceptions impact adoption decisions. So, internal IT support impacts adoption indirectly through perceptions of the characteristics of IT. Utilising IT can be a challenging, intimidating proposition for employees within an SME. Having internal IT support can help ease fears associated with learning to use and using IT. Simply having someone to turn to when facing difficulties will have a positive impact on perceptions of IT, making the use of IT less intimidating.

There may be another, more subtle, force at work however. As discussed earlier, most SMEs face a degree of resource poverty. Dedicating resources to IT sends a very strong signal to the members of the organisation that IT is important – so important that management is devoting valuable resources to support IT efforts. Similar statements can be made about the availability of internal IT training. Training in IT impacts a number of outcomes in the context of SMEs, including increased understanding of IT, and more frequent and more diverse use of IT applications (Raymond 1988). In the context of SMEs, internal support and training have been demonstrated to have positive impacts on perceived usefulness, which in turn impacts IT acceptance and use (Igbaria et al. 1997). Table 9.1 shows a number of organisational factors that have been included in empirical studies of SME IT adoption.

Environmental factors

The impact of a number of environmental characteristics on adoption and diffusion has been studied, although empirical support has been lacking (Kwon and Zmud 1987). According to Kwon and Zmud (1987) there are two perspectives regarding diffusion and the environment. The environment can be viewed as a source of information or as a stock of resources.

Table 9.1
Organisational Factors

Factor	References
Top management support	Premkumar and Roberts (1999); Igbaria et al. (1997); DeLone (1988)
Size	Premkumar and Roberts (1999); Igbaria et al. (1997)
IT expertise (overall)	Premkumar and Roberts (1999); Thong (1999); DeLone (1988)
IT expertise (CEO)	Thong (1999); Thong and Yap (1995)
Availability of slack resources	Iacovou et al. (1995)
Internal IT support	Igbaria et al. (1997); Raymond (1990)
Internal IT training	Igbaria et al. (1997); Raymond (1990)

Several environmental factors have been studied in the context of SME adoption of IT. Support for IT from external entities (vendors, suppliers, customers, governmental agencies or industry groups) has a positive impact on IT adoption (Premkumar and Roberts 1999). As noted earlier, SMEs often lack the resources required to adopt and implement advanced technologies. Being able to draw from outside sources for support is, in some cases, a critical aspect of the adoption decision. If such assistance is not available, many SMEs may simply not be able to adopt certain technologies.

External pressure is also related to IT adoption by SMEs. For example, many SMEs were pressured to adopt electronic data interchange when large customers basically demanded that all suppliers become EDI-compliant. In the early 1990s, small engineering and design firms in some locations were required to adopt CAD as a condition of being awarded government projects. It is not necessary for customers or governmental agencies to force adoption in order to influence adoption. In some cases, the pressure is much more subtle. It is not uncommon for larger organisations to offer incentives to their smaller partners in order to influence adoption decisions. For example, financial or technical assistance may be provided to SMEs that decide to adopt certain technologies.

Competition may also impact SMEs' IT adoption decisions. On the surface, it may seem that the amount of competitive pressure would be positively related to the adoption of IT. Information technologies may be appropriate responses to competition for at least two reasons. First, the clever application of IT can lead to competitive advantage. Second, IT has the potential to increase operational efficiency, making additional financial resources available for other measures to respond to competition. However, competitive pressure may, in some circumstances, lead to less adoption of

IT. This possibility stems from the general lack of slack resources experienced by many SMEs. If limited funds are available, and competitive pressure is increasing, the SME may feel that any available funds should be directed towards responding to the competition, which may not involve IT adoption. Interestingly, lack of free time also may be a reason for an inverse relationship between competition and IT adoption. When facing increasing competition, SME managers may feel that they need to spend their available time on responding to the competition, not on investigating IT adoption.

The strength of vertical linkages may also impact SME adoption of new technologies. When an SME has strong ties with larger organisations, such as those present in a franchise relationship, the larger partner possesses the resources to investigate new technologies. In addition, the larger organisation has the expertise and financial resources to refine the new technology for use in a particular setting. Finally, the larger partner may mandate the use of a particular IT by the SME (Premkumar and Roberts 1999). For example, an automated accounting system that automatically transmits daily accounting data to the franchiser may be required. Table 9.2 summarises the environmental factors related to SME IT use and provides references for supporting research.

Table 9.2
Environmental Factors

Factor	Reference
External support	Premkumar and Roberts (1999); Raymond (1990)
External pressure	Premkumar and Roberts (1999); Iacovou et al. (1995); Raymond (1990)
Competition/competitive pressure	Premkumar and Roberts (1999); Thong and Yap (1995)
Vertical linkages	Premkumar and Roberts (1999)

Innovation characteristics
An oft-studied area related to innovations is the impact of adopter perceptions of the characteristics of an innovation on its adoption and its diffusion rate. This impact is thought to be considerable (Rogers 1995; Lancaster and Taylor 1986; and Gatignon and Robertson 1985). Note that it is the potential adopters' *perceptions* of these characteristics rather than an expert's objective assessment of how an innovation rates on these characteristics that impacts the diffusion rate (Rogers 1995; and Lancaster and Taylor 1986).

Rogers (1995) lists five perceived characteristics of an innovation that can help to explain its adoption: relative advantage, compatibility, complexity, trialability and observability. Others have proposed additional characteristics that may influence adoption. Davis (1986) proposed a Technology Acceptance Model that includes the constructs of perceived usefulness and perceived ease of use. These are conceptually similar to Rogers's (1995) relative advantage and complexity (Moore and Benbasat 1991). Moore and Benbasat (1991) developed an instrument to measure seven constructs. These include Rogers's (1995) relative advantage, compatibility and trialability in addition to Davis's (1986) ease of use; they added the constructs image, result demonstratability and visibility. Table 9.3 provides definitions of a number of innovation characteristics that have been demonstrated to influence IT adoption. The table also provides appropriate references.

Three of the innovation characteristics listed above have been empirically demonstrated to influence adoption of IT by SMEs. Relative advantage, or any similar construct of usefulness or perceived benefit, impacts on SME IT adoption decisions. Simply put, the greater the advantage to be gained from adopting a technology, the more likely an SME is to adopt. A similar statement could be made regarding compatibility – the more compatible an SME perceives an innovation to be, the more likely it is to adopt that technology. Perceived complexity has an inverse relationship with adoption. As the perceived complexity of a technology increases, the likelihood of adoption decreases. The validity of all of these relationships has been demonstrated empirically in the studies listed in Table 9.4.

9.3.2 Technology Cluster Innovations

Most studies of the adoption of new technologies involve single technologies, rather than groups of related technologies. However, there is evidence that the adoption of one technology often influences the adoption of other, related technologies (LaRose and Hoag 1996). A technology cluster is 'one or more distinguishable elements of technology that are perceived as being closely interrelated' (Rogers 1995, p.15). Many information technologies are in fact clusters of related technologies. For example, a personal computer system actually comprises a number of related technologies such as the central processing unit, a monitor, a keyboard and so on. In fact, in the very early days of microcomputers it was quite common to purchase most of the system components separately. However, today a consumer purchasing a new computer is likely to purchase a bundled system. Organisations that offer such systems are intuitively taking advantage of the concept of the technology cluster. By understanding technology clusters, change agents wishing to influence the SME adoption of IT may be able to develop product or service bundles that take advantage of clustering.

There are a number of forms of technology clusters. These forms differ according to the nature of the relationships among the innovations that make up the cluster. A number of the possible forms are described below.

1.   *Complementary*: Technologies in a cluster may be complementary to one another (Chin and Moore 1991). In this case, one of the innovations cannot be used to

the fullest without adopting the other. For example, Silverman and Bailey (1961) found that adopting thicker planting density required adopting hybrid seed and fertilisation in order to improve yields.

2. *Similar function*: Technologies in a cluster can also be related in that they provide

Table 9.3
Innovation Characteristics

Innovation characteristic	Description	References
Relative	Degree to which an innovation is seen as being superior to its predecessor	Hebert and Benbasat (1994); Premkumar et al. (1994); Teo et al. (1995)
Complexity	Degree to which an innovation is seen by the potential adopter as being relatively difficult to use and understand	Teo et al. (1995); Cooper and Zmud (1990); Grover (1993)
Compatibility	Degree to which an innovation is seen to be compatible with existing values, beliefs, experiences and needs of adopters	Grover (1993); Eastlick (1993); Nedovic-Budic and Godschalk (1996); Taylor and Todd (1995)
Trialability	Based on adopters' perceptions of the degree to which an innovation can be used on a trial basis before confirmation of the adoption must occur	Rogers (1995); Lancaster and Taylor (1986); Teo et al. (1995)
Result demonstrability	Degree to which the results of using an innovation are perceived to be tangible	Hebert and Benbasat (1994); Moore and Benbasat (1991)
Visibility	The perception of the actual visibility of the innovation itself as opposed to the visibility of outputs	Moore and Benbasat (1991); Agarwal and Prasad (1997)
Image	Degree to which the use of the innovation is seen as enhancing to an individual's image or social status	Moore and Benbasat (1991)

similar, but different, functions (Chin and Moore 1991). Both air-bags and anti-lock brakes are similar in that they provide additional vehicle safety, but clearly provide different functions. It can be posited that an individual who adopts one because of an interest in safety will be more likely to adopt the other (Prescott and Van Slyke 1997).

3. *Common platform*: A common platform may also provide the link between innovations in a cluster. Automobile electric door locks and power windows are a good example of this relationship. Both share the common platform of electrical wiring in the doors, which makes adopting the door locks less expensive if the power windows are also adopted and vice versa (Chin and Moore 1991).

4. *Contingent*: A final possible relationship is found when one innovation's adoption is contingent on the adoption of another technology (Peterson and Mahajan 1978). For example, the adoption of a personal computer monitor is contingent on adopting a personal computer. Without adopting the personal computer adopting a monitor makes little sense.

So far, in this section we have attempted to provide a comprehensive view of SME IT adoption. In the remainder of the section we present a model of SME IT adoption that attempts to integrate the diverse research in this area.

Table 9.4
Innovation Characteristics in the Context of SMEs

Factor	Reference
Relative advantage (usefulness; benefit)	Premkumar and Roberts (1999); Igbaria (1997)
Compatibility	Premkumar and Roberts (1999)
Complexity (ease of use)	Premkumar and Roberts (1999); Igbaria (1997)

9.3.3 An Integrated Model of SME IT Adoption

As we have seen, there is a diverse set of factors that influence SMEs adoption of information technology. Classifying and integrating these factors results in the model shown in Figure 9.2. Our model is similar to that proposed by Prescott and Conger (1995). Similar models have been employed by Thong (1999), Premkumar and Roberts (1999) and others. Our contribution consists, in part, in the addition of the concept of technology clusters to the theory behind the model, and in the addition of indirect impacts on adoption. As can be seen from Figure 9.2, there are direct impacts on technology adoption from each of the categories of factors (environmental, organisational, perceived innovation characteristics, and the prior adoption of a related technology). In addition, however, there are also impacts between sets of factors. Previously in this section, we have discussed the direct impacts on adoption related to each category of factors. Now we turn attention to understanding the indirect impacts.

Two sets of factors, organisational characteristics and the adoption of a related technology, may impact SMEs' perceptions of the characteristic of an information technology, which in turn impacts adoption. Certain characteristics of the organisation may have an impact on the SMEs' perceptions of the innovation in question. For example, changes in the level of IT expertise may cause changes in perceptions of the complexity of a technology. The availability of internal training and support may also impact perceptions. The adoption of a related technology may lead to changes in the perceptions of an information technology. Consider the example of the adoption of inventory control software. If previously the SME adopted a related technology, such as accounting software, they may view the adoption of inventory control software differently. Relative advantage may be higher. Assuming that the previously adopted accounting software and the inventory control software are compatible, adopting the inventory control software not only brings the advantages of the inventory control software but may also allow automatic updating of data in the accounting software. Obviously, without the prior adoption of the accounting software, this advantage would not be present. Compatibility would also be impacted. The SME would be used to using an automated system for control purposes. As a result, the idea of using

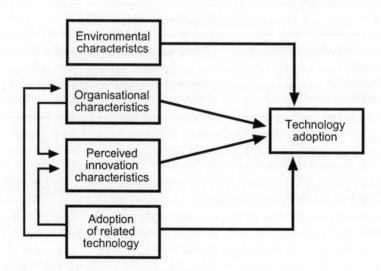

Figure 9.2   Integrated Model of SME Information Technology Adoption

an automated system for inventory control would be more compatible than if the accounting system were not adopted. Similar arguments could be made for the prior adoption lowering perceived complexity.

The adoption of other technologies in a cluster may also impact organisational characteristics. The primary characteristic impacted is that of IT knowledge. Depending on the relationship between the IT being investigated and previously adopted technologies in the cluster, any prior adoptions may have increased the IT knowledge of the SME. Using the accounting system example cited previously, the prior adoption of the accounting system would increase the IT knowledge available when considering the adoption of the inventory control system. Prior adoption may also impact the level of internal IT support available. The prior adoption may have required a degree of internal IT support, which is now present when considering the adoption of a new IT.

In the next section, we describe several categories of barriers to SME IT usage.

9.4   BARRIERS TO SME IT USE

Relative to their larger corporate counterparts, SMEs must address business issues with a relatively limited set of resources, which Welsh and White (1981) have referred to (in general) as 'resource poverty'. Similarly, many of the IT-related problems that SMEs face stem from a lack of resources. In this section, we discuss how resource poverty, in various areas, can translate into barriers to the SMEs' successful introduction of IT.

9.4.1   Lack of IT Knowledge Resources

From a technology perspective, one of the most critical problems facing SMEs is a lack of awareness of IT and how it can be employed. Though most people recognise the need to monitor technological advances, few employees can spare time from their regular responsibilities to actively ponder new technologies and how they might be utilised. Since SMEs often hire generalists, not specialists, few SME employees subscribe to technical journals. As such, SMEs are often blinded to technological advances deployed against them by their larger brethren. This can be particularly problematic for East Asian SMEs competing with firms who have operations in other nations where technological advances often take place. These multinational corporations can identify new technologies and introduce them into their organisations in the country where the advance occurred before introducing them into their operations in East Asia. This problem is exacerbated by the general lack of CEO and staff knowledge of IT in many developing countries (Foong 1999).

In addition, many SME managers have difficulty identifying business information that would improve their operations (Farkas-Conn 1999). They are often unaware of how specific technologies (for example, electronic mail) or use of technologies (for example, electronic commerce) can impact their organisations. For example, a study of British SMEs indicated that they tend to use technology to support operations rather than for decision making or strategic planning (Bridge and Peel 1999). Most used application software rather extensively but few used IT for strategic planning purposes, suggesting an inability to fully leverage their technology. Whether the result of a lack of formal education, or perhaps due to the time poverty discussed above, a general lack of planning is common in SMEs, often resulting in a short-term focus and a reactive (rather that proactive) approach to changing business conditions.

SME managers often suffer from a lack of management expertise (Lin et al. 1993), particularly in developing countries (Foong 1999). IT projects are often very complex, lengthy undertakings. Many SME managers do not have the project management skills required for projects of this magnitude. Moreover, the importance of top management support for successful IT introduction is well recognised. One can see the inherent difficulty in having managers unfamiliar with IT perform successfully in the role of technology champion and advocate.

9.4.2   Lack of Slack Financial Resources

Deploying IT can be expensive. Unlike many of their larger corporate brethren, SMEs conduct business operations with relatively limited financial resources (Thong 1999). They may also have restricted access to external sources of funds or have difficulty securing financing at reasonable interest rates. Therefore, SMEs often find it difficult to make the large capital outlays necessary to introduce IT into their organisations. It may also be difficult to get approval if a manager hoping to deploy IT cannot identify specific expected savings or revenues. In part due to SMEs' general lack of funds, SMEs often require a relatively speedy return on investment. Lack of funds also contributes to an SME's difficulty in building its technical infrastructure.

However, the situation may be changing. Farkas-Conn (1999) notes that the World Wide Web is offering SMEs new opportunities for forging strategic partnerships with large international banks, a development she feels will support global economic integration. This type of partnering may prove especially fruitful in East Asian countries whose financial services sectors are still developing.

9.4.3   Lack of Slack Human Resources

Many SMEs employ few if any IT specialists. This is often the result of their just not being competitive salary-wise. Similarly, managers tend to be generalists, not IT managers. SMEs often can spare neither funds nor their employees' time for IT-related training. This contributes to the lack of awareness of IT and IT trends discussed above. Additionally, employees find it difficult to dedicate time to long-term IT development efforts, though it is well known that user involvement in IT development efforts is critical to their success. Similarly, SME managers, particularly in smaller firms, often suffer from time poverty (Cragg and Zinatelli 1995), a condition typically brought about by managers having to perform many different types of activities (for example, sales, technician, supervisor) in a single workday. This can make it extremely difficult for employees to learn even basic computing skills, such as word processing.

9.4.4 Poor Access to IT Expertise

As mentioned above, SMEs often have few highly technical employees. IT specialists can be very expensive to employ; consequently, SMEs tend to have limited technical expertise in-house. Furthermore, highly qualified IT consultants are often prohibitively expensive. This lack of IT expertise can be particularly acute in rural areas. The problem is only exacerbated by the 'brain drain' from some countries, often to Silicon Valley in the United States. This can hinder the firm in a number of ways. Lack of IT expertise can make it difficult for SMEs to identify their information needs. This tends to inhibit their ability to identify which technologies to employ and how to best employ them. Moreover, successful requirements analysis and system design require specialised technical skills. Lack of IT expertise also can inhibit SME managers' ability to compare packaged software they might be considering.

9.4.5 Telecommunications

SMEs face technical, legal, and operational headaches with regard to telecommunications. National telecommunications infrastructures can vary from nation to nation, as well as regionally within individual countries. Though large corporations may build and maintain their own telecommunications networks, SMEs can rarely afford such luxuries. Consequently, they find themselves more dependent on external sources for their network access, increasing the difficulty of integrating telecommunications into their operations. SMEs operating in rural areas are especially dependent upon external telecommunications providers, whether private or public.

Though not unique to SMEs, those firms that conduct multinational operations face a daunting set of issues. Meeting varying legal requirements between countries regarding privacy, transborder data flows, and software licensing can introduce complexity to international systems, as can designing systems to properly handle exchange rates.

9.4.6 Section Summary

In this section, we have reviewed how various categories of resource poverty can become barriers to the successful introduction of IT into the SME. In the next section, we introduce some methods of overcoming these barriers.

9.5   OVERCOMING THE BARRIERS TO SME IT USE

The barriers to IT use by SMEs, lack of both slack financial and human resources, as well as a lack of knowledge among both employees and management, can be assisted by external sources. Consultants, not-for-profit organisations, business partners and governmental entities can provide both assistance and solutions to assist the SME in overcoming these barriers. This section discusses the four barriers and potential solutions based upon the external source.

9.5.1   Consultants and Vendors

Consultants and vendors have been valuable allies to SMEs in assisting with their implementation and use of IT. Consultants and vendors are often the only source of help available to the SME, and come at a cost. Consultants and vendors can be very costly as a substitute for internal IT expertise and support. Ideally, an SME should wean itself off the relationship with consultants or vendors, using them periodically as allies in helping to update the SME's IT resources.

IT is a fast-changing field. To the casual observer, it can seem very complex, almost mind-boggling. Vendors provide expertise in the form of quality shrink-wrapped software and hardware environments. Many vendors provide expertise as well, in the form of training and technical support. Vendors can provide high-quality support and services. However, the SME should have a plan to assess both short- and long-term use of a vendor's services.

Consultants can provide advice and management services for those IT areas the SME decides to outsource. Ideally, consultants have either few ties to specific products, or provide higher-quality training and technical support than the vendor. As with the vendor, the consultant often provides implementation services to the SME. Consultants can provide both expertise and independence to the SME. They can provide temporary relief in the form of high-level management services. In addition, large consulting organisations can provide assistance for a variety of specialised IT positions.

9.5.2   Not-for-profit Organisations

Not-for-profit (NFP) organisations can provide a variety of resources, depending on the nature of the organisation. Three different types of NFPs, and their potential contribution to the SME overcoming IT barriers, will be briefly discussed: foundations, trade, and quasi-public organisations.

Foundations can provide capital and expert volunteers to assist certain types of SMEs based upon the mission of the particular foundation. Trade organisations provide the SME with access to knowledge specific to their industry and IT. The organisations can also recommend consultants and vendors who have performed well for other members of the respective association, or that provide validated industry-specific solutions.

The third type, quasi-public organisations, can provide the SME with access to resources similar to those provided by trade associations and foundations. Often formed with governmental funding in addition to that provided by concerned citizens, quasi-public organisations can provide capital similar to foundations. However, quasi-public organisations can also function in a similar manner as trade associations, providing the SME with an opportunity to pool resources with others to develop necessary solutions, or to provide a means for a group of SMEs to share a common good – a pooled resource. An example of a successful quasi-public NFP, ACEnet, will be presented later in this section.

9.5.3   Trading Partners

The benefit of a long-term trading relationship with large organisations, such as mass retailers, provides great incentives for the SME to overcome barriers to using IT. Large partners often issue an ultimatum, 'either automate to our standards or lose our business'. The opportunity cost often compels the SME to obtain or provide the necessary funding to overcome the barriers to IT use. In addition, the trading partner often provides proprietary or customised applications that can furnish the SME with low-cost yet effective IT solutions. The SME can obtain competitive advantages by efficiently utilising the inter-organisational resources provided by a large trading partner.

9.5.4   Government and Education

Efforts to assist SMEs and the overcoming of barriers to IT utilisation are a matter of funding by government and education. This section will briefly discuss efforts within the United States to assist SMEs, focusing on the Small Business Administration (SBA) of the Federal government.

The SBA provides an array of assistance to the SME, notably financing and local outreach. Organised with a number of district offices, the SBA can provide financing in the form of loan guarantees. Local outreach is provided by a number (58) of small business development centres (SBDCs) with a minimum of one in each state, with four in Texas, and one each in Washington DC and four territories of the US. SBDCs are commonly, although not exclusively, associated with a state-funded higher educational institution. The mission statement of the SBDC includes the following:

The program is a cooperative effort of the private sector, the educational community and Federal, state and local governments. It enhances economic development by providing small businesses with management and technical assistance. (http://www.sba.gov/SBDC/mission.html)

The district offices, essentially subcontractors of the SBA, extend training and support services to the local small business community. In the SBDC, the SME has a readily available resource to assist it in overcoming barriers to the use of technology in the SBDC. In addition to training and consulting, SBDCs also offer outreach to disadvantaged SMEs, and those in specialised industries (for example, automakers).

9.5.5 Networking Strategy

The majority of the general strategies employed to assist the SME in overcoming IT barriers are based on traditional, hierarchical models. Foundations and governmental institutions have existed for years, and although they often provide excellent assistance in linking public and private resources, they typically have a top-down, not lateral, structure. Corporate trading partners tend to increase the switching costs for the SME by limiting their exposure to alternatives. A similar argument can be made for the assistance provided by both consultants and vendors.

One strategy employed to form a lateral linking of SMEs has been initiated by ACEnet, the Appalachian Center for Economic Networks, an organisation formed by private citizens with federal funding in the region that was the United States' colonial frontier. ACEnet focuses on providing a networking infrastructure for the local SMEs to interact with others in their geographic region. ACEnet proposes socio-economic strategies similar to the Mondragon Cooperative Corporation in Mondragon, Spain, holding that in addition to the economic justification of the SME there is also a social dimension that draws those in economically and socially distinct regions together.

ACEnet provides a service to the primarily rural, historically inaccessible, population of the Southeast Ohio region of the United States (Van Slyke et al. 2001). ACEnet has evolved from an organisation intent on bringing the SME up by its bootstraps, to one that has developed a cooperative network of SMEs in the region. ACEnet's outreach efforts include the development of public access to the Internet and the development of a technical centre for the local community. A combination of these two efforts provides ACEnet's member firms with an infrastructure for e-commerce. With structures such as ACEnet in place, the SME can begin to wean itself from the IT influence fostered by trading partners, vendors, and consultants. Structures like those provided by ACEnet can assist SMEs in the development of virtual organisations to provide members with competitive advantages and alternatives in their supply-chain management.

9.5.6 Summary

SMEs face a distinct set of barriers to the use of IT that must be overcome to effectively and efficiently utilise information and related technologies. Capital, both financial and human, as well as management and overall knowledge of IT can raise barriers to the use of IT. This section presented a discussion of four ways to assist the SME in overcoming barriers to IT. The SME can employ vendors and consultants to assist with knowledge of ongoing and complex IT issues. Foundations and government agencies can help provide the SME with necessary capital to develop their own knowledge resource and IT strategy. Not-for-profit organisations and government agencies can also help the SME.

Eventually, barriers to IT are overcome by the individual SME developing the organisational knowledge necessary to manage their specific IT environment. The more critical IT becomes to the operations of the SME, the more the organisation must commit to investment in this resource. Outside organisations can prove helpful to the SME in developing strategies to overcome knowledge barriers at all levels of the organisation. Until adequate human resources are dedicated to IT in SMEs by management, outsiders can assist when needed. Ultimately, the SME needs a framework to assess the impact of the barriers of IT within their own organisation, as well as a strategy to address removing the barriers. As with other strategic components of successful organisations, owners and managers of SMEs must be committed to the effective and efficient use of IT throughout their enterprise.

9.6   RECOMMENDATIONS FOR FACILITATING SME IT USE

A number of stakeholders may be interested in encouraging and facilitating information technology use by SMEs, including SME advisers, vendors, governmental organisations, and not-for-profit organisations. In this section, we discuss a number of recommendations for facilitating SME IT use. These recommendations are broken down according to stakeholder. Although we discuss recommendations for each stakeholder apart from the others, isolated programs are not sufficient, however. There is a need for constant interaction among SMEs, IT suppliers and policy makers (La Rovere 1996).

9.6.1   Advisers

As discussed earlier, SME managers often suffer from a lack of time and a lack of managerial expertise. These two factors may converge to lead SME managers to take an *ad hoc* approach to IT planning and acquisition, which often leads to incorrect decisions when evaluating IT. This *ad hoc* approach to IT development and acquisition is a particular problem in developing countires (Foong 1999). Advisers to SMEs should help SME managers take a careful, systematic approach to IT evaluation. Geisler (1992) recommends seven criteria for evaluating the acquisition, updating or replacing of IT. Below we list and briefly comment on each.

Capabilities of the IT system
Of course, one key to evaluating IT is to understand the capabilities of the IT in question. It is not sufficient to simply rely on the vendor's representation of the IT. It is also useful to contact current users to understand how they have utilised the system. In addition, research from secondary sources, such as product reviews, may prove useful when determining capabilities.

Match between the IT system and the organisation's needs

Once the capabilities of the system are understood, it is necessary to determine whether the capabilities match the organisation's requirements. Of course, this assumes that an analysis of the organisation's requirements has been conducted and an understanding of those requirements has been reached. This understanding can be difficult to achieve. Many SME managers have difficulty in articulating their needs, which makes them no different from many IT users. In our work with SMEs we find it useful to keep the requirements analysis as straightforward as possible. For example, in some cases we start with a three-tier categorisation of the requirements. The first category consists of those requirements that *must* be met. Any system that cannot provide these functions is rejected. The second category is made up of requirements that are not absolute necessities, but that the SME would be willing to pay to have met. The final category consists of requirements that the SME would like to have met, but would not be willing to pay for.

When determining SMEs' IT requirements it is important to understand that many SME managers lack broad experience. This may lead to a manager's not recognising some requirements. Advisers working with SMEs should endeavour to enlighten the SME with respect to system requirements. For example, one of the authors was working with a small engineering firm that wanted to automate their design function through the use of CAD. The manager in charge of the project did not understand the necessity of an arithmetic co-processor (which was not an integrated component as it is in most central processing units (CPUs) today). In his role as adviser, the author impressed upon the manager the critical nature of this component. As a result, the co-processor was elevated to 'must have' status. Once the requirements and the candidate system's capabilities are understood, the level of match can be determined. If no systems match the requirements, additional systems may need to be investigated, the requirements may need modification, or the project may have to be abandoned.

Price

Of course, the cost of the IT is an important factor. As noted earlier, in general SMEs suffer from a lack of slack financial resources. So, price is a critical aspect of any adoption decision. There may be cases in which the 'best' IT is beyond the capital resources of an SME. In such cases, a lesser IT may, out of necessity, be selected. Programs that assist SMEs in gaining access to capital may help alleviate price-based limitations. Even in these cases, a careful cost/benefit analysis should be conducted to ensure that the cost of the proposed IT is less than the expected benefits.

When examining costs, it is critical to not simply examine hardware and software acquisition costs. In most cases, acquisition costs are a relatively minor portion of the overall cost of implementing an IT. Other tangible and intangible costs may be incurred. Tangible costs include training, installation and customisation, among others, while intangible costs include lost productivity while learning the new system.

Adoption of IT by the workforce

The match between candidate technologies and the workforce should be examined from multiple perspectives. First, the adoption of the IT by the SME's current workforce must be considered. If the workforce lacks the skill to utilise the IT, the SME must either train current workers or acquire skilled workers. The costs of either action must be considered when evaluating the technology. In some cases, it may be preferable to accept a lesser system if it is more likely to fit with the current workers' abilities. Even when the current workforce is able to utilise the candidate system, workers may resist the change represented by the system. If so, the workers will also resist adopting the IT. Even if the IT is a perfect match with the SME's requirements, the system will do little good if the workforce refuses to adopt the IT.

A related issue is the availability of workers skilled in the use of the IT. At some point, most organisations that adopt a particular IT will have to hire new workers who are skilled in that system. If a relatively obscure IT was adopted, the organisation may find acquiring skilled workers difficult. One of the authors faced this situation when managing the IT for a small engineering firm. At the time, the firm was using an obscure word-processing package. The current clerical staff was able to use the program, but as the company expanded it became almost impossible to find workers with expertise in the use of that package. As a result, management decided to make the switch to a more mainstream program – one that was familiar to many potential workers.

Extendibility of the IT

Adopting new information technologies can be problematic for SMEs, for the many reasons discussed earlier in this chapter. Therefore, it is critical to maximise the useful lifetime of any IT that is adopted. As a result, SMEs (or those advising SMEs) should consider the extendibility of any technology under consideration. For example, a modular accounting package may be attractive. Such software allows the SME to add new modules in order to gain additional functionality. Perhaps the critical need at the moment is for an accounts receivable solution. If the accounts receivable software is part of a larger, modular package, inventory control can be added later without having to scrap the investment in the accounts receivable software. Considering the extendibility of hardware is also important. When evaluating a network server, for example, the ability to add storage capacity or additional processors as the SME grows can be paramount.

Compatibility of the IT

Two aspects of compatibility are important. First, the compatibility between the IT under consideration and the current practices, beliefs and experiences of the SME is important. These considerations were discussed in the section on innovation characteristics. Second, is the compatibility of the IT with those currently used by the SME. If not, additional expense may be incurred. Manual re-entry of data may be required in order to integrate incompatible systems. Middleware or other technology solutions may enable communication among incompatible systems, but this solution tends to be both expensive and complicated. Even when dealing with technologies that do not appear to require interaction, compatibility should be considered. Take the case of word processing and CAD. On the surface, it may seem that compatibility between these two disparate systems is not important. However, the ability to type long notes on a word processor, then transfer them onto a drawing in the CAD system saves significant time and effort.

Total life-cycle of the IT

The life of an information technology is rarely dictated by the length of time it takes for the technology to 'wear out.' Rather an IT generally is constrained by its economic life cycle, which is determined by when the IT outlives its economic usefulness (Oberlin 1996). Most readers have likely experienced the need to replace a computer that still works. The replacement is driven by the need to extend the functionality of the system beyond that which is economically feasible. It is common to hear such statements as 'It's cheaper to buy a new one than it is to upgrade this one'. When evaluating IT for SMEs, it is important to project the total life cycle of the IT. The capabilities of the IT as well as its extendibility must be considered. In some cases, it is a better decision to spend additional money on a more capable IT with a longer total life cycle than it is to save money on the initial purchase by purchasing an IT with a shorter life cycle. Of course, it is very difficult to determine the total life cycle of an IT. New developments and/or changing requirements can make an IT obsolete much sooner than anticipated. This points to the importance of extendibility discussed earlier in this section. SMEs and their advisers must use past experience, combined with current research, to make the most accurate life cycle estimate possible. It is critical to realise that this determination must be made within the context of the SME in question. Different SMEs have different needs, both current and future. As a result, a good decision for one may be a bad decision for another.

SME advisers should also keep the components of the Integrated Model (Figure 9.2) described earlier in mind when working with SMEs. For example, advisers should make SME managers cognisant of the critical nature of top management support in IT adoption. Managers who truly want to promote the use of IT within their organisations must not only make their desires known to employees, but they must also provide the necessary support in terms of resources and overcoming internal barriers. Otherwise, the IT implementation efforts may go for naught. In addition, it is important for advisers to emphasise the role of internal IT support in successful IT adoption. SME managers can improve the chances of success by providing IT support mechanisms inside the organisation.

It is also important to help SME managers understand the critical nature of IT expertise, both in terms of their own expertise and that of their employees. As discussed earlier, both CEO and organisational IT knowledge are positively related to IT adoption by SMEs. Advisers can also assist SMEs by helping them recognise opportunities to apply IT in useful ways. One aspect of the importance of IT knowledge is the ability to recognise such opportunities. Advisers can use their greater expertise and exposure to IT applications to help increase awareness of potential IT applications.

9.6.2 Vendors

Vendors also play an important role in SME IT use. Since SMEs represent a significant market for IT, many IT vendors have specific programs to market their products or services to SMEs. These vendors may also take some guidance from the material in this chapter. Knowledge of the barriers to IT use may allow vendors to address these barriers through special services offered to SMEs. For example, vendors could address the financial barrier by providing low-cost financing to SME customers.

The concept of cluster innovations discussed earlier may also help vendors design programs to reach SMEs. Vendors may wish to consider cluster innovation concepts when designing their product offerings. Offering carefully constructed bundles of products may influence SME adoption. For example, rather than offering the component pieces for a network separately, vendors could offer a network bundle. Of course, many vendors are already offering such bundles. However, through a deeper understanding of innovation clusters, vendors may be able to expand their coordinated offerings beyond the obvious. Vendors may also utilise the cluster concept by concentrating marketing efforts using clusters as a guide. For example, one potential cluster of technologies includes electronic mail and Web-based marketing, which are related (Van Slyke 2000). Vendors who are interested in promoting Web-based marketing to SMEs could concentrate their efforts on those SMEs that have already adopted electronic mail.

Awareness of the impact of perceptions of the characteristics of IT innovations may also help vendors design their marketing efforts. As shown in the Integrated Model (Figure 9.2), perceptions of the relative advantage, compatibility and complexity of an IT are related to its adoption. While vendors have traditionally touted the benefits (relative advantage) and ease of use (the inverse of complexity) of their products or services, casual observation suggests that less attention is given to perceptions of compatibility.

Vendors should also be aware of the importance of external support for IT. As discussed previously, external support has a positive impact on SME IT adoption. Vendors that have solid support programs for their products should be sure that they emphasise the existence of the programs when dealing with SMEs. Vendors without support programs have two options for addressing this weakness. First, the vendors could implement support programs. As an alternative, these vendors could partner with other service providers to provide support.

9.6.3 Governments

East Asian governments should play a significant role in encouraging IT use by the SME community. One role of government is to develop specific policies to diffuse IT to SMEs. Policies directed specifically at SMEs are necessary due to the tendency of SME managers to be less informed regarding the potential of IT (La Rovere 1996). La Rovere (1996) recommends a three-step approach to SME-oriented IT diffusion policy, as outlined below.

Step 1: Assess SMEs' situation in terms of the following:

- ability to raise capital

- relative cost of IT equipment

- managerial and accounting skills

- relationships with suppliers.

Step 2: Improve the SME IT infrastructure with respect to the deficiencies identified in Step 1.

Step 3: Ensure that there is a link between IT adoption and use by SMEs by:

- supporting the organisational development of SMEs

- upgrading the overall management and human resources of SMEs

- helping SMEs create an overall technological culture that promotes the constant search for improvements in the use of IT.

More general technology development efforts may impact SME IT use as a byproduct. An example is Malaysia's model 'intelligent city' Cyberjaya, which is located along Malaysia's Multimedia Super Corridor (MSC). Cyberjaya was designed to be a leading-edge multimedia centre with an infrastructure that would attract IT companies from around the world. Cyberjaya will enjoy a highly advanced telecommunications infrastructure complete with a broadband network, a 10gbs fibre-optic backbone and asynchronous transmission mode (ATM) switches. In addition, the backbone will connect to Japan, the United States, and Europe through direct, high-capacity fibre links (see <www.cyberjaya-msc.com> for additional details).

Although not specifically directed at SMEs, the Cyberjaya project may impact SME adoption of IT. As noted earlier, one barrier to SME adoption of IT in developing countries is the relatively poor telecommunications infrastructure in these countries. The Cyberjaya telecommunications infrastructure will be available to SMEs, thus overcoming this barrier for SMEs in that region.

The Cyberjaya project does not neglect SMEs, however. One aspect of the program calls for research and development grants for SMEs. While not specifically directed at IT adoption, these grants may make funds available for IT acquisition, which helps overcome financial barriers to IT adoption.

There are many examples of programs designed to assist SMEs in East Asia. The

China Centre for Business Cooperation and Coordination provides a wide range of services, including consultation and management training. The Korea Institute of Industry and Technology Information collects and disseminates technical information resources as well as providing other services. As noted earlier, the United States Small Business Administration, a federal government agency, assists SMEs through a distributed network of small business development centres. Many of these Centres provide assistance associated with IT.

9.6.4   Not-for-profit Organisations

The Appalachian Center for Economic Networks (ACEnet), which was discussed earlier in this chapter, provides very small businesses with a number of IT-related services. For example, ACEnet's Computer Opportunities Program is directed at the IT skills barrier. This program trains local students to provide IT services to area small businesses. ACEnet also has many other innovative SME-oriented programs. Readers interested in learning more about ACEnet are directed to Van Slyke et al. (2001), which provides a comprehensive discussion.

East Asia also boasts a number of non-governmental, not-for-profit organisations that provide IT assistance to SMEs. In Singapore the Association of Small and Medium Enterprises is a self-help organisation comprising SME managers. The Federation of Thai Industries provides a variety of services related to technology. While these organisations are not specifically oriented towards information technology, they do address IT issues. In contrast, the Small and Medium Industry Promotion Corporation, located in the Republic of Korea, is a not-for-profit organisation whose goal is to promote computerisation and automation in SMEs. To this end it provides technology training and other technology services to SMEs.

Whether by design or by accident, many organisations of this kind address the IT adoption issues noted earlier. For example, by providing external support for IT, some of these organisations influence IT adoption. The Small and Medium Industry Promotion Corporation's technology training services impact the organisational characteristic of IT knowledge, which in turn impacts SME IT adoption.

Those wishing to offer services that assist SMEs in their IT efforts would be well served to examine existing programs, such as those mentioned above. In addition, the Integrated Model (Figure 9.2), and the discussion of SME IT adoption barriers may provide guidance. It is important that services be designed to help SMEs overcome specific barriers. Some barriers may be beyond the reach of a single organisation. For example, improving the telecommunications infrastructure may require governmental intervention. However, single organisations have the ability to address other barriers, such as the IT knowledge barrier.

Organisations that desire to influence SME IT use should also pay heed to the role of perceptions of innovation characteristics. Programs can be designed to influence SMEs' perceptions of IT in a manner that improves chances for adoption. For example, educational programs such as seminars can point out the benefits of certain technologies, which may improve perceptions of relative advantage. Programs designed to build networks of SMEs may be particularly effective at influencing SME adoption of IT. In such networks, SMEs can learn from one another, and can cooperatively attack IT-related problems. More experienced members of the network can share their knowledge and experiences with the less experienced. Ideally, a synergy develops that benefits all SMEs involved. Successful networks hold the potential to impact several factors related to IT adoption. The network can act as an external support mechanism. In addition, through cooperative learning about IT, the IT knowledge of SMEs may increase. Further, the interactions within a network may have an impact on some SMEs' perceptions of the characteristics of IT innovations. By learning how peers are successfully utilising IT, some SMEs may increase their perceptions of the relative advantage of IT, for example.

9.7   CONCLUSIONS

In this chapter, we have discussed ways in which IT can be introduced into the SME. We described how and why the typical SME utilises various categories of information technology, from traditional systems to pre-packaged ('shrink-wrapped') software to emerging technologies like the World Wide Web. Our discussion also focused on how various factors of innovations, organisations and the business environment can influence IT adoption and diffusion within SMEs. In addition, we reviewed a number of barriers to successful IT adoption, as well as strategies for overcoming these barriers.

In today's fast-paced, global economy, IT can help SMEs remain viable. SMEs clearly can benefit from the appropriate adoption and use of IT. Determining IT requirements may be of paramount importance if SMEs are to be competitive. We hope this chapter will assist the SME owner or manager in understanding the importance of IT, as well as recognising how IT can affect their organisation (both positively and negatively). We hope also that the discussion can assist SME owners and managers in assessing and addressing their organisation's IT needs.

REFERENCES

Agarwal, R. and J. Prasad (1997), 'Role of Innovation Characteristics and Perceived Voluntariness in the Acceptance of Information Technologies', *Decision Sciences*, **28** (3), 557–82.

Anonymous (1990), *1990 Buyer's Guide and Directory: Computers in Accounting*, Boston, MA: Warren, Gorham & Lamont.

Bridge, J. and M. Peel (1999), 'Research Note: A Study of Computer Usage and Strategic Planning in the SME Sector', *International Small Business Journal*, **17** (4), 82–7.

Chin, W. and G. Moore (1991), 'Technology Clusters: An Empirical Investigation of the Adoption of Information Technology Applications by End Users', in *Proceedings of the Annual Conference of the Administrative Sciences Association of Canada Information Systems Division*, Niagara Falls, Ontario, Canada, May, pp. 80–9.

Cooper, R. and R. Zmud (1990), 'Information Technology Implementation Research: A Technology Diffusion Approach', *Management Science*, **36** (2), 123–39.

Cragg, P. and N. Zinatelli (1995), 'The Evolution of Information Systems in Small Firms', *Information & Management*, **29** (1), 1–8.

Davis, F. (1986), 'Perceived Usefulness, Perceived Ease of Use, and Use Acceptance of Information Technology', *MIS Quarterly*, **13** (3), 319–40.

Delone, W. (1988), 'Determinants of Success for Computer Usage in Small Business', *Management Information Systems Quarterly*, **12** (1), 51–61.

Eastlick, M. (1993), 'Predictors of Videotex Adoption', *Journal of Direct Marketing*, **7** (3), 66–74.

Farkas-Conn, I. (1999), 'New Strategic Partnerships between Large International Banks with Small- and Medium-sized Enterprises', *Bulletin of the American Society for Information Science*, June–July, pp. 11–14.

Foong, S. (1999), 'Effect of End-user Personal and Systems Attributes on Computer-based Information System Success in Malaysian SMEs', *Journal of Small Business Management*, **37** (3), 81–7.

Fuller, M. and E. Swanson (1992), 'Information Centres as Organisational Innovation: Exploring the Correlates of Implementation Success', *Journal of Management Information Systems*, **9** (1), 47–67.

Gatignon, R. and T. Robertson (1985), 'A Propositional Inventory for New Diffusion Research', *Journal of Consumer Research,* **11**, 849–67.

Geisler, E. (1992), 'Managing Information Technology in Small Business: Some Practical Lessons and Guidelines', *Journal of General Management*, **18** (1), 74–80.

Grover, V. (1993), 'An Empirically Derived Model for the Adoption of Customer-based Interorganisational Systems', *Decision Sciences*, **24** (3), 603–40.

Grover, V. and M. Gosslar (1993), 'The Initiation, Adoption and Implementation of Telecommunications Technologies in US Organisations', *Journal of Management Information Systems*, **10** (1), 141–63.

Hebert, M. and I. Benbasat (1994), 'Adopting Information Technology in Hospitals: The Relationship Between Attitudes/Expectations and Behaviour', *Hospital & Health Services Administration*, **39** (3), 369–83.

Hoffer, J. and M. Alexander (1992), 'The Diffusion of Database Machines', *Data Base*, **23** (2), 13–19.

Iacovou, C., I. Benbasat and A. Dexter (1995), 'Electronic Data Interchange in Small Organisations: Adoption and Impact of Technology', *MIS Quarterly*, **19** (4), 465–85.

Igbaria, M., N. Zinatelli, P. Cragg and A. Cavaye (1997), 'Personal Computing Acceptance Factors in Small Firms: A Structural Equation Model', *MIS Quarterly*, **21** (3), 279–302.

Kwon, T. and R. Zmud (1987), 'Unifying the Fragmented Models of Information Systems Implementation', in R.J. Borland and R.A. Hirschheim (eds), *Critical Issues in Information Systems*, New York: John Wiley, pp. 227–51.

Lancaster, G. and C. Taylor (1986), 'The Diffusion of Innovations and their Attributes: A Critical Review', *Quarterly Review of Marketing*, **11** (4), 13–19.

LaRose, R. and A. Hoag (1996), 'Organisational Adoptions of the Internet and the Clustering of Innovations', *Journal of Telematics and Informatics*, **13** (1), 49–61.

La Rovere, R. (1996), 'IT Diffusion in Small and Medium-sized Enterprises: Elements for Policy Definition', *Information Technology for Development*, **7**, 169–81.

Lin, B., J. Vassar and L. Clard (1993), 'Information Technology for Small Businesses', *Journal of Applied Business Research*, **21** (7), 20–27.

Mahajan, V. and R. Peterson (1985), *Innovation Diffusion Models and Applications*, Beverly Hills, CA: Sage.

Moore, G. and I. Benbasat (1991), 'Development of an Instrument to Measure the Perceptions of Adopting an Information Technology Innovation', *Information Systems Research*, **2** (3), 192–222.

Nedovic-Budic, Z. and D. Godschalk (1996), 'Human Factors in Adoption of Geographic Information Systems: A Local Government Case Study', *Public Administration Review*, **56** (6), 554–67.

Oberlin, J. (1996), 'Financial Mythology of Information Technology: Developing a New Game Plan', *CAUSE/EFFECT*, **19** (2), 10–17.

Peterson, R. and V. Mahajan (1978), 'Multi-product Growth Models', in J. Seth (ed.), *Research in Marketing,* Greenwich, CT: JAI Press, pp. 201–31.

Premkumar, G., K. Ramamurthy and M. Crum (1997), 'Determinants of EDI Adoption in the Transportation Industry', *European Journal of Information Systems*, **6** (2), 107–21.

Premkumar, G., K. Ramamurthy and S. Nilakanta (1994), 'Implementation of Electronic Data Exchange: An Innovation Diffusion Perspective', *Journal of Management Information Systems*, 11 (2), 157–86.

Premkumar, G. and M. Roberts (1999), 'Adoption of New Information Technologies in Rural Small Businesses', *Omega: International Journal of Management Science*, 27 (4), 457–84.

Prescott, M. and S. Conger (1995), 'Information Technology Innovations: A Classification by IT Locus of Impact and Research Approach', *Data Base Advances*, **26** (2/3), 20–41.

Prescott, M. and C. Van Slyke (1997), 'Understanding the Internet as an Innovation,' *Industrial Management and Data Systems*, **97** (3 & 4), 119–24.

Raymond, L. (1988), Impact of Computer Training on the Attitudes and Usage Behaviour of Small Business Managers', *Journal of Small Business Management*, **26** (3), 8–13.

Raymond, L. (1990), 'Organizational Context and IS Success', *Journal of Management Information Systems*, **6** (4), 5–20.

Rogers, E.M. (1995), *Diffusion of Innovations*, 4th edition, New York: Free Press.

Silverman, L. and W. Bailey (1961), *Trends in the Adoption of Recommended Farm Practices*, State College, Mississippi, Agricultural Experimental Station Bulletin 617.

Taylor, S. and P. Todd (1995), 'Understanding Information Technology Usage: A Test of Competing Models', *Information Systems Research*, **6** (2), 144 –76.

Teo, H., B. Tan and K. Wei (1995), 'Innovation Diffusion Theory as a Predictor of Adoption Intention for Financial EDI', *Proceedings of the Sixteenth Annual International Conference on Information Systems*, December, Amsterdam, pp. 155–65.

Thong, J. (1999), 'An Integrated Model of Information Systems Adoption in Small Businesses', *Journal of Management Information Systems*, **15** (4), 187–214.

Thong, J. and C. Yap (1995), 'CEO Characteristics, Organizational Characteristics, and Information Technology Adoption in Small Businesses', *Omega: International Journal of Management Science*, **23** (4), 429–42.

Tornatzky, L. and M. Fleischer (1990), *The Processes of Technological Innovation*, New York: Lexington Books.

Van Slyke, C. (2000), 'The Role of Technology Clusters in Small Business Electronic Commerce Adoption', *CollECTer 2000 Proceedings*, December 2000, Brisbane, QN, Australia.

Van Slyke, C., M. Kittner and F. Belanger (2001), 'ACEnet: Facilitating Economic Development through Small Business Electronic Commerce', *Annals of Cases on Information Technology Applications and Management in Organizations*, **3**, 1–20.

Welsh, J. and J. White (1981), 'A Small Business Is Not a Little Big Business', *Harvard Business Review*, **59** (4), 18–32.

WITSA (2000), *Digital Planet 2000: The Global Information Economy*, Vienna, VA: World Information Technology and Services Alliance.

10 Electronic Commerce and Small and Medium Sized Enterprises in East Asia

Boon-Chye Lee

10.1 INTRODUCTION AND BACKGROUND

The term electronic commerce, or e-commerce, is used to refer to the utilisation of any part of a cluster of related technologies to facilitate commercial transactions. Some of these technologies have been part of the commercial landscape for decades, being used in what has come to be known as B2B (business–business) e-commerce. For example, electronic data interchange (EDI) technology by organisations along different parts of a supply chain using proprietary systems has been in use since the 1970s. These tend to be limited to closed networks of organisations, usually involving a large organisation and its network of suppliers, and very specific in application. Because EDI requires expensive and complex customised software, and dedicated communication links, the principal users have been large firms and their principal suppliers. In general, small and medium enterprises adopting B2B e-commerce technologies have tended to be driven by necessity, in reaction to pressure by their larger clients who require such changes by their suppliers as part of efforts to streamline their operations. Most SMEs, however, have been left out of the EDI networks because they were unable to afford the large investments required.

More recently, non-proprietary systems over open networks have evolved. In particular, the advent of the Internet has dramatically reduced entry costs, making it possible for small and medium enterprises to take advantage of the technology without having to invest large sums of money to develop it independently. It has been estimated, for example, that the cost of Internet-based transactions is a tenth of those carried out by EDI (OECD 1999). While B2B transactions dominate e-commerce by far, and are expected to continue to do so, accounting for more than 80 per cent of e-commerce revenues (Mann, et al. 2000), B2C (business-to-consumer) and even C2C (consumer-to-consumer) applications are increasingly being made possible and economically viable. The benefits of e-commerce notwithstanding, it remains the case that, especially in East Asia as compared to Europe and the US, SMEs tend to have only a limited understanding of e-commerce and consequently either do not avail themselves of the technology or do not take full advantage of it.

Important official initiatives have also introduced a third player into the e-commerce landscape, the government and other state authorities, so that increasingly there is discussion of electronic transactions between government and individuals, and government and business. Indeed, government initiatives and leadership in this area are an important factor in educating the general public about e-commerce and its possibilities, and creating an overall environment conducive to the use of e-commerce technologies.

In this chapter we examine what electronic commerce has to offer SMEs in the economies of East Asia. We define the region loosely to include the countries on the western rim of the Pacific – namely, China, Hong Kong, Japan, South Korea, Taiwan, Vietnam, Singapore, Malaysia, Indonesia, Australia and New Zealand. The readiness of East Asian economies for electronic commerce is then examined, using the Economist Intelligence Unit's E-Business-Readiness Ranking as a point of departure for the discussion. Policy implications, particularly as they relate to SMEs, are also touched upon.

The chapter proceeds as follows. Section 10.2 identifies the opportunities and risks posed by e-commerce for SMEs. Section 10.3, specifically discusses issues arising from the adoption of e-commerce by SMEs. Section 10.4 discusses the preparedness of East Asian SMEs for the adoption of e-commerce. Finally, Section 10.5 presents a brief summary of the major conclusions from this chapter.

10.2 OPPORTUNITIES AND RISKS POSED BY E-COMMERCE

The Internet and e-commerce is in the process of bringing about fundamental changes in the conduct of commerce. These changes involve both product and process innovations, as well as new markets in time, geography and information. While the opportunities and potential gains are widely recognised, particularly by governments but also by businesses, there are also risks involved for SMEs. For example, e-commerce technologies have brought about an increasing use by firms (regardless of size) of external networks, thus eroding what has traditionally been a source of competitive advantage of SMEs (Narula 2001).

10.2.1 Microeconomic Aspects

It has been argued that because e-commerce reduces transaction costs and the economies of scale from vertical integration, it will tend to reduce the economically optimal size of firms (*The Economist* 2000a). At the micro level, the most obvious benefits offered by e-commerce to firms, irrespective of size, are in the expansion of market reach and cost reduction, including time saved by online processing of orders, lower stocks and automated collection of high-quality data. However, it is evident that the potential benefits are not uniform across industries. For example, while the potential benefits of moving to the Internet are great in the health-care industry because it is so information intensive and still largely paper based, and manufacturing firms would also benefit from improved information flow and restructuring of routine back-office functions, this is less true of the financial services industry because most of the benefits of automation have probably already been reaped (Litan and Rivlin 2000).[1]

OECD (2000a) cites surveys indicating that the main benefits SMEs associate with e-commerce include: strengthening customer relationships; access to new markets; optimising business processes; cost reduction; and creating new products and services. Other studies (for example, Poon and Swatman 1999; Premkumar and Roberts 1999; PriceWaterhouseCoopers 1999; and Van Slyke 2000) generally support these findings.

The prospective benefits to SMEs are potentially much more significant than for larger firms, because the former traditionally have often operated at a significant disadvantage to larger firms. For example, large firms often have direct access to domestic and international capital markets, while SMEs are by and large excluded because of the high fixed costs involved which militate against smaller-scale ventures. In addition, compliance with regulations often also involves fixed costs, which again disadvantages smaller-scale enterprises. E-commerce offers SMEs the prospect of a more level playing field denied them by virtue of lack of access to the economies of scale enjoyed by many large firms. Because high transaction costs can significantly impede access to important resources, and threaten the viability of a business, their reduction will promote the creation and expansion of SMEs.

On the other hand, lower transaction costs pose certain risks for firms performing intermediary roles. This is because functions which firms had previously found economical to outsource may now become economical to perform in-house. This phenomenon, sometimes referred to as 'disintermediation', endangers the survival of firms that have specialised in performing functions which may be under threat of rationalisation. The existence of many, perhaps most, SMEs hinges critically on the roles they play as intermediaries within larger supply or value chains. The longer the chains are, the greater the potential impact of e-commerce is likely to be as cost inefficiencies are exposed and rationalisation occurs. This is particularly the case in Asia where supply chains typically involve three or four intermediaries, twice as many as in Europe (Belson 2000).

The literature on the role of intermediaries in commerce generally has tended to take the approach of transaction cost economics. This approach regards the organisation of the process of getting a good from producer to end-user as a choice between two broad alternatives, hierarchies or markets (Williamson 1975). The process involves a series of steps, from the acquisition of inputs, to the manufacturing process, marketing of the good, and distribution to the final transaction that culminates in the good ending up with the final consumer. This series of steps is termed the value chain because at each step the set of inputs undergoes a process that adds value to it on its way to the end-user. Each step, or transaction, involves costs that may be characterised as transaction or coordination costs – the costs of coordinating the purchase of inputs, the manufacturing process, through the marketing, distribution and sale processes.

If transaction costs are sufficiently low, the producer would find it efficient to conduct all of these steps within the one organisation, and we would have a vertically integrated firm or hierarchy comprising the entire value chain. However, if sub-contracting any stage in the value chain to an external party would result in cost and/ or organisational efficiencies the producer will do so, and we would have an intermediary interposed into the value chain. In this case, because there may be any number of possible intermediaries that might perform this function for the firm, the firm is said to opt for a market solution for this particular step in the value chain.

This line of argument has been brought to bear on the analysis of the role of intermediaries in electronic commerce. Some writers (for example, Malone et al. 1987; and Benjamin and Wigand 1995) have suggested that implementation of e-commerce technologies would result in cost efficiencies that would precipitate a trend towards disintermediation, putting the survival of many traditional intermediaries at risk. More recent analysis (see Sarkar et al. 1995; Bailey and Bakos 1997; OECD 1997; and Schmitz 2000) indicates that this view is overstated and somewhat lopsided. For one thing, while it is true that there could be an increase in direct sales in an electronic environment, thus eliminating many traditional retailing and wholesaling operations, most of the steps in a transaction will still require institutional and distributional support of some kind (OECD 1997). In addition, much of the promise of the Internet lies in its potential not just to reduce the costs of carrying out the same transactions as before but also to restructure procedures and operations more efficiently, for example by improving information flows and better coordination of schedules resulting in reduced stock levels.

Part of the reason for the earlier pessimistic prognosis on intermediaries rests in the methodology of transaction-cost economics, which employs what has been described as an 'organisational comparative statics' approach (Dietrich 1994). This approach presupposes an institutional and organisational structure that alters little over time, if at all. In a dynamically evolving situation, the approach is ill-equipped to explain the organisational and institutional structures that are observed. This is particularly true for electronic markets which are rapidly changing and subject to constant innovation. In time, the prevailing metaphor of a supply chain or value chain may be superseded by that of a supply web more in line with the network characteristics of the Internet (Gross 1998). Under such circumstances, opportunities exist for niche operators to perform new intermediary functions quite different from those traditionally associated with physical products. As has been noted:

> [M]any forms of electronic commerce may not be sustainable unless new forms of intermediation develop to support the customer/supplier relationship. In some circumstances, intermediation can reduce transaction costs by adding value to product information and coordinating transaction support structures such as contract negotiation, credit, insurance, funds transfer and logistics. Indeed, one of the growth business areas in an electronic marketplace could well be in the field of intermediation – setting up businesses that coordinate all of the support mechanisms necessary to preserve buyer and seller confidence in the market. (OECD 1997, pp. 48–9)

Given the nascent state of development of e-commerce, it is not possible to present an exhaustive list of the business possibilities offered by the technology. However, even at this early stage, a number of business models have emerged that are suggestive of the possibilities offered by electronic commerce. A notable example of this has been the emergence in the virtual world of that most basic form of an intermediary, the broker, whose function consists solely in matching up buyers with sellers at a particular point in the value chain. The broker is often underrated because it is not perceived as contributing value to the chain, its primary function being to reduce search costs. With e-commerce technology, the broker has come into its own in such intermediaries as e-Bay, an Internet auction site. In addition to bringing together buyers and sellers across a wide range of goods, the company has managed to tap innovatively into e-commerce technologies in creating a model of decentralised, self-organised reputation creation and tracking among its clients by which customers provide testimonials about other customers they have dealt with in the past on e-Bay (Schoder and Yin 2000). In providing the means by which reputation can be established and checked, without actually performing that function itself, the company has gone some way towards overcoming problems of trust and reputation inherent in the electronic medium.[2] Innovative uses of e-commerce technologies such as this will characterise the nature of intermediaries in the virtual world.

The e-Bay example illustrates one aspect of the use of e-commerce technologies: how economies of scale can be redefined by small companies for products and services in markets which would otherwise be dominated by big companies. The networking capabilities of e-commerce offer another means by which smaller firms can obtain economies of scale. Groups of small firms, by pooling their purchasing orders, for example, can marshall sufficient economic power to negotiate better terms for themselves. Networking, through the sharing of information among members of the network, also offers a way of countering the informational asymmetries that smaller businesses often suffer from. This has potentially wide implications for the emerging economies of East Asia and elsewhere in the potential for these economies to catch up with the more developed ones.

Another form of asymmetric information is particularly pertinent to small and medium enterprises, especially in the context of B2C e-commerce, as they typically do not have reputations to trade on. The inability of consumers on the Internet to assess the quality of vendors' products gives rise to a form of market failure well known in economics as the 'lemon' problem. This suggests a role for intermediaries. To illustrate the argument, consider the case of a subscription for a bundled product, for example a magazine subscription. If the vendor has an established reputation for quality, this in itself may be a sufficient guarantee of quality. If not, however, a subscription would mean that the consumer is required to commit to a bundle of products of uncertain quality. There would not be many customers who are prepared to make such a commitment.

One mechanism to resolve this problem is to unbundle the magazine and allow consumers to purchase individual articles. Because the commitment required of the consumer is extremely short term in nature and minimal in terms of price, there would be much less reluctance on the part of consumers to try out the vendor's products. If the quality does not meet the consumers' expectations, they will be reluctant to make further purchases. The mechanism therefore also provides an incentive for the vendor to strive for quality. What makes this mechanism possible, however, is the availability of payment methods that are able to make very small payment amounts economically. Such methods are already available in various stages of development.[3]

What appears to be an emerging trend, the unbundling of products such as music and information, may be indicative of a growing demand on the part of consumers to pick and choose only those parts of previously bundled products like newspapers, magazines, research journals and compact disks that they want. The fact that the delivery of products of this nature can be effected over the Internet, thereby obviating the need for costly physical packaging (paper, ink, binding, plastic), means that the marginal cost of delivering each article or song will be driven down towards zero. The development of electronic money and its ability to process micro payments at low cost would be well placed to cater to the requirements of the emerging market in micro transactions. Perhaps more to the point, the ability to make micro-payments means that micro transactions are now economically feasible.

Thus, the music industry represents an example where e-commerce technology can bring about a change in the structure of intermediation, and where various kinds of value can be transferred via alternative delivery systems. Resulting in a situation where the control of different elements in the value chain could be shifted to different intermediaries.

While it is possible to focus on intermediaries using short-term contracts and micro-transactions to overcome the lemon problem in the case of products that can be unbundled, it is clear that there is also a role for other kinds of intermediary functions in this context which offer services for the authentication and certification of transactions – for example, trusted third parties which rely on their reputations to offer certification or guarantee services.

Thus, while the immediate impact of e-commerce will be on the efficiency of transactions as a result of transaction-cost reductions, additional impacts will see the restructuring of the value chain, including the transformation or elimination of traditional intermediaries and the creation of new intermediary functions, as well as the restructuring of processes.

While the development of low-cost Internet technologies provides opportunities to SMEs in the region to extend their activities into new domains, similar opportunities are presented to firms in other parts of the world. Firms in the region will, therefore, be less able to take advantage of lower labour costs as a source of competitive advantage.

10.2.2 Macroeconomic Aspects

From a macro-economic perspective, the benefits of technology to the overall macro economy, while not precisely articulated, are regarded as almost self-evident in the traditional economics literature. As early as the 1950s, the Solow–Swan neoclassical growth theory postulated that the long-run rate of economic growth is tied to the rate of technological advancement. Recent studies support this presupposition. For example, Jorgenson and Stiroh (2000) and Oliner and Sichel (2000) found that a combination of accelerating technical progress in high-tech industries and investment in information technology were driving recent productivity gains in the US. Other studies have attempted to quantify the effects of the application of e-commerce technology. Altig and Rupert (1999) present evidence suggesting that improving the access of a country's population to the Internet would be associated with an additional 4 per cent in GDP growth. An Australian government study indicates that greater use of e-commerce could result in a 2.7 per cent increase in GDP (DOCITA 2000). Brookes and Wahhaj (2000) estimate that B2B activity will enhance GDP by almost 5 per cent in the major industrialised countries within 10 years, and that the annual GDP growth rate during this period will be 0.25 per cent higher. However, these studies do not evaluate if the potential growth rate has permanently changed due to increases in factor productivity or, if it has, the underlying factors that have brought about this change.

In addition, Altig and Rupert (1999) urge caution in the interpretation of their findings. They interpret access to the Internet broadly as a general proxy for a range of factors that influence the rate at which economies adopt and absorb new technologies, and argue that:

> The very same elements that inhibit widespread public access to the Internet – high taxes, labour market policies that raise the cost of production, capital market imperfections and regulations that retard the creation of start-up enterprises, tariffs, and so on – are likely to more broadly interfere with optimising the promise of technological progress. In other words, economic infrastructure matters, and those policies and regulations that interfere with creative access to new technologies have a very real negative impact on the wealth of nations. (Altig and Rupert 1999)

The policy implications are that, in addition to ensuring adequate physical infrastructure, governments need to deal with the broad environmental factors that will determine whether people and businesses will ultimately embrace e-commerce as part of their lives. The economic infrastructure necessarily includes physical and legal components, but social aspects – including the general level of education in a country, issues of access – will also be crucial. These considerations are taken up in the following section.

10.3   THE ADOPTION OF E-COMMERCE BY SMES

SMEs adopting e-commerce can be classified into three categories (OECD 2000a, 2000b): (a) Internet start-ups that invent new ways of creating value added, new services and new business models; (b) SMEs already established in the physical world that seek to utilise the Internet in pursuit of expansion opportunities; and (c) groups of SMEs entering into partnerships either with large firms that are their customers or suppliers, or with industry-wide networks, or both.

PriceWaterhouseCoopers (1999) offers a more conceptual classification scheme based on the e-commerce capabilities of SMEs. Four categories or levels of SMEs are identified, representing the stages of e-commerce development through which firms may progress:

- Level 1: SMEs that possess very basic or no online capabilities.

- Level 2: SMEs with a Web site but no advanced capabilities such as order taking and processing.

- Level 3: SMEs that have Web sites with the capability to take orders and provide customer service.

- Level 4: SMEs with Web sites that are able to complete transactions and receive payments.

The OECD classification scheme recognises that SMEs can go directly from the outset to higher levels without evolving from scratch at Level 1.

PriceWaterhouseCoopers (1999) notes that raising the awareness of the potential benefits and opportunities of e-commerce is an important means of increasing the adoption of the technology by SMEs. It is equally important to address the perceived inhibitors to e-commerce adoption by SMEs. The results of the survey by PriceWaterhouseCoopers (1999) of participating SMEs reveal that the most important inhibitor was 'low customer e-commerce use', which more than 75 per cent of respondents rated either 'very important' as an inhibitor or 'somewhat important'. The next three most important inhibitors, each of which were rated by more than 65 per cent of responding SMEs as 'very important' 'somewhat important', were 'concerns about security', 'low supplier e-commerce use', and 'legal and liability concerns'.

PriceWaterhouseCoopers (1999, p. 18) report, however, that 'SMEs participating in the survey generally rated the importance of [the] barriers [to the adoption of e-commerce] well below the importance of the potential benefits'. It is noteworthy that two of the three most important inhibitors of e-commerce adoption ('low customer e-commerce use' and 'low supplier e-commerce use') have to do with a perceived lack of critical mass, which is a problem to a greater extent in Asia than in the more-developed economies of Europe and the US. It is in this area that government can play an important role, which is discussed in the following section as is the creation of a legal and regulatory regime to address the legal and liability concerns of businesses.

10.4   E-COMMERCE PREPAREDNESS IN EAST ASIA

The countries in the region represent a wide range of economies at varying stages of development and preparedness for what is often referred to as the 'New Economy'. The level of sophistication of the communications infrastructure capable of supporting e-commerce, for example, is widely divergent, as is the general level of education. These and other factors will be crucial in determining the rate of uptake of e-commerce in any country.

The Economist Intelligence Unit's (2000) assessment of 'e-business-readiness' is instructive as a guide to the relative preparedness of countries for the electronic age. Not surprisingly, at a global level, the United States was rated first, closely followed by the Nordic countries, Sweden, Finland and Norway. Among Asian countries, Singapore and Hong Kong are the clear leaders, together with Australia and New Zealand (see Table 10.1).

Two key factors entering into the rating scheme were accessibility (what the report calls 'connectivity') and the general business environment. Each takes into account a broad range of relevant factors. Additionally, in Asia, unlike the situation in the United States where private sector initiatives have led the way, it is the governments that have been the main promoters of e-commerce, reflecting the relative inability of private enterprise in the region to undertake such initiatives. Accordingly, the extent to which government is prepared or able to provide initiative, leadership and direction in electronic commerce is an important factor that needs to be taken into account. We discuss each of these factors below.

10.4.1   Accessibility

In general, accessibility factors have to do with the ease with which individuals and firms in the country are able to connect to the Internet and other vehicles to communicate and exchange information and goods with the rest of the world. It encompasses factors like the reliability of the electricity supply, and the cost and reliability of communications services and is strongly related to the quality of the

Table 10.1
'E-Business-Readiness' Rankings, Selected Countries

Country	Rank (out of 60 countries)	Business environment ranking, 2000–2004	Connectivity rating	E-business-readiness rating
USA	1	8.69	9	8.8
Singapore	8	8.55	8	8.3
Hong Kong	9	8.52	8	8.3
Australia	16	8.14	8	8.1
New Zealand	17	8.10	8	8.1
Japan	21	7.43	8	7.7
Korea	24	7.30	7	7.2
Taiwan	27	8.13	5	6.6
Thailand	28	7.27	5	6.1
Malaysia	32	6.91	5	6.0
Indonesia	38	6.16	5	5.6
Philippines	46	6.72	3	4.9
India	50	5.97	3	4.5
China	51	5.88	3	4.4
Vietnam	54	5.30	3	4.2

Source: Economist Intelligence Unit (2000).

telecommunications infrastructure. As the Economist Intelligence Unit (2000) argues:

> Of critical importance is the availability of various means to access the Internet – telephone lines, mobile phones, leased lines, and the like – and the relative quality, distribution and cost of these services. High levels of availability coupled with low costs would translate into a higher ranking, whereas low availability and high costs would yield a low connectivity score.

These factors are of particular relevance to the adoption of electronic commerce by SMEs in a country. Table 10.2 presents some indicators of accessibility, namely the level and sophistication of the telecommunications and computing infrastructure, and its use in selected countries in the region. In general, other things equal, the better the infrastructure, the faster the take-up rate of the Internet by the population. This will tend to be reflected not just in higher adoption rates of electronic commerce by SMEs but also in the extent to which B2C e-commerce activities are carried out in the country.

Table 10.2
Accessibility Indicators, Selected Countries in the Asia–Pacific Region

Country	Population (million)	GDP per capita (US$) (2000, projected)	Mobile phones per 1000 in 1997	Tele-phone lines per 1000	Personal computers per 1000	Internet hosts per 10 000, Jan 1999	Internet users per 1000
Australia	19.1	19 993	264	521	362.2	420.6	400
Brunei	0.3	13 555	na	247	na	na	152
China	1 260.0	845	10	86	6.0	0.14	14
Hong Kong SAR	7.1	23 891	343	576	230.8	122.7	362
Indonesia	224.8	759	5	29	8.0	0.8	7
Japan	126.5	36 485	304	494	202.4	133.5	213
S. Korea	47.5	10 526	150	441	150.7	40.0	326
Malaysia	21.8	3 901	113	203	46.1	21.4	57
New Zealand	3.8	13 944	149	490	263.9	360.4	342
Papua New Guinea	4.9	980	1	12	na	0.3	0.4
Philippines	81.0	1 024	18	39	13.6	1.2	5
Singapore	4.2	26 964	273	482	399.5	210.0	531
Taiwan	22.2	14 284	na	545	na	na	255
Thailand	61.2	2 072	33	86	19.8	3.4	15
Vietnam	78.8	341	2	27	4.6	0.0	1

Sources: World Bank (2000), Asia-Inc (2000).

The summary profile in Table 10.2 indicates that wide differences in the incomes and infrastructures exist between the various countries in the region.

Clearly some countries are better placed than others to take advantage of the opportunities offered by electronic commerce. For example, the countries with the highest rates of Internet penetration are Singapore (53 per cent of the population), Australia (40 per cent), Hong Kong (36 per cent) and New Zealand (34 per cent). The same countries have the highest numbers of personal computers for their populations, but with a slightly different ordering: Singapore (just under 40 per hundred population), Australia (36 per hundred), New Zealand (26 per hundred) and Hong Kong (23 per hundred). These and other factors relating to physical infrastructure are relevant in determining the extent to which firms in a country will be able to take advantage of e-commerce technologies.

At the same time, other aspects of the development process are also important. In Malaysia, for example, a huge investment of more than US$3.6 billion by the government to develop the physical infrastructure for its Multimedia Super Corridor has not been supported by a parallel program to develop the country's human resources in the relevant fields. Consequently, a shortage of trained personnel has become apparent, the result being 'an impressive infrastructure not sufficiently supported by human capital' (*Foreign Policy* 2001). This suggests that a wider concept of access than that used by the EIU (2000) study may be appropriate. Wilson (2000), for example, distinguishes between formal access and effective access to the technologies associated with the Internet and e-commerce as follows:

> Putting a computer in a school, or stringing a telephone wire to a village, is *formal* access. Ensuring that people in the village and in a developing country as a whole can actually pay for the services, can find relevant content, know how to use the technologies to satisfy their own needs, and are engaged and represented in the policy process, is *effective* access. Some global programs provide formal but not substantive and effective access.

10.4.2 General Business Environment

The extent to which privatisation and competition occurs in the telecommunications industry, and the regulatory framework governing business in that industry, are important aspects of the general business environment that will impact on the use and adoption of electronic commerce in a country.

As Spaanderman and Ypsilanti (1997, p.13) argue:

> The economic inefficiencies which often occur with limited competition in infrastructure can retard the growth of e-commerce applications and limit the economic and social benefits they can provide. Regulators ought therefore to accelerate and extend the process of market restructuring already underway and thus allow the development and integration of generic networks that can provide and support all types of services, including entertainment, telephony and e-commerce. Allowing such a convergence in networks will require a change in present day regulations away from those specific to broadcasting and telecommunication markets, and towards frameworks which place emphasis on open access to networks for all services. Network and service providers would be subject to fewer regulatory restrictions than is the case at the moment.

Although a great deal of deregulation of the telecommunication industries in the region has taken place in recent years, with these markets increasingly being opened to competition, in many countries they are still highly regulated. Restrictions on market access will obviously affect incentives to invest and the rate of expansion of infrastructural capacity.

An important aspect of the business environment is the existence of a legal and regulatory framework supportive of the use of electronic commerce, and which provides the requisite level of confidence to support electronic transactions. The extent to which the legal and regulatory system recognises and provides certainty and support to contracts entered into or otherwise transacted via electronic means is of crucial importance.[4] PriceWaterhouseCoopers (1999), for example, present evidence suggesting that SMEs in lower-GNP economies in the region were significantly more concerned about legal and liability issues than those in higher-GNP economies, possibly because of a relative lack of legal infrastructure for electronic commerce in the former. The lack of an adequate legal and regulatory infrastructure in this area can pose a significant barrier to e-commerce activities. In addition, the willingness and ability of government to enforce legal rights and obligations in areas such as intellectual property rights, in particular, will constitute an important aspect of the legal and regulatory climate in a country.

Given the borderless nature of e-commerce, a clear, consistent framework across national jurisdictions is also obviously desirable. With this in mind, the United Nations Commission on International Trade Law (UNCITRAL) completed work on the development of its Model Law on Electronic Commerce in 1996 (see UNCITRAL 1996). The Model Law offers national legislators a set of internationally acceptable rules as to how a number of legal obstacles to the development of electronic commerce may be removed, and how a more secure legal environment may be created for electronic commerce (ECEG 1998). Since then a number of countries around the world have passed laws, some closely modelled on the Model Law, although the response has been uneven, partly reflecting national differences in Internet access, usage and national priorities. As a survey of initiatives relating to electronic and digital signatures (an important aspect of e-commerce support technology) outside of the US noted:

> Some countries, like Germany and Japan, have, to date, focused only on the technical standards for the operation of a Public Key Infrastructure ('PKI'). Others, like Singapore and Malaysia, have spanned the entire range of issues associated with the legal effect of electronic signatures, the legal framework for the operation of a PKI, and the establishment of a regulatory apparatus to oversee Certificate Authorities ('CAs'). Indeed, one of the themes of this survey is that countries do not always agree on the required scope of electronic authentication legislation. (Internet Law and Policy Forum 1999)

Table 10.3 provides a list of electronic commerce legislative initiatives in East Asia. While it is not intended to be an exhaustive listing of laws that have a bearing on electronic commerce,[5] and in addition does not provide an indication of the differences in scope, emphasis and treatment of various issues by the various statutes listed, it is suggestive of the importance accorded to electronic commerce in various countries.

The existence of legislation to regulate the legality of online transactions is a vital component of a general business environment that is conducive to electronic

Table 10.3
Electronic Commerce Legislation in East Asia

Country	Legislation (enacted or proposed)	Date*
Australia	Electronic Transactions Act	June 1999
China	No separate e-commerce legislation	na
Hong Kong	Electronic Transactions Ordinance	January 2000
Indonesia	No separate e-commerce legislation	na
Japan	Law Concerning Electronic Signatures and Certification Services	May 2000
S. Korea	Electronic Transactions Law; Electronic Signatures Law	February 1999
Malaysia	Digital Signature Act	June 1997
New Zealand	Electronic Transactions Bill	Tabled October 2000
Philippines	Electronic Commerce Act	2000
Singapore	Electronic Transactions Act	July 1998
Taiwan	No separate e-commerce legislation	na
Thailand	Electronic Transaction Bill; Electronic Signature Bill	March 2000
Vietnam	No separate e-commerce legislation	na

Note: * Enactment date unless otherwise indicated.
Sources: Baker & McKenzie (2001); Ministry of Posts and Telecommunications, Japan (1999); van der Hof (2000); Wu (2000).

commerce, as well as an important indicator of the seriousness of the government's intentions regarding electronic commerce. By this measure, the East Asian countries at the forefront are Malaysia and Singapore, which were the first to pass wide-ranging legislation closely modelled on the UNCITRAL law, and Australia. While the scope of the latter's Electronic Transactions Act is restricted to certain transactions under federal laws, it is widely expected to lead to a more general legislative framework for regulating all online transactions conducted in Australia (Farrell and Yuen 2000).

10.4.3   The Role of Government

Government's role in the process of moving their economies into the New Economy is not limited to the fostering of a supportive regulatory and legal environment. The government can be a key player in actively encouraging the use of e-commerce technologies by example, as evidenced in the GeBIZ project in Singapore (*The Economist* 2000b). As significant players in many markets, governments and government departments at all levels can set the tone by adopting e-commerce in their own operations, in what have been referred to as B2G ('business–government') transactions (see, for example, UNCTAD 2000). PriceWaterhouseCoopers (1999) report that many SMEs surveyed for their study, identified government use of e-commerce for purchasing and procurement as an important priority and potential driver for the wider adoption and use of e-commerce by SMEs.

Governments are also increasingly making information and services available to the public on the Internet. This is an important factor in educating the general public in the use of the relevant technologies, creating a social environment where people in general are more comfortable with the technology. The spillover effects on to increased business adoption of e-commerce can be significant. Singapore's eCitizen service, which has been described by the US General Services Administration as 'the most developed example of integrated service delivery in the world',[6] aims in part to 'enhance the ability of the public to be increasingly familiar and comfortable with IT, which has become a critical component in the knowledge economy. Our people's openness to and skill with IT can offer a distinctive competitive edge to Singapore'.[7] Businesses can also be encouraged to use e-commerce technologies in a variety of ways, ranging from tax incentives, the provision of grants and requiring government suppliers to submit electronic bids when tendering for government contracts (PriceWaterhouseCoopers 1999).

Government can also play a role in an area of particular deficiency for SMEs – the lack of personnel, trained and able to implement and operate e-commerce technologies – by providing and/or subsidising training and practical assistance in this area to SMEs.

10.5 SUMMARY AND CONCLUSIONS

Electronic commerce technologies are bringing about dramatic changes in the way business is conducted, including innovations in products as well as processes, and in markets spanning both space and time. In doing so, it offers opportunities and risks to firms irrespective of their size. Encouraging SMEs to adopt these technologies entails not only informing them of the opportunities (and risks) provided by e-commerce, but also addressing the factors that tend to inhibit e-commerce adoption.

The countries of East Asia represent a diverse range of economies at various stages of development and preparedness for the 'New Economy'. In this respect, the role of the government is much more important in most of these countries than has been the case in the US and Europe. As important players in their respective economies, the uptake of e-commerce technologies by SMEs will be an important factor in determining their ability to compete in global markets. Factors determining the preparedness of economies to adapt in the transition to the 'New Economy' include accessibility, the general business environment, and the degree to which the government takes a proactive role in this area.

NOTES

1   Litan and Rivlin's (2000) observations relate to the US, and are probably broadly true of other developed economies as well. Within specific industries there would be more potential for e-commerce in the less-advanced economies of East Asia. The point is that the potential varies across different industries.
2   However, problems with less than objective customer reviews posted by some sellers themselves and their friends have forced a rethink of this system by the company.
3   See Lee (1998) for a discussion of Internet retail payment systems.
4   For a discussion of the legal issues, see ECEG (1997), de Zwart (1998), and generally the special issue of the *University of New South Wales Law Journal* (1998) on Legal Issues for the Information Age.
5   For example, in many countries, there are other regulations or statutes relating to intellectual property, privacy, crimes perpetrated with the aid of computers and so on, which are relevant to e-commerce.
6   Quoted in *The Economist* (2000b).
7   The education minister, Peter Chen, quoted in *The Economist* (2000b).

REFERENCES

Altig, D. and P. Rupert (1999), 'Growth and the Internet: Surfing to Prosperity?' *Economic Commentary*, Federal Reserve Bank of Cleveland, 1 September [at <www.clev.frb.org/research/com99/0901.pdf>].
APEC (1994), *Survey on Small and Medium Enterprises*, Singapore: APEC Secretariat.
Asia-Inc (2000), *Pacific Rim Lift-Out Map*, November, Hong Kong: Praxis Communications.
Bailey, J.P. and Y. Bakos (1997), 'An Exploratory Study of the Emerging Role of Electronic Intermediaries', *International Journal of Electronic Commerce*, **1** (3), Spring, 7–20.
Baker & McKenzie (2001), 'Electronic and Digital Signature Definitions: Country-by-Country Comparison Table of Enacted Legislation' [available at <www.bmck.com/ecommerce/countrycomp.htm>].
Belson, K. (2000), 'Asia's Internet Deficit', *Business Week*, 23 October.
Benjamin, R. and R. Wigand (1995), 'Electronic Markets and Virtual Value Chains on the Information Superhighway', *Sloan Management Review*, **36** (2), Winter, 62–72.
Brookes, M. and Z. Wahhaj (2000), 'The Shocking Economic Effect of B2B', Global Economics Paper No. 37, New York: Goldman Sachs.
Coppel, J. (2000), 'E-Commerce: Impacts and Policy Challenges', Economics Department Working Paper No. 252, Organisation for Economic Cooperation and Development (OECD).

Department of Communications, Information Technology and the Arts (DOCITA) (2000), *E-Commerce Beyond 2000*, Canberra: DOCITA.

De Zwart, M. (1998), 'Electronic Commerce: Promises, Potential and Proposals', *University of New South Wales Law Journal*, **21** (2) [available at <www.austlii.edu.au/au/other/unswlj/thematic/1998/vol21no2/dezwart.html>].

Dietrich, M. (1994), *Transaction Cost Economics and Beyond: Towards a New Economics of the Firm*, London: Routledge.

Economist, The (1999), 'Asia Online', *The Economist*, 17 April [available at <www.economist.com>].

Economist, The (2000a), 'A Thinker's Guide', *The Economist*, 1 April [available at <www.economist.com>].

Economist, The (2000b), 'Island Site: When It Comes to E-government, There Is Nothing to Match Singapore', *The Economist*, 22 June [available at <www.economist.com>].

Economist Intelligence Unit (EIU) (2000), 'Introducing the EIU's E-Business-Readiness Rankings', 4 May [available at <www.ebusiness.com>].

Electronic Commerce Expert Group (ECEG) (1997), 'Issues Paper No. 1', Attorney-General's Office, Commonwealth of Australia [available at <law.gov.au/aghome/advisory/eceg/ecegissue1.htm>].

Electronic Commerce Expert Group (ECEG) (1998), 'Electronic Commerce: Building the Legal Framework', Report to the Attorney-General, Commonwealth of Australia, 31 March [available at <//law.gov.au/aghome/advisory/eceg/single.htm>].

Farrell, C. and Yuen, A. (2000), 'Asia–Pacific Moves Up a Gear', *International Tax Review*, July–August, 39–42.

Foreign Policy (2001), 'Measuring Globalisation', *Foreign Policy*, January/February, 56–65.

Gross, N. (1998), 'The Supply Chain: Leapfrogging a Few Links', *Business Week Online*, 11 June.

Internet Law and Policy Forum (1999), 'Survey of International Electronic and Digital Signature Initiatives', 24 September [available at <www.ilpf.org/digsig/survey.htm>].

Jorgenson, D.W. and K.J. Stiroh (2000), 'Raising the Speed Limit: US Economic Growth in the Information Age', *Brookings Papers on Economic Activity*, **1**, 125–211.

Lee, B.C. (1998), 'Paying for Goods and Services in the Information Age: Implications for Electronic Commerce', in C.T. Romm and F. Sudweeks (eds), *Doing Business Electronically: A Global Perspective of Electronic Commerce*, London: Springer-Verlag, pp. 163–73.

Litan, R.E. and A.M. Rivlin (2000), 'The Economy and the Internet: What Lies Ahead?', Internet Policy Institute, November [available at <www.internetpolicy.org/briefing/litan_rivlin.html>].

Malone, T.W., J. Yates and R.I. Benjamin (1987), 'Electronic Markets and Electronic Hierarchies', *Communications of the ACM*, **30** (6), June, 484–97.

Mann, C.L., S.E. Eckert and S.C. Knight (2000), *Global Electronic Commerce*, Washington, DC: Institute for International Economics.

Ministry of Posts and Telecommunications (1999), 'Legal Provisions Relating to Electronic Signatures and Certification: Promoting Electronic Commerce and Otherwise Laying the Foundation for Network-based Social and Economic Activities', (with the Ministry of International Trade and Industry and the Ministry of Justice), Japan, 19 November [available at <www.mpt.go.jp/whatsnew/english/LegalProvisions-e.html>].

Narula, R. (2001), 'R&D Collaboration by SMEs: New Opportunities and Limitations in the Face of Globalisation', Maastricht Economic Research Institute on Innovation and Technology (MERIT), MERIT-Infonomics Research Memorandum Series No. 2001–012, May [available at <meritbbs.unimaas.nl/rmpdf/ 2001/ rm2001–012.pdf>].

OECD (1997), *Report of the Group of High-Level Private Sector Experts on Electronic Commerce*, Paris: OECD.

OECD (1999), *The Economic and Social Impact of Electronic Commerce: Preliminary Findings and Research Agenda*, Paris: OECD.

OECD (2000a), *OECD Small and Medium Enterprise Outlook*, Paris: OECD.

OECD (2000b), Realising the Potential of Electronic Commerce for SMEs in the Global Economy, Workshop 3, *Enhancing the Competitiveness of SMEs in the Global Economy: Strategies and Policies* (Conference for Ministers Responsible for SMEs and Industry Ministers), Bologna, Italy, 14–15 June.

Oliner, S.D. and D.E. Sichel (2000), 'The Resurgence of Growth in the Late 1990s: Is Information Technology the Story?', *Journal of Economic Perspectives*, **14** (4), Fall, 3–22.

Poon, S. and P. Swatman (1999), 'An Exploratory Study of Small Business Internet Commerce Issues', *Information and Management*, **35** (1), 9–18.

Premkumar, G, and M. Roberts (1999), 'Adoption of New Information Technologies in Rural Small Businesses', *Omega: International Journal of Management Science*, **27** (4), 457–84.

PriceWaterhouseCoopers (1999), *SME Electronic Commerce Study*, Telecommunications Working Group and Business Facilitation Steering Group, APEC, September.

Sarkar, M.B., B. Butler and C. Steinfield (1995), 'Intermediaries and Cybermediaries: A Continuing Role for Mediating Players in the Electronic Marketplace', *Journal of Computer-Mediated Communication*, **1** (3) [available at <www.ascusc.org/jcmc/vol1/issue3/sarkar.html>].

Schmitz, S.W. (2000), 'The Effects of Electronic Commerce on the Structure of Intermediation', *Journal of Computer-Mediated Communication*, **5** (3), March.

Schoder, D. and P.L. Yin (2000), 'Building Firm Trust Online', *Communications of the ACM*, **43** (12), December, 73–9.

Spaanderman, J. and D. Ypsilanti (1997), 'Infrastructures for Electronic Trade', *OECD Observer*, **208**, October–November, 13–15.

United Nations Commission on International Trade Law (UNCITRAL) (1996), 'UNCITRAL Model Law on Electronic Commerce with Guide to Enactment' [available at <www.uncitral.org/english/texts/electcom/ml-ec.htm>].

United Nations Conference on Trade and Development (UNCTAD) (2000), *Building Confidence: Electronic Commerce and Development*, United Nations Secretariat.

University of New South Wales Law Journal (1998), Special Issue on 'Electronic Commerce: Legal Issues for the Information Age', **21** (2) [available at <www.austlii.edu.au/au/other/unswlj/issues.html#V21N2THEME>].

Van der Hof, S. (2000), 'Digital Signature Law Survey', version of 5 December [available at <rechten.kub.nl/simone/ds-lawsu.htm>].

Van Slyke, C. (2000), 'The Role of Technology Clusters in Small Business Electronic Commerce Adoption', Proceedings of the Fifth CollECTeR Conference on Electronic Commerce, Brisbane, December.

Williamson, O.E. (1975), *Markets and Hierarchies: Analysis and Antitrust Implications*, New York: Free Press.

Williamson, O.E. (1985), *The Economic Institutions of Capitalism: Firms, Markets, Relational Contracting*, London: Macmillan.

Wilson, E.J. III (2000), 'Closing the Digital Divide: An Initial Review', Internet Policy Institute [available at <www.internetpolicy.org/briefing/ErnestWilson0700.html>].

World Bank (2000), *Entering the 21st Century: World Development Report 1999/ 2000*, London: Oxford University Press.

Wu, R. (2000), 'Electronic Transactions Ordinance – Building a Legal Framework for E-commerce in Hong Kong', *Journal of Information, Law and Technology*, Issue 1 [available at <elj.warwick.ac.uk/jilt/00–1/wu.html>].

11 SMEs and Regional Labour Markets: Major Trends Since 1997

Peter van Diermen

11.1 INTRODUCTION

In 1995 the Rialdi family in Sukabumi Udik, Jakarta operated a prosperous garment business producing jeans for the local Jakarta and regional Java markets.[1] The family employed 12 young men in their small factory incorporated at the back of the residential home. The business also provided work for the wife, three sons and daughter in addition to the father's role as owner. By early 1998, the family had ceased manufacturing. The father had found work as a cutter in another nearby garment factory. The youngest son who was still at school had ceased work altogether. The two older sons worked periodically for other nearby garment factories depending on the demand for labour. The daughter had found work in a nearby commercial laundry and the wife operated a stall at a nearby local open-air market.

Of the 12 workers, three had stayed on in Sukabumi Udik and found work in other small garment factories. A further seven had returned to the village to be with family and seek work. Of these seven, over a period of eight months, four had drifted back to Sukabumi Udik after some time spent in the village without finding work, or finding work that paid less than they were earning in the city. Not all of these men, however, were being employed full time and at least one had returned several times to the village when no work was available. Of the seven returnees, one person had stayed on in the village and now worked on the family land and helped in the small general store owned by his aunt. The two remaining returnees had also left the village but had moved on to other cities and the people in Sukabumi Udik's garment district had lost contact with them. Finally, of the remaining two workers, one now worked as a salesperson in a garment kiosk at the nearby Pasar Baru market and the other worked as a street vendor selling noodles.

The above scenario is repeated, literally millions of times across the Southeast Asian region. In millions of SMEs across the region, family members and workers alike are being made redundant, employed, reemployed, changing occupations or dropping out of the workforce. In countries as varied as South Korea, Indonesia, Malaysia, the Philippines and Thailand, SMEs and their workers responded to the 1997 financial crisis. In each of these countries the broad impact of the crisis has been the same – a flight of capital out of the country, a devaluation of the currency, problems in the banking sector and corresponding impact in the real sector. Further, while significant differences exist between countries, generalisations can be made about the crisis impact on SMEs and their workers across the region.

SMEs in Southeast Asia are significant for their contribution to production but are even more significant for their contribution to employment. In all of Southeast Asia, SMEs are normally more significant for their contribution to national employment than their contribution to GDP. Therefore, this chapter focuses on the impact the 1997 financial crisis had on SMEs' contribution to regional labour markets. The chapter's analysis is extended to the five countries previously mentioned. While not providing a complete coverage of the region, it is, nevertheless, sufficient to provide a comprehensive picture. Further, it should be noted, the generalisations made in this chapter do not imply universal trends. In many of the five countries there are national specific developments that add, modify or contradict the story being told here. Therefore, an attempt is made in this chapter to also incorporate specific local details in describing and analysing more general trends.

As illustrated in the opening case study, several trends can be identified within SMEs' regional labour markets. First, labour markets have been very flexible in coping with the crisis. This, however, is not a new phenomenon. SME labour markets have always been extremely dynamic and labour within these market segments continue to use a variety of coping strategies. Second, there has been a general downward shift in size and informality. As workers have been laid off in large-scale manufacturing, services and the building sector, many of them have moved into self-employment. Moreover medium sized companies have generally found it more difficult to operate, and smaller more flexible units of production have grown in number. Third, there has been a shift of labour out of some sectors and into others. This has been in response to changing patterns of demand for goods and services as well as changing availability and costs in production inputs. Fourth, there has been a feminisation of SME labour markets. Women have remained in employment, or found work to supplement family income. The feminisation of the SMEs workforce also relates to the moving down in scale of economic activity. Women take on a variety of work to supplement household income. Fifth, and related to the feminisation of the workforce, has been the growing casualisation of the workforce. The SME labour market has always been highly casualised, but this trend has been accelerated with the financial crisis and the increase in economic uncertainty for SME entrepreneurs. Sixth, traditional support mechanisms, primarily based around rural–urban networks are breaking down under the heavy strain of sudden and high demands being placed on them. Moreover, several decades of 'modernisation' have also weakened these coping mechanisms. Finally, in an attempt to stop in-migration of workers, national boundaries within the regional SME labour market have become more important. The incentive for migrants in surplus labour economies to seek employment in other countries has increased, corresponding to the incentive for traditional recipient labour markets to close their borders to these workers.

Before examining the above trends it is important to provide some understanding of the relative contribution of SMEs to the regional labour market. This is provided in Section 11.2. Section 11.3 explores in some detail seven trends apparent in regional SME labour markets, and provides country-specific case-study and statistical evidence for each of the seven trends. Finally, the chapter's conclusions are presented in Section 11.4, which focuses on policy implications and possible future scenarios for SME regional labour markets.

11.2   SMES' CONTRIBUTION TO REGIONAL LABOUR MARKETS

During and after the 1997 financial crisis, national SME labour markets played a key role in labour absorption. As can be seen from Table 11.1 below, in all five countries, SMEs' share of employment rose significantly. In each of the five countries, this rise coincided with a period when national unemployment rates were also escalating. Thus, during the time of rising unemployment, the trend was for SMEs to account for a greater proportion of employment, signifying their importance in the labour market. Proportional growth of the SME sector during the crisis contradicts the Anderson (1982) model, which is based on historical observation. It predicts that over time the SME sector in relation to large-scale activity should begin to decline. Such a deviation from the model reinforces the flexible nature of SME regional labour markets and their significant role in national economies. A word of caution is, however, necessary in reading Table 11.1. The table does not allow for direct comparison between countries because different years are used and, more importantly, different definitions of small-scale activity and economic sectors are used. Nevertheless, the table provides an overview for illustrating the significant role of SMEs in labour absorption during and after the crisis.

Table 11.1 provides information about the relative growth in SME employment but does not indicate if real growth took place during a time of rapidly rising unemployment. Nevertheless, based on widespread anecdotal evidence and Table 11.1, it is suggested that more jobs were being lost in the large-scale sector relative to the SME sector. Under conditions of rapidly rising unemployment real growth in the SME sector may have only been small or could have been negative, but proportionately smaller than that in the large-scale sector. Moreover, Table 11.1 provides national aggregate figures and hides the dynamic changes happening within the SME sector. The literature on SMEs indicates that the sector is extremely dynamic, with a large number of entrants and exits occurring even during good times. Therefore, in the rest of this section a closer look will be taken at each of the five country labour markets.

Table 11.1
Before and After the Crisis: SMEs' Contribution to National Labour Markets and National Unemployment Rates

	Employment as % of total		Unemployment rate (%)	
Country	Before Crisis	After Crisis	Before Crisis	After Crisis
Indonesia	Year 1994	Year 1997	Year 1996	Year 1999
	15.4	19.4	4.8	6.4
S. Korea	Year 1996	Year 2000	Year 1996	Year Feb. 1999
	73.2	78.5	2	8.6
Malaysia	Year 1995	Year 2000	Year 1995	Year 1999
	36.2	39.2	2.8	4.5
Thailand	Year	Year 1998	Year Feb.1996	Year Feb.1999
	na	62	2	5.2
Philippines	Year 1995	Year	Year 1996	Year 1998
	32	na	7.4	13.1

Note: Korea's employment per cent is for all sectors, for Malaysia, Indonesia and the Philippines employment per cent is given for manufacturing only. Different definitions of small and medium enterprises are used. For Korea up to 300 employees is considered an SME, for Malaysia up to 200 employees, for Thailand fewer than 200, for Indonesia only small enterprises in manufacturing with more than five and fewer than 20 people have been included, and in the Philippines fewer than 100 employees defines an SME.

Sources: Various. International Labour Organisation (ILO) published data, Indonesia's Central Bureau of Statistics (BPS), Asian Development Bank (ADB) and World Bank published figures have been used. Thailand's Central Bank figures and Korea's National Statistics Office (NSO) data as well as UN statistical division data have been used.

Of the five countries Indonesia has the largest labour market. It was also the economy most severely affected by the financial crisis. For Indonesia, the financial crisis turned into an economic, social and political crisis that the country is still coming to terms with in the year 2001. Its labour market was also severely affected by the crisis. Table 11.2 provides an aggregate picture of the country's labour force in real numbers. From Table 11.2 it can be seen that the labour force continues to grow, driven by demographics. Large numbers of new workforce entrants will continue to enter the market. The participation rate has remained approximately the same, while, conservatively estimated, the number of people looking for work has risen to over 6 million.

Various estimates suggest that the number looking for work is much larger than official figures reveal. Furthermore, jobs lost during the height of the crisis occurred primarily in large-scale industries. Ahmed (1999, p. 5) suggests that, in 1998, during the height of the crisis, one in every five jobs was wiped out and that most of these

Table 11.2
Indonesia's Employment Statistics, 1997–99

Activity	1997	1998	1999
Labour force	89 602 835	92 734 932	94 847 178
Labour force participation rate	66.34%	66.63%	67.22%
Working	85 405 529	87 672 449	88 816 859
Looking for work	4 197 306	5 062 483	6 030 319
Unemployment rate	4.68%	5.46%	6.36%

Source: BPS National Labour Force Survey 1997, 1998, 1999.

losses occurred in large-scale industries. He further suggests that these workers did not remain unemployed but moved into the informal sector and other positions of underemployment. Suryahadi and Sumarto (1999) provides additional insight and support for the proposition that most displaced workers have moved into the informal or SME sector. Suryahadi and Sumarto (1999, p. 11) indicates that along with these changes, between May 1997 and December 1998, the incidence of poverty increased by 38.2 per cent. The increase in household poverty has primarily occurred through a reduction in household income. The decline in income was, however, less a function of household members becoming unemployed but related more to a decline in individual income earned from lower-paid work and underemployment.

Other significant changes occurred in the composition of the workforce. Data from Indonesia's National Labour Force Survey also support the thesis that workers moved into smaller-scale activity. Between 1997 and 1999 a 10 per cent increase, some 2 million more workers, occurred in self-employment. Between 1997 and 1998 self-employment assisted by family members also increased from 17.9 million to 19.7 million workers. To complete the picture, the number of full-time employees, a significant number of whom work in large-scale enterprises, fell from 30.3 million to 29.3 million. Shifts also occurred between the main branches of industry. Employment in the agriculture, forestry and fishing sector and the service sector increased significantly, while construction, mining and electricity, gas and water fell. In 1998 employment in manufacturing dipped suddenly, but in 1999 returned to 1997 levels.

In contrast to Indonesia, South Korea's labour market is normally one of labour shortage. In 1996 Korea's labour force grew from 21.2 million to 21.9 million workers. Of those in the workforce 20.8 million were employed and 420 thousand were unemployed, giving an unemployment rate of 2 per cent. By mid-1999 this had changed to 20.6 million employed and 1.4 million (6.2 per cent) unemployed.

South Korea's SME sector has been significantly influenced by government policy. Pre-1975 government policies favoured large-scale diversified conglomerates at the expense of SMEs. However, by the early 1980s the government had taken a more scale-neutral development approach. As a result, by the 1990s, Korea had an increased share of small enterprises. But also, by the early 1990s the *chaebols* had significant overcapacity and major structural problems.

By 1993 the growth of the SME sector was such that close to 20 per cent of all employment was generated in enterprises with fewer than 10 workers. Those enterprises employing more than 10 but less than 50 accounted for another 27 per cent, and enterprises with 50 or more but fewer than 100 workers accounted for a further 11 per cent of employment. Thus, a total of 58 per cent of all employment occurred in the SME sector employing fewer than 100 workers.

Despite the large number of workers employed in the SME sector, since 1990, the relative proportion of the workforce employed in industries with fewer than 200 workers has been declining. Using 1990 as a base year the Industrial Bank of Korea estimated that by the end of 1996, employment in SMEs had declined to 89.6 per cent of the 1990 figure. However, as can be seen from Table 11.1, this trend was reversed during the financial crisis when SME employment grew as a percentage of total employment.

The unemployment figures for Korea can be broken down further. As shown in Table 11.1, unemployment increased sharply between 1996 and 1999, and this occurred primarily in the *chaebol* sector. However, within the SME sector, over the same period, the largest increases in unemployment occurred in the light manufacturing industry sector. Those SMEs that were export oriented tended to shed the least amount of labour. In general, export-oriented SMEs were more competitive and more flexible than their larger counterparts. This is reflected in South Korea's trade figures. Small and medium exporters increased their proportion of total trade from 41.8 per cent in 1996 to 45.7 per cent in 1999. It is likely that the SMEs' position will be strengthened even further over the next few years as the government's reform packages for the corporate and financial sector start to have an impact.

Malaysia, similar to Korea, has moved from being a labour surplus economy to having a tight labour market and relying on migrant workers. Through most of the 1990s Malaysia experienced very rapid economic growth. From 1991 to 1996, real GDP grew at an average of 8.7 per cent per year. Much of this economic growth was attributable to exports of industrial products. These industrial exports have weak domestic linkages and rely heavily on imported inputs. Overall, the Malaysian economy has a narrow economic base and has recently lost some of its competitiveness as the labour market has tightened and real wages have outpaced productivity.

But, unlike Korea, much of Malaysia's migrant workers come from Indonesia. Around 20 per cent of Malaysia's workforce comes from across the straits and provides the country with a buffer against rapid fluctuations in the labour market, such as occurred during the 1997 financial crisis. During the crisis, migrant workers, many of them illegal entrants, were dismissed and sent home. The loss of jobs primarily occurred in low-skilled and low-paid work in large factories as well as SMEs. These migrants lessened the impact of the financial crisis on Malaysian workers.

In 1995, Malaysia's official labour force consisted of 8.1 million people, of which 7.9 were employed, giving the country an unemployment rate of 2.8 per cent. By 2000 the labour force had grown to 9.3 million, with 9.1 million employed, increasing unemployment for a short period in 1999 to 4.5 per cent before returning in 2000 to only a marginally higher rate of 2.9 per cent. Of all the states in Malaysia, only Sabah and Sarawak, at 5.7 and 4.1 per cent respectively, had significantly higher rates of unemployment. Overall, the large number of migrant workers has cushioned the impact of the crisis. In terms of large versus small, it has been estimated that most job losses occurred in the large export-oriented enclaves. Malaysian workers in the SME sector did not experience massive restructuring. However, during 1998, for the first time in several years, real wages declined by 2.3 per cent compared to real growth in 1996 and 1997 of 5.8 and 4.2 per cent, respectively. The decline in real wages is likely to have had the greatest impact on Malaysian workers in SMEs, who normally earn substantially less than workers in large-scale industries.

During the 1990s, Thailand, like Malaysia, experienced a tight labour market. While Thailand has also had a significant number of migrant workers, the impact of the crisis was not the same as it had been for Malaysia. Primarily, migrant workers accounted for a smaller proportion of the workforce and came from a more dispersed regional and ethnic background. Further, surplus labour also came from the north-eastern part of the country where wages are substantially lower. Bangkok dominates Thailand's economic landscape and draws labour from all the provinces. As a result, much of the job losses that occurred in and around Bangkok also had an impact on the relatively poor northeastern part of Thailand. Returning migrants from Bangkok tended to push up unemployment rates in the poorest parts of Thailand, thereby exacerbating the 1997 crisis impact on rural Thailand.

Looking at Thailand's aggregate employment figures it can be seen that in August 1996, prior to the crisis, employment numbered 32.2 million from a workforce of 32.7 million. The 353 thousand unemployed equalled an unemployment rate of just 1.1 per cent, indicating a tight labour market. By May 1998, almost a year after the crisis began in Thailand, unemployment had grown to 5 per cent, or equal to 1.6 million people looking for work (Thailand's National Statistical Office). However, latest national figures (August 2000) show that this rate has more than halved to 2.4 per cent. A noteworthy feature of the Thai economy is the large numbers of open unemployed. In Indonesia, where the crisis was much more severe and the proportion of actual unemployment much larger, the number of those openly registering as unemployed was much smaller.

While difficult to measure, it appears that the largest job losses occurred in the formal large-scale sector. Despite the sudden increase in unemployment, Thailand's SMEs continued to grow in numbers. Watcharaphun (2000, p. 168) notes that the SME sector grew by an average rate of 6.1 per cent during the crisis period. However, closures and start-ups were also much higher than pre-crisis. In particular, SME domestic consumption-oriented enterprises did much worse than export-oriented enterprises (Chirathivat and Chantrasawang 2000, p. 85). Within Thailand, in terms of the broad impacts of the crisis, SMEs in the southern part of the country did not do as well. During 1997–98, and in contrast to the growth of SMEs for the country as a whole, the southern part experienced a decline in total numbers of SMEs.

The final and fifth country reviewed is the Philippines. The SME sector, like those in its near neighbours, accounts for a dominant proportion of the workforce. SMEs accounted for 67 per cent of all employment in the manufacturing and service sectors. The SME sector tends to be dominated by small enterprises, with very few medium enterprises. It is suggested that this is a reflection of the policy environment that tends to favour large enterprises despite the barrage of programs for SMEs.

Like Indonesia, the Philippines is a labour surplus economy. However, unlike Indonesia, the financial crisis did not cause widespread economic contraction and massive unemployment. Prior to the crisis, in October 1996, the Philippines' labour force consisted of 29.6 million people, of which 27.4 million were employed (Philippines National Statistics Office), giving an unemployment rate of 7.4 per cent. Of those employed in October 1996, nearly 20 per cent were underemployed.[2] By October 1999 the labour force had grown to 32 million of which 29 million were employed, giving an unemployment rate of 9.4 per cent, an increase of 2 per cent over the 1996 figures. By October 1999 underemployment had also increased to over 22 per cent, an increase of more than 2 per cent. Like the other countries reviewed, anecdotal evidence indicated that many of the job losses occurred in the large-scale sector while the informal small-scale sector grew.

In terms of the Philippines' SME employment, several trends can be observed. First, as already noted, the impact of the crisis was not as severe as in other parts of Southeast Asia. Second, general observation indicates that the impact it did have was far greater in the formal, urban, large-scale segments of the economy. Third, as in many other labour surplus countries, the crisis saw a movement of workers from the formal sector to the informal/SME sector. Fourth, the financial and construction sectors were the hardest hit, while the service sector suffered the least. Fifth, and finally, male unemployment increased more rapidly than female, and for those remaining in work hours worked increased more rapidly for females compared to males (Lim 2000, p. 1304).

11.3 MAJOR TRENDS IN SME REGIONAL LABOUR MARKETS

Having described each of the five countries' contribution to SME regional labour markets, it is now possible to return to the seven trends identified earlier and provide more details for each as well as statistical evidence and case-study examples. Before doing so, some introductory remarks are necessary to the section. It is apparent from the above discussion that there are some major differences between and within the five countries. It follows from this, that the seven major trends will not be equally apparent or appear in some of the countries. Furthermore, in some cases the trends described were in existence before the crisis and merely became accelerated, or more pronounced, during and after the crisis. Finally, despite these caveats, the seven trends are significant observable changes that are, or have, taken place in Southeast Asia. Below, then, each of the seven trends is described in more detail.

First, the trend towards highly flexible SME labour markets has been identified. By its very nature the SME sector is extremely dynamic because of the low entry and exit barriers. The large number of SMEs competing in any one market segment and the resulting tight profit margins, means that small macroeconomic fluctuations in national economies have always resulted in large numbers of entry and exits. Furthermore, at the micro level SMEs throughout Southeast Asia continue to be based on the family unit. As family circumstances change, these entrepreneurs have adjusted their activity accordingly. These characteristics are carried over into very flexible labour markets. Most workers in the SME sector have little job security and tend to be highly mobile in shifting between employers in the same sector. Further, in industries where skill levels are low, movement is possible between different industries, or, as is often the case, between industry and agriculture.

Similar to entrepreneurs, workers' continuing reliance on the extended family creates additional flexibility in SME labour markets. In most of Southeast Asia, the extended family (household) continues to be the primary economic unit. Strategies for survival are based around the household unit. The outcome of such a strategy allows some members to be underemployed or temporarily out of work. This results in labour having a greater range of choices than would otherwise be possible.

During, and immediately after, the crisis workers in the SME sector were not so much faced with new economic conditions, but more an acceleration and increase in scale of change. This is particularly true for labour surplus economies such as Indonesia and the Philippines. In the Philippines the economy slowed, and workers displaced in some segments of the economy found work in others or became self-employed. In Indonesia, where the scale of restructuring in the SME sector was much greater, there was rapid exit and entry of SMEs. For example, during the height of the crisis it was reported that 200 small *tahu* (soybean cake) producers in the town of Banjarnegara near the West Java–Central Java border had exited the industry. Their demise was caused by the steep rise in the price of soybeans, the basic raw material for tahu (*Suara Pembaruan Daily* 1998). Similarly, many small clove cigarette (*rokok kretek*) producers in Central Java terminated their operations as a result of the steep rise in the price of their raw materials (van Diermen et al. 1998, p. 30). In contrast, the export-oriented SME furniture industry in Jepara, Central Java, increased in terms of numbers of enterprises and workers employed (*KOMPAS Daily* 1998, p. 9). These examples illustrate the highly dynamic nature of the SME sector, and the flexibility required in the associated labour market to accommodate such changes.

Second, a downward shift in size and informality was identified. As workers were displaced from large enterprises they sought new employment. Initially this was in the same industry and geographical location. However, given the extent of the decline in large-scale industries, few opportunities existed for employment in those industries. Alternative markets for labour grew in medium-scale, small-scale and the micro/informal sectors.

Increasingly, across much of Southeast Asia, consumer spending adjusted to lower incomes by maintaining spending on essential goods and services, and, where possible, shifting to lower-quality products. As consumers shifted to cheaper commodities and lower quality goods, produced primarily by SMEs, labour demanded by this segment of the market also increased.

Within the SME sector employment redistribution occurred from medium to small enterprises and to the micro/informal sector. On the supply side, massive unemployment in large-scale industries created a pool of surplus labour many of whom entered the informal sector – employer of last resort – out of necessity. On the demand side the decline in purchasing power by workers caused a substitution effect to domestically produced lower-quality and lower-priced goods, most often supplied by the informal/cottage enterprise sector. Enterprises that weathered the crisis best were SMEs catering for the export market using very few imported goods, and businesses producing low-priced essential commodities and products for the mass domestic market. In particular, SMEs in the agricultural sector producing for export markets grew most rapidly and hired more workers. As the World Bank (2000, p. 117) noted in its recent report on the crisis, 'Informal work increased considerably as labour shifted out of the formal sector and into self-employment, unpaid family work, and agriculture'.

Third, labour shifted out of some economic sectors and into others. Before the 1997 financial crisis, across Southeast Asia, labour's share in the agricultural sector had been falling, while the industry and service sectors had experienced long-term growth. Similarly, in most Southeast Asian countries, industrial wages in real terms had risen throughout much of the 1990s. After the financial crisis, structural adjustment saw workers shift out of industry and into the agricultural sector. For the first time in several years countries like the Philippines, Malaysia, Thailand and Indonesia had their proportion of employment in the smallholdings agriculture sector increase and large scale industry decrease. In other words, adjustment occurred from large-scale industries to SMEs in the agricultural sector.

In many cases, as the value of local Southeast Asian currencies declined against the US dollar, internationally traded commodities produced by small holders increased in value. This provided a booming agricultural market in rubber, cocoa, sugar, soybeans and coffee. In contrast, specific sectors in decline included the construction industry. Throughout Southeast Asia, construction was one of the first and hardest hit sectors. The financial crisis was partly fuelled by an over-priced and over-supplied commercial property sector. In Thailand and in Indonesia, commercial property values plummeted. Only in 2000 did construction recommence on some of the half-finished projects in Bangkok and Jakarta.

Other sectors that declined included the services sector, while the subsector of trade increased. Generally, as the crisis affected household incomes, expenditure on services was reduced. However, as workers lost their jobs in factories, a significant number moved into commodity and essential product trading to make a living. In many cases women traded agricultural products in local markets in order to increase household incomes.

The structural adjustment in the labour market was primarily fuelled by livelihood strategies. Labour moved out of inefficient oversupplied markets, such as the construction industry, and shifted to essential commodities such as agriculture. As Tubagus (1998, p. 364) argues for Indonesia, a highly flexible labour force has responded to economic fundamentals by moving from inefficient sectors to internationally competitive sectors. This corresponded to a shift in consumer demand from expensive goods and services into commodities and essential goods. For example, in much of Southeast Asia, expenditure on furniture was reduced as a larger proportion of shrinking household incomes was spent on commodities such as rice. Moreover, the corresponding labour market adjustments were possible because a significant proportion of the urban labour force remained circular migrants with strong ties to the rural sector.

Fourth and fifth, in response to the crisis there has been a feminisation and casualisation of the SME labour market. Several preliminary observations should be made before substantiating these claims. First, the rate at which the two processes of feminisation and casualisation occur is highly dependent on country specifics (Horton 1996). For example, countries such as Thailand and the Philippines have always had much higher female participation rates than other Asian countries. Second, both processes occurred before the crisis in different locations to different degrees. However, during and after the financial crisis the process became more prominent. Third, SMEs generally have a more casual labour market than large enterprises. Despite extensive labour legislation in most Southeast Asian economies, SMEs are less likely to adhere to regulations and enforcement by governments is minimal. Despite these caveats, SME labour markets have continued towards greater feminisation and casualisation.

In the Philippines, a study by Lim (2000, p. 1285) found that economic growth during the 1990s increased opportunities for women to participate in the labour force. During the financial crisis of 1997/98, male-dominated industrial and tradable sectors declined faster than the female-dominated service sector. Women were less likely to be made unemployed than men. At the same time, Lim found women who remained in work were more likely to increase their hours of work compared to men who remained in work. Similarly, a study by Horton and Mazumdar (1999, p. 2) found, across Southeast Asia, that women and children were likely to increase their employment, particularly in the informal sector, as part of a household coping strategy.

Related to the feminisation of the workforce has been the growing casualisation of the workforce. The SME labour market has always been highly casualised, but this trend has been accelerated with the financial crisis and a general increase in uncertainty. SME labour markets have always been very flexible, partly demonstrated by the high number of SME start-ups and closures (Sussangkarn et al. 1999, pp. 3–9). During and after the crisis, start-ups and closures increased dramatically. This increase also reflects an increased rate of labour employment and retrenchment. For every SME start-up and closure there is an associated labour market adjustment. Moreover, start-ups and closures are the tip of industry sector 'icebergs', with many more established SMEs adjusting labour requirements.

Sixth, the financial crisis has placed a severe burden on rural–urban networks. Rural–urban circular migration pattens are an important feature of many Southeast Asian economies. They reflect individual and, more importantly, family livelihood strategies. Over the last several decades, patterns of rural–urban migration have intensified as transportation and telecommunications networks have become more efficient, and the agricultural sector has undergone structural change.

During the financial crisis, rural–urban migration movement increased in both directions. First, in the immediate aftermath, when a large number of factories closed, migrants returned home to rural areas. However, as the crisis continued, many of the returnees found opportunities in the village little better, or indeed worse, than those in the cities they had come from. Moreover, as the recent droughts and economic decline in parts of the rural sector affected the countryside, many families found it more difficult to support returnees. The result was a significant number of migrants returning to the city.

The impact of the crisis on rural–urban networks and their ability to cope has varied greatly between and within countries. In Thailand, immediately after the collapse of several large financial institutions, the rural northeast experienced a massive influx of workers from Bangkok. However, as the rural economy began to slow down and remittances from the city dried up, many migrants returned to Bangkok. As Crispin and Gaew (1999, p. 22) note:

> Thailand's migration cycle has sharply reversed. Many of those who left Bangkok two years ago have returned, putting pressure on the overcrowded city's social services and raising levels of desperation.

In Indonesia, a similar, but less-intensive, pattern can be observed. Firman (1999, p. 78) notes that there has been an increase in the number of migrants returning to the countryside, placing an additional burden on rural households. However, he is uncertain whether this will weaken or strengthen rural–urban networks. Other evidence suggests that Indonesia's rural–urban networks are breaking down. Suhendar (1998, p. 7) notes that many returnees in the districts around Bandung city do not have the skills to farm and are, therefore, unable to be absorbed into the rural workforce.

Seventh, across Southeast Asia the economic crisis resulted in national boundaries taking on greater significance, either in preventing labour entry or as obstacles to workers seeking higher-paid labour markets. From the mid-1980s onwards labour flows across national boundaries were important for the region's long-term growth. Throughout the 1980s and 1990s, tight labour markets in Japan, Korea, Singapore, Malaysia and Thailand relied on labour surplus markets. Labour came from several countries including many of the socialist Southeast Asian countries but also primarily from the Philippines and Indonesia. Furthermore, as Athukorala and Manning (1999, p. 2) note, a significant proportion of these foreigners worked in SMEs.

Following the financial crisis, all the regional governments made efforts to return foreign workers in order to increase the opportunities for their own workers. In Malaysia, Thailand and South Korea the governments rounded up illegal workers and repatriated them (Athukorala and Manning 1999, p. 219). These governments also made efforts to prevent new entrants coming in and seeking work. Legal migrant workers were also discouraged through new regulations.

In the short term, national government efforts have been effective in repatriating workers and discouraging new workers from coming. Nevertheless, in the long term, there are important pressures that might see the resumption of migrant flows. First, wage differentials have not declined and will continue to encourage both legal and illegal migration. Second, many of the jobs vacated by migrants in the SME sector are those that local workers have shunned and are unlikely to take up (Athukorala and Manning 1999, p. 219). Third, SMEs are likely to face growing wage bills in replacing illegal foreign workers with locals. This has led businesses to lobby their governments to ease the restrictions on foreign labourers. For example, in South Korea the small business lobby has pressured the government to ease restrictions (Kim Jung Min 2001, p. 63).

11.4   CONCLUSIONS AND POLICY IMPLICATIONS

It is difficult to generalise the impact the crisis had on labour markets across Southeast Asia. In general, employment declined more in the large-scale formal sector than in the SMEs sector. In many cases the small informal employment sector grew as it absorbed displaced labour from the large manufacturing sector. The impact, however, varied between rural and urban areas and between labour shortage and labour surplus economies. Impacts also varied depending on the proportion of labour provided by foreign workers. As a rule, the greater the proportion of foreign workers the smaller the impact on the local labour market. Despite these and other dissimilarities, this chapter has tried to outline some of the major impacts the crisis had on regional labour markets. In particular, it highlighted seven major trends that could be observed to various degrees in all of the regions' labour markets.

Several important issues are worth flagging at this point. The impact of the crisis on unions and their role in the SME sector is a significant topic worth further investigation. Over the last decade unions have gained a greater importance within large-scale industrial activity. Across much of East Asia, as a result of more than a decade of economic growth, unions' influence has increased. In Indonesia, for example, unions have, since the early 1990s, become more active, and by the late 1990s strikes and labour unrest had increased significantly in the country. While in Malaysia, unions have been partly responsible for the rapid growth in real wages.

This influence, while traditionally limited to large-scale economic activity and the public sector, had slowly begun to influence SMEs. Existing labour legislation was slowly being extended to medium sized enterprises, and workers within medium sized companies were becoming more aware of their rights. Since the crisis, however, existing labour legislation has often been relaxed. For example, in Thailand, a series of amendments have been considered to the Labour Protection Act of 1998, and minimum wage regulations have been relaxed. Moreover, the bargaining position of labour has been weakened by the high unemployment rates and large number of corporate failures. The result has been to increase the dualism and inequality within the labour market. These issues, however, are being played out in different ways in various locations and will need to be more fully examined elsewhere.

A second important issue not dealt with in this chapter, but of some magnitude, is the issue of child labour and SMEs. In Southeast Asia, for much of the 1990s, the practice of child labour had been on the decline and was primarily limited to unpaid work in family businesses and concentrated in rural areas. However, in response to the crisis, child labour has been on the increase in several Asian countries. Families have withdrawn children from school, as they could no longer afford the cost. Also, families used child labour as a survival strategy of diversifying income sources. On the demand side, as the enforcement of labour laws has become more relaxed and employers have sought out cheaper labour, the demand for child labour has increased, particularly in the less regulated SME sector. In some places the strategy has been a short-term response; however, the long-term consequences of such a strategy for children and the labour force need to be analysed and more detail is required than is possible here.

Other issues that deserve further mention include the decline in real wages, estimated by some to be in the range of 30 to 50 per cent (Sussangkarn et al. 1999), and health and safety issues and the role of micro finance. All of these topics are worth further investigation in relation to regional SME labour market responses to the crisis.

Finally, it is worth mentioning that in many Southeast Asian economies government policy makers are focusing on SMEs as a solution to the crisis. In both Thailand and Indonesia, for example, the government has explicitly identified growth of the SME sector as leading the economic recovery. Such emphasis has important implications for regional SME labour markets.

NOTES

1   This vignette is sketched from an extensive 1995 survey of the Sukabumi garment cluster and a 1998 follow up survey of the area. In addition, between 1995 and 2000 several short informal visits were made to the area (van Diermen 1997).

2   Defined as those working less than 40 hours a week and wanting more hours.

REFERENCES

Ahmed, I. (1999), 'Indonesia's Crisis and Recovery: The Myths and Reality', Occasional Discussion Paper Series No.1, Jakarta: ILO, April.

Anderson, D. (1982), 'Small Industries in Developing Countries: A Discussion of Issues', *World Development*, **10** (11), 913–48.

Athukorala, P.C. and C. Manning (1999), *Structural Change and International Migration in East Asia: Adjusting to Labour Scarcity*, Melbourne: Oxford University Press.

Chirathivat, S. and N. Chantrasawang (2000), 'Experience of SMEs in the Financial Crisis in Thailand', in M.A. Abdullah and M.I.B. Baker (eds), *Small and Medium Enterprises in Asian Pacific Countries: Volume I: Roles and Issues*, New York: Nova Science Publishers.

Crispin, S.W. and W.N. Gaew (1999), 'Thailand: Cycle of Despair', *Far Eastern Economic Review*, **162** (38), 23 September, 22.

Firman, T. (1999), 'Guest Editorial, Indonesian Cities under the "Krismon": A Great Urban Crisis in Southeast Asia', *Cities*, **16** (2), 69–82.

Horton, S. (1996), *Women and Industrialisation in Asia*, London: Routledge.

Horton, S. and D. Mazumdar (1999), 'Vulnerable Groups and the Labour Market: The Aftermath of the Asian Financial Crisis', World Bank, ILO, Japan Ministry of Labour, Japan Institute of Labour Seminar, Tokyo.

Kim Jung Min (2001), 'Hard Labour: Attempts to Improve Life for the Vast Army of Illegal Workers are Meeting Tough Resistance', *Far Eastern Economic Review*, **164** (12), 29 March, 63.

KOMPAS Daily (1998), 22 March.

Lim, J.Y. (2000), 'The Effects of the East Asian Crisis on the Employment of Women and Men: The Philippines Case', *World Development*, **28** (7), 1285–306.

Suara Pembaruan Daily (1998), March.

Suhendar, E. (1998), 'Villages Under the Crisis', Workshop paper, International Workshop on the Impacts of the Economic Crisis on Labour in Indonesia, Akatega, Bandung, 12–14 July.

Suryahadi, A. and S. Sumarto (1999), 'Update on the Impact of the Indonesian Crisis on Consumption Expenditure and Poverty Incidence: Results from the December 1998 Round of 100 Village Survey', SMERU Working Paper, Jakarta, Small Medium Enterprise Response Unit (SMERU), August.

Sussangkarn C., F. Flatters and S. Kittiprapas (1999), 'Comparative Social Impacts of the Asian Economic Crisis in Thailand, Indonesia, Malaysia and the Philippines: A Preliminary Report', *TDRI Quarterly Review*, **14** (1), 3–9.

Tubagus, F.D. (1998), 'Social Impact of the Indonesian Economic Crisis', *The Indonesian Quarterly*, **26** (4), 325–64.

van Diermen, P. (1997), *Small Business in Indonesia*, London: Ashgate.

van Diermen, P., Kian Wie Thee, M. Tambunan and T. Tambunan (1998), 'The IMF

50-point Program: Evaluating the Likely Impact on SMEs', A Report for The Asia Foundation, Jakarta: The Asia Foundation.

Watcharaphun, P. (2000), 'Liquidity Problems of Small Businesses in Thailand', M.A. Abdullah and M.I.B. Baker (eds), *Small and Medium Enterprises in Asian Pacific Countries: Volume I: Roles and Issues*, New York: Nova Science Publishers.

World Bank (2000), *East Asia: Recovery and Beyond*, Washington, DC: World Bank.

12 From Miracle to Crisis and Beyond: The Role of Entrepreneurship and SMEs in Asia

Hock-Beng Cheah

12.1 INTRODUCTION: SMES AND THE DEVELOPMENT PROCESS IN ASIA

The economies of many Asian countries do not rely significantly on the activities of large firms engaged in the production of radically innovative goods and services, promoted by creative entrepreneurs. Instead, their international competitiveness has been based, especially in the early phases, principally on the production (and export) of unskilled, labour-intensive, and relatively low-value-added goods and services. These economies have been dominated by adaptive entrepreneurs, engaged in small-scale enterprise, product and process imitation, subcontracting and spatial arbitrage. Nevertheless, this has not prevented several Asian countries from 'catching up' with previously more economically developed and technologically advanced nations. Indeed, the causes of the significant shifts in competitive advantage, including the diffusion of technology from more-advanced countries, can be attributed to the power of adaptive entrepreneurship,[1] assisted in some cases by the supportive and protective efforts of governments, that enabled Asian countries to catch up rapidly with the more advanced industrial countries.

For instance, a prominent characteristic of Hong Kong's industrial structure is that each industry has only a few large undertakings and a large number of small concerns whose activities are largely responsive to buyers' orders, especially to those from original equipment manufacturers or to subcontracted orders from other firms (Ho 1992, p. 111). In 1950, the average size of a manufacturing firm was approximately 55 persons per establishment. By 1992, the average size was 14 persons per

---

This chapter benefited from the helpful comments of two anonymous reviewers.

establishment (Hong Kong Government Industry Department 1991, p. 17). Thus, over time, the small firms had increased their dominance. Indeed, the average size of Hong Kong's industrial undertakings, which was small by international standards, had actually become smaller over a period of rising prosperity. Thus, the perception that the dominance of SMEs is only a characteristic of an early stage of development, and that these establishments are destined to be eliminated progressively, is not true.

Small manufacturers in Hong Kong survive on small profit margins by being flexible, alert to economic changes, and responding rapidly to market needs (Chau 1993, p. 25). Cheng (1982, p. 50) remarked that Hong Kong's manufacturing firms are 'capable of accepting orders subject to widely differing requirements as to amount, date of delivery and special specifications, and there is a constant attempt to develop new lines of products in response to change in the world market'. The small-scale enterprises play an indispensable part in this regard. For small firms, with limited overheads, machinery and personnel, the opportunity cost of shifting to other sectors and new activities is relatively low.

Furthermore, most Hong Kong manufacturers adopt a short-term planning perspective. They do not commit themselves to long-term investments. Decisions are made on an *ad hoc* basis. They rush into the manufacture of the most popular products that have low value added, low profit margins but a quick return (Cheung 1982).

Sit and Wong (1989, p. 27) noted that 'flexibility and diversity of products through small changes in design, creating a new variety of products within the same industries and filling existing market niches are significant elements behind the dynamics of the Hong Kong manufacturing industry'. Referring to this practice as 'guerrilla capitalism', Lam and Lee (1992, p. 109) reported that small and medium family-owned firms succeeded by exploiting market opportunities using the strategy of a guerrilla force: seek out an opportunity for high profit margins, develop a formula, exploit it by rapidly flooding the market before the established firms can respond, make profits over the short term, and then leave the market for another one, before competition forces the price down to the point where they are no longer profitable without large-scale investments in technology or infrastructure.

In China, the bulk of the SMEs are in the non-state sector, which includes a broad range of enterprises from urban collectives, to town and village enterprises (TVEs), private and individual enterprises, and foreign funded enterprises; the last comprising joint ventures and wholly foreign-owned enterprises (Cheah 2000a, p. 165). According to Jefferson and Rawski (1994, p. 61), 'Chinese manufacturers are enmeshed in multi-layered innovation ladders that link international firms and their Chinese branches to small and unsophisticated township and village enterprises through the agency of state-managed factories, laboratories, and universities'.[2] Several studies indicate that the non-state sector has been more dynamic, grew faster, and has surpassed the state sector in terms of output, employment and exports (Goodhart and Xu 1996, pp. 5–6; East Asia Analytical Unit 1997, pp. 355–73). Despite this, the non-state enterprises had poorer access to: bank finance; technology; skilled employees and managers; adequate transport and distribution facilities; and face more government impediments.

In this situation, non-state enterprises have had to operate more flexibly and efficiently. Through strategies of imitation, subcontracting, wheeling and dealing, and other adaptive strategies, enterprises in this sector have sought to cope with, and to overcome, their difficulties.[3]

Many enterprises in this sector have capitalised on the lower cost of Chinese labour to gain competitive advantage in low-value-added manufacturing assembly and production, reliant on relatively simple skills and mature technology. They have contributed to China's growing competitiveness in unskilled labour intensive activities in recent years. To succeed, this development did not involve creative entrepreneurship, only relatively minor, incremental and evolutionary adaptations. The relative ease of this development was also a significant factor in the speed and extent of the growth of this sector, once government permitted its emergence.

Foreign funded enterprises now constitute a significant and growing constituency in this sector. They have facilitated and promoted the influx of simple manufacturing activities, and subcontracting, capitalising on the large pool of lower-cost labour and other advantages. In this respect these enterprises are transferring and replicating adaptive activities and strategies previously employed in other rapidly growing countries in the region.

The most important foreign investors in China have been overseas Chinese entrepreneurs (see Goodhart and Xu 1996, p. 36; Weidenbaum and Hughes 1996; Haley et al. 1998). These entrepreneurs generally began as small Chinese family businesses (CFBs) in Hong Kong, Taiwan, Singapore and other countries in Southeast Asia,[4] developed into significant Chinese family business networks (CFBNs) in the Asian region and, more recently, these CFBNs have begun to extend their activities globally.[5]

The origins and mode of operation of these enterprises illustrate the concept of adaptive entrepreneurship very well. Most CFBs began as small traders, itinerant vendors, artisans or subcontractors; and many of the entrepreneurs had previously been employed as migrant labourers, small farmers, or employees of other private enterprises (see Wang 1991; Rolls 1992, 1996).[6] Their initial business ventures commenced on a small scale, on an individual basis or a partnership, and often had to rely on support from family members or other persons linked by clan, locality of origin, dialect or guild affiliation.

'Most overseas Chinese businesses remain relatively small; [however] over time, the total size of all a family's business may add up to a large conglomerate' (Haley et al. 1998, p. 117). Indeed, over time, the successful overseas Chinese entrepreneurs have diversified into a wide range of products, services, industries and locations. For instance, these entrepreneurs ventured from trading into restaurants and hotels, real estate management and property development, banking and insurance, transportation, agribusiness (rubber, sugar, palm oil and pineapple plantations), manufacturing (food products, textiles and clothing and electronics), and a host of other activities within as well as between countries (see Haley et al. 1998, pp. 58–9). Consequently, 'The net result of these cross-border investment flows by the overseas Chinese community has been the rapid emergence of a Chinese-based economy that is the epicenter for industry, commerce, and finance in Southeast Asia' (Weidenbaum and Hughes 1996, p. 16). In the process, the CFBNs have built up aggregate assets estimated at more than US$500 billion (Weidenbaum and Hughes 1996, p. 25).

The management and decision-making methods of CFBs remain somewhat traditional, unorthodox and even esoteric in certain respects (compared to modern Western business management methods). One reason offered for their success is that membership in the extensive intra-Chinese trading network enables the CFBs to 'economise on the 'high transaction costs' associated with doing business in China and elsewhere in Southeast Asia' (Weidenbaum and Hughes 1996, pp. 52–3). This method of operation is particularly apt for undertaking incremental and evolutionary innovations in uncertain and unstable environments.

In such environments, CFBs, acting as adaptive entrepreneurs, seek to discover profitable discrepancies, gaps, mismatches of knowledge and information that others have not yet perceived and exploited, and to capitalise on the opportunity for gain or advantage which that discovery provides. In that process the CFBs generate more knowledge about the situation, reduce the gap between themselves and the market leaders through a process of 'catching up', and reduce the general level of uncertainty over time (for themselves, and often for others, too). Through activities such as arbitrage, speculation, risk-taking, incremental and evolutionary innovation, production of generic or no-brand goods, or even through gross or outright imitation, the CFBs seek to respond quickly and flexibly to perceived market signals and opportunities ahead of others. Such activities distinguish them as adaptive entrepreneurs. Over time the CFBs create wealth for themselves and others, promote development, and generate a tendency towards equilibrium.

From this perspective it is not surprising that the CFBs, adaptive entrepreneurs *par excellence*, have invested substantially in China. While the historical, ethnic and cultural affinities of the CFBs have been helpful and contributory factors (see Haley et al. 1998, pp. 28–69), it is the capabilities and experiences of the CFBs as adaptive entrepreneurs, familiar with operating in uncertain and unstable situations, characterised by significant 'informational void', that are of particular relevance and value in China and other similar situations as it seeks to manage the transition from a planned towards a more market-oriented economy.[7]

Empirical research has indicated (see Cheah and Yu 1996, among others) that the CFBs and their associated networks in Hong Kong and elsewhere have also invested in China to maintain or to extend the viability of their small-scale economic activities. Such activities have been very flexible, and they enable firms to survive on relatively small profit margins by being able to respond quickly to changes in market conditions. With limited overheads, machinery and personnel, the opportunity cost of shifting to other sectors and to new activities is relatively low for such firms. The opening up of the special economic zones and other accessible production locations in China has extended the opportunity and the scope for such firms to operate.

Such strategies and activities have contributed significantly to economic development in Hong Kong, China and other Asian countries. At the macro level, evidence on changes in revealed comparative advantage presented by Toshio Watanabe and others point to significant changes in competitiveness between different countries in various industries; and to the occurrence in Asia of a catching-up process in the 'flying geese pattern' (see Akamatsu 1961; Yamazawa et al. 1991; Watanabe 1992, pp. 148–60). Empirical analysis of United Nations trade data also shows that there have been significant shifts in competitive advantage between countries in the Asia–Pacific region in five trade categories: agricultural resource-intensive exports; mineral resource-intensive exports; unskilled labour-intensive exports; human capital-intensive exports; and technology-intensive exports (Cheah 1995). Over the 1965–93 period the findings suggest that the natural resource-rich countries, the USA, Canada and Australia are maintaining or improving their competitiveness in natural resource-based exports, while the Asian countries are losing ground in those areas but rapidly gaining ground in areas where labour, skilled and unskilled, and technology are the principal resources.[8]

One result of the process of 'catching up' by Japan and other Asian countries has been the corresponding rise in their general standard of living. The evidence indicates that Japan, in particular, together with Hong Kong, Singapore and South Korea, have narrowed the gap with and, in some instances, surpassed the developed Western countries such as the USA, Canada and Australia based on comparisons of per capita gross national product, the human development index and indicators of welfare levels (Cheah 1995). This represents a significant shift in the balance of growth, wealth and power in the world. While many different factors contributed to this shift, this chapter explores in particular the role of adaptive entrepreneurship and the contribution of SMEs in the economic development process.

The chapter proceeds as follows. Section 12.2 focuses upon different forms of adaptive entrepreneurial strategies that have been adopted among SMEs in Asia which has enabled them to grow and evolve as the economies within which they operate develop. Section 12.3 analyses the Asian crisis in the context of a Schumpeterian perspective of catching up and slowing down in the development process. Section 12.4 looks at the new dynamics of production, and the movement towards a diversified production system. Finally, Section 12.5 provides a summary of the major conclusions from this chapter.

12.2 FORMS OF ADAPTIVE ENTREPRENEURIAL STRATEGIES AMONG ASIAN SMES

Earlier creative innovations in previously more advanced Western industrial nations provided many opportunities for adaptive entrepreneurship in Asia. Adaptive entrepreneurs capitalised upon these opportunities through strategies such as product and process imitation, subcontracting and spatial arbitrage, undertaken by both local and foreign enterprises.[9]

12.2.1 Imitation

Imitators may capitalise on the success of others in various ways. While imitators have not invented a product or a service, they may be able to improve it and position it better. In this way, imitation adds new product attributes so that the modified product or service is somewhat different from the original and/or caters for a slightly different market niche.

Imitation may be seen as a form of 'strategic followership' (Hagedoorn 1989, p. 91). It is a strategy that is available when the market becomes more stable. As the market segments are more easily identified, marketing research can establish consumer preferences more clearly. This strategy enables firms to reduce the level of risk that they face.[10]

Imitation strategies may take various forms. These include: reverse engineering, entrepreneurial spin-offs, product and process licensing, serving as original equipment manufacturers, and even counterfeiting. Nevertheless, to prosper, imitators must possess some competitive advantage not available to the original innovators. In developing countries this may include lower production costs derived from cheaper product development and labour costs. In addition, because imitators may face keen competition from other actual or potential imitators in the industry, they may need to be more efficient. In this respect they may face continuing pressures to modify the product, and to improve the production and distribution processes further.

In the electronics industry, Hobday (1995, p. 1189) noted that 'latecomer innovation began with incremental improvements to the manufacturing process. As competencies were learned minor innovations to product designs were made, and eventually some new products were offered to the market'. Through this process, Asian manufacturing firms learned to innovate. Over time the improved products offered by the latecomers could even be significantly superior to the original.

Similarly, Hong Kong's manufacturers traditionally have received technical know-how from foreign agents operating in Hong Kong, learnt through imitation, and relied upon trading firms to market their products. According to Davies et al. (1993, p. 12), 'Hong Kong's manufacturing industries traditionally are oriented towards incremental, rather than radical change, technological followership rather than leadership and cost reduction rather than product differentiation'. They have competed in world markets on the basis of their capacity to manufacture at low cost and their flexibility to meet changing patterns of demand at very short notice. In aggregate terms, Hong Kong continues to have significant competitive advantage in the export of unskilled labour-intensive goods. Although this competitive advantage has been eroded since the 1960s, it has not been surpassed by increased competitive advantage in the export of other, more technically sophisticated, goods.[11]

12.2.2 Subcontracting

Subcontracting has been another significant feature of the economic development process in many Asian countries, ranging from Japan to Hong Kong (Ho 1992, pp. 111, 117), Taiwan, South Korea, Malaysia, Thailand and China. It enables firms to find a niche for themselves by serving some of the needs of other, often larger, firms. Smaller firms may have cost advantages in producing simple parts and components, in assembling diversified products, or in providing industrial services to customers with specific requirements. By participating in a process of co-production with the contractor, the subcontracting firm can also gain significant advice, assistance, and access to a variety of resources, to the mutual benefit of both parties. By these means the growth and performance of the subcontractor may be facilitated and enhanced significantly.[12]

Like the imitators, subcontractors must also be able to draw upon competitive advantages not available to the other firms that contract for their products or services. For instance, subcontractors may be able to produce more efficiently or at lower cost by employing simpler technology or labour-intensive techniques operated by cheaper and lower-skilled labour. They may also be capable of producing in smaller batches or being able to change their output mix more flexibly and quickly than the contractors. Thus, small manufacturers survive on small profit margins by being alert to changes, and by responding rapidly to market needs (Chau 1993, p. 25).[13]

From the early stages of Hong Kong's industrialisation, many trading firms contracted with small local factories to produce the goods that they traded. A survey by King and Man (1979, pp. 58–9) revealed that small factories in Kwun Tong and in Hong Kong depended to a significant degree on subcontracts from larger firms, and marketed their products through wholesalers, merchants or export houses. Similarly, Woronoff (1980, pp. 142–5) observed that many small firms belonged to original equipment manufacturers, producing for companies overseas or multinationals. Import–export houses provided technical advice and assistance in the designing and the marketing of a small factory's products, and helped small manufacturers to secure loans. More recently, Ho (1992, p. 117) noted that a large number of small firms in Hong Kong have acted as subcontractors for larger manufacturing concerns and export houses producing components or complete products.

Unlike the subcontracting system in Japan, which is based on a steady relationship, subcontracting in Hong Kong is based on short-term convenience (Sit et al. 1979, p. 345). Firms resorted to subcontracting when they did not possess the required capabilities, and also when orders exceeded their available capacities (see Sit et al. 1979, p. 345). In some cases, firms might have no production site at all. They simply operated an office for administrative purposes, and subcontracted all orders that they received. Ho (1992, p. 117) concluded that, just like Japan's early industrial development, small-scale enterprises in Hong Kong are well integrated into the economy through the widespread practice of subcontracting, and this contributes to the efficiency of the manufacturing sector and the maintenance of Hong Kong's competitive edge in export markets by reducing production costs. Subcontracting is also an important feature of the adaptive response of Hong Kong manufacturers to rapid changes and fluctuations in export markets.

12.2.3   Spatial Arbitrage

Adaptive entrepreneurs engage in spatial arbitrage when (a) they buy goods at a lower price and subsequently sell them to customers in a different location at higher prices (arbitrage traders); (b) they shift production activities from a location where production and operating costs are higher to other areas where the corresponding costs are lower (arbitrage producers). Arbitrage traders are widely observable in the large numbers of marketplaces, departmental stores, emporiums and shopping centres, and import–export ventures in almost all Asian countries. Arbitrage producers are represented by the large number of multinational corporations operating in Asia, as well as by local and foreign firms that establish subsidiaries and production facilities in different regions within a country.

Hong Kong's manufacturers maintained their competitive edge by being alert to cost reduction opportunities. In particular, when they experienced an erosion of cost competitiveness, they moved parts of their operations to lower-cost regions. Previously they shifted production to countries like Indonesia, Thailand, Malaysia and Taiwan in order to reduce costs (Chen 1983, p. 91). In more recent years, China's 'open door policy' presented Hong Kong producers a closer opportunity for maintaining cost competitiveness through access to cheaper land, abundant supplies of cheaper labour and even to cheaper qualified engineers. By combining the lower-cost advantages in other Asian countries with Hong Kong's marketing expertise, Hong Kong's entrepreneurs have been able to capitalise on the significant spatial competitive differentials in the region. This did not require them to undertake any radical innovations, only the ability to perceive profitable opportunities for arbitrage activities.

Asian countries offer numerous profitable opportunities for arbitrage traders because of the imperfection of many markets. Similarly, international and regional disparities have provided numerous opportunities for arbitrage production, to achieve lower production and operating costs. This has encouraged American, European and increasing numbers of Asian multinational firms to establish subsidiary plants and production joint ventures in various Asian countries and regions. Over time, as some Asian countries develop more quickly than others, the relative cost structures change, and this leads to new possibilities for arbitrage in both trade and production. The flow of foreign direct investments initially from the USA and Europe to South Korea, Taiwan, Singapore, Malaysia, Thailand and the Philippines, followed by subsequent foreign direct investments from Japan, South Korea, Taiwan, Singapore and Hong Kong to Indonesia, Vietnam, China, India, Sri Lanka and other Asian countries, reflects these changing dynamics.

12.2.4 Diversification

In the early stages of their development, Asian countries had relatively large populations, unskilled and low-wage labour, limited capital, and limited access to modern technology. Initially, the population engaged mainly in agricultural activities such as farming and fishing, or in entrepôt trade and retail activities in Singapore and Hong Kong. With the initiation of a process of industrialisation, entrepreneurs shifted resources from the agricultural sector to the manufacturing sector; initially into labour-intensive manufactures such as plastic products, textiles and garments, footwear, and simple electronics products and components (Ting 1985, p. 9).

Over time, several Asian countries have moved away from labour-intensive, simple technology, low value-added industries, and turned towards higher-value-added, more-skilled and technology-intensive industries, and established their own internationally renowned market brands. This has been spurred by a general rise in wages and other costs. Producers from some Asian countries are now able to supply good-quality products at relatively low cost. Consequently, entrepreneurs from the more-developed Asian countries have increasingly shifted their investments and production activities abroad, into lower-cost production locations as well as into the final markets for their products. This process has created further changes in the regional and international division of labour.

Thus, over time, the activities of adaptive entrepreneurs also led to a diversification into new economic activities: from farming and fishing to light industries, from simple commerce and retail activities to heavy industries, property development, banking and financial services, and the information technology industry. This has accompanied and promoted a parallel process of structural change in the economy: from agricultural-based activities to the rise of manufacturing, and the growing prominence of the service sector. While Japan, South Korea, Taiwan and Singapore have sought to develop more sophisticated manufacturing bases, Hong Kong enterprises have diversified more significantly into the service sector (Chen 1989, p. 36). This process involved both intra-sectoral and inter-sectoral changes in the economy in these countries. As a result of the diversification activities of the entrepreneurs, resources have been shifted from the manufacturing sector to real estate, financial and other service activities. Each profitable shift in activity by the entrepreneurs enhanced the value of the resources they employed.[14]

These examples of experiences of SMEs in Hong Kong, China, and other Asian countries, together with the activities of the CFBs in the region, demonstrate the important role of entrepreneurship in economic development and, specifically, the role of adaptive entrepreneurship. These experiences suggest that SMEs can play an important and continuing role in the development process, even at higher income levels. The ability of such enterprises to prosper through such strategies as subcontracting, imitation, arbitrage and diversification, also help to provide flexibility and dynamism to the economy.

12.3   THE CRISIS: A SCHUMPETERIAN PERSPECTIVE OF CATCHING UP AND SLOWING DOWN IN THE DEVELOPMENT PROCESS

The rapid post-Second World War growth of Japan and other Asian countries may be attributed, among other things, to the power of adaptive entrepreneurship, the diffusion of technology from more-advanced countries and, in some cases, the supportive efforts of governments, which enabled Asian countries to catch-up rapidly with the more advanced industrial countries (see Wade 1990; MacIntyre 1994). These developments were facilitated earlier by the favourable post-war international economic environment and US goodwill. Specifically, in the immediate decades after 1945, several Asian countries benefited from the creation of the Bretton Woods system of fixed exchange rates, and the increasing liberalisation of world trade. These were influenced by liberal and supportive US policies, which were influenced by Cold War politics. These developments were very significant for the development of various Asian countries and for Europe too (see Hersh 1993; and Schwartz 1994, p. 205). In this environment, governments in the Asian region also actively promoted national production capabilities and competitiveness.

Asian newly industrialising countries (NICs) benefited from their pursuit of an export-oriented industrialisation strategy, and from the influx of direct foreign investments. This strategy capitalised upon the growth in the international economy and contributed significantly to domestic growth and development. The rising employment and wage levels contributed to improvements in living standards, while the proliferation and growth of local private and state enterprises strengthened indigenous productive capacity and expanded the bases for local capital accumulation.

One result of these developments has been a significant rise in the intensity of competition, resulting from rapidly expanding production capacity. This has led to a tendency towards deflation. Deflationary tendencies arise from price cutting among a host of products and industries. These have ranged from agricultural commodities to petroleum products, integrated circuits and computers, which have all experienced substantial falls in prices.

The intensification of competition has also encouraged Japanese and other Asian firms to place increased emphasis on product and process innovation, and to undertake their own foreign direct investments. However, many competitors have directed their efforts at promoting the same activities, products or industries. The contrast between the high degree of complementarity in the economies of the USA, Europe and Japan in the 1950s, and the increased competition resulting from the convergence of economic capabilities in the 1990s was highlighted by Lester Thurow (1993, pp. 29–30). See also Solman and Friedman (1982); Brain (1999). This intensified the tendency for zero-sum situations to arise.

At the same time the achievements of the Asian countries, especially Japan, Hong Kong, Singapore, Taiwan, South Korea, Malaysia and others, also helped to undermine their previous competitive advantages. This occurred through rising wage rates as a consequence of higher levels of employment and growing labour shortages, appreciation of their currencies, as well as increasing capital outflows in the form of direct foreign investments into both developed and developing economies. These culminated in the so-called Asian economic crisis that was precipitated in August 1997, with lingering effects that continue to the present.

Contrary to the beliefs of conventional, neo-classical economics, development does not occur in a continuously harmonious process of evolutionary change, and these developments can be appreciated better from a Schumpeterian perspective. Unlike the conventional approach, the Schumpeterian approach expects development to be an uneven and discontinuous process characterised by changing phases.[15] Schumpeter conceived of the development process as passing through the phases of recovery, boom, recession and depression. For him, each recovery is powered by a new group of products, industries and technology.[16] These constitute the new starting points of the development process, and it is the diffusion and maturation of the earlier products, industries and technologies that bring each cycle of development to its end. In Schumpeter's conception, these dynamic processes and their associated changes do not lead to a situation of history merely repeating itself in recurring cycles; rather, these developments lead to fundamental changes in the economic system, that is to its transformation.

Moreover, for Schumpeter, the new generally does not arise from the old, nor does it operate largely to complement the latter; instead the new competes with the old for resources, markets, as well as in shaping the very forms and directions of development. Thus, the different growth experiences of 'slowing down' of the mature economies and 'catching up' by the emerging economies, leads to a relative convergence of economic structures and productive capacities. The tendency for a relative convergence of economic structures and production capacities, over time, observed, among others, by Knies (1853, p. 117), League of Nations (1945) and Hoffmann (1958, p. 147) is likely to create major structural problems for at least three reasons.

First, the expansion of existing capacity is generally less difficult than the initial efforts to establish production capability, where none had previously existed. Second, the establishment and expansion of productive capacity are both easier than the dissolution of this capacity, once it has come into existence (see Salter 1966, p. 22). Consequently, the problems of surplus capacity can easily become endemic (see Downie 1958, pp. 117–20; Strange 1979; and Strange and Tooze 1981). Third, the existence of substantial surplus capacity and the accompanying recession is likely to slow down the rate of implementation of technical innovations (Downie 1958, p. 119). This then contributes to prolonging the problem of surplus capacity and, with it, the intense competitive pressures in industry.

Excess capacity in the production of final consumer goods leads, in time, to the extension of the problem to capital goods; and the resolution of this domestic problem in one country through exports, eventually reproduces the problem at the international level. This and, in particular, the rapidity of the late-developers' forward surge, at particular phases in the international development process, creates Schumpeter's 'swarm-effect' on a world scale. The general consequences associated with this would be a marked rise in the level and intensity of competition, severe profit squeeze, ending of the boom, a slide into recession, a 'shake-out' of competitors within the system, and the 'end' of development.[17]

The economic recession ('crisis') is a generalised one; its causes are fundamentally structural (or systemic) in nature; and, from a Schumpeterian perspective, its resolution is likely to require dynamic discontinuities in the development process – that is, development takes new forms and directions. This could produce substantial modifications in the international division of labour and, consequently, significant shifts in the balance of growth, wealth and power.

The shifts in the growth centres result partly from the problems of economic maturity among the leading economies, which contribute to their relative 'slowing down' in the development process. In contrast, various factors assist a process of 'catching up' by later developers. Together, these lead to a situation of relative convergence in the world economy that creates a 'swarming effect' on a world scale. These result in the intensification of competition, recession, crisis in the world economy and stresses on international economic relations.[18] The difficulties would only be reduced through significant institutional and structural changes, accompanied by technological, organisational and other innovations. These changes provide the foundation for the emergence of new leaders in the world economy, whose rapid growth generates a relative divergence of economic structures, the re-establishment of complementarity between countries, and lays the foundation for a (another) period of harmonious international economic relations (Cheah 1987, pp. 18–43).[19]

This perspective provides a useful general framework for viewing developments in the world economy, and among Asia–Pacific economies in particular. It helps us to identify the, changing, bases for complementarity and conflict in the region, and to consider also how the processes of economic transformation can be managed better.

From this perspective the recent economic difficulties experienced by several Asian countries have a more fundamental systemic cause. While many observers, including the International Monetary Fund (IMF), have placed the blame on 'crony capitalism', poor banking practices, property speculation, currency speculation, authoritarian governments and corruption (IMF Staff 1998), these were at best precipitating factors in the crisis (see Gray 1998b; Hamilton 1998; Walker 1998; Brain 1999; Yamakage 1999, pp. 33–4; and Cheah 2000b). Indeed, these factors were also present much earlier, even during the catching-up phase.[20] It was only when the global effects of catching up led to proliferation of substantial excess productive capacity in a host of industries and countries, and severe competitive pressures in the global economy, that the basis emerged for a general crisis to be precipitated.

Furthermore, while some groups and countries have made significant progress in raising their living standards in the 20th century, the President of the World Bank has recently admitted that 'the fact remains that progress is too slow'.[21] However, it has also been contended in various circles that the difficulties lie not just in the relatively slow pace of the development process but, more significantly, in the very nature of the development model that has been adopted so far. It is a model in which excessive emphasis has been placed on the economic aspects, a model that has generated significant inequities, a model that is not meaningful for the large majority of the world's population, and a model that may not be sustainable in the longer term (see Hodson 1972; Illich 1973; Schumacher 1974; Chossudovsky 1997; Harman and Porter 1997; Douthwaite 1999; Theobald 1999; UNEP 1999).

The economic, social and ecological problems cited above constitute a broader crisis of development. They have provoked a critical questioning of present forms and processes of development, and have led to a search for better and more viable alternatives. At the same time, competitive and other pressures are transforming the dynamics of production, shifting from 'mass production' to 'lean production' and beyond. This transformation offers significant possibilities for ameliorating and, perhaps, even eventually eliminating the problems that have been encountered.

12.4 THE NEW DYNAMICS OF PRODUCTION: TOWARDS A DIVERSIFIED PRODUCTION SYSTEM (DPS)

Over time there has been an evolution from craft production to mass production to lean production (see Piore and Sabel 1984; Womack et al. 1990; Streeck 1991; Kotha 1996), with ongoing changes in the direction of what may be termed as 'diversified production'.[22] These developments have helped to promote and to intensify changes in the outcomes of the production process along five distinct dimensions: time, space, matter, type and price.

12.4.1 Time

The new dynamics of production are leading to outcomes where there is a tendency that customers are served the product or service that they desire in the shortest possible time. Improvements in this capability lead to a tendency where the desired product or service becomes available at any time. This can be seen in the examples of home delivery of pizza in the case of products, and home banking in the case of services. In the ultimate, it generates a tendency towards immediate gratification of consumer wants the moment they are conceived. To facilitate this possibility, organisations will need to endeavour to create 'real-time structures; structures that change continually in tiny increments, not in large static quantum jumps. Each change is so minute that the overall effect is one of a structure in constant, seamless motion' (Davis 1987, p. 41).

12.4.2 Space

The miniaturisation of products has led to a dramatic shrinking of the space that they previously occupied. This is illustrated most vividly by the evolution of mainframe computers to palm-size computers, but the process is also observable in many other products; for instance, the encapsulation of the 32-volume contents of *Encyclopaedia Britannica* within two CD-ROMs. This spatial contraction has generally been accompanied by increased, not reduced, product capability, functionality, sophistication and, consequently, value. Miniaturisation and portability means that transportation constraints are reduced tremendously, such that products and services can be more easily delivered any time, any place and everywhere. The growth of the Internet is only one means through which this process is being spread and intensified. Consequently, 'The meaning of market "place" is being fundamentally transformed for both the seller and the buyer' (Davis 1987, p. 56).

12.4.3 Matter

Another significant outcome is the development of products that use fewer or no materials, for instance new digital cameras that do not require film. An even more significant development in the shift away from materials is related to the rapid expansion of services in the economy. This has accelerated the shift away from tangibles such as physical resources towards intangibles, no matter, such as information. This has the important consequence that economic activity is shifting away from resources that are potentially and/or actually finite, to resources, for example information, that are potentially and/or actually infinite. Indeed, the increasing importance, value added, of intangibles attaches both to goods as well as services. According to Davis (1987, p. 99), 'in the new economy, both inputs (resources) and outputs (goods and services) are increasingly intangible, and value will increasingly be attached to intangibles'.

12.4.4 Type

Another significant change resulting from the new dynamics of production is the increasing range and diversity of products and services. This can be observed in the evolution from the corner grocery store to supermarkets, to shopping emporiums and shopping malls. Indeed, customers are now capable of being offered not just a range of goods and services produced in one location, but from throughout the globe. This is complemented by the shift from mass production towards mass customisation (see Davis 1987, pp. 140–90; and Pine 1999). In the ultimate, the tendency is that customers will be able to have any kind (type) of good or service tailored to their specific desires or specifications, at any time and any place.

12.4.5 Price

Finally, in the price dimension, there is a deflationary tendency (see Davidse 1983, pp. 127–8; Makridakis 1989; Shilling 1998), leading first towards a general fall in prices; and second, to a growing number of products and services becoming available at no charge. Software that is freely and legally available to be downloaded from the Internet provides examples of the latter. This does not mean that no revenues will be available to private producers of such goods and services, only that not all aspects, parts, of the products and services that are provided in the private sector will be transacted for a price. Nevertheless, it is intriguing that it may be postulated as a general tendency that goods and services will become progressively cheaper, and that many privately produced goods and services will assume the characteristics of public, 'free', goods.

The characteristics of the outcomes of the old versus the new dynamics of production thus may be summarised as in Table 12.1. Indeed, the refinements of the mass production and lean production over time, have contributed both directly and indirectly to these new dynamics of production.

Table 12.1
Tendencies Flowing from the Old and New Dynamics of Production

Dimension	Tendencies from mass production	Tendencies from diversified production
Time	The product or service is available only at specific or limited times.	The product or service is available at any time.
Space	The product or service is available only at specific or limited locations.	The product or service is available anywhere (everywhere).
Matter	The product is tangible and bulky.	The product is miniaturised, or intangible and immaterial, or available as a service.
Type	The product or service is available only in specific or limited forms.	The product or service is available in multiple or customised forms.
Price	The product or service is available at a price.	The product or service is available at no charge.

While adaptive entrepreneurial strategies will continue to dominate the scene, to cope effectively with these changes in the production process from mass production to lean production and beyond, SMEs and other organisations will need to be concerned with the imperatives flowing from the tendencies generated on the five dimensions of the shift towards diversified production. In this regard, SMEs and other organisations will also need to devote greater emphasis in the future to three key aspects in their entrepreneurial efforts: diversity, sustainability and creativity.

12.4.6 Diversity

As organisations increase or change the range of their products and services, and expand the scale and extend the locations of their operations, management will tend to encounter greater diversity among their markets, their employees, as well as among their customers (Fernandez 1993, p. 291). Marketing departments have long realised the importance of taking account of differences in customer tastes and preferences, and managers are increasingly alert to distinctive conditions in different production locations as well as the importance of managing effectively the ethnic, cultural and other significant differences among their employees in diverse locations (see Kossek and Lobel 1996; Cope and Kalantzis 1997; Bertone, Esposto and Turner 1998).
   From this perspective,

> Managing diversity is a corporate strategy directly tied into the business strategy for managing organisational change and improving productivity in the 1990s and beyond ... As today's work forces and customer bases in Japan, the United States, and the EC countries continue to evolve and become more diverse in terms of race, gender, age, sexual orientation, culture, language, religion, disabilities, and other characteristics, it is necessary for corporations to shift their emphasis from homogeneity to diversity in their approach to managing people and courting different customer markets. (Fernandez 1993, pp. 291–2)

The reported benefits from this are: 'work-team heterogeneity promotes more critical strategic analysis, creativity, innovation, and high-quality decisions and solutions. ... given a creative task, heterogeneous groups adopted multiple strategies and identified more solutions than did homogeneous groups' (Fernandez 1993, pp. 284–5). These results flow partly from the combination of the strengths of different cognitive styles contained in heterogeneous groups (Kirton and de Ciantis 1989, pp. 95–6).

12.4.7 Sustainability

Previously, sustainable development had largely been deemed to be a concern of governments and non-business organisations, or of no concern at all. However, this is no longer the case (see Wolfensohn 1997; World Bank 1999, pp. 87–105), and increasingly business organisations, including SMEs, must incorporate sustainability issues into their planning and operational activities.

Sustainability, or the concern for long-term viability, covers three main dimensions: (a) economic viability (that is, business activities must be economically profitable), (b) social viability (that is, in addition to individual or private gain, the activities must also promote community and societal well-being, for instance by reducing social divisions, inequity and conflict), and (c) ecological viability (that is, the activities must also be ecologically friendly and not damaging to the environment).

Economic profitability has been a traditional concern of private firms. However, at present and in the future, this concern can no longer be pursued with a narrow focus (see Ayres 1996; Harman and Porter 1997; Prahalad 1997). Private firms can and should also address more directly the issue of poverty and social inequity (see Yunus 1984; Khandker 1996; Ravallion and Wodon 1997; and World Bank 2000). Indeed, more fundamentally, it has been argued that, 'The only feasible answer to ever-increasing underdevelopment is a response to basic needs that is planned as a long-range goal for areas which will always have a different capital structure' (Illich 1973, p. 365; see also Harmon 1996; Theobald 1999, pp. 37–62). Finally, the private sector has to be more concerned about both the immediate environmental effects and the long-term ecological impact of their activities (see Stiglitz 1997; Wolfensohn 1998; and UNEP 1999), for dangers to the global environment also generate significant costs and problems for private enterprise.

12.4.8 Creativity

At any time, there are opportunities for both adaptive and creative entrepreneurship. However, it has been argued that the balance between these shifts over time has changed (Cheah 1994). For most of the post-war decades adaptive entrepreneurship served Japan and other Asian developing countries well, as they embarked on a catching-up process behind the western industrial countries (Cheah 1998a). However, as the gap narrowed the benefits from, and the opportunities for, adaptive entrepreneurship have diminished. Consequently, firms in Japan and the other Asian industrialising economies will need to devote greater attention to creative entrepreneurship, that is, the effective commercialisation of more radical innovations (Tatsuno 1990; Basadur 1992).

To achieve a major re-evaluation and re-orientation of business objectives and strategies, and to take into account the need to manage for diversity and for sustainability, firms will need to become significantly more creative in their corporate vision, as well as in their planning and operational efforts (see de Bono 1992; Gibson 1997; and Porter 1997). Furthermore, firms will need to be more effective in managing the transitions between the evolutionary and the revolutionary modes in the entrepreneurial process, so as to be able to recognise and to avoid the potential errors and failures in the different phases of that process (see Cheah 1998b). Efforts to meet this and other aspects of the new dynamics of management and production will lead to an evolution towards a diversified production system (DPS).

The DPS will incorporate the three principles of diversity, sustainability and creativity, and be effective in responding to the challenges of change on the five dimensions of time, space, matter, type and price, identified above. At the micro level the DPS will have to be integrated into the culture of the firm. At the macro level, conditions for the effective establishment and consolidation of the new DPS depend on national and international efforts to recreate complementarity and flexibility to the global economy. Indeed, the DPS may itself be a significant means for promoting these conditions.[23]

12.5   CONCLUSION

Much of the concern about the so-called 'Asian' crisis that was precipitated in Thailand in August 1997 has focused on its financial aspects – currency depreciation, the flight of foreign capital, bank insolvency, crony capitalism and other corporate malpractices. However, the Asian financial crisis is part of a broader global economic and development crisis. Consequently, the resolution of the crisis will require not simply changes in private sector and public sector financial practices. It will also involve revolutionary transformations in production and development processes. Just as SMEs played a significant part in the earlier 'catching-up' process preceding and leading up to the crisis, so too it is necessary for SMEs in Asia and elsewhere to adjust to the ongoing changes and contribute to the improvements in economic and development outcomes.

For the world has started the 21st century still markedly divided between the rich minority and the poor majority. This is not a morally desirable situation. It is arguably also not practically sustainable. At the same time, ecological problems are also threatening the viability of present development processes in the world.

This situation raises fundamental questions about the processes of creation and distribution of wealth and resources, and about the possibilities for a satisfactory quality of life for the world's population. How can we generate and equitably share an abundance of wealth and other resources in a sustainable way? Specifically, how do we manage the processes of innovation and organisational change so as to transform this situation into a state of sustainable abundance? This presents both an intellectual challenge, to formulate appropriate concepts and analytical frameworks, as well as practical challenges, to create, for instance, more effective organisational structures, decision-making processes and reward systems.

In this regard, SMEs had earlier played an important part in Asian development in general, and in particular in the transition from craft production towards mass production and lean production. They will continue to contribute significantly in the shift towards diversified production, which offers significant possibilities for more economically, socially, and ecologically sustainable production processes.

The significant changes in domestic and international economies in the last two decades have altered the economic conditions for many enterprises and the development prospects for many countries. In particular, the problem of convergence of economic structures needs to be resolved by finding means to regenerate complementarity through promoting divergence of economic structures and activities. Solutions need to be found through entrepreneurial ingenuity at the enterprise level, through national programs, and through international collaboration and coordination. Consequently, the development outcomes will be determined only partly by the efforts of individual firms and governments.

Nevertheless, the forces that have been unleashed by competition and intensified by the recent economic crisis are generating pressures for organisations to respond to the new dynamics of production in at least five dimensions (time, space, matter, type and price). To respond effectively, organisations will also need to devote greater emphasis to the management of diversity, sustainability and creativity. These changes and responses will in time revolutionise the forms and operations of private enterprise, national economies as well as the global economy.

In this context possession of an understanding of the dynamic forces of change, within local economies as well as in the global economy, would assist SMEs to have a better perspective of the existing and emerging opportunities and threats. Consequently, they would be better prepared to respond appropriately, in terms of their choice, timing and implementation of innovation strategies, to the changing environment in the new millennium.

NOTES

1   'Adaptive entrepreneurship' refers to the many different forms of incremental innovation, such as product and process imitation, subcontracting, and spatial arbitrage. It is contrasted to 'creative entrepreneurship' which results in radical innovations (see Cheah 1993).
2   More importantly, it has been argued that, 'The erosion of entry barriers associated with China's industrial reform has created a domestic product cycle in which new products, materials and processes introduced by innovative state firms are adopted by non-state enterprises which use their cost advantages to erode state sector profits and force state industry toward fresh innovations' (Jefferson and Rawski 1994, p. 61. See also, Yan 1995; and Christerson and Lever-Tracy 1997).
3   For a revealing personal account of entrepreneurial wheeling and dealing, see Ye (1996, pp. 106–17).
4   Significantly, 'the family enterprise tends to be the basic economic unit in Southeast Asia' (Weidenbaum and Hughes 1996, p. 53). Indeed, 'In large measure, the bamboo network consists of cross-holdings of privately owned family-run, trade-oriented firms, rather than the huge publicly owned manufacturing corporations that are typical in the US, Japan, and Western Europe' (Weidenbaum and Hughes 1996, p. 27). This situation has undoubtedly contributed to 'crony capitalism' in the region; although it is not the only form

of crony capitalism (that is, business activities based on informal preferential relationships), and crony capitalism in diverse forms is also found widely outside Asia.

5   According to Weidenbaum and Hughes (1996, p. 5): 'It is becoming increasingly clear that the ancient Chinese trading tradition can adjust very well to the high-tech world economy that is currently dominated by the United States, Japan, and Germany, and that this Chinese approach to economic development can generate unprecedented wealth'.

6   See the origins of the business empires of the Wuthelam Group, the Charoen Pokphand Group and others (Haley et al. 1998, pp. 93–4 and 124–5).

7   Despite the capabilities of the CFBs, and their attraction to China, it is worth noting that 'Even the most aggressive overseas Chinese investors concede that business on the mainland is a risky proposition (as it has also been elsewhere in Southeast Asia). China is still an authoritarian nation, ruled by leaders with a great deal of arbitrary power' (Weidenbaum and Hughes 1996, p. 16).

8   Several industry- and firm-level studies in the car, electronics and other industries also provide supporting evidence of changes in competitiveness between firms in different countries (see Majumdar 1982; Dertouzos et al. 1989; Womack et al. 1990; Sprague 1993; and Hobday 1994).

9   The dominance of SMEs in Hong Kong's economy provides many illustrations of these strategies.

10 In the consumer electronics industry, Matsushita had adopted such a strategy of being a 'second-mover' (Bolton 1993, p. 32). The company deliberately chose to enter the market later, watching and waiting until a rival had introduced a new product and achieved consumer acceptance before producing improved versions of the product which it sold at lower prices.

11 A survey by the Hong Kong Government Industry Department and Census and Statistics Department (1991, pp. 84–8) revealed that 88 per cent of manufacturing establishments in Hong Kong did not undertake R&D. Of these, 79 per cent reported that they were not planning to do so in the future. Only 12 per cent carried out R&D regularly. These firms were largely involved in the electronics, garment, watches and clocks, food and beverages industries. Most of them were larger firms. In terms of R&D expenses, only 36 per cent of the establishments spent 5 per cent or more of their total annual revenue on R&D. About 42 per cent of the establishments spent less than 5 per cent, and 22 per cent of the establishments had no fixed R&D budget. Indeed, more creative product innovation strategies seemed to be less successful. Consequently, Hong Kong's overall manufacturing technology has generally lagged behind the other Asian newly industrialising economies (Chen 1985, p. 37; Ng 1988, p. 39). With a good communications network, managerial skills, and a hybrid of Western and Chinese culture, Hong Kong entrepreneurs have specialised in sourcing, quality control, testing, packing and coordinating functions.

12   Klein (1977, p. 179) noted that subcontracting generates important advantages 'not only for static efficiency, but also for dynamic efficiency. The smaller the units in which competition can take place, the easier it is to enter an industry; and with easier entry, competition is more likely to thrive'.

13   According to Woronoff (1980, p. 170), 'The foreign investors thought they were very clever in using Hong Kong's cheap and docile labour and they earned very handsome profits on their investments ... But surely, more and more local manufacturers were springing up, either former employees going into business on their own or a local industrialist who hired the necessary technicians to run a plant. Whereas Hong Kong was once dependent on foreign components to manufacture transistor radios, by the mid-1960s it could do without them. In electronics ... Hong Kong was merely supposed to produce parts, which would be sent back to more mature industrial countries like America, Japan or Germany, to be assembled into highly sophisticated products. Oddly enough, soon locally made calculators, almost as good and certainly cheaper, were appearing on the market. Finished products began to include cassette-recorders, televisions, intercoms, memory telephones, home computers and all the latest gadgets, along with an increasing range of highly sophisticated parts and components, and ultimately the "chips". Moreover, many companies stopped being just subcontractors and began to sell under their own name.'

14   By the beginning of the 1980s, Hong Kong had become host to scores of multinational banks, foreign exchange dealers, security houses and other non-bank financial institutions conducting a wide range of retail and wholesale services. In 1990, the tertiary sector accounted for nearly 80 per cent of the total GDP, and employed 63 per cent of all workers. In this manner adaptive entrepreneurship has helped to shift Hong Kong's economy away, first from the traditional fishing and agricultural activities in the 1950s and 1960s into manufacturing, and then to finance and other services in the 1970s and 1980s, and from a traditional entrepôt port towards a modern international trading and financial centre (Chau 1993, p. 16).

15   From a Schumpeterian perspective, evolutionary change is periodically disrupted by revolutionary changes in the economy. Schumpeter's perspective of the development process emphasises the reality of change through competition, displacement or elimination, and through a general transformation of the economy. Moreover, owing to the dynamic and competitive nature of the development process, development, in Schumpeter's conception, does not occur continuously and evenly over time and place. Instead, the phenomenon is primarily an episodic, transient and discontinuous one. For Schumpeter, generalised economic fluctuations (economic cycles) are an integral aspect of the competitive development process (see Schumpeter 1934, 1939, 1946).

16   Schumpeter warned that 'industrial change is never a harmonious advance with all elements of the system moving or tending to move in step. At any given time, some industries move on and others stay behind; and the discrepancies

arising from this are an essential element in the situations that developed'
(Schumpeter 1939, pp. 101–2).

17   During this phase the tendency for a shift from productive investments into
highly speculative investments ('casino capitalism'), highlighted earlier by
Strange (1986) and more recently by Soros (1998), becomes increasingly
pronounced.

18   During such periods, mercantilist practices and ideology become more
prominent; and so too does the tendency for conflict to occur, under a variety of
guises (see Huntington 1993; and Gray 1998a).

19   During such periods, *laissez-faire* policies and ideology come into vogue again.

20   The Asian 'miracle' was always less miraculous and more flawed than it was
made out to be by its admirers; and it always had its critics, the most recent
being Lingle (1997), Garran (1998) and Backman (1999). Despite the
protestations of the critics, in the past institutions such as the IMF, the World
Bank and the Asian Development Bank largely overlooked, deliberately ignored,
or treated as inconsequential, the deficiencies that they have recently attributed
as the principal causes of 'the Asian crisis'.

21   Specifically, 'With three billion people still living under US$2 a day, with
growing inequity between rich and poor, with forests being degraded at the rate
of an acre a second, with 130 million children still not in school, with 1.5 billion
people still not having access to clean water, and two billion people not having
access to sewage [facilities], we cannot be complacent. More than this, we must
be concerned that 80 to 90 million people are being added annually to our planet,
mainly in the developing world. Two billion more souls must feed themselves
by the year 2025, hampered by wars, with growing inequity, and with distortions
of economies and politics as evidenced in crises from Indonesia to Russia and
from Latin America to Africa. With the reduction in Overseas Development
Assistance and current instability in the international financial markets, there is
much to be concerned about' (Wolfensohn 1999).

22   Indeed, Christerson and Lever-Tracy (1997, p. 584) suggest that rural industrial
areas in China resemble the industrial districts of the Third Italy in many ways:
'They are globally competitive in producing for fast-changing fashionable market
niches. They are marked by networks of relatively autonomous small firms
which are at least partially locally owned and managed and which often take
part in high-value activities such as design and marketing. They display high
degrees of local government involvement in small enterprises, and are embedded
in trust relationships among suppliers, investors and clients. This suggests that
it is indeed possible for flexible industrial districts to emerge in developing
peripheral areas distant from design centres, established parts suppliers and
sophisticated markets.'

23   In general, while significant benefits will flow from the emergence and diffusion
of the DPS, some caveats are necessary: in some situations the DPS may intensify
existing problems and disparities. Indeed, success in promoting and responding

to the DPS is by no means assured everywhere. Consequently, further efforts need to be devoted, analytically and in practical terms, to establish the dynamics and consequences of the impact of the DPS, and to determine the appropriate strategies and measures to maximise the benefits, while minimising or avoiding the negative and harmful effects.

REFERENCES

Akamatsu, K. (1961), 'A theory of unbalanced growth in the world economy', *Weltwirtschaftliches Archiv*, **86** (2), 196–217.

Ayres, R. (1996), 'Technology, progress and economic growth', *European Management Journal*, **14** (6), 562–75.

Backman, M. (1999), *Asian Eclipse: Exposing the Dark Side of Business in Asia*, New York: J. Wiley.

Basadur, M. (1992), 'Managing Creativity: A Japanese Model', *Academy of Management Executive*, **6** (2), 29–42.

Bertone, S., A. Esposto and R. Turner (1998), 'Diversity and Dollars: Productive Diversity in Australian Business and Industry', CEDA Information Paper no. 58, Melbourne: Committee for Economic Development of Australia (CEDA).

Bolton, M. (1993), 'Imitation Versus Innovation: Lessons to be Learned from the Japanese', *Organizational Dynamics*, Winter, pp. 30–45.

Brain, P. (1999), *Beyond Meltdown: The Global Battle for Sustained Growth*, Melbourne: Scribe Publications.

Chau, L.L.C. (1993), *Hong Kong: A Unique Case of Development*, Washington, DC: World Bank.

Cheah, H.B. (1987), *International Competition in the Pacific*, Singapore: Institute of Southeast Asian Studies.

Cheah, H.B. (1993), 'Dual Modes of Entrepreneurship: Revolution and Evolution in the Entrepreneurial Process', *Creativity and Innovation Management*, **2** (4), 243–51.

Cheah, H.B. (1994), 'Creativity in the Entrepreneurial Process', in S. Dingli (ed.), *Creative Thinking: A Multifaceted Approach*, Malta: Malta University Press, pp. 134–49.

Cheah, H.B. (1995), 'Changes in competitive advantage in East Asia and the Pacific: Causes and Consequences', International Economic Conflict Discussion Paper No. 87, Economics Research Center, School of Economics, Nagoya University, Japan.

Cheah H.B. (1998a), 'Catching Up: Adaptive Entrepreneurship and Economic Development in Asia', in Y. Takahashi, M. Murata and K.M. Rahman (eds), *Management Strategies of Multinational Corporations in Asian Markets*, Tokyo: Chuo University Press, pp. 243–63.

Cheah, H.B. (1998b), 'Entrepreneurial Development: Understanding and Managing

Change in the Entrepreneurial Process', *Journal of Enterprising Culture*, **6** (1), 25–47.

Cheah, H.B. (2000a), 'Raising the Dragon: Adaptive Entrepreneurship and Chinese Economic Development', in F.-J. Richter (ed.), *The Dragon Millennium*, London: Quorum, pp. 163–81.

Cheah, H.B. (2000b), 'The Asian Economic Crisis: Three Perspectives on the Unfolding of the Crisis in the Global Economy', in F.-J. Richter (ed.), *The East Asian Development Model*, London: Macmillan, pp. 97–116.

Cheah, H.B. and T. Yu (1996), 'Adaptive Rsponse: Entrepreneurship and Competitiveness in the Economic Development of Hong Kong', *Journal of Enterprising Culture*, **4** (3), 241–66.

Chen, E.K.Y. (1983), 'Multinationals from Hong Kong', in S. Lall (ed.), *The New Multinationals: The Spread of Third World Enterprises*, Chichester: John Wiley, pp. 89–136.

Chen, E.K.Y. (1985), 'Maintaining Hong Kong's Prosperity', *The China Business Review*, September/October, pp. 37–41.

Chen, E.K.Y (1989), 'Hong Kong's Role in Asian and Pacific Economic Development', *Asian Development Review*, **7** (2), 26–47.

Cheng, T.Y. (1982), *The Economy of Hong Kong*, revised edition, Hong Kong: Far East Publications.

Cheung F.K. (1982), 'A Study of Management Practices of Small-scale Electronics Industry in Hong Kong', MBA thesis, University of Hong Kong.

Chossudovsky, M. (1997), *The Globalisation of Poverty: Impacts of IMF and World Bank Reforms*, Sydney: Pluto Press.

Christerson, B. and C. Lever-Tracy (1997), 'The Third China? Emerging Industrial Districts in Rural China,' *International Journal of Urban and Regional Research*, **21** (4), 569–88.

Cope, B. and M. Kalantzis (1997), *Productive Diversity*, Annandale: Pluto Press.

Davidse, J. (1983), 'Characteristics of growth and limitations in electronics', *Technological Forecasting and Social Change*, **24** (2), 125–35.

Davies, H., J. Ling and F. Cheung (1993), 'Product Design and the Location of Production: Strategic Choice in Hong Kong Manufacturing', *Academy of International Business*, **3**, 1–14.

Davis, S. (1987), *Future Perfect*, Reading, Mass.: Addison-Wesley.

de Bono, E. (1992), *Sur/petition: Going Beyond Competition*, London: Fontana.

Dertouzos, M., R. Solow and R. Lester (1989), *Made in America: Regaining the Productive Edge*, Cambridge, Mass.: MIT Press.

Douthwaite, R. (1999), *The Growth Illusion: How Economic Growth Has Enriched the Few, Impoverished the Many and Endangered the Planet*, Gabriola Island: New Society Publishers.

Downie, J. (1958), *The Competitive Process*, London: Duckworth.

East Asia Analytical Unit (1997), *China Embraces the Market*, Canberra: Department of Foreign Affairs and Trade.

Fernandez, J. (1993), *The Diversity Advantage: How American Business Can Out-perform Japanese and European Companies in the Global Marketplace*, New York: Lexington.

Garran, R. (1998), *Tigers Tamed: The End of the Asian Miracle*, Sydney: Allen & Unwin.

Gibson, R. (ed.) (1997), *Rethinking the Future*, London: Nicholas Brealey.

Goodhart, C. and C. Xu (1996), 'The Rise of China as an Economic Power', Centre of Economic Performance, Discussion Paper No. 299, London: London School of Economics and Political Science.

Gray, J. (1998a), 'Global Utopias and Clashing Civilisations: Misunderstanding the Present', *International Affairs*, **74** (1), 149–64.

Gray, J. (1998b), 'World Bank Attacks Management of Crisis', *Australian Financial Review*, 4 December, p. 26.

Hagedoorn, J. (1989), *The Dynamic Analysis of Innovation and Diffusion: A Study in Process Control*, London: F. Pinter.

Haley, G., C.T. Tan and U. Haley (1998), *New Asian Emperors*, Oxford: Butterworth-Heinemann.

Hamilton, G. (1998), 'Asian Business Networks in Transition: What Alan Greenspan Does Not Understand About the Asian Financial Crisis', keynote speech to a Workshop on Asian Business Networks, 31 March–2 April, at the National University of Singapore.

Harman, W. and M. Porter (eds) (1997), *The New Business of Business: Sharing Responsibility for a Positive Global Future*, London: Berrett-Koehler Publishers.

Harmon, J. (1996), 'Culturally Sustainable Development Policy: A Lesson from Japan', *LBJ Journal of Public Affairs*, **8** (1) [available at <//uts.cc.utexas.edu/~lbjjpa/1996/harmon.htm>].

Hersh, J. (1993), *The USA and the Rise of East Asia since 1945*, New York: St Martin's Press.

Ho, Y.P. (1992), *Trade, Industrial Restructuring and Development in Hong Kong*, London: Macmillan.

Hobday, M. (1994), 'Technological Learning in Singapore: A Test Case of Leapfrogging', *Journal of Development Studies*, **30** (3), 831–58.

Hobday, M. (1995), 'East Asian Latecomer Firms: Learning the Technology of Electronics', *World Development*, **23** (7), 1171–93.

Hodson, H. (1972), *The Diseconomies of Growth*, London: Pan.

Hoffmann, W.G. (1958), *The Growth of Industrial Economies*, Manchester: Manchester University Press.

Hong Kong Government Industry Department (1991), *Survey on the Future Development of Industry in Hong Kong: Statistical Survey of Manufacturers, 1984–1989*, Hong Kong: Government Printer.

Huntington, S. (1993), 'Clash of civilisations', *Foreign Affairs*, **72** (3), 22–49.

Illich, I. (1973), 'Outwitting the "Developed" Countries', in H. Bernstein (ed.), *Underdevelopment and Development*, Harmondsworth: Penguin, pp. 357–68.

IMF Staff (1998), 'The Asian Crisis: Causes and Cures,' *Finance and Development*, **35** (2), 18–21.

Jefferson, G. and T. Rawski (1994), 'Enterprise Reform in Chinese Industry', *Journal of Economic Perspectives*, **8** (2), 47–70.

Khandker, S. (1996), 'Grameen Bank: Impact, Costs and Program Sustainability', *Asian Development Review*, **14** (1), 97–130.

King, Y.C. and P. Man (1979), 'Small Factory in Economic Development: The Case of Hong Kong', in T.B. Lin (ed.), *Hong Kong: Economic, Social and Political Studies in Development*, New York: M.E. Sharpe, pp. 31–64.

Kirton, M.J. and S. de Ciantis (1989), 'Cognitive style in organisational climate', in M.J. Kirton (ed.), *Adaptors and Innovators: Styles of Creativity and Problem Solving*, London: Routledge, pp. 79–96.

Klein, B.H. (1977), *Dynamic Economies*, Cambridge, MA: Harvard University Press.

Knies, K. (1853), *Die Politische Okonomie vom Standpunkte der Geschichtlichen Methode* [*Political Economy from the Historical Point of View*], Braunschweig.

Kossek, E. and S. Lobel (eds) (1996), *Managing Diversity: Human Resource Strategies for Transforming the Workplace*, Oxford: Blackwell.

Kotha, S. (1996), 'From Mass Production to Mass Customisation: The Case of the National Industrial Bicycle Company of Japan,' *European Management Journal*, **14** (5), 442–50.

Lam, D. and I. Lee (1992), 'Guerrilla Capitalism and the Limits of Statist Theory: Comparing the Chinese NICs', in C. Clark and S. Chan (eds), *The Evolving Pacific Basin in the Global Political Economy*, London: Lynne Rienner Publishers, pp. 107–24.

League of Nations (1945), *Economic Instability in the Post-war World: The Conditions of Prosperity after the Transition from War to Peace*, Princeton, NJ: Princeton University Press.

Lingle, C. (1997), *The Rise and Decline of the Asian Century: False Starts on the Path to the Global Millennium*, Hong Kong: Asia 2000.

MacIntyre, A. (1994), *Business and Government in Industrializing Asia*, Ithaca: Cornell University Press.

Majumdar, B.A. (1982), *Innovations, Product Development and Technology Transfer: An Empirical Study of Dynamic Competitive Advantage, the Case of Electronic Calulators*, Washington, DC: University Press of America.

Makridakis, S. (1989), 'Management in the 21st Century', *Long Range Planning*, **22** (2), 37–53.

Ng, Y.C. (1988), *Hong Kong on the Turning Point*, Taipei: Commonwealth Publishing Co.

Pine, B.J. (1999), *Mass Customization: The New Frontier in Business Competition*, Boston: Harvard Business School Press.

Piore, M. and C. Sabel (1984), *The Second Industrial Divide: Possibilities for Prosperity*, New York: Basic Books.

Porter, M. (1997), 'Creating Tomorrow's Advantages', in R. Gibson (ed.), *Rethinking the Future*, London: Nicholas Brealey, pp. 48–60.

Prahalad, C.K. (1997), 'Strategies for Growth', in R. Gibson (ed.), *Rethinking the Future*, London: Nicholas Brealey, pp. 62–75.

Ravallion, M. and Q. Wodon (1997), 'Banking on the Poor: Branch Placement and Non-farm Rural Development in Bangladesh', World Bank Working Paper no.1858, Washington, DC: World Bank.

Rolls, E. (1992), *Sojourners*, St Lucia: University of Queensland Press.

Rolls, E. (1996), *Citizens*, St Lucia: University of Queensland Press.

Salter, W.E.G. (1966), *Productivity and Technical Change*, second edition, Cambridge: Cambridge University Press.

Schumacher, E.F. (1974), *Small is Beautiful: A Study of Economics as if People Mattered*, London: Abacus.

Schumpeter, J.A. (1934), *The Theory of Economic Development*, New York: Oxford University Press.

Schumpeter, J.A. (1939), *Business Cycles*, 2 volumes, New York: McGraw-Hill.

Schumpeter, J.A. (1947), 'The Creative Response in Economic History', *Journal of Economic History*, **7** (2), 149–59.

Schwartz, H. (1994), *States versus Markets*, New York: St. Martin's Press.

Shilling, A.G. (1998), *Deflation*, Short Hills, NJ: Lakeview Publishing Company.

Sit, V. and S.L. Wong (1989), *Small and Medium Industries in an Export-Oriented Economy: The Case of Hong Kong*, Hong Kong: Centre of Asian Studies, University of Hong Kong.

Sit, V., S.L. Wong and T.S. Kiang (1979), *Small Scale Industry in a Laissez-Faire Economy: A Hong Kong Case Study*, Hong Kong: Centre of Asian Studies, University of Hong Kong.

Solman, P. and T. Friedman (1982), *Life and Death on the Corporate Battlefield: How Companies Win, Lose, Survive*, New York: Simon & Schuster.

Soros, G. (1998), *The Crisis of Global Capitalism*, New York: Public Affairs.

Sprague, J. (1993), *Revitalizing US Electronics: Lessons from Japan*, Boston, MA: Butterworth-Heinemann.

Stiglitz, J. (1997), 'Stepping toward Balance: Addressing Global Climate Change', speech by the Chief Economist of the World Bank to the Conference on Environmentally and Socially Sustainable Development, 6 October, Washington, DC.

Strange, S. (1979), 'The Management of Surplus Productive Capacity', in N.M. Kamrany and R.H. Day, (eds), *Economic Issues of the Eighties*, Baltimore, MD: John Hopkins University Press, pp. 226–46.

Strange, S. (1986), *Casino Capitalism*, Oxford: Blackwell.

Strange, S. and R. Tooze (1981), *The International Politics of Surplus Capacity*, London: Allen & Unwin.

Streeck, W. (1991), 'On the Institutional Conditions for Diversified Quality Production', in E. Matzner and W. Streeck (eds), *The Socio-economics of Production and Full Employment*, Aldershot, UK: Edward Elgar, pp. 21–61.

Tatsuno, S. (1990), *Created in Japan: From Imitators to World-class Innovators*, New York: Harper & Row.

Theobald, R. (1999), *We DO have Future Choices: Strategies for Fundamentally Changing the 21st Century*, Lismore: Southern Cross University Press.

Thurow, L. (1993), *Head to Head*, New York: Warner.

Ting, W.L. (1985), *Business and Technological Dynamics in Newly Industrializing Asia*, London: Quorum Books.

UNEP (1999), *Global Environment Outlook 2000*, Nairobi: United Nations Environment Program.

Wade, R. (1990), *Governing the Market: Economic Theory and the Role of Government in East Asian Industrialisation*, Princeton, NJ: Princeton University Press.

Walker, W.C. (1998), 'Contagion: How the Asian Crisis Spread', Economics and Development Resource Center (EDRC) *Briefing Notes* no. 3, Manila: Asian Development Bank.

Wang, G. (1991), *China and the Overseas Chinese*, Singapore: Times Academic Press.

Watanabe, T. (1992), *Asia: Its Growth and Agony*, Honolulu: East–West Centre.

Weidenbaum, M. and S. Hughes (1996), *The Bamboo Network*, New York: Free Press.

Wolfensohn, J. (1997), 'Towards Global Sustainability', remarks by the President of the World Bank to the United Nations General Assembly Special Session on the environment, 25 June, New York.

Wolfensohn, J. (1998), Speech by the President of the World Bank to the Cambridge Business and Environment Program, 17 November, London.

Wolfensohn, J. (1999), 'A Proposal for a Comprehensive Development Framework', statement to the Board, Management and staff of the World Bank group, 21 January.

Womack, J., D. Jones and D. Roos (1990), *The Machine that Changed the World*, New York: Harper.

World Bank (1999), *Entering the 21st Century: World Development Report 1999/2000*, New York: Oxford University Press.

World Bank (2000), *Attacking Poverty: World Development Report 2000/1*, Washington, DC: World Bank.

Woronoff, J. (1980), *Hong Kong: Capitalist Paradise*, Hong Kong: Heinemann.

Yamakage, S. (1999), 'Crisis, Co-operation and the Power Triangle in the Asia-Pacific Region', in C.Y. Ng and C. Griffy-Brown (eds), *Trends and Issues in East Asia 1999*, Tokyo: IDRI/FASID, pp. 33–50.

Yamazawa, I., A. Hirata and K. Yokota (1991), 'Evolving patterns of comparative advantage in the Pacific economies', in M. Ariff (ed.), *The Pacific Economy: Growth and External Stability*, Sydney: Allen & Unwin, pp. 213–232.

Yan, S.P. (1995), 'Export-oriented rural enterprises', *JETRO China Newsletter* no. 118, pp. 8–22.

Ye, S. (1996), *The Year the Dragon Came*, St Lucia: University of Queensland Press.

Yunus, M. (1984), 'The Grameen Bank in Bangladesh', *Group-based Savings and Credit for the Rural Poor*, Geneva: ILO.

13   Small Chinese Businesses after the Asian Crisis: Surviving and Reviving

Constance Lever-Tracy and David Ip

13.1   INTRODUCTION

How rapidly the pendulum of fashion swings, especially in prescriptions for business success. It is only a few years since small and medium enterprises were being discovered as the wave of the future, lauded for their 'entrepreneurship' and 'flexibility'. Their weight in the economies of industrialised countries, after declining for a century, was seen to be rising again from the mid-1970s, and evidence emerged of increasing autonomy, innovation and technical competence. Their 'cooperative competition', in the industrial districts of the 'Third Italy' or the integrated production networks of Taiwan, or in the Township and Village Enterprises of coastal China, was contrasted with the 'sclerotic' and bureaucratic 'dinosaurs' represented by large 'Fordist' corporations and state enterprises (Pyke et al. 1990; Orrù 1991; Storper and Scott 1992) which were instructed to decentralise and spin off.

We now see daily reports of a renewed wave of mergers and acquisitions, sometimes encouraged or mandated by governments (as with Malaysian banks' restructuring), each competing with the last to be the largest on record, accompanied by claims that only thus can they compete in the new global economy. It is, however, unclear if this is really the logic of history and technology, and some have suggested that such mergers are a fashion of dubious economic or financial benefit (Sirower 2000). A somewhat different question is whether this indicates also a new global climate, increasingly unfriendly to small and medium enterprises at the other end of the spectrum. Even if the merger of giants leaves a subcontracting system intact, will it lead to small firms becoming increasingly squeezed, dependent and insecure, and with fewer prospects for autonomous growth?

Before the Asian crisis struck, a strong case was being made that the 'Asian economic miracle' itself could be largely credited to the dynamism of the mainly small and medium diaspora Chinese capitalists networking across East and Southeast

Asia and into China, with connections extending to Silicon Valley, Vancouver, Sydney and elsewhere around the world (Redding 1990; Hamilton 1991; Kotkin 1993; Yamaguchi 1993; Lever-Tracy et al. 1996; and Hsing 1998).

The pundits seized on the crisis to discredit the family management, personal networks and risk-taking diversification of Asian capitalism, and its failure to produce 'world-class' multinational corporations. Asian family businesses, whether owned by small capitalists or as part of the hundreds of firms comprising a tycoon's conglomerate, were seen as unable to compete with professionally managed corporations, strictly focused on their 'core' business, and it was expected that many would be taken over and knocked into shape by Western management. In an article called 'Merge or Perish', for example, Hiscock predicted that 'Asia's family-owned conglomerates could face a lonely death if they don't find a [Western] partner' (*The Australian*, 20 April 1999, p. 32). While the Western takeovers in practice made little headway, it seems that with the recovery from the crisis, more balanced alliances with Western corporations are increasing and there are signs of a new wave of intra-Asian mergers and acquisitions (*FEER*, 20 April 2000, pp. 66–7).

During the crisis, the critical focus was on the tycoons and their 'crony ties', and on their diversified conglomerates with their accumulated mountains of opaque debt for speculative ventures. It seemed likely, however, that the mass of small and medium family firms would have similar weaknesses and would probably have been even worse affected by the crash. Many commentators argued that Asian economic recovery would depend on a thoroughgoing restructuring that would take years.

The recovery was some time coming, but once it took hold, by mid-1999, it accelerated beyond expectations, and predictions and estimates of economic growth in East and Southeast Asia had to be repeatedly revised upwards. The fall and rise and the shifting hierarchy of the tycoon families and their conglomerates are regularly reported, and can be tracked, for example, through the ranked lists of Forbes Magazine and *Yazhou Zhoukan* (Tracy 2000). Less is known about the multitude of smaller family firms – their vulnerability and their resources in a crisis, how they fared, and whether they have been changed by the experience. How far were they destroyed, weakened or subjugated? How far were they able to shield themselves from property, currency and stock market collapses and from the cessation of bank lending? Might the recovery itself in some ways be attributed to their own survival strategies? Have the survivors retreated into a tradition-bound conservatism or is it possible that there will be a new swing of the pendulum and we will again be talking of a new wave of economic growth driven by the dynamism of small and medium firms?

The remainder of this chapter proceeds as follows. Section 13.2 conducts a brief overview of the study being conducted by the authors that forms the basis of this chapter. Section 13.3 discusses in detail the impact of the regional crisis upon the sample of SMEs interviewed for the study, and their responses to it. Section 13.4 identifies a number of defensive strategies adopted by the SMEs and mechanisms that assisted them in surviving the crisis. Section 13.5 analyses the importance of entrepreneurial drive in enabling the sample of SMEs to remain in business despite the inhospitable business environment within which they were operating. Finally, Section 13.6 presents a summary of the major conclusions from this chapter.

13.2   THE STUDY

This chapter is a report on 25 open-ended interviews with ethnic Chinese small and medium business owner–managers, in Taiwan, Hong Kong and Australia, carried out in late 1999 and early 2000. This is a report on work still in progress, leading eventually to 120 interviews in these three economies and also in Singapore. The interviews were carried out, generally in Chinese languages, by the researchers themselves in Hong Kong and Australia and by a local interviewer in Taiwan (where they were recorded and sent back to the researchers for translation). The interviews were obtained through snowballing introductions, starting with individuals known to the five interviewers personally (through friends, family, colleagues or students) or from earlier research and then moving out to other respondents introduced by these. The requirement was that they be currently involved in the management of their own business, and that it have some transnational dimension to its activities such as trade or offshore production. Respondents were not clustered in any particular occupation or industry, or any particular district in the four cities covered. The group was not, however, selected in any statistically representative fashion and generalisations from the findings must be made with great care. Little can be said about precise frequencies. At most it might be suggested that features common in the group may be presumed to be not uncommon in the wider population. The range of experiences should give some indication of the extent of differences to be found more widely. Where features are absent or very rare, we might presume that they are probably uncommon, at least among sections of the Chinese business community in these countries. As part of a wider study, which will also include analysis of statistical data and more representative survey material, such qualitative findings aim to provide questions for further study and also some indications of causation, perceptions and motives.

The interviews discussed the experiences of respondents and the way they perceived their own weaknesses and strengths in the context of the Asian financial crisis. Many respondents were active in more than one line of business. At the time of the interviews ten of the respondents had manufacturing as their main business, mostly employing fewer than 100 workers, with the largest two employing 400 and 1000 workers. One of these had production located in Taiwan and Vietnam and all the remainder carried out at least some of their production in Mainland China. Seven had been primarily involved with international commerce as traders, import export agents or shipping agents. One was a factory builder (for Taiwanese-owned ventures in China). One was in aquaculture and two owned a number of retail outlets (including a restaurant and a number of shopping centres). Whether or not they saw themselves as directly affected by the regional crisis, all had felt its impact through the mood of insecurity that permeated the region in which they and their friends were active and had themselves felt threatened at some time or another.

These interviews were restricted to survivors, people who were currently still operating a business. Furthermore we must assume that those who felt they had reason to be proud of their achievements were more likely to be nominated and introduced by others and more likely to agree to an interview. Nor can we expect that the promise of anonymity will always induce people to speak fully about their own failures and mistakes. We have sought to balance this a little by asking respondents also to tell us about the experiences of unnamed acquaintances.

No method of enquiry can present a fully valid picture but where silences and falsifications are the issue, personal introductions and in-depth conversations may often obtain a more valid picture than quantitatively more reliable techniques. The interviews themselves are part of a wider study into the impact of the crisis on diaspora Chinese businesses, including an analysis of macro data, a larger structured survey of foreign joint ventures in China and a multi-pronged monitoring of the fortunes of larger firms and tycoon families.[1]

13.3   SMALL AND MEDIUM BUSINESSES AND THE CRISIS

13.3.1   Big Business and the Crisis

A number of our respondents, particularly in Taiwan, understood the crisis as a problem created and mainly experienced by big businesses. In Taiwan there has historically been a clear divide between the big business sector, supported by the Kuomintang party and the state, and the main body of small businesses, most often made up of ethnic Taiwanese, who have been in the forefront of export-oriented industrialisation (Hamilton 1997). Five Taiwanese respondents nominated the instability of government-supported large firms in crisis as a primary explanation for the differing vulnerability of entire economies, contrasting Taiwan with other countries in the region.

> The main cause [of the crisis] is over-borrowing, especially in countries where enterprises are dependent on government support ... In Taiwan, where most enterprises are SMEs, the government is shielded from the storm. (TW7)[2]

> South Korea's economy was controlled by 50 *chaebols*. Yet they had more liabilities than assets. It was no surprise that the country was in trouble. Taiwan is fortunate because the energy of Taiwan's economy comes from SMEs. Most SMEs rely on their own capital. (TW5)[3]

> Taiwan is an economic community of SMEs. They know what to do when a crisis strikes, with their own ingenuity rather than being reliant upon

government intervention. That is why most Taiwanese businesses have survived the crisis. On the contrary, the *chaebols* in South Korea had to depend on the support from their government and the banks. It was not surprising to see the domino effect taking place when a chaebol started having problems. (TW6)[4]

[The crisis was] caused by countries with weak economies dominated by large corporations propped up by their national government. For example, when Hyundai, Daewoo or Samsung were in trouble, many of the small SMEs closely tied in with them also suffered great losses. Fearing that they would be unable to make payments, even enterprises in China were not willing to accept contracts and orders from Japan, the Philippines and Thailand. (TW8)[5]

The South Korean government's continual direct involvement in propping up the *chaebols* to keep expanding regardless of economic performance could only bring failure to the businesses and the whole economy. (TW11)[6]

It was also the Taiwanese in particular who made a qualitative distinction between the networks of SMEs and the influential connections of tycoons and big companies.

I am referring to a more dubious relationship between the government and big businesses and not situations relating to friendship or family. What I am saying is that if you are in financial difficulties, it's fine if you go to ask your friend or relative for help. But it would be inappropriate for one to ask for special privileges from the government simply because you have special connections with some government officials. They are not always reliable anyway. I know of many big corporations that, at one time, could almost get whatever they wanted from the government. But when their business started to go downhill, few government officials were willing to stick their neck out. (TW1)[7]

TW4[8] and TW11 also felt such connections might be unreliable in a crisis.

The big corporations have [political] connections. So do the enterprises controlled by the Nationalist Party [KMT] … I think there is a difference between connections (*guanxi*) and network (*renmo*). Your network is more organic, like your friends and neighbours. Connections are more instrumental and they require deliberate cultivation. In times of crisis, I am not sure if your connections are willing to help you overcome your problems, but your network will try to help. (TW4)

13.3.2   Respondents' Experiences in the Crisis

In contrast, the story these respondents told of their own experiences in the crisis were of surprisingly limited damage. Ten said they had been negatively affected to some extent (but only three significantly so), ten had been completely unaffected and five said the crisis had benefited them The worst affected were HK10[9] who had had to sell his garment factory in China to the Chinese 'for a dime' and OZ1[10] who lost half a million Australian dollars on a failed fashion boutique, embarked on just as the crisis struck. Both, however, were proud that they had not lost so badly that they could not make a new start.

Another seven spoke of temporarily slowed growth and expansion plans postponed, rather than of any decline or serious problems. TW10[11] had abandoned a project to open a new office in Malaysia and TW2[12] (who described his business as 'not badly affected') had abandoned some traditional markets in Indonesia and Thailand, fearing he might not be paid. Ten respondents, three Taiwanese, one in Hong Kong and six in Australia (two of whom were exporting to the region and one dependent on the custom of Chinese immigrants in Australia) were emphatic that they had experienced no impact from the crisis at all.

It is a truism that it is an ill wind that blows no good and from every crisis there emerge winners as well as losers, the former often at the expense of the latter. Five respondents, four in Hong Kong and one in Taiwan, had benefited directly from the crisis. These had still growing markets in the West, especially for innovative or higher-tech products, or found the demand for their low-end electronic products reviving in Asia, as substitutes for more expensive alternatives. HK1[13] thought the crisis had given his business in a sunset industry 'a new lease of life for a few extra years'. Even where their customers were able to demand lower prices, these respondents had been able to pass this on, with advantage, in lower payments for materials and labour and in more extended credit by their suppliers. Some were able to take over the customers of those who had been less efficient or financially prudent and gone under, or who were in countries where the currency collapse prevented them obtaining their needed inputs or credit.

When the W.I. trading company in Hong Kong closed its doors HK6,[14] facing unemployment and knowing her ex-employer's connections in Brazil, had decided to use her own savings to start an export agency. She examined the client networks inherited from her old company and found a number of small buyers the company had not bothered to deal with very much. She contacted them and found that they were eager to import from her. Their orders were never really big, but they were reliable in making payments, and ordered from her consistently. Her new business was now flourishing, although it was constrained from expanding by lack of access to capital. She concluded that 'This has taught me that big is not always beautiful and, in times of crisis, being small is not necessarily a disadvantage'.

Our respondents were, as we noted, in part self-selected as survivors and may have sought to downplay their own losses. Yet the picture of survival and of readiness to start again meshes well with the macro evidence of rapid recovery in the region, which has contradicted so many gloomy predictions. Nor did they present their own experience as unique. When we asked whether they knew personally any others whose business had suffered from the crisis, eight could not think of any and only seven (four in Hong Kong, two in Taiwan and one in Australia) could bring to mind anyone they knew who had actually been ruined by it. Most of these were said to have mortgaged their businesses in order to speculate on the stock or property markets or were already on a downward slide for other reasons, but some had been hit by the bankruptcy of major customers in Southeast Asia, especially Indonesia. HK4[15] remarked that 'I know people in my field of business [electrical manufacturing] who were suffering great financial difficulties but somehow they managed to stay in business'. 'People found it harder to export, but are still surviving.' (OZ20)[16]

13.4   DEFENSIVE STRATEGIES OF SMALL AND MEDIUM BUSINESSES

13.4.1   Conservatism

Our respondents spoke often of the handicaps resulting from their small size, especially the difficulty in raising capital, in the absence of support from banks and government, as well as the pressures of powerful contractors and customers, and the limited professional expertise at their disposal. Yet some of these could, with hindsight, be seen as strengths in disguise. Most, as we saw, had been relatively unaffected by the crisis or had revived quickly, and they largely attributed this to their own efforts.

> I'm an old hag in this industry and I've seen lots of ups and downs ... There's very little luck involved. If you're like me who has survived for so long, you have already learned the tricks to stay away from trouble. (HK1)

The advantages attributed to SMEs in a financial crisis seemed to be of two kinds. First, the low debt and self-reliance of small firms could be seen, at least with hindsight, as an insulation against the disastrous consequences of sudden credit droughts and the bursting of speculative bubbles. While this mode of operating had been perhaps initially objectively imposed by the absence of bank and government support, it became incorporated into a collective conservative ethic of autonomy, family responsibility and productivism. Second, their long-term, trust-based personal relationships with customers and suppliers could provide some security and, when necessary, extended credit, so long as too much was not expected of them.

> If we had borrowed heavily to expand we would have been in deep trouble. I heard stories about other people who are not in my business who had to flee or

> disappear because they defaulted on all kinds of repayments. We are doing all right because we only have a very small loan from the bank. (HK8)[17]

> I would not borrow money to start a new business… I would only transfer money from my reserves to get it up and running. (TW10)

Such financial conservatism also makes possible significant contraction without disaster:

> When our business is good, we operate our factory in full capacity. When the situation is a bit dull, we operate in 70–80 per cent capacity. We have very low personnel and general expenses. If we find that business is really bad, we stop ordering raw materials and decrease our production until a recovery is visible. (TW2)

If debt-based expansion was seen as a cause of the crisis, even more damaging to economies and to businesses was short-term speculation especially if it relied on borrowing. Seventy per cent of all respondents (six in Hong Kong, four in Australia and six in Taiwan) were critical of speculation in stocks and property as a primary cause of the Asian crisis, of business failures by people they knew or as a hazard to 'serious' 'honest' businesses.

> I think it is a matter of over extension of credit. First you had the speculation boom in Japan and Taiwan, then spreading to the rest of Southeast Asia. Property and share prices were hot and they provided the perfect playground for Soros. When the foreign hot money retreated, the governments had to devalue their currencies. (TW4)

The 'easy money' and 'get rich quick' temptations of such activities were condemned in ethical terms, separated by a moral divide from responsibility to family, personal control over ones own fate and gains made through hard work.

> The lure of fast money was powerful. (HK10)

> It [speculation] is too risky … I feel that I have to be responsible to my father and my family to carry on the family's business … At least I can say I haven't failed my father's expectations. (HK8)

> I never speculate on properties or shares because I have real responsibilities to my family and relatives. They gave me so much support in getting this business off the ground, the least I could do is to make it viable, safe and credible. (HK9)[18]

Speculation and productive enterprise were contrasted as incompatible.

> When you are involved in manufacturing [*shi ye*, literally means real or concrete business], you shouldn't gamble with your business. (HK9)

> I am not interested in speculative activities, like buying and selling shares … I believe in good, honest investment. (TW6)

> I wouldn't put any money from my core business into speculating on shares or properties. I know that when they crash, I would have nothing left. I won't have a business anymore. (HK4)[19]

The big companies, who were best positioned to play such games, were also likely to be the biggest losers.

> Most people who lost their shirts … were the people who had to spend big to prop up the value of the shares of their own businesses, such as National Automobiles, Hanshen and Guangsan Department Stores. They were the ones who were manipulating the stock markets, inflating their assets by re-mortgaging their own shares to contract bigger loans, normally worth 70 per cent of their value, and use the money to purchase another piece of property … when the market started to dip … they became extremely precarious in making repayments. And when the market continued to tumble, the whole thing collapsed. (TW1)

Small businesses could protect themselves by avoiding such activities.

> Sticking with what you do – not gambling away your business in speculating properties or stock market. Of course, speculation is quick, easy profit but only if you are lucky. I refused to play the game and that's why now I'm still a small fry in this business. (HK1)

While several admitted to being tempted they congratulated themselves on resisting.

> Every one I know in Hong Kong back then was persuading me that I should give up my business in Australia and return there to speculate on properties and the share market because it was easy money … I was tempted. (OZ3)[20]

> I must admit that there were times I was absolutely disheartened by the fact that it was so easy to make money by speculating on properties. … one could easily make $100 000 just for standing in line overnight to get into the

developer's office to buy a flat off the plan ... Now people say that I am having the last laugh ... (HK4)

Even the few who admitted to some speculative activities dissociated themselves from those who allowed them to endanger their real business.

They were gambling with their businesses, and I wasn't. They were not diversifying their business – in fact, they were shifting into speculating full time. (HK10)

In general respondents indicated that such activities breached a shared code of values, and that shame would prevent such people from seeking assistance from their friends when in trouble

You don't want to help ... anyone who comes to you to borrow money to pay their gambling debts. (TW2)

I only helped those who deserved to be helped. Like those who genuinely had business difficulties. (TW5)

13.4.2   Trust-based Networks

The high level connections of big firms were perceived as both a temptation to unsound practices and as an unreliable support in a crisis.

We heard stories that even when you thought you had 'good connection' with banks, they would not treat you any different from any other client – no personal favours, no exceptions. I suppose they would have to behave that way because in times of crisis, who could risk their necks for you? (HK4)

Lacking assistance from government and banks, 21 respondents had benefited from advice and support from personal networks of kin and friends, and from establishing long-term trust with proven, reliable suppliers and customers. Unlike those of large firms and tycoons, the networks of SMEs were praised. Twelve respondents (two from Hong Kong, three from Australia and seven from Taiwan) believed or knew from experience that such networks could be a valuable support in a crisis. 'Friends are more appreciated when you are in difficulty' (OZ20). Five had actually themselves given or received financial assistance when in need.

We just wanted to develop a mutual system of support and information exchange so that we could develop strategies to help each other out of our predicaments. (TW8)

We've also been fortunate because we have very good, loyal clients who have been supporting us all along since I started my own business. Mind you, their loyalty is hard earned because it is the result of a long-term relationship based on trust. (HK9)

The only kind of relationship I treasure is the one related to my clients, friends, upstream and downstream partners. These are the relationships that must be well maintained. (TW2)

My upstream partner supplies me with raw materials, my downstream partner is responsible for marketing and retail and we have been working as a production network for ten, fifteen years. As a network we are almost working like a big corporation, but we don't have the pressure of a big corporation, especially in terms of capitalisation and risks. Simultaneously, when we work as a network, we also have a better chance to survive. (TW1)

Among my friends in Taiwan, we helped each other during the crisis. We gave them jobs and we lent them money to help them tide over the difficult times. (TW4)

Cash-flow problems were ameliorated by suppliers allowing longer repayment credit to regular, trusted customers. Eight people spoke of credit extensions, which sometimes were crucial in allowing a business to stay afloat. In this mutual aid and good business combined.

What saved us from going down was the fact that... given the connections I had accumulated from my previous job in the same field, it was relatively easy for me to ask for an extension to pay for the shipment. (OZ7)[21]

Only those people downstream [the retailers] are not in direct competition with you. So, if they have financial trouble, I would still supply them my products, I would give them more time to make repayments. They are your clients and your friends. If they are in trouble, you should give them a hand. (TW2)

The grapevine was highly valued even by those who stressed autonomy. 'Being independent is most important' asserted TW11, but added that 'we often share our business experiences with friends', and TW11 had relied on it to warn him of potential clients with shaky finances.

Yet the help provided by such networks in a crisis had limits, as seven respondents stressed. Both the scale of financial need of those in trouble and the fact that everyone was having problems often precluded direct financial help and the shared values of autonomy discouraged people from asking, except as a last resort.

> I don't think one can rely too much on networks to solve one's business problems … In business, people will have to look after their own interest first before they can help you, even if you are their best friend or closest relative. There is a distinction between *renqing* (sentiment) and *daoli* (principle). Network is about sentiments, allowing you to enjoy special privileges among a certain group of like-minded people, but when things get tough you should also know that the principle is to look after yourself and not relying on using sentiments to ask people to bail you out especially in a crisis situation when everyone is almost in the same boat facing similar threats. That's why one cannot abuse the principle by over reliance on sentiments. Once you abuse it, you will be excluded from the network. No one will want to see you again. (OZ2[22])

> Few people would ask you for monetary help during this time because they also know that things are tight all round. (TW2)

Indeed arguably the networks themselves could not survive if too many demands were made on them.

The consensus among our respondents was that a financially conservative strategy, before and during a crisis, was the best defence. Avoid speculation; minimise debt and have as little to do with banks as possible; maintain a cash reserve for bad times and conserve capital for future uses; beware of too much risk! Sustain long-term personal and business networks, without expecting too much from them! But such conservatism represents only one dimension of the views and responses of our respondents.

13.5   CONTINUING ENTREPRENEURIAL DYNAMISM

13.5.1   Coexistence of Conservatism and Entrepreneurship

It is not, however, through conservatism that small and medium Chinese businesses in Asia had played their major role in economic development and the entry of China onto the world market. They have, rather, been renowned for entrepreneurship, an innovative search for new products, methods, designs and markets and for a diversification which combines existing activities with quite different, new and often risky ventures.[23]

Arguably, this willingness to venture into unknown territory was a major source of the dynamism of East Asian economies in the years before the crisis. Over the pre-crisis period of rapid growth there was also a substantial upgrading of products and technology, and moves upward from contracting to OEM production* and then to increasing their own design input and aspiring to their own brand names (Hobday 1995; Gereffi and Hamilton 1996). Innovation and calculated risk taking are not so common among small businesses, and seem to require the encouragement of an entrepreneurial culture as well as mutually supportive institutions such as business networks. How far has the crisis tipped the balance away from these and towards conservatism and self-sufficiency?

Our respondents, despite the widespread expression of financially conservative sentiments, and the advocacy of 'keeping low in lean times' (TW11), had not abandoned their entrepreneurial drive. Only six had limited themselves to one product or activity over the previous few years and were not seeking to diversify or upgrade their activities or to find or develop new products, new markets or new methods, either as a response to uncertainty or as a continuation of prior practices. There was widespread awareness that too limited a range could leave them trapped in a declining or overcompetitive sector and render them vulnerable in a crisis.

Entering new fields and new markets demanded investment of money and of time to acquire new skills and develop trust in new networks. But even those who had shied away from such risks seemed apologetic, giving age or lack of resources or an especially cautious temperament as the reason for avoiding what they knew might be the wiser, though riskier, path.

HK1 had thought of moving from the sunset industry of making portable radios into toys, but felt he would not now have the time in the six years before he intended to retire to build the new networks required or to recoup the high capital costs. TW1 had similarly considered doing something new but rejected the idea.

> It is correct to say diversification is good for minimising risks but if you finance your projects by overborrowing that becomes extremely risky ... If I had lots of money I certainly would diversify. However ... diversification is a bottomless pit.

Few had unmixed feelings. The same business culture that enjoined productive conservatism at the same time promoted entrepreneurship, and each individual had to juggle their own combination which varied with temperament. The received wisdom, cited by many, was that even a conservative strategy must involve 'not putting all your eggs in one basket'. If a crisis made some established markets unreliable, it might be better to cut them off and find new ones. If there were pressures on profit margins it may be necessary to move production to places where costs were lower or to move out of overcompetitive 'sunset' industries and into new ones. Innovation

---

*   OEM stands for an original equipment manufacturer, who is responsible for subcontracting, coordinating and carrying out all the processes for a finished product, to the detailed (or sometimes) sketchy design requirements of a brand-name contractor.

might be a necessity for moving ahead or just keeping up. At the same time such moves were hampered by shortage of capital and the difficulty and risks of borrowing.

> I think one should diversify and not be too conservative. One should always look for the opportunity to expand overseas and diversify your market. Otherwise you will not grow. Nevertheless, one should not overdiversify. One should not spend more than 30 per cent of the business' capital for that purpose. (TW4)

> I do not oppose people diversifying into other businesses but you can do so only when you make sure your core business is secure. (HK4)

> It is a good thing not to put everything in one basket. But it is equally important to know what you do best and not lose sight of that. (OZ4)[24]

> I like diversification ... People did say to me that diversification involves risks but I am fairly cautious, I test things out first a bit. (OZ6)[25]

> You should take advantage of opportunities but also pay attention to risk management, have some reserves and contingency plans. (OZ20).

13.5.2 Diversification

A strategy of diversification is the hinge that links together the two seemingly contradictory principles of conservatism and entrepreneurship. This involves combining, under common ownership (but often in formally independent ventures), different products, activities and markets. The diversity is on the one hand an insurance policy but on the other it allows for experimentation and trial and error, while protecting a familiar terrain. In a rapidly changing and unpredictable world big leaps can be made, while allowing for a gradual transition if they are successful and a retreat if necessary. In our earlier research on Chinese business, over the last decade, we have found diversification of both large and small owners to be ubiquitous. In this survey it is clear that the crisis has not halted this tendency, which remained widespread.

Respondents who were import–export agents in Australia had moved from importing building materials to carpets, had added Chinese teas to herbal imports and had changed from a focus on wool to iron-ore exports and the import of agricultural machinery. Taiwanese manufacturers had added fabric printing to the manufacture of synthetic textiles, the development of new designer containers to standard bottles and had started to produce machinery parts (for themselves and others) that they had previously subcontracted. One respondent in Hong Kong, after developing and making a range of innovative lighting products and a device for watching TV in 3D, was shifting from a focus on manufacture to one based on licensing their production, with transfer of designs, equipment and components, to manufacturers around the world. Others had moved from clothing manufacture to the import of pharmaceuticals and health foods and from computer retail and servicing to the testing and sale of a newly invented organic fertiliser (in France, Malaysia, Vietnam and Taiwan). HK9 combined manufacture of leather products with the ownership of rental properties; OZ4 owned shopping centres as well as having shares in a restaurant and a karaoke club; TW4 built factories for Taiwanese in China as well as investing in a fruit orchard there, and TW8 owned a shipping agency as well as having interests in a rubber factory, a restaurant and a discothèque and, perhaps in the future, an orchard. Both HK9 and TW1 had installed new machinery in order to produce better-quality products (plastic bottles and leather bags), aimed at upmarket niches. Both, however, planned to retain their established mass production facilities and markets as well.

With this strategy failures can be limited and accepted. OZ3, when we interviewed him in 1993, was combining a printshop, a newsagency and a curio shop. When we spoke to him again seven years later, these were both ticking over but he had also been running a Chinese video rental business. This had closed down in 1998 when the spread of the Internet and cheap video compact disks (VCDs) from Hong Kong reduced demand.

> I don't regret to closing it down. I always believe in diversifying your business especially if you can afford to expand. In this case, I didn't lose any money and I enjoyed the experience. It just didn't make money for me. I think for what its worth, it's better to seize the opportunity and try things out rather than let it go by. Who knows, you might not have the same opportunity again in your life. I don't think one should stick to 'core business' too often. Sure, if that's what's giving you the security and your livelihood, you should stay in it. But if you could afford to try something different, you should give it a go. You'll never know if you never try. You may say that's kind of risky, but everything you do involves a certain amount of risk. As long as you don't put your 'core business' at risk, there's no harm diversifying yourself.

His latest venture was to open a restaurant, with the help of his sister-in-law's experienced advice and contacts.

OZ1 had been operating a prawn farm that was struggling, with Japanese demand in the doldrums. She decided to open a fashion boutique, leaving the aquaculture in the hands of other family members, but she had misjudged the Australian market, and although her friends' custom kept the venture afloat for a year she finally sold it with a loss of half a million Australian dollars and retreated back into the earlier business. This was now doing better as they had become more experienced and had also made efforts to find new markets for seafood, and a diversification into abalone exports. She described the shop as an 'honourable failure ... Despite the financial loss, we are doing okay because we didn't lose our shirt'.

13.5.3   Networks and Entrepreneurship

We have noted above how networks could be an important, although necessarily limited, resource for survival. Such networks were often even more important for the ability to change direction, providing advice, information and personal introductions for new products and markets. 'Network is ... about giving you extended access to information and opportunities' (OZ2).

The positive evaluation of the contribution of such networks was almost unanimous. One Taiwanese respondent thought the cultivation of networks, even in China, was 'a waste of time', but he was a solitary voice. Nineteen believed, or knew from experience, that they were useful, even indispensable in starting or running a business.[26]

> Recently I joined the Taiwanese Business Association and met new contacts. In times of an uncertain economic future, I think everyone is keen to cooperate with one another to minimise unnecessary competition and willing to share market information and develop business strategies that are able to bring benefits to all. The advice I get from others has been very useful. (TW10)

> I didn't have many difficulties in my new business because ... I have developed a string of connections that I could rely on, in terms of giving me leads for distribution ... (HK10). I have received no assistance from either the Taiwanese or the Chinese government. Friends in my network introduced me to new clients and new agents. They're helpful to my business. (TW8)

Three had set up their own businesses during the crisis on the basis of the contacts they had made as employees with suppliers and customers (in two cases in failing businesses).

> My business has been having a smooth run since it started. I consider myself extremely lucky because I am strategically placed to develop a good network and have a good distribution base [the clinic]. I meet an awful lot of people first as patients, then they became my friends. They came from various backgrounds and they were always very helpful if you needed any information. I am truly blessed because many of my business opportunities were offered to me by my patients. When I decided to import Chinese herbal remedies into Australia, the idea actually was suggested by several of my patients. They even gave me suggestions as to how I should run my import business and some of them gave me leads to contact suppliers. (OZ6)

> You could say that I could not have started my own business without connections. My relatives are important to back me up financially, but more

important are the suppliers and their willingness to give me an exclusive dealer/ distributorship. In China, particularly, you wouldn't be able to accomplish anything if you don't have the right connections. (OZ7)

The differing career paths of OZ20 and OZ21[27] give an indication of the importance of networks for changes of direction. We interviewed them first in 1993 when both had high hopes for exporting wool to small end users in China. OZ21, an immigrant from Malaysia, was by far the most experienced of the two, working in partnership with a mainland Chinese who had good contacts. OZ21 was herself from China, with friends there but no business background or financial resources. Shortly thereafter, it seems, this kind of trade declined and then collapsed, under pressure from new tariffs and from cut price Russian competition. At the same time OZ20 lost contact with his Chinese partner. He rejected an opportunity to put money into property development near Shanghai because 'We didn't have people over there, it was too much risk', and thereafter he abandoned projects in China.

OZ20 on the other hand was clearly prospering when we interviewed her again in 2000, and had diversified successfully into more promising fields of trade with China. She was still 'Working through long term connections in China, not through the phone book ... I try to deal with people on a basis of trust', and she had been able to move successfully into a wide variety of other import and export activities involving iron ore, wheat, education and machinery.

13.5.4 Restructuring

Most of our respondents had been taking a variety of new initiatives but, although the pathways opened by networks may lead in new directions, these may often seem random or eccentric, deriving from accidental meetings and chance conversations. Can we obtain from these interviews any indications of overall trends or wider restructuring? Directions taken by several respondents may provide some hints.

Seven respondents had turned to the still growing Chinese domestic market, developing or seeking products for it. One had withdrawn from markets in Indonesia and Thailand and was hoping to develop new alliances for distribution in the Middle East and Canada. Several were moving out of sunset manufacturing and into supplying new kinds of demand which they predicted would grow in the future: two were now trading Chinese medicines, therapeutic teas and mushrooms and Western pharmaceuticals and health foods to what they both described as increasingly health conscious ageing populations in Hong Kong and Australia; three were making or trading new products aimed at growing environmental problems that they saw as of increasing concern to governments – organic fertilisers, recycling machinery and water purifiers.

A number of respondents were seeking to improve or upgrade their skills, technology or modes of operating. Three Taiwanese had recently been shifting more production and technical work into China to cut costs and one of these was also looking to move some production to Singapore, Malaysia or the Philippines to reduce the perceived political risk of too much investment in China.

Four manufacturers were taking steps to improve the quality of their products, to incorporate more of their own design, to promote their own brand name or to cater to a more discerning segment of the market. Five respondents claimed to have improved on the performance of erstwhile competitors or employers, whom they had taken over or displaced, by establishing more long-term and trustworthy ties with suppliers and customers. Three were seeking to adopt Western professional management systems and to enter into partnerships with Western companies in order to gain such expertise.

13.6   CONCLUSIONS

Our findings must be very tentative because of the, as yet, small number of respondents and the unavoidably non-representative nature of our selection procedures. Precise distributions cannot be relevant in such a study. What we have found, however, is a seemingly almost consensual coexistence, in the immediate post-crisis period, of both conservative and entrepreneurial values and strategies in varying combinations.

Conservative prescriptions call for small-business people to ensure a sound cash flow and cultivate long-term networks; avoid high-risk speculation aimed at getting rich quick; avoid debt that cannot be repaid if things go wrong, and above all make sure that the existing core business is sheltered from the implications of failure. On the other hand such measures alone cannot guarantee safety, not to speak of growth and success. All your eggs in one basket is generally recognised as a foolish way to court disaster; in a changing world thriving activities can become sunset industries, new competition can eliminate profits and prosperous markets can be hit by crisis.

With enthusiasm or resignation almost all respondents knew that they might have to diversify, upgrade or change direction, but that they must do so with caution, and most said they were trying to tread this fine line. Most had continued to seek new products, markets and methods and were making some contribution to a restructuring of their economies. The rapid recovery in the economies of the region matches well the picture we have found.

NOTES

1   Funded by Australia Research Council. Carried out by David Ip, Richard Lam, Constance Lever-Tracy and Noel Tracy.
2   Taiwan interviewee number 7.
3   Taiwan interviewee number 5.
4   Taiwan interviewee number 6.
5   Taiwan interviewee number 8.

6   Taiwan interviewee number 11.

7   Taiwan interviewee number 1.

8   Taiwan interviewee number 4.

9   Hong Kong interviewee number 10.

10 Australian interviewee number 1.

11 Taiwan interviewee number 10.

12 Taiwan interviewee number 2.

13 Hong Kong interviewee number 1.

14 Hong Kong interviewee number 6.

15 Hong Kong interviewee number 4.

16 Australian interviewee number 20.

17 Hong Kong interviewee number 8.

18 Hong Kong interviewee number 9.

19 Rita Ho, who has carried out an unpublished study of the relationship between Chinese business and gambling (Ho 1997), suggests that there may be a bifurcated business culture, with one group inclined to gambling in business affairs, and the other (mainly those involved in manufacturing) averse to it. Both groups felt there was likely to be some incompatibility between speculative and productive activities (personal communication).

20 Australian interviewee number 3.

21 Australian interviewee number 7.

22 Australian interviewee number 2.

23 A reviewer of this chapter has suggested that diversification may be a declining practice, appropriate for low-skilled activities and owners with limited education. Historical accounts suggest, rather, that diaspora Chinese have tended to move away from narrow occupational niches originally ascribed to groups defined by dialect and place of origin. Our earlier study of Chinese and Indian immigrant businesses in Australia, found high levels of education and did not clash with pervasive strategies of diversification (Lever-Tracy et al. 1991, pp. 71–7). In the current study also, while some wished to restrict their diversification broadly to fields for which higher education had prepared them, others were happy to be more randomly flexible and opportunistic. Those most inhibited, who felt most restricted to the familiar, were the older and less-educated respondents.

24 Australian interviewee number 4.

25 Australian interviewee number 6.

26 One woman described them as necessary to her own identity and ability to start a new life after a broken marriage. Her biggest frustration, she said, was not having her own contacts, because every friend she had was her ex-husband's friend. Only when she had built her own personal network did she feel she was a person herself again, able to get on with her own life and to establish her own, now thriving, business.

27 Australian interviewee number 21.

REFERENCES

Gereffi, G. and G. Hamilton (1996), 'Commodity Chains and Embedded Networks: The Economic Organisation of Global Capitalism', paper presented at the Annual Meeting of the American Sociological Association, New York.

Hamilton, G. (ed.) (1991), *Business Networks and Economic Development in East and Southeast Asia*, Hong Kong: Centre for Asian Studies, University of Hong Kong.

Hamilton, G. (1997), 'Organisation and Market Processes in Taiwan's Capitalist Economy', in M. Orru, W. Biggart and G. Hamilton (eds), *The Economic Organisation of East Asian Capitalism'*, Thousand Oaks, CA: Sage Publications, pp. 238–91.

Ho, Rita (1997), 'Diaspora Chinese Business: A Chop Suey of Speculative and Rational Features', Honours thesis, Department of Sociology, Flinders University of South Australia.

Hobday, M., (1995), *Innovation in East Asia: The Challenge to Japan*, Cheltenham, UK: Edward Elgar.

Hsing, Y.T. (1998), *Making Capitalism in China: The Taiwan Connection*, New York: Oxford University Press.

Kotkin, J. (1993), *Tribes: How Race, Religion and Identity Determine Success in the New Global Economy*, New York: Random House.

Lever-Tracy, C., D. Ip, J. Kitay, I. Phillips and N. Tracy (1991), *Asian Entrepreneurs in Australia: Ethnic Small Business in the Chinese and Indian Communities of Brisbane and Sydney*, Canberra: Office of Multicultural Affairs, AGPS.

Lever-Tracy, C., D. Ip and N. Tracy (1996), *The Chinese Diaspora and Mainland China: An Emerging Economic Synergy*, Basingstoke: Macmillan/St. Martins.

Orrù, M. (1991), 'The Institutional Logic of Small-firm Economies in Italy and Taiwan', *Studies in Comparative International Development*, 26 (1), Spring, pp. 3–28.

Pyke, F., G. Becattin, and W. Sengenberger (eds) (1990), *Industrial Districts and Inter-Firm Cooperation in Italy*, Geneva: IILS.

Redding, S.G. (1990), *The Spirit of Chinese Capitalism*, Berlin: Walter de Gruyter.

Sirower, M. (2000), *The Synergy Trap: How Companies Lose the Acquisition Game*, New York: Simon & Schuster.

Storper, M. and A. Scott (eds) (1992), *Pathways to Industrialisation and Regional Development*, London: Routledge.

Tracy, N. (2000), 'Weathering the Storm: Structural Changes in the Chinese Diaspora Economy', in D. Ip, C. Lever-Tracy and N. Tracy (eds), *Chinese Business and the Asian Crisis*, Aldershot: Ashgate/Gower, pp. 163–83.

Yamaguchi, M. (1993), *The Emerging Chinese Business Sphere*, in Nomura Asian Perspectives Monograph Series, no. 11 (2).

Periodicals/newspapers:

FEER (Far Eastern Economic Review)
Forbes Magazine
The Australian
Yazhou Zhoukan

14   Connections, Culture and Context: Business Relationships and Networks in the Asia–Pacific Region

Liz Fulop and David Richards

14.1   INTRODUCTION: CULTURE, NETWORK FORMS AND SMES

Business structures and relationships are influenced by many social and economic factors, but are significantly influenced by culture, particularly values. According to Lessem (1998, p. 46), 'Cultures earn their livings, produce and develop effectively, that which their members most value. To believe that a particular task is valuable is a necessary prelude to doing it well'. In many Western countries, business networks, comprising SMEs,[1] have been mainly formed through interventions of third parties, such as industry associations, industry bodies, development boards or governments or through a combination of these agents. In Australia and New Zealand, for example, it makes little sense to talk of networking and SMEs without addressing the issue of government sponsored business network programs. In the case of Australia, a number of specific network types have emerged as a result of the targeting that occurred in government funded business network programs. Similarly, in New Zealand, the Joint Action Group (JAG) was the initial impetus for network formation, but was later augmented by a 'hard network' program developed through government funding and aimed specifically at SMEs (Ffowcs-Williams 1998).

The same seems to apply in some other countries in the Asia–Pacific region,[2] such as Korea, where the *chaebol* has been supported by government initiatives directed at encouraging large organisations to form networks, which, until recently, excluded SMEs. The *keiretsu* in Japan involves both large firms and SMEs and emerged through government legislation in the early 1940s that forced SMEs to become subcontractors to large manufacturing firms (Shadur and Kienzle 1995, p. 450). A variety of network forms exist in Japan, including those dominated by SMEs that have emerged since the 1980s through the support and patronage of various government departments and their officials (Shadur and Kienzle 1995, p. 454). For the purposes of this chapter, we use the term 'contrived network' to describe those networks which have been formed largely through the intervention of third parties.

By contrast, in most of East and Southeast Asia, business network relationships are organic and have not required, or been given, deliberate help from outside agencies. Indeed, SMEs may refuse to be helped by schemes that exist to facilitate networking (Chee 1990). This is because, in most of the region, cultures are relationship oriented, rather than principle or contract oriented: '*the relationship comes before the contract*' (Hampden-Turner and Trompenaars 1997, p. 178, emphasis in original). The overseas Chinese, who form an ethnic minority yet play a commanding economic role[3] in many countries of East and Southeast Asia, have as a dominant form the family business linked into a series of informal networks. This provides the archetype of how relationships and networks link to advance the business interests of SMEs. These networks are very extensive and able to cross national boundaries, including into Mainland China, yet are not influenced by governments, but rather by a complex system of kinship and extended family ties. We use the term 'organic network' to describe those networks that have been formed largely *without* the intervention of third parties.

A large part of the explanation for these different forms of networking lies both in cultural influences and the institutional arrangements that reinforce cultural differences between nations. One helpful way to understand the context of culture was developed by Hall (1976), who distinguished between *high-* and *low-context cultures*. In high context cultures the external environment is very important, many things are hidden and meaning is conveyed indirectly. In low context countries the environment is less important, things are made more explicit and meaning is often conveyed directly. Although Hall does not clearly place different countries within his model, others such as, for example, Hofstede (1991) and Mead (1998, p. 30), have undertaken such a categorisation.

For Mead, high-context cultures include China, Japan, Korea, Vietnam and other Asian countries, countries around the Mediterranean and in the Middle East. They are characterised by: long-lasting relationships; implicit, shared and indirect communication codes; personal authority with loyalty to superiors and subordinates; spoken (rather than written) agreements; clear distinctions between insiders and outsiders, and with cultural patterns that are slow to change. By contrast, low-context cultures include the Anglo countries (Australia, Britain, Canada, New Zealand and the United States), Scandinavia and Germany. These cultures are characterised by short-term relationships; explicit, logical and direct communication codes; bureaucratic and diffuse authority with impersonal relationships; written (rather than spoken) agreements based on legal systems; imprecise distinctions between insiders and outsiders, and with cultural patterns which are more adaptable to change.

Hall's model, although not empirically based, has many similarities to and resonates significantly with those of Hofstede (1991) and Trompenaars (Hambden-Turner and Trompenaars 1997), both of which are supported by comparative data. These cultural models are useful in understanding how members of different cultures develop business relationships, negotiate with insiders and outsiders and implement contracts (Mead 1998, p. 31): 'For example, Hall's model helps explain why family companies in high-context Southeast Asian cultures differ so widely from their equivalents in low-context Anglo cultures'.

Before turning to the two network forms described above, it is necessary to explore in more detail the dynamics of network formation, highlighting how culture continually intercedes to create distinct national variations. However, here we try to avoid the danger of the ill-defined and simple cultural models that can be seen in explanations of economic performance, both before and after the collapse of the Asian economies in the late 1990s (Buchanan et al. 1998).

The remainder of this chapter proceeds as follows. Section 14.2 focuses upon the different types of networks that have been identified in the literature, and their key characteristics, as well as those most applicable in the context of the East Asian economies. Section 14.3 focuses upon one type of networking system, organic networking, which is prevalent in the context of Chinese family business. Section 14.4 outlines an alternative networking system, prevalent in the context of Western societies, based on contrived networking and looks at this in the context of business networks in Australia. Section 14.5 focuses upon the role of networking and networking programs in assisting SMEs to enter international markets. Finally, Section 14.6 presents a summary of the major conclusions from this chapter.

14.2   NETWORK DYNAMICS

The literature on business networks is noted for the overabundance of global and often complex overviews of networking or inter-organisational relations (Benson-Rea and Wilson 1994; Buttery and Buttery 1994, 1995; Grandori and Soda 1995; Ebers and Grandori 1997; Human and Provan 1997; Nooteboom 1997; and Buttery et al. 1999). Few, if any, of the aforementioned authors attempt to distinguish between network dynamics at the local or national level from those that come into play in a cross-cultural context. Nor does this literature attempt to distinguish network dynamics in SME-based networks from those dominated by larger organisations.

Of the theorists mentioned above, perhaps Nooteboom's approach is the one that offers some bridging concepts between local network dynamics and the cross-cultural context. While it can be argued that Nooteboom did not develop his approach to networks in the context of SMEs, his framework does complement studies that have looked at network dynamics of SMEs, although none have included the cross-cultural context (for example, Buttery and Buttery 1995; Fulop with Kelly 1995, 1997a, and 1997b; Johannisson and Mønsted 1996;and Nesheim and Reve 1996).

Nooteboom draws on a number of theoretical perspectives to identify the key elements of network formation and performance that are described in Figure 14.1. He argues that his contingency approach accounts for the key dimensions of networking and can also lead to some testable propositions. The framework is used here for descriptive purposes, as its fundamental assumptions are not based on SME studies.

In developing the framework, for example, Nooteboom starts from the premise that networks are formed to achieve certain goals based on particular strategic options that collaborative solutions could offer businesses. The framework assumes order, logic and rationality in how businesses make decisions about joining a network and formulating their strategies. In the case of SMEs, this would be a questionable assumption in the cross-cultural context as the discussion of the Chinese family business below reveals. Furthermore, studies of contrived networks in Australia have shown that SME owners do not actively seek out network relations. Instead they are usually either co-opted or enticed by a third party and they are less likely to join on

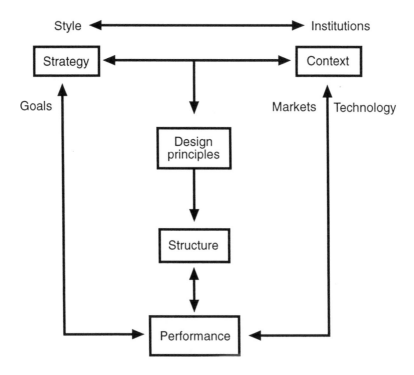

Source: Nooteboom (1997), p. 3.

Figure 14.1   Nooteboom's Framework

their own initiative or through personal contacts with other business owners (Buttery and Buttery 1995; Fulop with Kelly 1997b). SMEs in organic networks, on the other hand, do actively seek out relationships through their own initiative or personal contacts with other business owners. Nooteboom's framework does, however, identify the strategic importance of identifying common goals in collaboration and thus gaining ongoing commitment to networking.

In studies undertaken by Buttery and Buttery of SME-based networks in Australia, developing common goals, openness and trust were given high rankings by network participants as being important to a network's success. Yet Buttery and Buttery (1995) and Fulop with Kelly (1997a, 1997b, and 1995) have found that the incidence of planning in these SME networks was limited and often left to a third party, such as a consultant or network broker. Few SMEs in these two studies had strategic plans that included joining a business network. The attraction of government funds was often the major catalyst.

For Nooteboom, style translates into a preference for one style of governance over another. Others refer to this as the climate in the network (Buttery and Buttery 1995) and this can range from being highly bureaucratic and legalistic to informal and based on a 'hand shake' or 'accepting someone's word'. Nooteboom assumes that most networks, even those of SMEs, will have certain legally binding arrangements, especially as funding bodies require that such agreements be drawn up. Following on from this, Nooteboom's treatment of context (see Figure 14.1) is of particular interest to cross-cultural collaboration. At the institutional level, context can cover a range of factors and Nooteboom (1997, p. 17) identifies ten of these. From these he develops four key propositions, the first of which refers to the legal infrastructure (laws, contracts, enforcement rules) in which collaboration takes place. Nooteboom argues that if this infrastructure is poor, then governance may not be feasible and so collaboration is unlikely to succeed. Second, if contractual attitudes are highly legalistic then the cost of establishing legally based governance mechanisms is likely to be excessive and inhibit collaboration. Third, when contractual attitudes and practices are relational or personal and morality is familial, clan based or based on similar exclusionary affiliations, then entry barriers are likely to be high and collaboration very difficult for outsiders. Lastly, he cites the differences between text-based and voice-based attitudes as creating problems in collaboration inasmuch as some forms of collaboration might allow for protest, complaints or dissenting voices while others do not.

In cross-cultural collaborations, these four factors provide a useful context for analysing the poor performance of many SME international joint ventures. Lane and Beamish (1990, p. 87) observe that many Western companies 'seek co-operative ventures as a "quick fix" to global competitiveness without understanding the relationships being established and the behavioural and cultural issues involved'. Successful international alliances and collaborations require managers to develop improved skills in collaborative working, communicating with others and coping with ambiguity (Richards 1997). Cross-cultural cooperation cannot be taken for granted and requires changes in attitudes, specific training and practice, in order to learn to behave cooperatively, particularly for Western cultures. Culture influences how willing you are to trust a possible international joint-venture partner. Shane (1993) studied perceptions of transaction costs in partners of American companies in 38 countries. He found evidence that partners from *low-power distance* cultures (Hofstede 1991) were more likely to trust in joint venture partnerships. However, if trust is low in *high-power distance* cultures, then partners need greater control, are afraid of paying higher transaction costs, and prefer to be on their own. In theory, partners are more likely to agree on business matters when their cultures are compatible and thus a venture formed 'by partners of similar cultures stands a greater chance of succeeding than one between dissimilar cultures' (Mead 1998, p. 335).

Nooteboom (1997, p. 9) conceives of structure as the range of forms that inter-firm relations can take. We believe that it is the mode of governance, identified under structure, which has significant ramifications for cross-cultural collaborations with SMEs. Nooteboom suggests that governance involves four elements that come into play in interorganisational collaborations. First, control refers to the extent to which bureaucratic or legal regulation and monitoring mechanisms are put into place to deal with threats of opportunism. Legal forms of contracting, he argues, are costly and inflexible and do little to foster trust (Nooteboom 1997, pp. 9, 17; de Laat 1997). This is particularly true in the high-context cultures of Asia (Hall 1987) where, as we will see, agreements between people are based on relational trust and are 'spoken' rather than 'written'. After a contract has been signed in China or Japan the partner may request further changes. This, Hall points out, causes Western indignation, particularly he says to Americans who 'regard a contract as binding, a stable element in a changing and uncertain world' (Hall 1987, pp. 128–9). Second, he mentions loyalty, based on particular norms and values, habituation or bonds of family, kinship, friendship and clans that help build trust-based relations and help reduce opportunism. Third, he mentions that the extent and unity of partner values can ensure stronger dependence in collaboration and greater mutual understanding. Lastly, he mentions binding, which is affected by exit barriers or how easy these are to enforce and at what cost, and the cost of losing one's reputation from behaving opportunistically.

Much of Nooteboom's discussion of governance revolves around the important issue of trust. While trust is generally thought to be all-important between business partners, particularly in networking and relationships in international and cross-cultural contexts, the reality is that different cultures are more or less willing to trust in a negotiation or relationship and are more or less suspicious of the other. Hofstede's work predicts that cultures having a need for strong *uncertainty avoidance* would exhibit suspicion and aggressiveness to strangers (out-group members) while demonstrating high levels of trust to friends (in-group members) (Hwang 1987; Redding 1990; Hofstede 1993, 1991; and Gabrenya and Hwang 1996). Shane (1993) found that cultures which were high in *power distance* (Hofstede 1991, 1993) had low degrees of interpersonal trust, but this is inevitable as cultures which strongly distinguish between 'we' and 'they' will find trust impossible in hierarchical relationships. Relatives are much more trustworthy. These findings provide further help in explaining the networking preferences of Asian, particularly Confucian, cultures.

Trompenaars and Hampden-Turner (1997, p. 45), using Talcott Parsons' distinction, found that in *universalist* cultures, where behaviour is based on universal and abstract rules and principles (as in Anglo cultures, Germany and Switzerland), 'a trustworthy person is one who honours their word or contract'. However, in *particularist* cultures, where judgements are made according to the nature of the particular relationship between people, a trustworthy person is one who respects the demands of the relationship. Southeast and East Asian cultures are characterised by *such relational personalism* that typically will judge trust in this way. Indeed, in such cultures the demand for written contracts is a sign of mistrust, since they are only necessary when both parties are trying to maximise their own advantage at the expense of the other.

Thus, trust can include a range of different elements in the Western business context (as the extensive literature on networking reveals), but might have different meanings in cooperative or collaborative arrangements in other countries. This argument has been put forward in the case of the Japanese *keiretsu*. Elements such as reputation, prior association, reciprocity and fair dealing are considered the key to explaining how trust underpins network formation in Western societies (Ring and Van de Ven 1994), but might have completely different meanings, or even be meaningless, in other cultures. Moreover, there are a whole range of non-verbal elements, customs, rituals and practices that also contribute to developing business relations that are often ignored in Western societies (Hall 1976), and that are likely to be highly complex in multicultural societies.

We now turn to a more detailed consideration of network forms across a select number of countries in the Asia–Pacific region to explore the dominant network types found among SMEs. We examine overseas Chinese family business as an example of the dominant regional form – *organic networking* – and contrast this with Australia as an example of the practice of *contrived networking,* which is a minority form in the region. In this analysis we present somewhat polarised ideal types of network relationships and recognise that superficial similarities may disguise considerable differences. For example, although clusters of family-owned SMEs appear to be the defining feature of the Taiwanese economy, there is also evidence of large corporations being 'crucial in the development and sustenance' of this small-firm system (Orrù 1997, p. 347). Indeed, we agree with Orrù that: 'While showing that East Asian economies are not all of one kind, the researchers have forgotten that Western economies are not all of one kind either' (Orrù 1997, p. 342). Orrù argues 'that similar economic structures can be found in different cultural areas' and demonstrates this by finding 'remarkable similarities' in the small-firm organisations in Italy and Taiwan (Orrù 1997, p. 342). Nevertheless, the cultural similarities that Orrù finds tend to confirm the arguments of this chapter rather than contradict it.[4]

14.3   ORGANIC NETWORKING: THE CHINESE FAMILY BUSINESS

The family businesses run by the overseas Chinese in Southeast Asia reflect their high context and collectivist culture (see Mead 1998, p. 381).

- Relationships tend to be long-lived.

- Collectivist loyalty is expected between family members, and communication is effective between them.

- The family are insiders and are clearly distinguished from outsiders who pose a threat from which they are protected by the loyalty and cohesion of family members.

- Family and patronage loyalties, rather than bureaucratic norms, determine family relationships.

Redding, in his illuminating 1990 study of the overseas Chinese entitled *The Spirit of Chinese Capitalism*, argues that the origin of the system is found in the history of Chinese society. This had no formal laws, only formal networks of powerful people guided by general principles of Confucian virtue (Hofstede 1993, p. 86). Authority was powerful and arbitrary, so the only reliable protection was one's extended (and usually extensive) kin network. The overseas Chinese then took this system of beliefs and values with them and found that it was very well adapted to countries where they were usually minorities, often envied and threatened by the potential for ethnic persecution.

The Chinese communities share Confucian values, a written language and an insecure past, but they do not constitute a homogeneous group. They settled at different times, in different countries, from different parts of China and are still divided into different subcultural, clan and language groups.

14.3.1   Relational Personalism

Chinese social behaviour has been characterised in a number of ways, but the term 'relational personalism' used by Gabrenya and Hwang (1996, p. 311) seems to capture the complexity well. It is striking, they say, how the evidence from China shows great parallels with other relational personalist cultures such as the Arabs and Japanese (1996, p. 315). Chinese social interaction is normally seen as 'collectivist' (cooperative or harmonious) in many social situations and many empirical studies have supported this description, but Chinese social behaviour can be also 'individualist' (competitive, antagonistic) in other contexts (Gabrenya and Hwang 1996, p. 311; and Leung 1996, pp. 257–8). The nature of this tension provides some illumination of the complexity of Chinese culture and its influence on business behaviour.

14.3.2   Relationships

The fundamental belief underlying Chinese collectivism is that the 'futures of individuals from the same group are inter-related and that each person's well-being depends upon the results of collective effort' (Leung 1996, p. 258). Individuals believe that acting in the interests of the group and conforming to the norms of the group will result in group harmony and prosperity. Personal relationships play a crucial role in Chinese society. The concept of relational personalism begins with a basic distinction between in-group members (insiders, *shu*, literally 'cooked') and out-group members (outsiders, *sheng*, literally 'raw') with the family (*jia*) an extra special in-group (Gabrenya and Hwang 1996, p. 311). Crucial to this is the core idea of Confucianism, '*ren*', which is an insistence that we should practice a hierarchical love tied to intimacy of relationships (Hwang 1987). Although making a clear distinction between types of relationship, the Chinese believe that in all cases the relationship comes first and holds a value that is greater than money. Indeed 'Chinese business people regard business relationship networks as a commercial investment or a form of insurance' (Wang et al. 1998, p. 36).

14.3.3   Social Networks

The collective nature of Chinese society results in a preference for getting things done through interpersonal relationships, or *guanxi*. People are linked in complex networks of *guanxi,* through which they navigate their social worlds. *Guanxi*, as well as meaning personal or informal relationships, can also be translated as 'connections'. The social networks expand as the individual grows up and gains connection in education, occupation and residence. Unlike what happens in Western, particularly Anglo, societies, 'these relationships persist long after the groups are dissolved or no longer have face-to-face interaction, forming lifelong rich rewards of *guanxi*' (Gabrenya and Hwang 1996, p. 312).

   Because these social networks are relatively permanent they are characterised by the importance and enforceability of the Chinese conception of *reciprocity* and *retribution (bao)*. Western societies emphasise short-term, symmetrical reciprocation in exchange relationships while people in Confucian societies believe that relationships are for the long term and will extend into the unforeseeable future (Hwang 1987; Yum 1988; Hofstede 1991; and Hampden-Turner and Trompenaars 1997). The concept of *bao* covers both positive and negative events and therefore either reciprocity or retribution may extend into the very long term. Hwang analysed the implications of this long-term reciprocity for people involved in particular relationships. For example, he observed that, 'Among the most intimate, gratefulness is not verbalised' so that Chinese people find it awkward to thank a friend for every little favour (Gabrenya and Hwang 1996, p. 312). This can annoy Western friends who expect to be thanked for providing a meal or giving a lift, but the Chinese person believes such thanks are insincere and will not provide them.

The development of networks of *guanxi* requires the presence of intermediaries. Research by Chang and Holt (1991) found that there are four common methods of establishing *guanxi* with another: appealing to kin relations; pointing to a previous association; using in-group connections or mediators; or social interaction requiring social skills such as the ability to play the '*renguing*' (favour) game described by Hwang (1987). Yum (1988) found that intermediaries are useful in bringing out-group members together into new relationships. Chinese kin, for example, act as brokers in aiding their relatives to make contact with people outside the kinship network, but American kin do not (Blau et al. 1991).

14.3.4 Networking with Insiders

As Mead (1998, p. 378) says, 'when business is based on relationships of trust, transaction costs are low'. It is widely accepted that the business success of the Chinese community in Southeast Asia is significantly related to the cohesive qualities of its social relationships (Redding 1990). Immediate members of the family are the most trusted, the extended family is the next most-trusted group and distant family members provide access to distant markets. Networks are formed within the family, then the village, clan and ethnic group. Hakka Chinese prefer to deal first with other Hakka, then with the Hokkien and so on. Brown (1995, p. 8) shows that, for example, in the early years of the twentieth century 'the Hakka rice networks of South Vietnam sought to prevent buyers and sellers using non-Hakka networks. Even French merchants had to use the Hakka marketing system'.

14.3.5 Networking with Outsiders

Well-placed connections with government and the wider business community are greatly valued and cultivated. Relationships are formed with both Chinese and non-Chinese government and business leaders who can offer support and protection, access to potential business deals and to confidential information. Strong informal links are made with suppliers, subcontractors and customers (Redding 1990, pp. 205–6).

The problem with depending upon informal networks is that they are, naturally, very context bound. Thus Chinese business people are at a disadvantage in unfamiliar business environments, where they have few prior connections or networks. This applies particularly in the West where information is more evenly and dispassionately distributed than it is in Asia. For example, Chinese companies setting up abroad often get into difficulties because they do not go through the systematic strategic stage-by-stage development process that Western firms use (Rodrigues 1995, pp. 14–16; Mead 1998, p. 379). Cultural factors that provide an advantage in one's own environment may prove a handicap in someone else's. Thus, both Asian and Western business techniques require adaptation to work in the other's culture and both will need local partners and intermediaries, familiar with local ways.

Chinese family businesses, as a rule, do not join contrived networks, especially government-sponsored trade associations, partly because they are suspicious of bureaucratic agencies, especially if they are linked to taxation authorities and partly because they do not need to. Mead quotes Chee (1990) as finding that there was only one association for 20 000 SMEs in Malaysia, and also observes that efforts to encourage specialisation through SME networking in the People's Republic of China (PRC) were also unsuccessful (Mead 1998, p. 380). This Chinese hostility to official networking does not appear to be found in some other Asian cultures, for example Japan and Korea (Mead 1998, p. 380).

14.4 CONTRIVED NETWORKING – BUSINESS NETWORKS IN AUSTRALIA

SMEs in low-context, individualistic and competitive countries, such as the United States and Australia, have begun to participate in cooperative, multifirm interorganisational relationships modelled on those in Continental Europe. One of the significant characteristics of these networks is that they were deliberately created (Human and Provan 1997). Australia provides a good example of the Western (Anglo) approach to networking. In 1994 the Australian government introduced 'The Principles of Industry Policy' in its major policy document called *Working Nation* (Commonwealth Government, May 1994). Australia was one of a number of OECD countries to introduce an industry policy to manage microeconomic reforms and push a range of reform agendas aimed at changing the competitive nature of Australian businesses (Metcalfe 1993). A business networks program was launched in 1994 specifically targeting SMEs. Australia has over 50 per cent of its workforce employed in this sector and it is an expanding area for job creation. Policy documents such as *Working Nation* reflected a fundamental belief in government circles that, given an increasingly global and international economy, SMEs on their own were no longer sufficiently entrepreneurial or competitive to survive in the changing world of business. Networking was seen as one important way of making SMEs more export driven and international in outlook. A national business networks program strategy was chosen for a number of reasons, a key one being the influence in policy circles of Michael Porter's book, *Competitive Advantage of Nations* (1990). Porter had, *inter alia*, successfully promoted the idea of networks and industry clusters or districts as core elements of nations being internationally competitive. However, the option of forming industry clusters or districts in Australia was limited because of a number of factors. Chief among these were the following: lack of industry concentration; few original equipment manufacturers (OEMs) to drive changes in supplier firms; the majority of firms operated at the low end of the market (that is, not elaborately transformed manufacturers: ETMs); exports were dominated by primary commodities; and industry associations were not providing services to businesses, especially SMEs, to help them export (AMC 1990; Benson-Rea and Wilson 1994; and Ffowcs-Williams 1998).

The success of SME-dominated network programs, especially in increasing export earnings among SMEs, particularly in Denmark and Norway, also provided the impetus for a national networking program in Australia. AusIndustry, which was part of the then Department of Industry, Science and Tourism (DIST), established the Business Networks Program (BNP) in 1994 with a AU$38million budget allocation. The BNP ran from 1995–98 with approximately 250 networks still operating when the program ended. It was modelled after the Danish BNP and included the use of network brokers and the establishment of a three-phase, three-year pilot program (see Nielsen 1993, 1996). Over its five years the program funded 400 networks spread across 31 industry sectors (AusIndustry 1996a, p. 10; Dean 1996, p. 12; Sinclair 1999).

Networks were funded to employ accredited and trained network brokers or consultants for the initial three years of a network's operations (see AusIndustry 1995). The 'network broker' concept formed the lynchpin of the BNP, although a number of the BNP networks moved very quickly from having a network broker to employing their own network managers. A number of networks had formed, or were already in the process of developing their networks, prior to the introduction of the BNP. State governments and other federal departments had also funded network programs creating multiple funding opportunities for many networks. It was not uncommon for network brokers to form networks with businesses that had no prior association or history of collaboration (Fulop with Kelly 1997a).

Exporting was a key target of the BNP, as was job creation, but later import replacement was included once it was acknowledged that many SMEs were unable to satisfy local demand, let alone enter international markets. By definition, the BNP favoured businesses with between 15 and 100 people, depending on the industry sector. A network had to have at least three members, only one of which could be a large organisation, thus ensuring that SMEs dominated the BNP. However, many of the businesses participating in the BNP were not SMEs, but microbusinesses (employing one or two people). Many of these microbusinesses concentrated on simple processing and were unlikely to export or be the source of major job creation opportunities.

The BNP focused on forming horizontal networks, with the key target being joint marketing for export (Sinclair 1999, p. 4). It was only later in the program that product innovation and forming value chain relationships (that is, vertical networks) were targeted. Indeed, empirical studies undertaken in Australia found that by far the most common network being formed was the *complementary service network* (see Buttery and Buttery 1995; and Fulop with Kelly 1997a). This type of network predominantly served the marketing and sales needs of members (see also Nesheim and Reve 1996, p. 368, for a similar observation in Norway). The network's activities had no significant importance to, or impact on, the core operations of the members' individual businesses and, therefore, network members had low interdependence and commitment to the network. A high failure rate was reported across this network type (Buttery and Buttery 1995; and Fulop with Kelly 1997b). A complementary service network usually brought together a mix of businesses to undertake such things as joint training, quality programs, trade fairs and information exchange. Such a network was usually thought of as a 'soft' network because it did not require businesses to invest heavily in the network and success or performance of the network did not produce measurable outcomes (for example, increased sales).

Another common network identified in the two studies was the *pooled service network*. This network usually involved businesses, or even an entire industry sector, developing joint marketing, especially for overseas markets, or joint distribution strategies, such as is found in the wine industry. The pooled service network usually included competitors as well as non-competitors and businesses that had no prior history of collaboration or working together. For example, evidence suggests that where a pooled service network had attempted to export to Asia and was dominated by competitors, it reported only limited success in exporting. Being a service network, it displayed many of the same characteristics of the complementary service network except that it was not uncommon for the members to contribute substantial funds to run the network. The network was rarely seen as being core to improving its members' businesses (Fulop with kelly 1987b).

Another less common network type found in the aforementioned studies was the *pooled operations network* (Buttery and Buttery 1995; Fulop with Kelly 1997b). This network usually comprised businesses that were competitors in one key area of operation who came together to gain advantage predominantly from economies of scale (for example, joint development of costly new technology) or economics of scope (for example. introduce a more diverse product range). They were usually drawn together for a variety of commercial reasons, a common one being a crisis or threat to segments of an industry. An example in Australia was the network developed among certain sections of the oyster industry in South Australia where growers' livelihoods were threatened by the restricted practices of mainland distributors (Fulop with Kelly 1997c). The level of competition in these networks was often a cause of conflicts, power struggles, instability and failure. While competitor networks were common in Australia and in other OCED countries, they were not encouraged in the Japanese *keiretsu* (Nooteboom 1997, p. 6).

A subsequent study of more mature business networks in the BNP found evidence of the complementary operations networks or vertical networks (Fulop 2000). This network type, also identified by Buttery and Buttery (1995), included businesses that were able to provide the necessary skills and knowledge to develop new products or services often unrelated to any one business's primary activity or core business. Competition was low or non-existent while dependency was high among members. An interesting feature of this network was the degree to which it could integrate the activities of member businesses into the network proper to form a new commercial entity (Nooteboom 1997). The case study in this chapter (see below) describes a complementary operations network that also had overseas network partners in Malaysia and involved businesses that had prior commercial associations and involvement with each other.

Over the last decade, the Australian government supported, and continues to support, SMEs and networking initiatives through a range of programs both within and external to the BNP. Joint action groups (JAGs) or 'hard networks' were also set up in Australia and included both SMEs and large organisations. JAGs were only formed where businesses could identify specific market or project opportunities that would benefit all members and were export oriented (Lisners 1995, p. 16). The JAGs were seen as complementing the BNP and one of the more publicised of these was the Furniture JAG whose 100 plus members succeeded in exporting products to Japan. The BNP also had an Asia–Pacific Economic Co-operation (APEC) Manufacturing Networks initiative to encourage networks, through funding of up to AU$200 000, to develop cross-border networks, especially complementary ones with Asian partners particularly in the high-tech area (AusIndustry 1996b, p. 12). Other more recently targeted network programs have included the Supply Chain Program, linking large organisations and SMEs in supply chain relationships, and the Value Chain Program involving a small number of projects that show high interdependence among businesses and can achieve bottom line results (Sinclair 1999, p. 4). These programs were augmented by others funded by the Federal government that have focused on commercialisation and innovation, as opposed to joint marketing, which was the key focus of the BNP (Sinclair 1999, p. 4). State governments also fund a variety of programs that include networks. It is difficult to ascertain how successful the BNP has been, especially in terms of getting large numbers of SMEs to export. A formal evaluation of the program was due for completion in 2000.

While we have examined the differences between organic and contrived forms of networking in the national context, the challenges facing networks entering into overseas markets, either in networks or as individual firms, presents another important element to the discussion of SMEs and the influence of culture.

14.5 SMES, NETWORKS AND INTERNATIONALISATION

The majority of government-funded SME network programs and initiatives in OECD countries have been aimed at assisting businesses to form local networks in order to create a critical mass for entering international markets. Studies of networking in OECD countries reveal that a major reason why SMEs join networks is to export and become international in orientation (Fulop with Kelly 1997b; Nesheim and Reve 1996; Reve 1995; Weaver 1997; and Buttery and Buttery 1995). Other reasons include the following: gaining know how and knowledge; cost reductions; opportunities to specialise; risk reduction; increased product and market scope; market development, including local markets and import replacement; improved management skills and knowledge; and an increased power base, such as in purchasing. The case study below illustrates how SMEs can use networks to enter overseas markets. It presents one of the earliest networking success stories for the BNP in Australia and reveals how both organic and contrived elements of networking were used both to form the network and develop an international partnership. It shows how network dynamics change and evolve over time, and that succeeding both nationally and internationally has strong cultural underpinnings. The nature of organic ties in the Western context does not easily translate into other cultural settings and vice versa. Thus, the Australian network formed an 'arm's-length' relationship with its Asian partner to develop their joint venture drawing on relationships formed over many years.

Businesses that seek to go international can choose a partner(s) in another country to form a joint venture, strategic alliance or other forms of partnership, such as franchising and licensing (see Nooteboom 1997, p. 10; Buttery et al. 1999). As mentioned above, our case study exemplifies the 'overseas partnership' approach – the hardest and least popular form of internationalisation among SMEs. More commonly, SMEs employ overseas agents or intermediaries and open an office in a foreign country. Forming local networks in order to enter overseas markets creates added complexities and challenges that single businesses do not have to face. Australian SMEs have formed successful joint ventures in Asia (see Maitland et al. 1999) without being members of local business networks. Network arrangements that work in a national context are not necessarily ideal for internationalising activities, and the network form itself is likely to be difficult to adapt to cross-cultural contexts. The success of the Proen network in entering Asia demonstrates one approach to internationalisation in the network context and highlights very clearly the limitations that culture places on what is feasible for SMEs in this context.

Box 1: Proen

Proen Design Australia was one of the first SME networks in Australia to achieve success. It was formed through government funding as a *complementary operations network*. It received its initial funding from the South Australian government and also joined the BNP in stage three of the program. By 1997 Proen was active in Malaysia and the US and was in the process of opening interstate offices. Three South Australian businesses – two micro-businesses and one large organisation – were the principal and equal stakeholders in Proen prior to its restructuring in 1997. One foundation member had exited the network to be replaced by another member. The CEO of the large organisation was also chairperson of another highly successful and innovative business network in South Australia. This gave Proen the added advantage of having other networking experiences to draw upon. The members of Proen had a very sophisticated and well-thought-out networking philosophy.

By late 1997 the network was in the process of integrating one of the foundation businesses along with two new businesses into Proen. These three businesses acquired a 75 per cent shareholding in Proen. The two other businesses became minority shareholders. Proen was turning into a new business. When Proen was formed, the structure of the network was vertical and through the network members were able to offer clients a range of supporting services that included: identification of market needs for industrial and consumer products; products and industrial design; design and manufacture of tooling and special-purpose equipment to manufacture the product; improvements to existing products and process; plant start-ups and equipment for production purposes; prototyping and product management.

Proen Design Australia was formed following a network feasibility study by a consultant and a business plan was completed in late 1993. The consultancy work, funded by the South Australian Centre for Manufacturing (SACFM), was in response to a South Australian government study into business opportunities in Southeast Asia. The study indicated that there were substantial opportunities in Singapore and Malaysia for product design, toolmakers and providers of associated services.

All of the principals had previously collaborated on a number of projects and joint ventures and were fully aware of each other's capabilities. Following the initial meeting of the group, it was decided to undertake a planning session to identify market products and services. It soon became apparent that Malaysia should be the target market for several reasons. One of the principals had already worked for a number of clients in Malaysia and knew the country and the culture, and Singapore was soon to be already well serviced in the area of product design, product management and toolmaking. Moreover, the Malaysian government had released its *Vision 2020* policy statement, which announced that Malaysia was to become a fully industrialised nation within 25 years.

After some personal research conducted in Malaysia, it became apparent that to succeed in the chosen market, the network would need to establish a presence in the market and focus its efforts on key companies. To meet the requirement of an established presence, a joint-venture agreement was sought. Namas Moor Sdn. Bhd. emerged as an attractive partner and one with whom there were personal associations. The company had interests in a graphic design company and the capabilities of the group were complementary to those of Proen Design Australia. After extensive correspondence and negotiation, the principals of Namas Moor visited Adelaide in February 1994 to sign a Heads of Agreement. A joint-venture company was formed and launched in June 1994 by the Premier of South Australia.

Proen Design Australia became a 50 per cent shareholder in the joint venture company, Proen Design Asia Sdn. Bhd. Namas Moor's chairperson was also Chair of the Stock Exchange, with extensive business contacts, and her family was involved in the management of Proen Design Asia. The Malaysian joint venture was run as a separate business and operated in its own right providing opportunities for its Australian partners where possible. The Malaysian partners provided the knowledge and experience of doing business in Asia while the Australian counterpart provided the technical components of product design, tooling design and manufacture as well as exploring future technologies. All publicity and promotion of Proen Design Asia was undertaken by the Malaysian partner and was published in both English and Malay.

Shortly after its formation, Proen Design Asia won a contract to design and product manage the development of a new telephone kiosk for the Malaysian Telephone Utility, and, in August 1994, another major tooling contract was won. The company negotiated a contract for design and tooling and held discussions with other Malaysian-based tooling firms to establish joint-venture operations. The joint venture was seen as desirable because the Malaysian market was very demanding and returns on tooling were poor because of very tight margins. Strategically, Proen Design Australia concentrated on its local markets and expanding interstate and used its overseas partner to source local business opportunities.

The principals of Proen Design Australia also successfully negotiated agreements for the commercialisation and product management of Australian developed medical technology in the US. The network was, however, shifting from supporting the businesses in the network to becoming a business in its own right. The network was seen as a transitory stage of business growth.

Proen Design Australia was accepted into Stage Three of the BNP and was assisted with partial reimbursement of operating costs. The network experienced considerable growth. Each of the participating businesses employed more staff and generated foreign business as a result of belonging to the network.

The critical success factors, identified for the network by key participants, were: high degree of trust between the members; complementary activities and capabilities; knowledge of target market; focused efforts on target clients; establishment of a joint venture with limited financial exposure and risk; using local presence in markets, and funding support during the early stages. While the network used a network broker, as a part of the funding arrangement with the BNP, it did much of the work itself in getting the network up and into Asia (King 1995; and Fulop 1998).

Most Western businesses, particularly SMEs, seek to internationalise using a 'gradualist approach' that entails exporting through distributing a product in an overseas market (Rodrigues 1995, p. 10). This is termed a 'vendor strategy' where overseas companies or agents are approached to sell a consumer product (Rodrigues 1995, p. 11). Rodrigues points out that exporting through a vendor strategy represents the quickest, though not necessarily the most successful, way to internationalise and is a first step in learning about another country and working out whether or not greater commitments can or should be made (Rodrigues 1995, p. 5). Not every business goes down this route; instead, some, such as Proen, 'leapfrog' by forming a partnership, such as a joint venture or non-equity strategic alliance, as the first step in internationalising.

However, Rodrigues argues that internationalisation strategies or moves are influenced by several factors, such as: 'psychic distance' or closeness of markets relative to one's own country. Attitudes of governments to foreign investment, including ease of entry relating to special treaties, trade missions and so on, are also important factors as are a range of other institutional concerns discussed below. Many of these factors cannot be easily influenced or changed once a business 'arrives' in a country and have to be understood or addressed well before contemplating an internationalisation strategy. Based on her study of how Brazilian SMEs handled their moves into PR China, Rodrigues concluded that there are five critical areas that affect how internationalisation strategies turn out. The advantage of Rodrigues's analysis, unlike many other studies, is that it was undertaken in the light of the experiences of SMEs in Asia, instead of the usual focus on multinational corporations (MNCs) or large organisations.

The first of these factors relates to the 'entering approach and the asymmetries in intentions and interests'. This asymmetry was especially evident when long-term partnerships were being sought as opposed to the short-term strategy of setting up distribution and sales outlets through agents. Rodrigues (1995, p. 11) also found that the perceived status and influence of government officials from the investor's country played a part in helping or hindering new entrants. Furthermore, being overly cautious and slow in committing to any business transaction or having a short-term orientation could signal different and, at times, negative intentions. The second factor affecting internationalisation strategies refers to the internationalisation experience of the businesses involved. New entrants tended to choose exporting of products while more experienced exporters were likely to seek partnerships, as indeed the Proen case also reveals (Rodrigues 1995, p. 12). Moreover, lack of international experience often meant businesses published marketing brochures and service manuals and so on in one language only – a mistake not made by Proen. Many businesses also failed to obtain relevant and salient market information, used their own assumptions to gain access to very foreign different markets, and tended to overestimate the competitiveness of their products.

The third factor was a lack of inter-firm and inter-country knowledge which Rodrigues (1995, pp. 13–14) says contributed to huge problems in negotiation processes. These obstacles tended to enlarge differences in interests and culture by introducing high levels of uncertainty and ambiguity into negotiations (see also Maitland et al. 1999, p. 19). Lack of local knowledge also often meant that critical information about a partner's capabilities, reputation, financial strength and competitiveness was not obtained and that suitable agents and intermediaries and points of access to markets (for example, trade fairs versus direct marketing) were not selected. Fourth, Rodrigues (1995, pp. 14–16) referred to the problem of a lack of mutual understanding in internationalisation strategies. Mutual understanding refers to such things as attitudes, interests and expected behaviour, including methods of communication. In her study, Rodrigues found that the intricacies of institutional and bureaucratic systems, and the collective dimensions embedded in complex and dispersed systems of decision-making, were least understood by foreign businesses. These businesses were also unlikely to possess the crucial intercultural competencies of mutual understanding, such as the ability to communicate effectively and 'read' cultural nuances, as well as being able to deal with different perceptions of power and status.

As already discussed, networks or associations in China are based on different norms and expectations requiring that outsiders use different means to build collaborative relationships. Rodrigues described how in China building a *guanxi* network meant using an intermediary, such as a consultant, foreign agent or Hong Kong trading company, and being prepared to pay commissions and various associated costs that come with having these intermediaries or third parties. She found that the cost of such services was prohibitive for SMEs from developing nations.

Finally, the competitiveness of the foreign investor was a critical factor and included not only the ability to compete on price, which was and is vital in Asia, but also having experience in managing large contracts involving subcontracting arrangements. This also entailed having knowledge of how bids and contracts were won, including the role of governments in these processes, as well as being able to access and influence the bidding and tendering processes, which again was likely to be costly for SMEs (Rodrigues 1995, p. 17).

14.6 CONCLUSION

In a Western culture, one's identity is closely linked to what one has achieved. In a culture where group membership is emphasised, distinction is made between in-group and out-group and identity is established on the basis of people to whom one is related. Collectivists behave towards members of their in-groups with more intimacy and to their out-groups with less intimacy than do individualists (Triandis 1990; and Hofstede 1991). Thus the kind of short-term interaction typical of an individualist's 'network' of useful 'contacts' is seen as offensive by collectivists (Triandis 1990). Nevertheless, SMEs in individualistic cultures need some kind of contrived networking, since this usually does not occur organically, particularly when doing business in collectivist cultures. Similarly SMEs from collectivist cultures need contrived networks to enable them to do business in individualistic cultures, and with other people who are not in their in-groups.

However, there is a need to rethink the contrived networking systems. Perhaps the notion of the *infinite game* used by Hampden-Turner and Trompenaars (1997) is helpful here. This view stems from ancient traditions in the East that seek unity in diversity and complexity. 'Infinite games are preferred by cultures which dislike confrontation, prefer conversation to debate, are shy and respond indirectly to questions and believe in the values of harmony. This includes China, Japan, Indonesia, Thailand and most of the economies managed by the Chinese' (Lessem 1998, p. 51). As we have seen in such countries the mutual relationship comes before, and takes precedence over, the contract and its terms. *Wa* (harmony), *guanxi* and dynamic reciprocity, where favours escalate on both sides, are more important than contract terms. 'Where changing circumstances render contract terms onerous to one or both parties, let the terms be changed'. The mutual relationship, that made the contract initially, takes precedence over the terms negotiated (Hampden-Turner and Trompenaars 1997, p. 178). A relationship is long term; a contract is not and is like a banister on stairs, Hampden-Turner and Trompenaars say, 'to be gripped only in emergencies' (1997, p. 181).

Networks that are contrived as interventions to help SME development often reflect a Western approach which is task focused, convergent and goal directed. Perhaps future initiatives should be based on the principles of the infinite game, metaphorically centred in organic networks, where clusters beget clusters and knowledge passes from one to another. Lessem recommends that '[a] consensus orientation, ultimately, is vital to the building of the clusters, in which victory in one game contributes to victories in clusters of games or one infinite game. These are typically joined by horizontal technologies which act as catalysts ... Clustering also greatly increases the chance of fortuitous and creative connections, combining competition with co-operation' (Lessem 1998, pp. 55–6). The use of such organic forms will be vital in creating and sustaining business networks in the Asia–Pacific region.

NOTES

1   We do not define SMEs in any specific way (for example, number of employees, amount of turnover) because these descriptions vary from country to country and across industry sectors.
2   But this may be an illusion, as Lessem argues (1998, p. 55). See later discussion.
3   They represent less than 6 per cent of the population throughout the region of Southeast Asia (Mead 1998, p. 376) yet command a gross national product (GNP) greater than Australia's (Hofstede 1993, p. 86).
4   For example, Orrù (1997, pp. 354–5) finds that in both Italy and Taiwan personal ties in the conduct of business are very important and that small firms rely on personal, especially family, relationships.

REFERENCES

AusIndustry (1995), *Network Broker's Manual*, Canberra: AGPS.

AusIndustry Business Networks Program (1996a), 'A Review of Business Networks Program', *Network News*, 6, December, 12.

AusIndustry Business Networks Program (1996b), 'APEC Manufacturing Networks Initiative', *Network News*, 6, December, 10.

Australian Manufacturing Council (AMC) (1990), 'Networking and Industry Development', discussion paper, Canberra: AMC.

Benson-Rea, M. and I.M. Wilson (1994), *Final Report to: Ministery of Commerce, Networks in New Zealand*, Auckland, NZ: University of Auckland.

Blau, P.M., D.C. Ruan and H. Ardelt (1991), 'Interpersonal choice and networks in China', *Social Forces*, 69, 1037–62.

Brown, R.A. (1995), 'Introduction: Chinese Business in an Institutional and Historical Perspective', in R.A. Brown (ed.), *Chinese Business Enterprise in Asia*, London: Routledge, pp. 1–26.

Buchanan, I.C., C. Boulas and B. Raj Gopi (1998), 'Asian Paradox: Miracle, Myth and Financial Crisis', *Monash Mt. Eliza Business Review*, 1 (2), July, 24–45.

Buttery, E. and A. Buttery (1994), *Business Networks*, Melbourne: Longman Business and Professional.

Buttery, E. and A. Buttery (1995), *The Dynamics of the Network Situation*, Canberra: AusIndustry.

Buttery, E., L. Fulop and A. Buttery (1999), 'Networks and Interorganizational Relations', in L. Fulop and S. Linstead (eds), *Management: A Critical Text*, Melbourne: Macmillan, pp. 414–63.

Chang, H. and G.R. Holt (1991), 'More than Relationship: Chinese Interaction and the Principle of Kuan-hsi', *Communication Quarterly*, 39, 251–71.

Chee, P.L. (1990), *Development of Small Scale Businesses in Developing Countries*, International Department, Institute of Small Business, University of Göttingen.

Commonwealth Government (1994), *Working Nation: Politics and Programs*, Canberra: AGPS.

de Laat, P. (1997), 'Research and Development Alliances: Ensuring Trust in Mutual Commitments', in M. Ebers (ed.), *The Formation of Inter-organizational Networks*, New York: Oxford University Press, pp. 146–73.

Dean, J. (1996), 'Review of Business Network Programs', *AusIndustry Business Networks Program Network News*, 6, December, 12, Canberra.

Ebers, M. and A. Grandori (1997), 'The Forms, Costs and Development Dynamics of Inter-organizational Networking', in M. Ebers (ed.), *The Formation of Inter-Organizational Networks*, New York: Oxford University Press, pp. 265–86.

Ffowcs-Williams, I. (1998), 'Stimulating Local Clusters', *Regional Policy and Practice*, 7, 13–18.

Fulop, L. (1998), *Next Generation Networks – A Preliminary Study*, Canberra: AusIndustry.

Fulop, L. (2000), 'A Study of Government Funded Small Business Networks in Australia', *Journal of Small Business Management*, **38** (4), 87–92.

Fulop, L., with J. Kelly (1995), *A Survey of Industry Network Initiatives in NSW – Final Report*, A Strengthening Local Economic Capacity Project (SLEC), Canberra: A Commonwealth Department of Housing and Regional Development Initiative.

Fulop, L., with J. Kelly (1997a), *An In-depth Study of Business Networks in Australia: Summary Report*, Vol. 1, North Sydney, NSW: Australian Business Chamber, May.

Fulop, L., with J. Kelly (1997b), *An In-depth Study of Business Networks in Australia: Summary Report*, Vol. 2, North Sydney, NSW: Australian Business Chamber, May.

Fulop, L., with J. Kelly (1997c), *An In-depth Study of Business Networks in Australia: Summary Report*, Vol. 3, North Sydney, NSW: Australian Business Chamber, May.

Gabrenya, W.K. and K.K. Hwang (1996), 'Chinese Social Interaction: Harmony and Hierarchy on the Good Earth', in M.H. Bond (ed.), *The Handbook of Chinese Psychology*, Hong Kong: Oxford University Press, pp. 309–21.

Grandori, A. and G. Soda (1995), 'Inter-firm Networks: Antecedents, Mechanisms and Forms', *Organization Studies*, **16** (2), 183–214.

Hall, E.T. (1976), *Beyond Culture*, New York: Anchor Press/Doubleday.

Hall, E.T. (1987), *Hidden Differences*, New York: Anchor Press/Doubleday.

Hampden-Turner, C. and F. Trompenaars (1997), *Mastering the Infinite Game*, Oxford: Capstone.

Hofstede, G. (1991), *Cultures and Organizations: Software for the Mind*, London: McGraw Hill.

Hofstede, G. (1993), 'Cultural Constraints in Management Theories', *Academy of Management Executive*, **7** (1), 81–94.

Human, S.E. and K. Provan (1997), 'An Emergent Theory of Structure and Outcomes in Small-firm Strategic Manufacturing Networks', *Academy of Management Journal*, **40** (2), 368–403.

Hwang, K.K. (1987), 'Face and Favor: The Chinese Power Game', *American Journal of Sociology*, **92**, 944–74.

Johannisson, B. and M. Mønsted (1996), 'Networking in Context – SMEs and Networks in Scandinavia', Plenary Presentation of the 9th Nordic Small Business Conference, Lillehammer, Norway, 29–31st May.

King, G. (1995), 'Proen Design Australia', AusIndustry Business Networks Program, *Network News*, **2** (October), 32.

Lane, H.W. and P.W. Beamish (1990), 'Cross-cultural co-operative behaviour in joint ventures in LDCs', *Management International Review*, Special issue, **30**, 87–102.

Lessem, R. (1998), *Management Development through Cultural Diversity*, London: Routledge.

Leung, K. (1996), 'The Role of Beliefs in Chinese Culture', in M.H. Bond (ed.), *The Handbook of Chinese Psychology*, Hong Kong: Oxford University Press, pp. 247–62.

Lisners, K. (1995), 'Soft and Hard Networks – Joint Action Groups', AusIndustry Business Networks Program, *Network News*, **3**, December, 16, Canberra.

Maitland, E., S. Morgan and S. Nicholas (1999), 'Cooperative Strategies by Australian Firms in China', paper presented at the Workshop on Organizational Collaboration, Department of Management, University of Melbourne, 15–16 December, pp. 1–29.

Mead, R. (1998), *International Management: Cross-cultural Dimensions* (2nd edition), Oxford: Blackwell.

Metcalfe, L. (1993), 'Government's New Role in Managing Competitiveness', *Australian Journal of Public Administration*, **25** (3), 269–80.

Nesheim, T. and T. Reve (1996), 'Business Networks and Knowledge Dissemination: Output from the Norwegian Business Network', *Business Networks Business Growth*, Canberra: Commonwealth of Australia. pp. 364–80.

Nielsen, N. C. (1993), 'Network Co-operation: Achieving SME Competitiveness in a Global Economy', National Seminar for Networks, 11–12th October, Adelaide: South Australian Centre for Manufacturing.

Nielsen, N. C. (1996), 'Issues in Structuring Networks', *Business Networks Business Growth*, Canberra: Commonwealth of Australia, pp. 355–62.

Nooteboom, B. (1997), 'Design of Inter-firm Relations: Goals, Conditions, Problems and Solutions', paper presented at the 13th EGOS Colloquium: Organizational Responses to Radical Environmental Changes: sub-theme 2 – Inter-Organizational Networks and Radical Environmental Change, 3–5 July, Budapest University of Economic Sciences: Budapest, pp. 1–26.

Orrù, M. (1997), 'The Institutional Logic of Small-firm Economies in Italy and Taiwan', in M. Orrù, N. Biggart and G. Hamilton (eds), *The Economic Organization of East Asian Capitalism*, Thousand Oaks, CA: Sage, pp. 340–97.

Porter, M. (1990), *The Competitive Advantage of Nations*, New York: Free Press.

Redding, S.G. (1990), *The Spirit of Chinese Capitalism*, Berlin and New York: de Gruyter.

Reve, T. (1995), 'Networks – the Norwegian Way: An Evaluation of the Norwegian Business Network Program', AusIndustry Business Networks Program, *Network News*, **3**, (December), 10–12.

Richards, D. (1997), 'Developing Cross-cultural Management Skills: Experiential Learning in an International MBA Programme', *Management Learning*, **28** (4), December, 387–407.

Ring, P. S. and A.H. Van de Ven (1994), 'Developmental Processes of Co-operative Interorganizational Relationships', *Academy of Management Review*, **19** (1), 90–118.

Rodrigues, S.B. (1995), 'Negotiations for Strategic Alliances: Brazilian Firms Entering the Chinese market', Proceedings of the European Group for Organizational Studies

Colloquium, Sub-Theme: Local versus Global Rationality, 6–8 July, Istanbul, Turkey, pp. 1–22.

Shadur, M. and R. Kienzle (1996), 'Developments in Business Networks in East Asia', *Business Networks–Business Growth*, Canberra: Commonwealth of Australia, pp. 449–62.

Shane, S. (1993), 'The Effect of Cultural Differences in Perception of Transaction Costs on National Differences in the Preference for International Joint Ventures', *Asia–Pacific Journal of Management*, **10** (1), 57–69.

Sinclair, N. (1999), 'Business Networks in Regional Australia. An Overview of Government Business Networks Programs and Analysis of their Impact on Regional Economies – from a Practitioner's Perspective', paper presented at the Australian and New Zealand Regional Science Association International Conference, Newcastle, New South Wales, 19–22 September.

Triandis, H.C. (1990), 'Theoretical Concepts That are Applicable to the Analysis of Ethnocentrism', in R.W. Brislin, *Applied Cross-cultural Psychology*, Newbury Park, CA: Sage, pp. 34–55.

Trompenaars, F. and C. Hampden-Turner (1997), *Riding the Waves of Culture*, London: Nicholas Brealey.

Wang, Y., X.S. Zhang and R. Goodfellow (1998), *Business Culture in China*, Singapore: Butterworth-Heinemann Asia.

Weaver, K.M. (1997), 'Why Firms Choose to Cooperate', AusIndustry Business Networks Program, *Network News,* **8** (September), 6–8.

Yum, J.O. (1988), 'The Impact of Confucianism in Interpersonal Relationships and Communication Patterns in East Asia', *Communication Monographs*, **55**, 374–88.

15 Franchising: An Interdependent Alternative to Independent SMEs

Leo Paul Dana, Hamid Etemad and Richard W. Wright

Franchising is the single most successful marketing concept ever.
– John Naisbitt

15.1 INTRODUCTION

Drivers of globalisation are removing the barriers that formerly segmented the respective domains of small and large firms (Dana et al. 1999a, 1999b). Consequently, it is increasingly difficult for independent, small firms to thrive on their own. In contrast, franchising is a system that assists inexperienced owner-managers who might otherwise fail on their own. As a result, franchising – a contractual agreement between a relatively large franchiser (the principal), and a smaller franchisee (the agent) – is becoming an increasingly popular means of cooperation among firms.

Franchising is a form of licensing, through which the franchiser provides a marketing program to a smaller-scale entrepreneur. This includes a brand name and logo, trademarks, products, service standards, technical expertise, advertising and methods of operation. Such arrangements allow franchisees – small-scale entrepreneurs – to integrate into the networks of the larger franchisers, with tested marketing and operational strategies as well as economies of scale. For the franchiser, franchising provides an inexpensive and profitable means for expansion. New symbiotic relationships are thus created, allowing firms to achieve the expanded reach and efficiencies associated with internationalisation more rapidly and effectively than they could on their own.

In Western business systems, collaborative arrangements between small firms and large firms have traditionally been transaction based; in other words, they can be terminated at the will of either (usually the larger) party. Franchising, as illustrated in this chapter, is characterised instead by interdependence, with each party relying on the other in a sustained, ongoing manner. In a truly symbiotic relationship, neither party can compete effectively without the continued contribution of the other. We see, therefore, that franchising is very relevant to SMEs. In 1998, the Society of Franchising and the *Journal of Business Venturing* embarked on a joint project to bring the fields of entrepreneurship and franchising closer together (Dant and Kaufmann 1998).

The remainder of this chapter proceeds as follows. Section 15.2 conducts a review of the literature relating to the importance of networking for SME business development. Section 15.3 is concerned with analysing the contribution that franchising can make for firms with limited resources to expand internationally – by means of franchisees. Section 15.4 discusses how and why franchising works. Section 15.5 briefly discusses the Franchise Agreement, while Section 15.6 identifies the advantages of franchising for the franchiser. Section 15.7 looks at franchising from the perspective of the franchisee. Section 15.8 identifies some of the important factors necessary to become a successful franchisee. Section 15.9 analyses an interesting case study of franchising in the airline sector while Section 15.10 identifies the Singaporean experience with franchising. Finally, Section 15.11 presents a summary of the major issues raised in this chapter as well as their implications for SMEs.

15.2   NETWORKS

The literature on networks of small firms is very rich. Aldrich and Zimmer (1986) suggested that networking may be an essential requirement for entrepreneurial success. Aldrich et al. (1987) found network accessibility to be significant in predicting the success of business start-ups. Others who have found networks to be central to entrepreneurial activity include: Aldrich (1989); Aldrich et al. (1984); Birley (1985); Boissevain and Grotenbreg (1987); Carsrud et al. (1986); Dubini and Aldrich (1991); Johannisson (1987); Olm et al. (1988); Shaver and Scott (1991); and Werbner (1984).

Evidence of the growing importance of networking in a specifically international context is provided by Dunning (1995) and by Holm et al. (1997). Iyer and Shapiro (1999) demonstrated how expatriate ethnic entrepreneurs leverage their membership in local ethnic networks, in the countries to which they had emigrated, to import from their country of ethnic origin; these business people thus infused international activity into the supply and value chains of the social/ethnic networks in both countries.

Here are a few examples of marketing networks among small businesses. First, of two million enterprises in Japan, only 1 per cent are large firms. About 80 per cent of the workforce is employed by *chusho kigyo*: retail firms with up to 30 employees, wholesalers with up to 100, or others with up to 300 employees or with share capital not exceeding 100 million yen. Yet, Japan is a country in which large size is usually desirable in industrial activity: an old proverb teaches, 'When seeking a shelter, look for a big tree'. Applied to entrepreneurs, this philosophy means, 'Join a network!'. Indeed, rather than competing with large firms entrepreneurs in Japan cooperate with them, serving as suppliers, assemblers, distributors and service providers in intricate *keiretsu* network relationships based on shared cultural beliefs of obligation, indebtedness and loyalty (Dana 1998, 1999a).

Second, and similarly, the development of one million small firms in South Korea – in manufacturing, trading, transportation, construction and services – allows small firms to specialise, and to achieve efficiencies due to scale economies in producing the components which they provide to the huge companies at the centre of each chaebol group. This phenomenon has led to an elaborate, mutually-beneficial system of collaboration with a large number of very small firms supplying a small number of very large *chaebol* firms, which in turn compete globally (Dana 1992, 1994–5).

Third, and along similar lines, several large corporations in France have encouraged qualified employees to quit their jobs in order to establish their own independent firms, which then receive supply contracts from their former employers. Major corporations involved in such schemes include: Alcatel Alsthom, Banque Nationale de Paris, Electricité de France-Gas de France, Hewlett-Packard, the French Post Office, Renault, and Sanofi. This process of rationalisation helps the large firms become more efficient, while the newly created ventures gain a platform for growth and indirect internationalisation through the large firms. The new ventures remain free to provide services to other large companies, even competitors.

Finally, in the Philippines, small-scale entrepreneurs in the agro-food sector have been linking up into networks with larger firms, and those networks of firms are supplemented in turn by networks of networks. For instance, the Villasis Mango Growers Association is a network of large and small firms. The Federation of Co-operatives for Pangasinan brings together several such networks of mango growers. In the same region, Ilocos Norte Federation of Agribusiness Co-operatives does the same for vegetables. A similar network is the Christian Farmers Kilusang Bayan for Credit and Allied Services. The networks attain sufficient size and capability to enter international markets and to compete globally, which the small firms alone could not.

Franchising likewise creates networks of small firms, distributing a proven product and/or service on behalf of a larger enterprise. Examples include McDonald's, KFC, Hertz, Holiday Inn, Marks & Spencer, and British Airways.

15.3   THE GLOBAL ENVIRONMENT

Traditionally, internationalisation was usually depicted as a gradual, incremental process. The Uppsala Model (Johanson and Wiedersheim-Paul 1975) identified stages of progressive internationalisation. Similar models were developed by: Bilkey and Tesar (1977); Johanson and Vahlne (1977); Newbould et al. (1978); Cavusgil (1980, 1984); and Bartlett and Ghoshal (1989). It should be noted, however, that the rapid globalisation of markets (Levitt 1983) and of competition (Ohmae 1989, 1990) is dramatically reducing that time span, and constraining the ability of small firms to control their own development paths. Franchising is an ideal way for a firm with limited resources to expand internationally – by means of franchisees. The result is a network of firms sharing a symbiotic relationship.

Marketing, today, increasingly involves symbiotic networks of large and small firms. Reynolds (1997) noted that the recent expansion of markets has not been associated with an expanded role for larger firms. Instead, smaller firms are filling niche roles (Buckley 1997). Oviatt and McDougall (1994, p. 46) concluded: 'the facile use of low-cost communication technology and transportation means that the ability to discover and take advantage of business opportunities in multiple countries is not the preserve of large, mature corporations'.

Franchising can enhance the competitiveness of franchisers – whether established or new – and it gives opportunities to franchisees. By distributing on behalf of high-volume, larger firms, entrepreneurs can achieve their own scale economies. As the smaller franchisees become more competitive, by capturing scale economies not possible without their franchisers, the franchisees in turn gain competitiveness by integrating those economies into their own value chains. Large, established franchisers increasingly achieve efficiency by incorporating smaller franchisees, into their networks. There is a symbiosis between franchisers and franchisees, with the larger firms providing niche opportunities for the entrepreneurs in their networks.

15.4   HOW AND WHY FRANCHISING WORKS

Franchising is a method of distribution of goods and services, whereby a franchiser expands by means of a network of franchisees. For franchisers, franchising is a means to rapid market penetration at a low capital cost. For the franchisees, it is a way to buy into an existing business network. Franchising helps both franchiser and franchisee to obtain economies of scale. There are two basic types of franchises. One can franchise a trade name, as is done with auto dealerships, and petrol service stations. The other basic type of franchise involves business formats, such as McDonald's and Bodyshop.

Not every business is franchiseable; the concept works only when it can be duplicated in many different locations. Key components of franchising include a proven prototype and market demand; a strong management team; a distinctive identity; well-developed site selection criteria; an effective marketing program; a proven method of management; and a comprehensive training program, including field support staff. Franchising has been exceptionally popular since society has become brand driven; people trust brands and recognise logos as representing quality, cleanliness, and standardised good service.

15.5　THE FRANCHISE AGREEMENT

The franchise agreement is the business contract, which serves as the basis of the relationship between franchiser and franchisee. This document indicates terms and conditions of business operations; it also stipulates what each party will provide. For instance, it defines the assistance to be provided by the franchiser, and the related fees. The document typically states the franchise fee, the site evaluation fee, working capital requirements, building costs, leasing agreements, necessary equipment and fixtures. It also states royalties and advertising contributions, each as a percentage of gross sales, and the frequency of payments. As well, a franchise agreement explains company policies and practices, including franchiser controls. In addition, it states the availability of employee training, the expense involved, and who is responsible for paying it.

15.6　THE FRANCHISER'S PERSPECTIVE

For the franchiser, franchising presents several advantages. Franchisees pay franchisers for rights and also for products; thus, franchising is a source of capital and profit for franchisers. Franchisers delegate management to franchisees, thus allowing for faster growth. As franchisees make purchases through franchisers, the franchisers attain greater economies of scale than they would otherwise. Thus, franchising gives a franchiser greater bargaining power as a buyer. The franchiser thus expands the franchise network, while maintaining control over prices, products and service. Franchisees are committed to sharing costs of advertising. Franchising thus helps franchisers expand rapidly with minimum resources, capital or staff, benefiting from the resources of a wider network. In the case of McDonald's in India, the concept succeeded only after modification by a local entrepreneur who understood the local market (Dana 1999b). Finally, franchising also allows a franchiser to expand into traditionally protected and still restricted foreign markets, bypassing barriers against foreign ownership; only by franchising was British Airways able to obtain local traffic rights within South Africa (Dana 2000a).

15.7　THE FRANCHISEE'S PERSPECTIVE

Williams (1999) showed that beginners are more likely to buy a franchise than are former business owners. This can be explained by the fact that franchisers sell a complete package for the individual with no business experience. Advantages of franchising, from the franchisee's perspective, include commitment from the franchiser, which involves a support system. The franchisee is assisted with location selection, design start-up, operations and advertising. The franchiser provides the product, and the service quality. The franchisee obtains access to economies of scale, thanks to the franchiser's network. The franchiser also provides access to expertise, experience, training and marketing. What this means for the franchisee is a higher chance of success, thanks to a shorter learning curve and an established trademark/ servicemark provided by the franchiser. Also, bank financing often favours franchised businesses.

There are, nevertheless, disadvantages to being a franchisee. Innovation is stifled, as the franchisee must adhere to the franchiser's system. The franchisee has less freedom than has an independent entrepreneur. Franchisees pay a substantial fee upfront (sometimes in the US$500 000 range), and profits are diluted. Advertising and promotional fees may be 6 per cent of gross sales, in addition to royalties, often 8 per cent of gross sales. Furthermore, binding franchise agreements include a non-competitive clause. Perhaps the greatest concern is that a bad incident at one franchisee may adversely affect sales at other franchisees.

15.8   HOW TO BECOME A SUCCESSFUL FRANCHISEE

Franchising is not for everyone. A potential franchisee should fully understand the commitment and limitations involved. Important questions to reflect upon include:

- What is the kind of business I would like to be in?

- Can I work within the limits of a franchise system?

- What types of business are succeeding these days, with every indication that they will continue to succeed?

- What is the best franchise for me?

- Is someone offering a franchise in my area of interest, which I believe will help me succeed, and that I can afford?

Such a critical self-assessment is most useful for the potential franchisee. It is important to weigh the advantages and the disadvantages involved in franchising, and to have appropriate expectations. Franchising limits risk, but likewise reduces potential. The potential franchisee should select a compatible franchiser, in an appropriate sector. Mutual trust is involved, between franchiser and franchisee. Both parties must agree on terms and conditions. It is also important to be comfortable with the initial start-up fee and subsequent royalty fee. Banks and franchisers are often keen to provide start-up capital. Success at one location does not guarantee it at another. Poncho Taco succeeded in California, but failed in Canada. American fast food succeeded in Malaysia and Singapore, but only after adapting to respect Islamic eating rules.

15.9   HOW FRANCHISING SPREAD TO THE AIRLINE
SECTOR

Franchising has appeared even in the airline industry – a sector into which few people expected it to expand. It evolved out of subcontractual agreements. Subcontracting involves an agreement in which one company contracts a specific segment of its business operations to another firm, allowing each firm to focus on its competitive advantage, and to leverage the core competency of the other. Specifically, larger international carriers, more efficient at long-haul flights, rely on the services of small-scale carriers, with smaller aircraft, to access and service small niche markets in which the smaller carriers are more efficient. Significant cost reductions are achieved through the use of more specialised aircraft, while seamless service is offered to the customer. The small carrier may have added cost advantages of not being unionised, and of having a more community-focused corporate culture. As an integral part of a larger network, smaller carriers can focus on specialised services and avoid scale-dependent operations to the mutual advantage of both.

Allegheny Airlines pioneered the concept of subcontracting flights to independent firms, to which it assigned its own two-letter designator. The airline developed a hub in Pittsburgh and introduced new routes. Deregulation allowed Allegheny Airlines to concentrate on its most profitable routes, mainly between hubs, using jet aircraft. Yet many other routes were still important as they provided feeder traffic and thus enlarged the customer base. Rather than discontinue service to minor airports, Allegheny maintained under contract a network of small, independent carriers that provided flights, under the brand name Allegheny Commuter, on behalf of Allegheny Airlines. Independent contractors included: Chatauqua Airlines, Fischer Brothers Aviation, Henson, Ransome Airlines, South Jersey Airlines and Suburban Airlines. This collaborative network enabled Allegheny Airlines (later USAir and more recently, US Airways) to focus on expanding its presence, without abandoning low-density routes to smaller communities. This concept also proved beneficial to Allegheny's associated entrepreneurs (such as Mr and Mrs Ransome, the owner–managers of Ransome Airlines), as it provided them access to long-haul travellers and scale-dependent operations (for example, reservation and information systems), which Allegheny provided efficiently. The members of the Allegheny network saved costs and improved their competitiveness in terms of expanded network reach, lower ticket prices, and higher satisfaction among customers who benefited from the seamless services provided by the network. When Allegheny changed its name to USAir it kept the Allegheny Commuter network, which eventually became USAir Express. The benefits associated with such cooperative networking would soon impact the dynamics of airline competition, forcing others to emulate it:

> Trans World Airlines (TWA) established the Trans World Express network of commuter feeders. Air Midwest, Resort Air and Resort Commuter provided

this service. In addition, until being absorbed by USAir, Piedmont Airlines had a code-sharing arrangement with TWA, whereby a Piedmont flight would be listed also as a TWA flight.

American Airlines, originally opposed to code sharing, launched its American Eagle program in November 1984. Members have included numerous small firms, such as: AVAir, Air Midwest, Chaparral Airlines, Command Airways, Executive Air Charter, Metro Express II, Metroflight, Simmons Airlines and Wings West Airlines.

United Airlines started sharing its (UA) designator in 1985 with Appleton-based Air Wisconsin, Seattle-based Horizon Air and Fresno-based WestAir. In 1986 Aspen Airways (operating Convair 580 turbo-props between Denver and Aspen) also became a United Airlines code-sharer. United lost Horizon when this contractor was acquired by Alaska Airlines.

As deregulation spread from the US to Canada and Europe, so did the principle of creating alliances and networks between large international airlines and small local subcontractors (Dana 2000b). In Canada, Air Canada set up a family of Air Canada Connectors, including Air Alliance, Air BC, Air Nova and Air Ontario, as well as Austin Airways (Canada's oldest airline, established as a family business in 1934). Eventually, several other small firms, including Alberta Citylink, British Midland, and Central Mountain Air, also became code-share partners.

International franchising is a more recent innovation in the quest to market airline services internationally. As is the case with subcontracting, franchising is an effective way by which one airline can cooperate with another to expand beyond its own resource base. A franchise agreement expands on subcontracting, often allowing the franchisee to use the franchiser's name and airline code, and to operate aeroplanes painted in the livery of the franchiser. Unlike subcontracting, franchising may allow an airline to effectively enter the restrictive domestic markets of foreign countries through its local franchisees.

In May 1996, British Airways (BA) signed its first franchise agreement with a small, regional carrier outside the United Kingdom. It allowed Sun-Air, a Danish airline, to paint its fleet in the livery of BA, and its cabin crew to wear BA uniforms. Two months later BA signed a similar franchise agreement with Comair, a small firm in the Republic of South Africa. In the case of airline franchising the franchiser benefits from rapid expansion into local markets without heavy capital investment. It also bypasses barriers against foreign ownership. The franchisee benefits from the brand name, technical expertise and scale-dependent benefits, including the expanded passenger base of the franchiser. For the franchisee operating a small airline, such a cooperative relationship provides access to international passengers that would require much greater resources to attain independently.

15.10 THE SINGAPORE EXPERIENCE

A&W, Avis, Hertz, Hilton, Hyatt, KFC, McDonald's and Pizza Hut pioneered franchising in Singapore. Budding franchises include: Bee Cheng (meat), Old Chang Kee (curry puffs), NTUC Fairprice, Kinderland Educare Services, Melandas Casa and Palm Beach Seafood. Franchising is growing rapidly in Singapore. During the mid-1990s, franchise sales in Singapore were only 5 per cent of GNP, quite low compared to 38 per cent in the US. Then the Trade Development Board spearheaded the vision to make Singapore 'an international franchise hub with total support capabilities, showcasing international franchises, which are either developed locally or brought in from abroad'.

In February 1998, the new International Franchise Enterprise Program (IFEP) was launched, to give Singaporean companies a higher level of support in development and marketing of franchise concepts. The Singapore Franchise Association expects 175 firms to join the industry before 2001.

15.11 CONCLUSIONS AND IMPLICATIONS FOR SMES

Knight (1921) argued that entrepreneurs undertook risk. To Schumpeter (1934) entrepreneurs were innovators. Today, franchising is an ideal alternative for those who dislike risk and for those who are not innovators. Williams (1999) suggested that entrepreneurs who buy franchises have lower skills than those who launch new ventures. Today, everyone who wishes to become an entrepreneur can become self-employed. Indeed, times have changed, and franchisees can thrive as interdependent agents of franchisers.

Figure 15.1 depicts this movement towards the new, interdependence paradigm. The figure shows, for example, that a larger firm may trade off a part of the independent management control associated with its large size, in order to gain flexibility and scale economies which will enable it to become more efficient and hence more competitive. Similarly, smaller firms may elect to sacrifice some of their autonomy by integrating into the larger firm's franchise network. By each trading off some of their independence, both franchisees and franchisers can improve their competitiveness.

Table 15.1 further expands into other potential dimensions of that conceptual framework. It compares the traditional modes of international involvement with the emerging interdependence paradigm on several key dimensions.

Thus, globalisation is transforming the competitive environment of small and large firms alike. In the more segregated competitive arenas of the past, managers of smaller firms could remain local if they wished, reasonably insulated from the forces of international competition.

If they chose to expand, they could acquire and internalise the resources needed

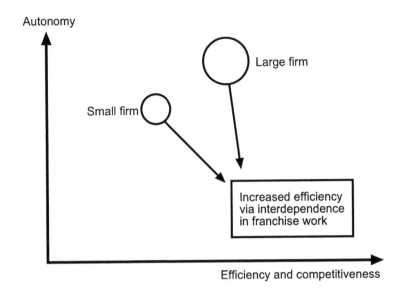

Figure 15.1   Autonomy/Efficiency Trade-off

to do so, incrementally over time. In the new intensified competitive environment, entrepreneurs must achieve world-class efficiencies in order to survive, whether or not they actually compete globally. They can no longer afford the luxury of achieving these efficiencies gradually, through a sequential evolution, using their own resources. Instead, many small firms are achieving cost reduction and expanding their market reach indirectly by linking their operations into the value chains of large firms, to the mutual benefit of both parties. Franchising is one means of participating in a global network.

Franchising allows firms to achieve symbiotic relationships in which franchisers and franchisees rely on each other to attain world-class competitiveness for their entire network. The resulting increase in efficiency enables the network as a whole to compete more effectively and to gain market share globally. The days when small firms could operate independently, in relatively protected environments, are waning. Networks – and even coalitions of networks – now compete for global market share. The implications largely contradict conventional thinking about the independent growth and management of SMEs. The global environment calls for new strategies, often involving a trade-off between independence and efficiency. Smaller firms may still depend heavily on the scale of large firms to achieve their initial efficiency gains.

Franchisees can draw upon the pooled capabilities and knowledge stock of their entire network, instead of developing the required knowledge themselves. Building upon such enabling knowledge networks – mirroring the physical networks of the firms – is a new strategic competence which is bound to challenge SME managers, especially those still oriented towards fully independent operations. The consequences of this paradigm shift from independence towards interdependence are far-reaching.

Table 15.1
The Rise of Franchising

	Traditional business	**The age of franchising**
1. **Policy environment**	• Closed, protected markets limited internationalisation	• Open, competitive markets encourage international-isation and international franchises
2. **Ownership and control**	• Full or majority ownership viewed as necessary for access to capabilities and for control • Need for control enforced adversarial system • Enabled independent learning and evolution	• Fee for service and relation-based understandings provide access to capabilities • Control viewed as hindrance to flexibility
3. **Mode of competition**	• Independent firms competing against each other	• Coalition of networked firms (franchisees) competing against other chains
4. **Popular *modus operandi***	• Independent, orderly growth through ownership and evolution of internal capabilities	• Rapid growth through franchising
5. **Implications/ observable results**	• Controlled expansion over time at tolerable costs and risks for each firm, independently	• Rapid expansion in short time through franchise networks

REFERENCES

Aldrich, Howard E. (1989), 'Networking among Women Entrepreneurs', in O. Hagen, C. Rivehum and Donald L. Sexton (eds), *Women-owned Businesses*, New York: Praeger, pp. 103–32.

Aldrich, H.E., T.P. Jones and D. McEvoy (1984), 'Ethnic Advantage and Minority Business Development', in R. Ward and R. Jenkins (eds), *Ethnic Communities in Business: Strategies for Economic Survival*, Cambridge: Cambridge University Press, pp. 189–210.

Aldrich, H.E., B. Rosen and W. Woodward (1987), 'The Impact of Social Networks on Business Foundings and Profit in a Longitudinal Study', in Babson College (eds), *Frontiers of Entrepreneurship Research*, Wellesley, MA: Babson College, pp. 154–68.

Aldrich, H.E. and C. Zimmer (1986), 'Entrepreneurship through Social Networks', in D.L. Sexton and R. W. Smilor (eds), *The Art and Science of Entrepreneurship*, Cambridge, MA: Ballinger, pp. 3–24.

Bartlett, C.A. and S. Ghoshal (1989), *Managing Across Borders: The Transnational Solution*, Boston, MA: Harvard Business School Press.

Bilkey, W.J. and G. Tesar (1977), 'The Export Behaviour of Smaller Sized Wisconsin Manufacturing Firms', *Journal of International Business Studies*, **8** (1), 93–8.

Birley, S. (1985), 'The Role of Networks in the Entrepreneurial Process', in Babson College (eds), *Frontiers of Entrepreneurship Research*, Wellesley, MA: Babson College, pp. 325–37.

Boissevain, J. and H. Grotenbreg (1987), 'Ethnic Enterprise in the Netherlands: The Surinamese of Amsterdam', in R. Goffee and R. Scase (eds), *Entrepreneurship in Europe: The Social Process*, London: Croom Helm, pp. 105–30.

Buckley, P.J. (1997), 'International Technology Transfer by Small and Medium-sized Enterprises', *Small Business Economics*, **9**, 67–78.

Carsrud, A.L., C.M. Gaglio and K.W. Olm (1986), 'Entrepreneurs – Mentors, Networks and Successful New Venture Development: An Exploratory Study', in Babson College (eds), *Frontiers of Entrepreneurship Research*, Wellesley, MA: Babson College, pp. 229–43.

Cavusgil, S.T. (1980), 'On the Internationalisation Process of Firms', *European Research*, **8**, 273–81.

Cavusgil, S.T. (1984), 'Differences Among Exporting Firms Based on Their Degree of Internationalisation', *Journal of Business Research*, **12** (2), 195–208.

Dana, L.P. (1992), 'Changes in the South Korean Model: Toward More Entrepreneurship and Innovation', *Entrepreneurship, Innovation, and Change*, **1** (3), 303–11.

Dana, L.P. (1994–5), 'A Comparison of Policy on Entrepreneurship in Taiwan and Korea', *Orientations: Journal of East Asia Studies*, **1**, 83–94.

Dana, L.P. (1998), 'Small But Not Independent: SMEs in Japan', *Journal of Small Business Management*, **36** (4), October, 73–6.

Dana, L.P. (1999a), *Entrepreneurship in Pacific Asia: Past, Present and Future*, Singapore: World Scientific.

Dana, L.P. (1999b), 'McDonald's (Japan) Ltd.', *British Food Journal*, **101** (5–6), May, 496–9.

Dana, L.P. (2000a), 'British Airways plc', in D.W. Cravens, B. Merrilees and R.H. Walker (eds), *Strategic Marketing Management for the Pacific Region*, Roseville, Australia: McGraw-Hill, pp. 323–33.

Dana, L.P. (2000b), 'Federal Express Corporation: Facing International Marketing Challenges in Asia Pacific', in D.W. Cravens, B. Merrilees and R.H. Walker (eds), *Strategic Marketing Management for the Pacific Region*, Roseville, Australia: McGraw Hill, pp. 334–44.

Dana, L.P., H. Etemad and R.W. Wright (1999a), 'The Impact of Globalisation on SMEs', Global Focus, 11 (4), 93–105; available at <?xml:namespace prefix = o ns = "urn:schemas-microsoft-com:office:office" />.

Dana, L.P., H. Etemad and R.W. Wright (1999b), 'The Theoretical Foundations of International Entrepreneurship', in R.W. Wright (ed.), *International Entrepreneurship: Globalisation of Emerging Businesses*, Stamford, CN: JAI Press, pp. 3–22.

Dant, Rajiv P. and Patrick J. Kaufmann (1998), 'Introduction to the Special Section on Franchising', *Journal of Business Venturing*, **13** (1), January, 1–2.

Dubini, Paola and Howard E. Aldrich (1991), 'Personal and Extended Networks are Central to the Entrepreneurship Process', *Journal of Business Venturing*, **6** (5), 305–13.

Dunning, J.H. (1995), 'Reappraising the Eclectic Paradigm in an Age of Alliance Capitalism', *Journal of International Business Studies*, **26** (3), 461–91.

Dunning, J.H. (1999), 'The Emerging Knowledge Network of International Entrepreneurship', *Global Focus*, **11** (3), pp. 55–62.

Holm, D.B., K. Eriksson and J. Johanson (1997), 'Business Networks and Cooperation in International Business Relationships', in P.W. Beamish and J.P. Killing (eds), *Cooperative Strategies: European Perspectives*, San Francisco: New Lexington Press, pp. 242–66.

Iyer, G. and J.M. Shapiro (1999), 'Ethnic Entrepreneurship and Marketing Systems: Implications for the Global Economy', *Journal of International Marketing*, **7** (4), 83–110.

Johannison, B. (1987), 'Towards a Theory of Local Entrepreneurship', in R.G. Wyckham, L.N. Meredith and G.R. Bushe (eds), *The Spirit of Entrepreneurship*, Vancouver, BC: Faculty of Business Administration, Simon Fraser University, pp. 1–14.

Johanson, J. and J.E. Vahlne (1977), 'The Internationalisation Process of the Firm – A Model of Knowledge Development and Increasing Foreign Market Commitments', *Journal of International Business Studies*, **8** (1), 23–32.

Johanson, J. and F. Wiedersheim-Paul (1975), 'The Internationalisation of the Firm: Four Swedish Cases', *Journal of International Management Studies*, **12** (3), 36–64.

Knight, F.H. (1921), *Risk, Uncertainty, and Profit*, New York: Houghton Mifflin.

Levitt, T. (1983), 'The Globalisation of Markets', *Harvard Business Review*, May–June, pp. 92–102.

Newbould, G.D., P.J. Buckley and T.C. Thurwell (1978), *Going International – The Experience of Smaller Companies Overseas*, New York: John Wiley & Sons.

Ohmae, K. (1989), 'The Global Logic of Strategic Alliances', *Harvard Business Review*, March–April, pp. 143–54.

Ohmae, K. (1990), *The Borderless World*, New York: Harper Collins Books.

Olm, K., A.L. Carsrud and L. Alvey (1988), 'The Role of Networks in New Venture Funding of Female Entrepreneurs: A Continuing Analysis', in Babson College (eds), *Frontiers of Entrepreneurial Research*, Wellesley, MA: Babson College, pp. 658–9.

Oviatt, B.M. and P.P. McDougall (1994), 'Toward A Theory of International New Ventures', *Journal of International Business Studies*, **25** (1), 45–64.

Reynolds, P.D. (1997), 'New and Small Firms in Expanding Markets', *Small Business Economics*, **9** (1), 79–84.

Schumpeter, J.A. (1934), *The Theory of Economic Development*, Cambridge, MA: Harvard University Press.

Shaver, K.G. and L.R. Scott (1991), 'Person, Process, Choice: The Psychology of New Venture Creation', *Entrepreneurship, Theory and Practice*, **16** (2), 23–64.

Werbner, P. (1984), 'Business Trust: Pakistani Entrepreneurship in the Manchester Garment Trade', in R. Ward and R. Jenkins (eds), *Ethnic Communities: Strategies for Economic Survival*, Cambridge: Cambridge University Press, pp. 166–88.

Williams, D.L. (1999), 'Why do Entrepreneurs Become Franchisees? An Empirical Analysis of Organisational Choice', *Journal of Business Venturing*, **14** (1), January, 103–24.

Index

A share(s), 97, 103–104, 106
adaptive
    entrepreneurs, 228, 232–3
    entrepreneurship, 227, 229, 233–4, 241
agribusiness, 227
alliances, 305
America(n), 48, 51–2, 54–5
Andean Group, 51
APEC, 2, 35–6
    survey, 4
aquaculture, 255, 267
Arrow's Law, 44, 49, 55
Asia Pacific Economic Cooperation
    (APEC), 158, 287
Asian
    Development Bank, 90, 116, 121, 129
    economic crisis, 2
    crisis, 3–6, 8, 27, 29, 38, 260
    currency, 21
    financial crisis, 32, 83–6, 89–92, 95,
        242, 255
Australia(n), 1, 6, 8, 95–7, 100–102, 109–
        11, 113, 131, 134, 136, 191, 198,
        200, 203, 229, 255, 258–62, 266,
        268–9, 274–80, 284–7, 289
automotive industry, 73

bad debts, 91
Bangladesh, 44
Bank
    credits, 36
    Indonesia, 88
banking system, 96
bankruptcy laws, 78
barrier to entry, 48
bilateral
    aid financing, 90
    trade, 91
biotechnology, 47, 134
Brazil, 258
Bretton Woods, 234
Britain, 58, 275
Brunei, 2, 200

business
    development services, 77–8
    linkages, 67–8
    vertical linkages, 67
    networks, 227, 264, 274, 276, 284, 286
    plans, 75, 78
    small scale, 72

Cambodia, 62, 70, 74
Canada, 58, 229, 269, 275, 303, 305
capital, 176, 178, 180, 184, 210, 233, 235,
        258, 264, 266, 302
    account liberalisation, 23, 25
    accumulation, 22, 234
    costs, 265
    flows, 25, 28
    long-term flows, 26
    goods, 66
    inflows, 23, 25, 38
    short-term flows, 27
    short-term inflows, 29
    intensive, 56
    intensive industries, 57
    intensity, 58
    market(s), 29, 114, 116, 119, 192, 196
    private inflows, 25
    structure, 241
cash flow, 270
casualisation, 219
Central Java, 67, 76
chaebol(s), 214, 256–7, 274, 300
child labour, 222
China, 1, 6, 8, 12, 17–20, 22, 50–51, 54, 84,
        95–8, 100, 104–108, 113–14, 129,
        134–6, 191, 200, 203, 228–33, 253–
        8, 264, 267, 269–70, 275, 279, 281,
        284, 291–3
Chinese, 50, 103, 106
    computer industries, 3
    joint venture, 121
    Taipei, 131
clustering, 64, 67
cluster(s), 6, 7, 46, 48, 62–4, 68–9, 75–7,

312